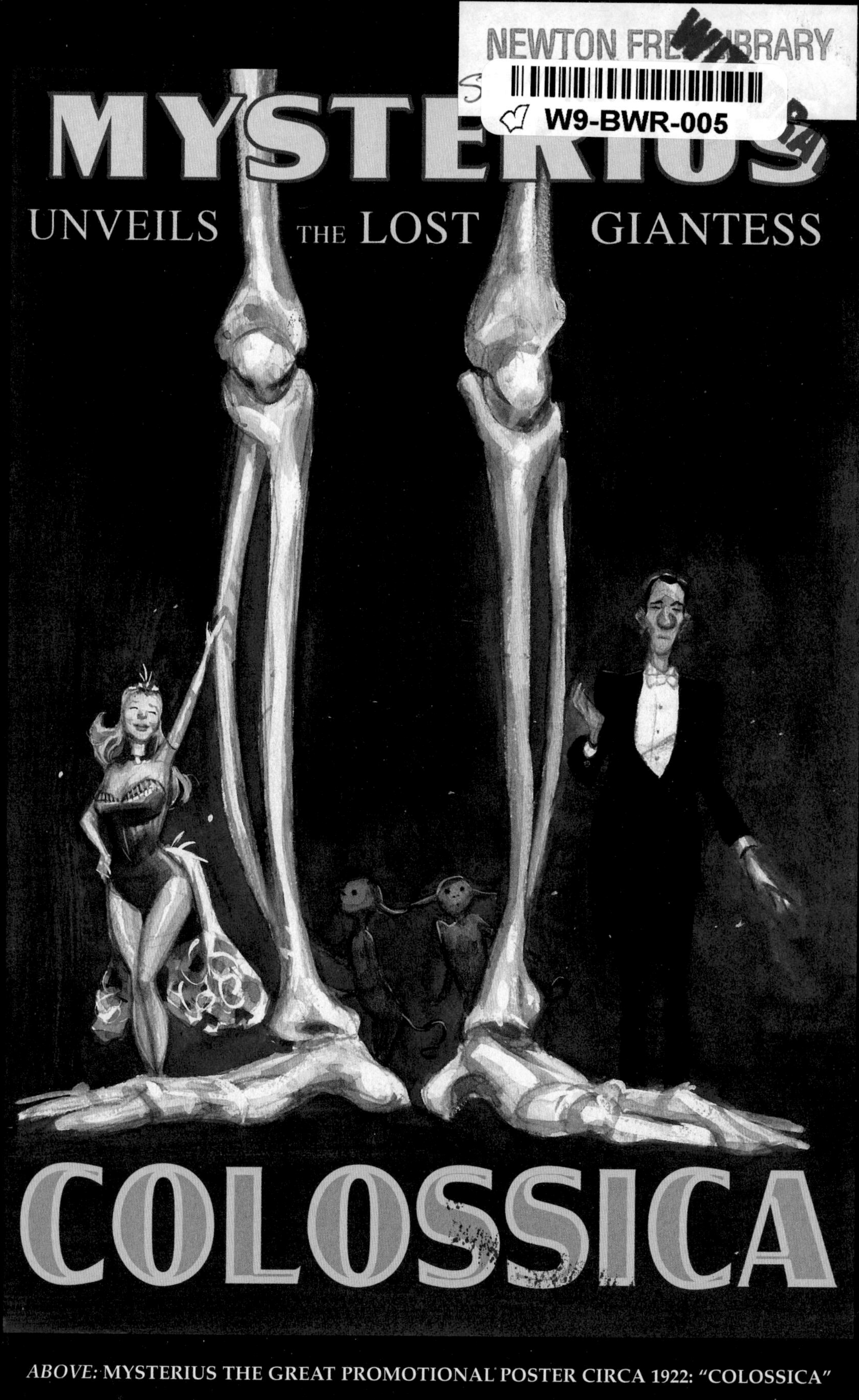
MYSTERIUS
UNVEILS THE LOST GIANTESS
COLOSSICA

ABOVE: MYSTERIUS THE GREAT PROMOTIONAL POSTER CIRCA 1922: "COLOSSICA"

Writer: **Jeff Parker**
Artist: **Tom Fowler**
Colorist: **Dave McCaig**
Letterer: **Saida Temofonte**

Special Thanks to **Chris Caroc**

WildStorm is pleased to present MYSTERIUS AND THE MISSING DIVA, previously available only to those few whose grandparents had the good taste to subscribe to the pulp magazine *Diabolic Tales*. Our copy was incomplete due to a poorly maintained slate roof, but we believe the three pages and accompanying illustrations presented throughout this edition are a worthy reminder of the glorious past of the pulps and the magician known to this day as Mysterius.

Left: Illustration from the original table of contents page for *Diabolic Tales*, published March 1935

Jim Lee	Editorial Director
Hank Kanalz	VP – General Manager
Ben Abernathy	Editor – Original Series
Kristy Quinn	Editor
Ed Roeder	Art Director

DC COMICS

Paul Levitz	President & Publisher
Richard Bruning	SVP – Creative Director
Patrick Caldon	EVP – Finance & Operations
Amy Genkins	SVP – Business & Legal Affairs
Gregory Noveck	SVP – Creative Affairs
Steve Rotterdam	SVP – Sales & Marketing
Cheryl Rubin	SVP – Brand Management

SUSTAINABLE FORESTRY INITIATIVE Certified Fiber Sourcing
www.sfiprogram.org

MYSTERIUS, published by WildStorm Productions. 888 Prospect St. #240, La Jolla, CA 92037. Compilation, prose story & new art Copyright © 2010 Jeff Parker and Tom Fowler. All Rights Reserved. Originally published in single magazine form as MYSTERIUS #1-6 © 2009 Jeff Parker and Tom Fowler. All Rights Reserved.

DC Comics, a Warner Bros. Entertainment Company.

ISBN: 978-1-4012-2670-1

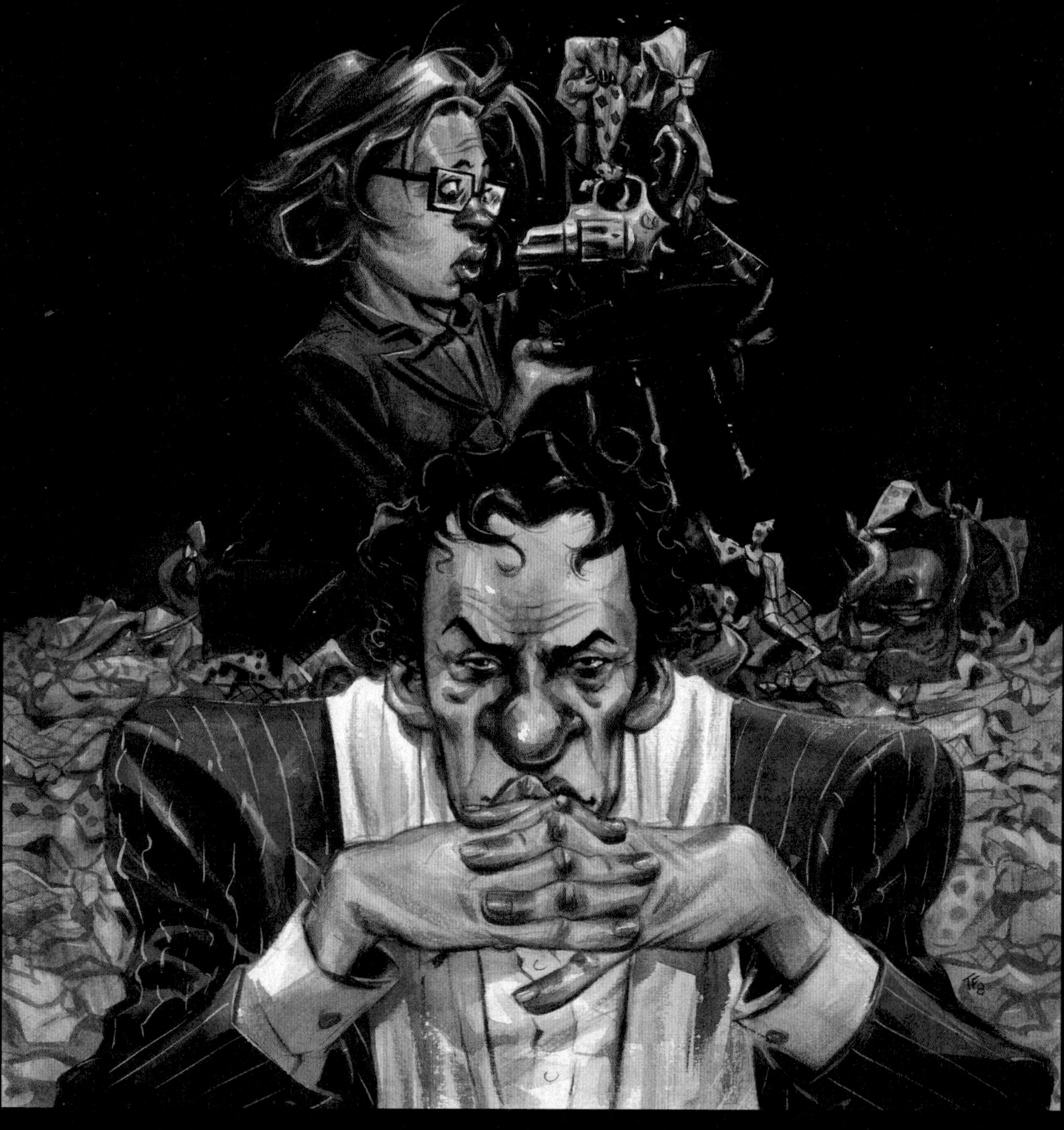

CHAPTER ONE: MYSTERIUS THE MAGNIFICENT

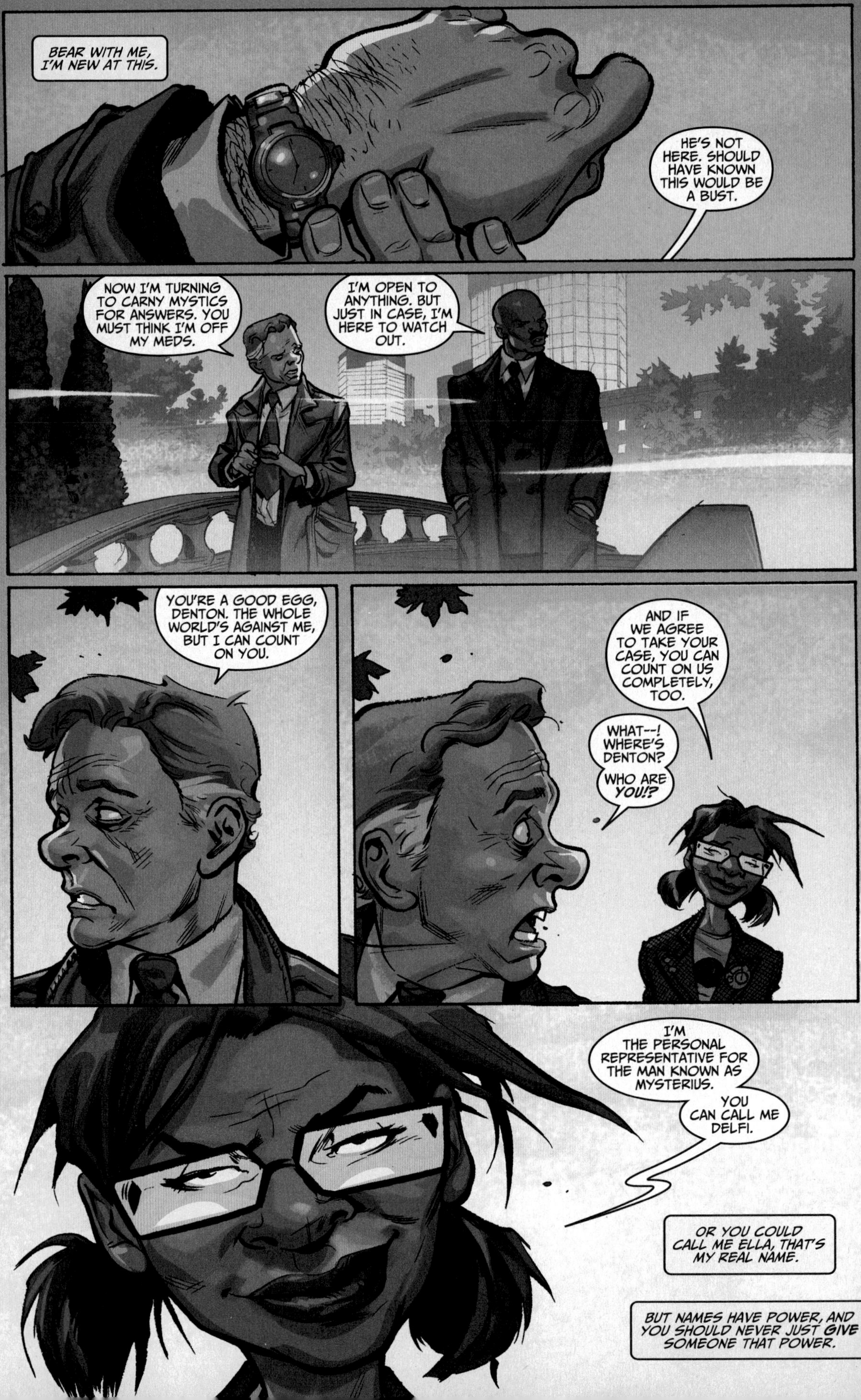
BEAR WITH ME, I'M NEW AT THIS.
HE'S NOT HERE. SHOULD HAVE KNOWN THIS WOULD BE A BUST.
NOW I'M TURNING TO CARNY MYSTICS FOR ANSWERS. YOU MUST THINK I'M OFF MY MEDS.
I'M OPEN TO ANYTHING. BUT JUST IN CASE, I'M HERE TO WATCH OUT.
YOU'RE A GOOD EGG, DENTON. THE WHOLE WORLD'S AGAINST ME, BUT I CAN COUNT ON YOU.
AND IF WE AGREE TO TAKE YOUR CASE, YOU CAN COUNT ON US COMPLETELY, TOO.
WHAT--! WHERE'S DENTON?
WHO ARE YOU!?
I'M THE PERSONAL REPRESENTATIVE FOR THE MAN KNOWN AS MYSTERIUS.
YOU CAN CALL ME DELFI.
OR YOU COULD CALL ME ELLA, THAT'S MY REAL NAME.
BUT NAMES HAVE POWER, AND YOU SHOULD NEVER JUST GIVE SOMEONE THAT POWER.

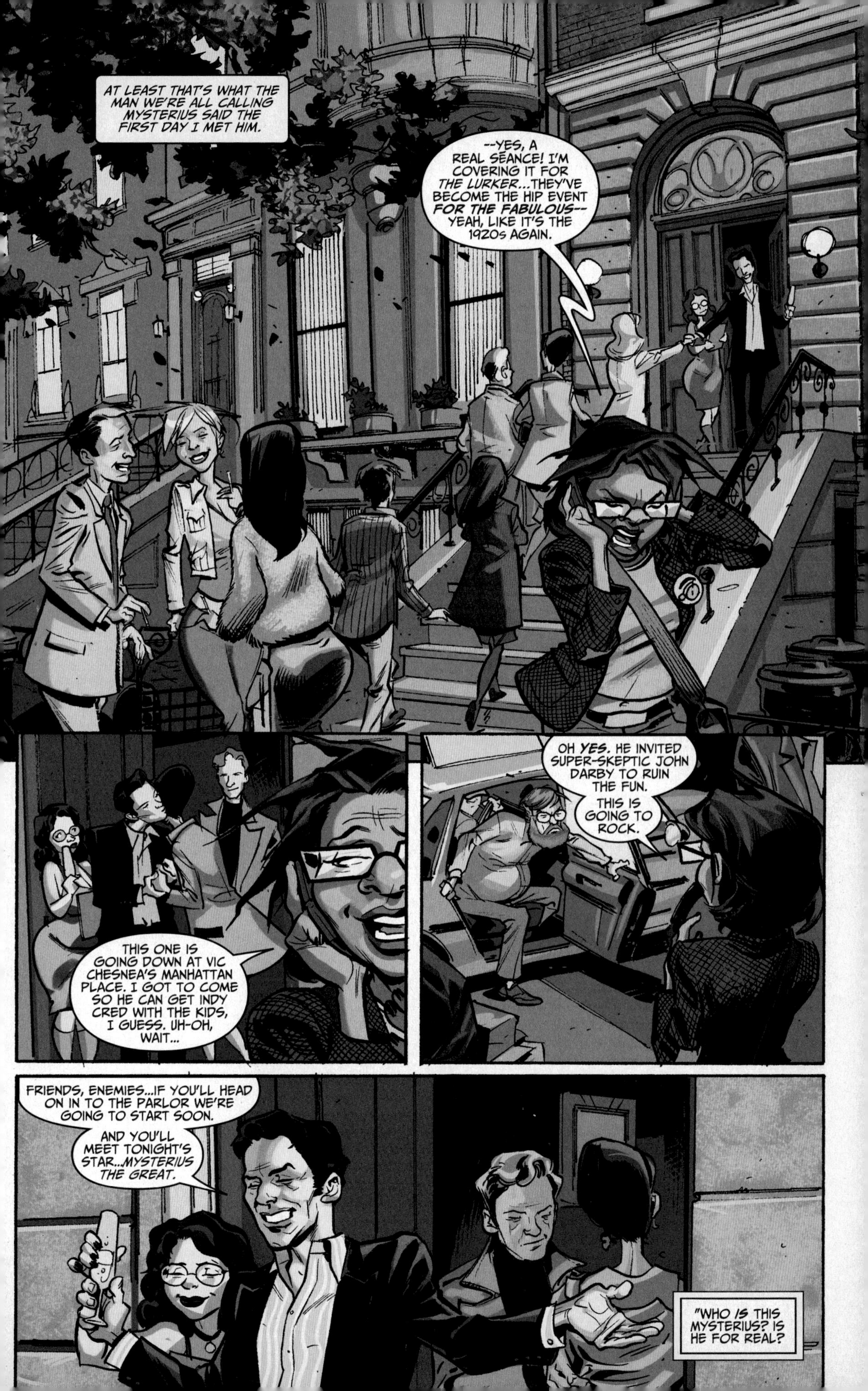
AT LEAST THAT'S WHAT THE MAN WE'RE ALL CALLING MYSTERIUS SAID THE FIRST DAY I MET HIM.
--YES, A REAL SÉANCE! I'M COVERING IT FOR THE LURKER...THEY'VE BECOME THE HIP EVENT FOR THE FABULOUS--YEAH, LIKE IT'S THE 1920s AGAIN.
THIS ONE IS GOING DOWN AT VIC CHESNEA'S MANHATTAN PLACE. I GOT TO COME SO HE CAN GET INDY CRED WITH THE KIDS, I GUESS. UH-OH, WAIT...
OH YES. HE INVITED SUPER-SKEPTIC JOHN DARBY TO RUIN THE FUN.
THIS IS GOING TO ROCK.
FRIENDS, ENEMIES...IF YOU'LL HEAD ON IN TO THE PARLOR WE'RE GOING TO START SOON.
AND YOU'LL MEET TONIGHT'S STAR...MYSTERIUS THE GREAT.
"WHO IS THIS MYSTERIUS? IS HE FOR REAL?

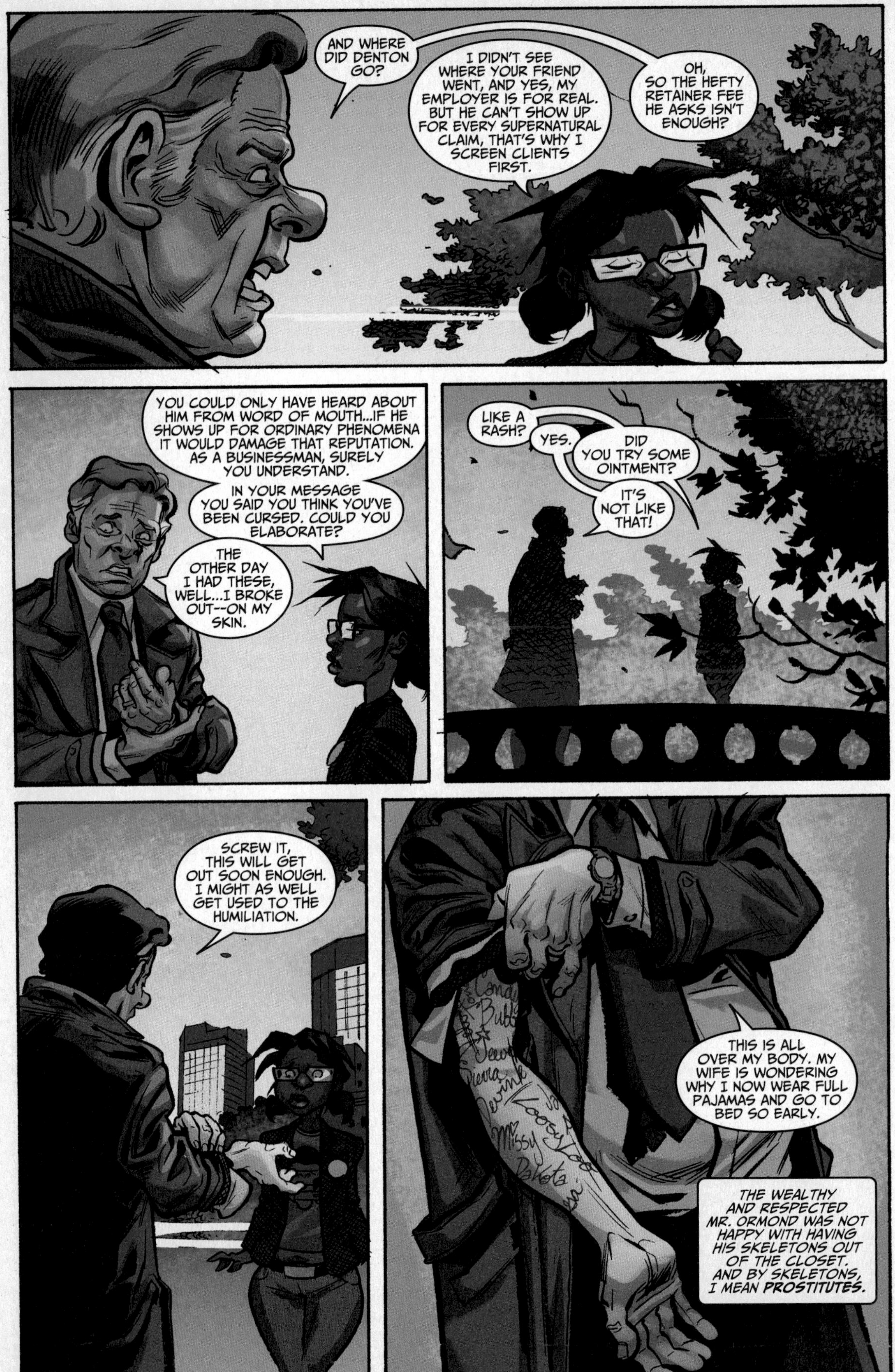
AND WHERE DID DENTON GO?
I DIDN'T SEE WHERE YOUR FRIEND WENT, AND YES, MY EMPLOYER IS FOR REAL. BUT HE CAN'T SHOW UP FOR EVERY SUPERNATURAL CLAIM, THAT'S WHY I SCREEN CLIENTS FIRST.
OH, SO THE HEFTY RETAINER FEE HE ASKS ISN'T ENOUGH?
YOU COULD ONLY HAVE HEARD ABOUT HIM FROM WORD OF MOUTH...IF HE SHOWS UP FOR ORDINARY PHENOMENA IT WOULD DAMAGE THAT REPUTATION. AS A BUSINESSMAN, SURELY YOU UNDERSTAND.
IN YOUR MESSAGE YOU SAID YOU THINK YOU'VE BEEN CURSED. COULD YOU ELABORATE?
THE OTHER DAY I HAD THESE, WELL...I BROKE OUT--ON MY SKIN.
LIKE A RASH?
YES.
DID YOU TRY SOME OINTMENT?
IT'S NOT LIKE THAT!
SCREW IT, THIS WILL GET OUT SOON ENOUGH. I MIGHT AS WELL GET USED TO THE HUMILIATION.
THIS IS ALL OVER MY BODY. MY WIFE IS WONDERING WHY I NOW WEAR FULL PAJAMAS AND GO TO BED SO EARLY.
THE WEALTHY AND RESPECTED MR. ORMOND WAS NOT HAPPY WITH HAVING HIS SKELETONS OUT OF THE CLOSET. AND BY SKELETONS, I MEAN PROSTITUTES.

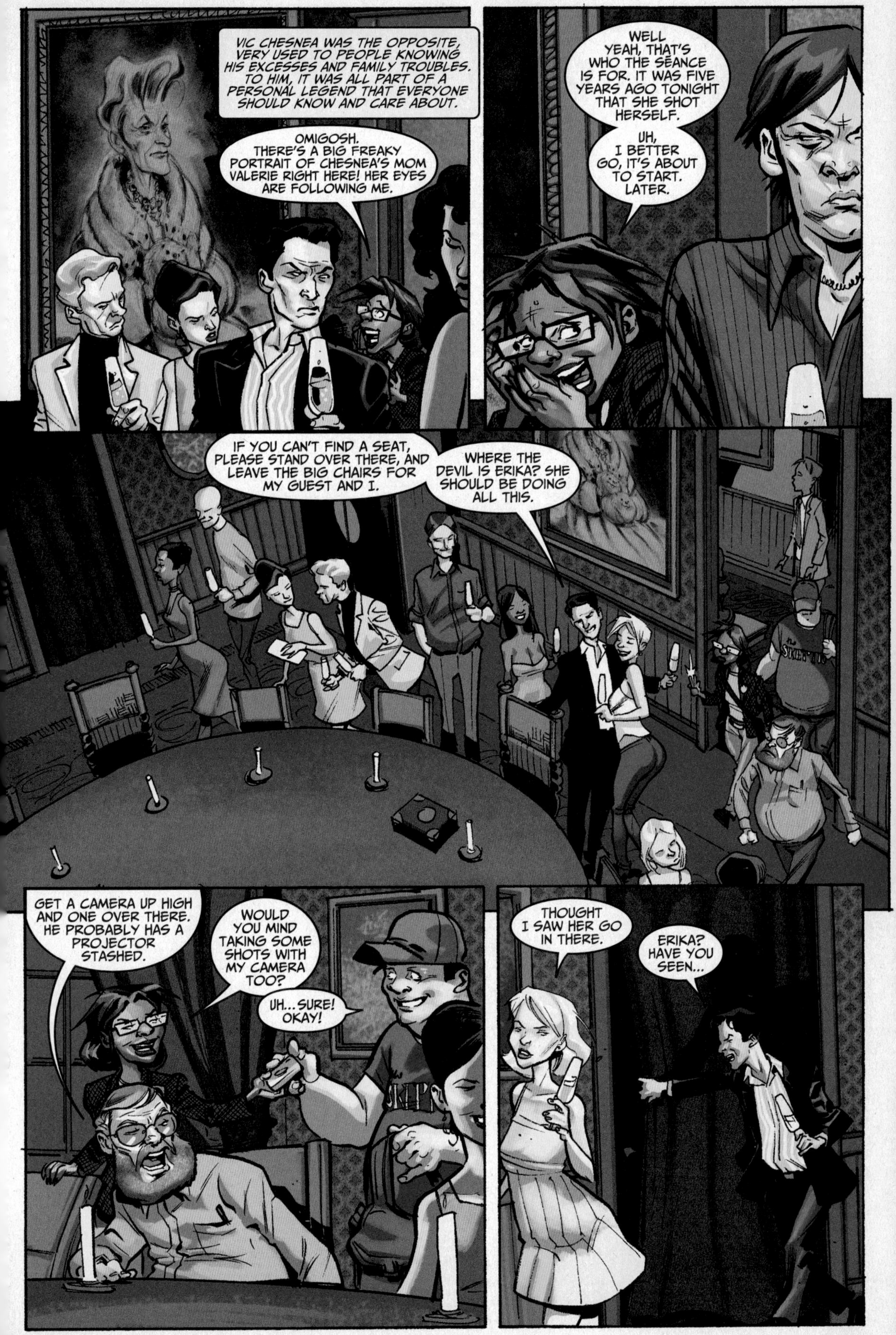
VIC CHESNEA WAS THE OPPOSITE, VERY USED TO PEOPLE KNOWING HIS EXCESSES AND FAMILY TROUBLES. TO HIM, IT WAS ALL PART OF A PERSONAL LEGEND THAT EVERYONE SHOULD KNOW AND CARE ABOUT.
OMIGOSH. THERE'S A BIG FREAKY PORTRAIT OF CHESNEA'S MOM VALERIE RIGHT HERE! HER EYES ARE FOLLOWING ME.
WELL YEAH, THAT'S WHO THE SÉANCE IS FOR. IT WAS FIVE YEARS AGO TONIGHT THAT SHE SHOT HERSELF.
UH, I BETTER GO, IT'S ABOUT TO START. LATER.
IF YOU CAN'T FIND A SEAT, PLEASE STAND OVER THERE, AND LEAVE THE BIG CHAIRS FOR MY GUEST AND I.
WHERE THE DEVIL IS ERIKA? SHE SHOULD BE DOING ALL THIS.
GET A CAMERA UP HIGH AND ONE OVER THERE. HE PROBABLY HAS A PROJECTOR STASHED.
WOULD YOU MIND TAKING SOME SHOTS WITH MY CAMERA TOO?
UH...SURE! OKAY!
THOUGHT I SAW HER GO IN THERE.
ERIKA? HAVE YOU SEEN...

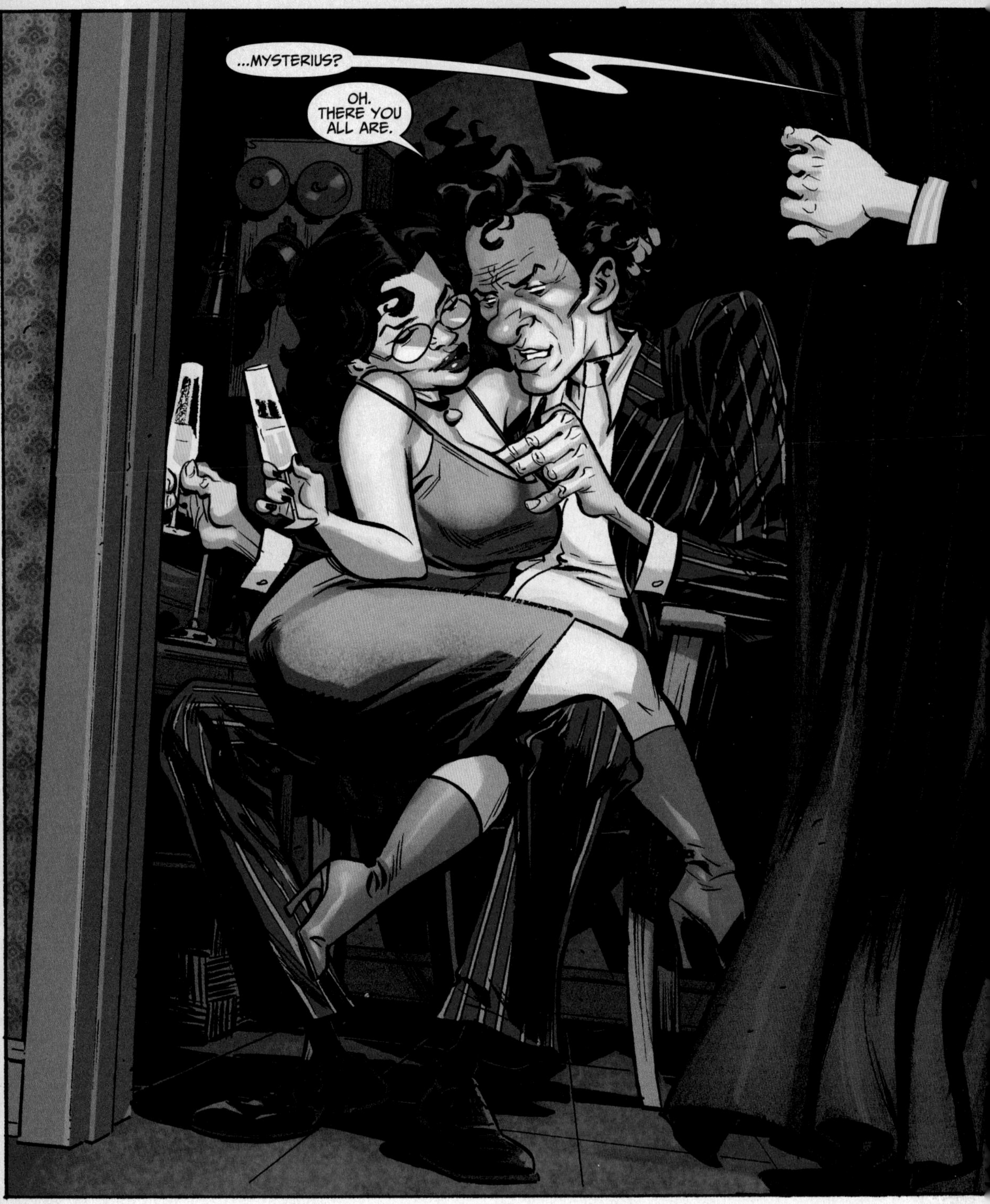
...MYSTERIUS?
OH. THERE YOU ALL ARE.

YOUR MISSING EARRING, MY DEAR.

WOW!

MR. MYSTERIUS, IF YOU'RE FINISHED HANDLING *MY* PERSONAL ASSISTANT, I THINK THE GUESTS ARE READY FOR THE MAIN EVENT.

OUR SPECIAL GUEST WAS UNLOCKING MORE SECRETS OF THE UNIVERSE, I THINK.

HAH!

CLAP CLAP CLAP CLAP

LADIES AND GENTLEMEN... MYSTERIUS THE GREAT.

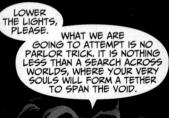

LOWER THE LIGHTS, PLEASE. WHAT WE ARE GOING TO ATTEMPT IS NO PARLOR TRICK. IT IS NOTHING LESS THAN A SEARCH ACROSS WORLDS, WHERE YOUR VERY SOULS WILL FORM A TETHER TO SPAN THE VOID.

NOW, GREAT MYSTERIUS, WHY DO WE HAVE TO HOLD HANDS IN THE DARK WITH CANDLES? WHAT DO THE SPIRITS CARE?

IT'S A SIMPLE PRINCIPLE, REALLY.

YOU ALL HAVE SOULS--WITH THE POSSIBLE EXCEPTION OF MR. DARBY--AND JOINING TOGETHER IN A LOOP OR CIRCUIT GIVES ME A *"SPIRIT ENGINE"* TO DRIVE TO THE AFTERLIFE.

USUALLY THE MORE THE BETTER, BUT I FIND IT'S HARD TO KEEP ANY GROUP BIGGER THAN THIS ON POINT OR TO STOP LETTING GO.

THAT'S MOST IMPORTANT-- DO NOT BREAK THE CIRCLE DURING THE SEANCE.

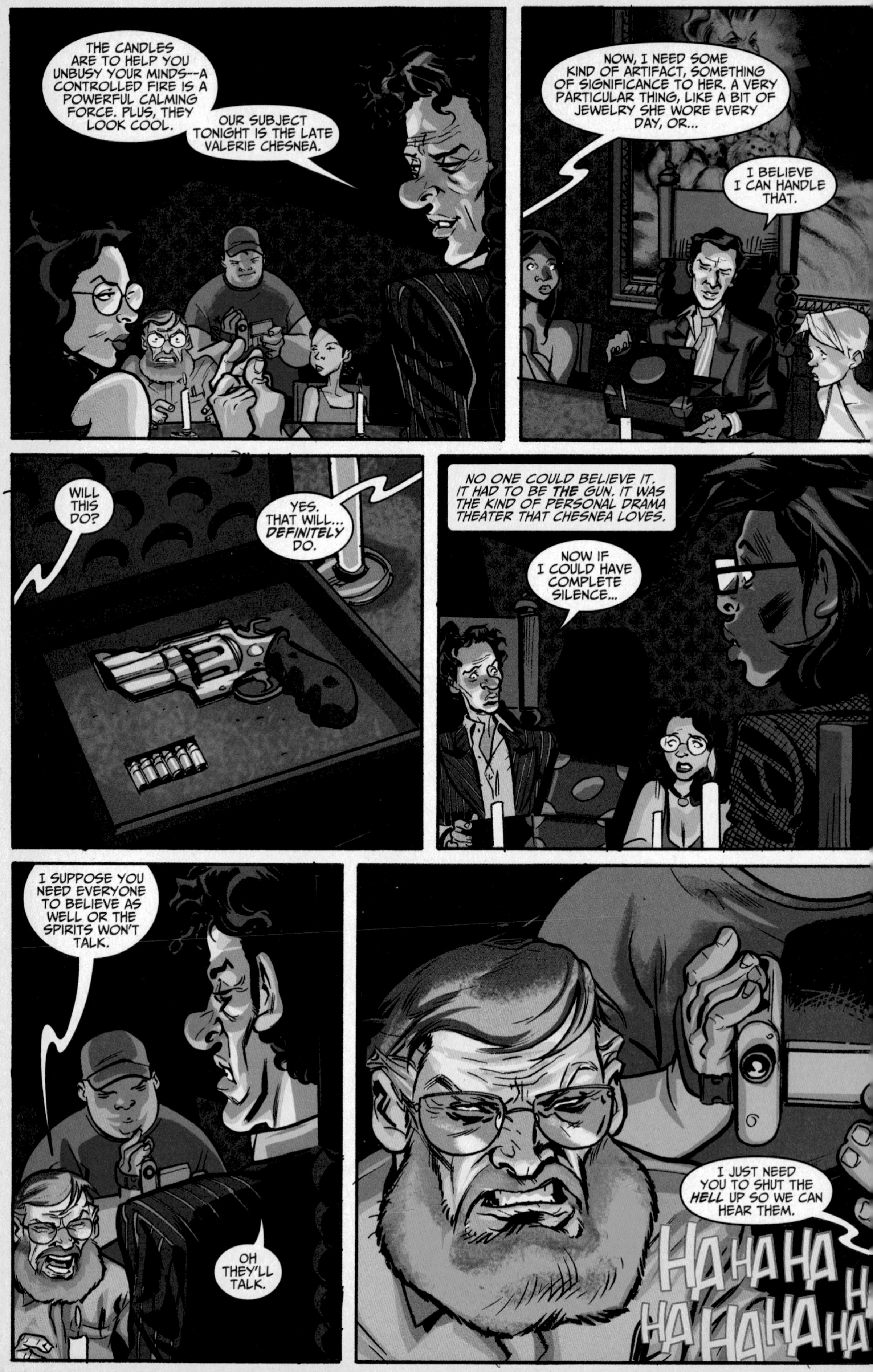
THE CANDLES ARE TO HELP YOU UNBUSY YOUR MINDS--A CONTROLLED FIRE IS A POWERFUL CALMING FORCE. PLUS, THEY LOOK COOL.
OUR SUBJECT TONIGHT IS THE LATE VALERIE CHESNEA.
NOW, I NEED SOME KIND OF ARTIFACT, SOMETHING OF SIGNIFICANCE TO HER. A VERY PARTICULAR THING, LIKE A BIT OF JEWELRY SHE WORE EVERY DAY, OR...
I BELIEVE I CAN HANDLE THAT.
WILL THIS DO?
YES. THAT WILL... DEFINITELY DO.
NO ONE COULD BELIEVE IT. IT HAD TO BE THE GUN. IT WAS THE KIND OF PERSONAL DRAMA THEATER THAT CHESNEA LOVES.
NOW IF I COULD HAVE COMPLETE SILENCE...
I SUPPOSE YOU NEED EVERYONE TO BELIEVE AS WELL OR THE SPIRITS WON'T TALK.
OH THEY'LL TALK.
I JUST NEED YOU TO SHUT THE HELL UP SO WE CAN HEAR THEM.
HAHAHAHA HAHAHAHAHA

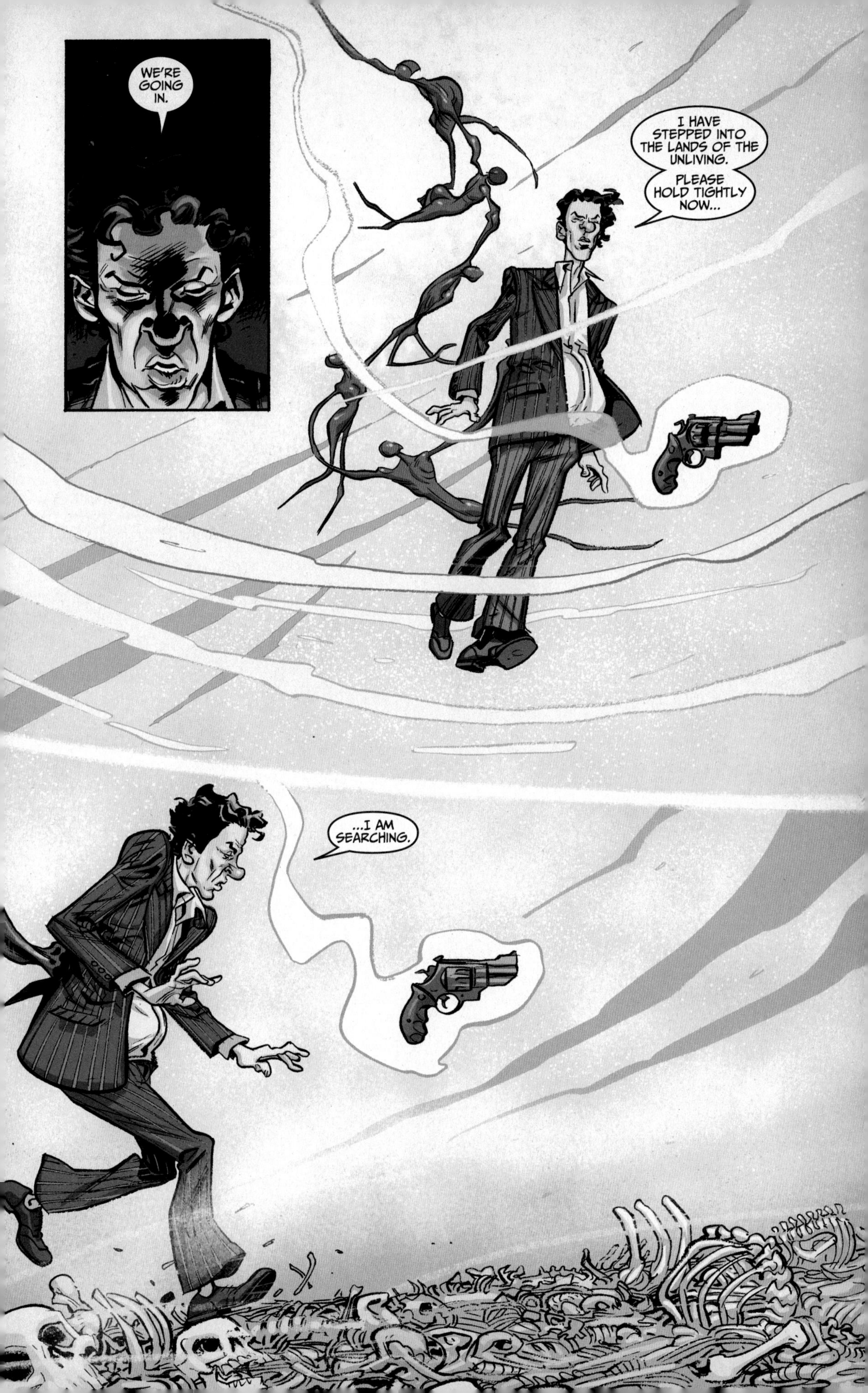
WE'RE GOING IN.
I HAVE STEPPED INTO THE LANDS OF THE UNLIVING.
PLEASE HOLD TIGHTLY NOW...
...I AM SEARCHING.

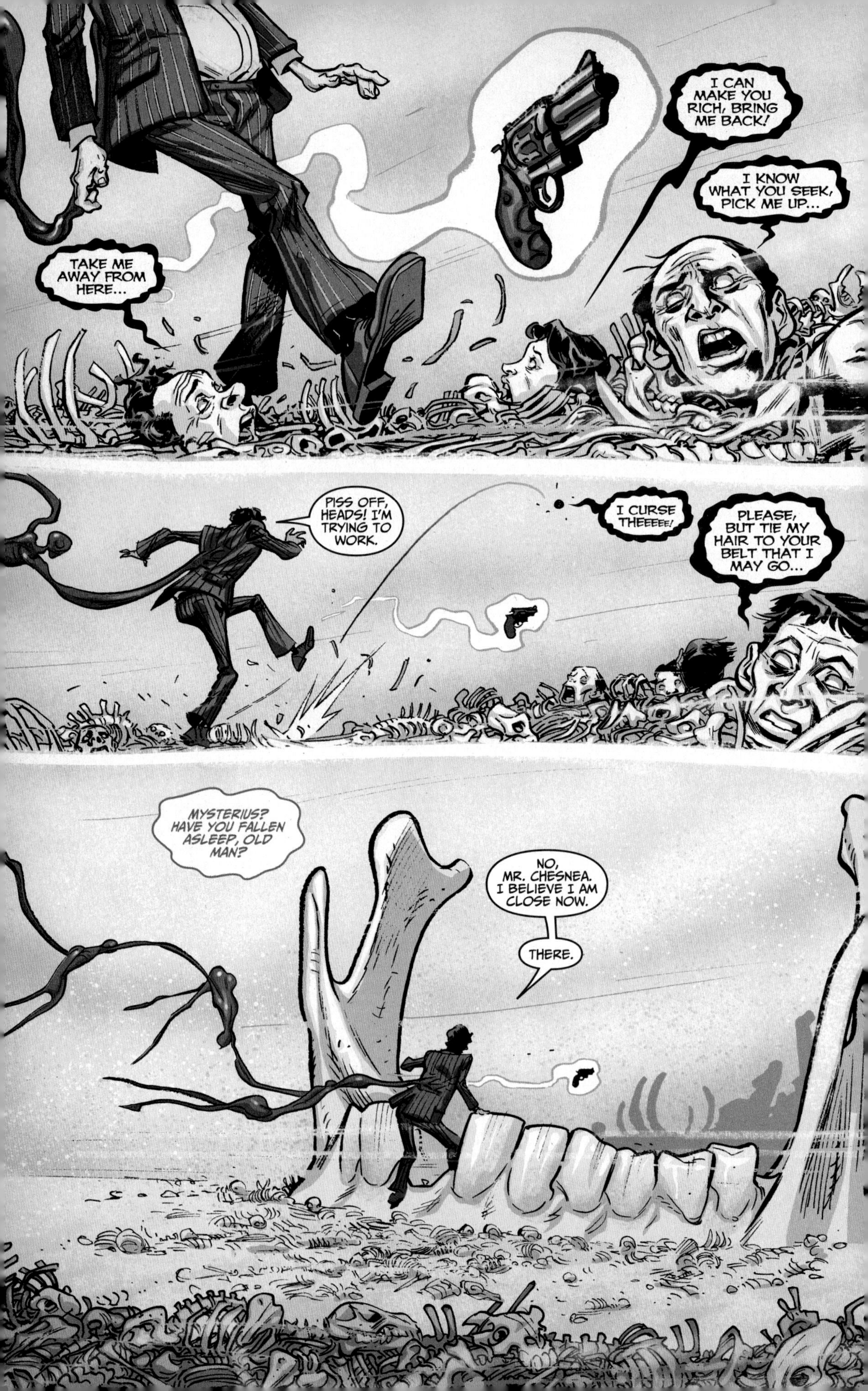
TAKE ME AWAY FROM HERE...
I CAN MAKE YOU RICH, BRING ME BACK!
I KNOW WHAT YOU SEEK, PICK ME UP...
PISS OFF, HEADS! I'M TRYING TO WORK.
I CURSE THEEEEEE!
PLEASE, BUT TIE MY HAIR TO YOUR BELT THAT I MAY GO...
MYSTERIUS? HAVE YOU FALLEN ASLEEP, OLD MAN?
NO, MR. CHESNEA. I BELIEVE I AM CLOSE NOW.
THERE.

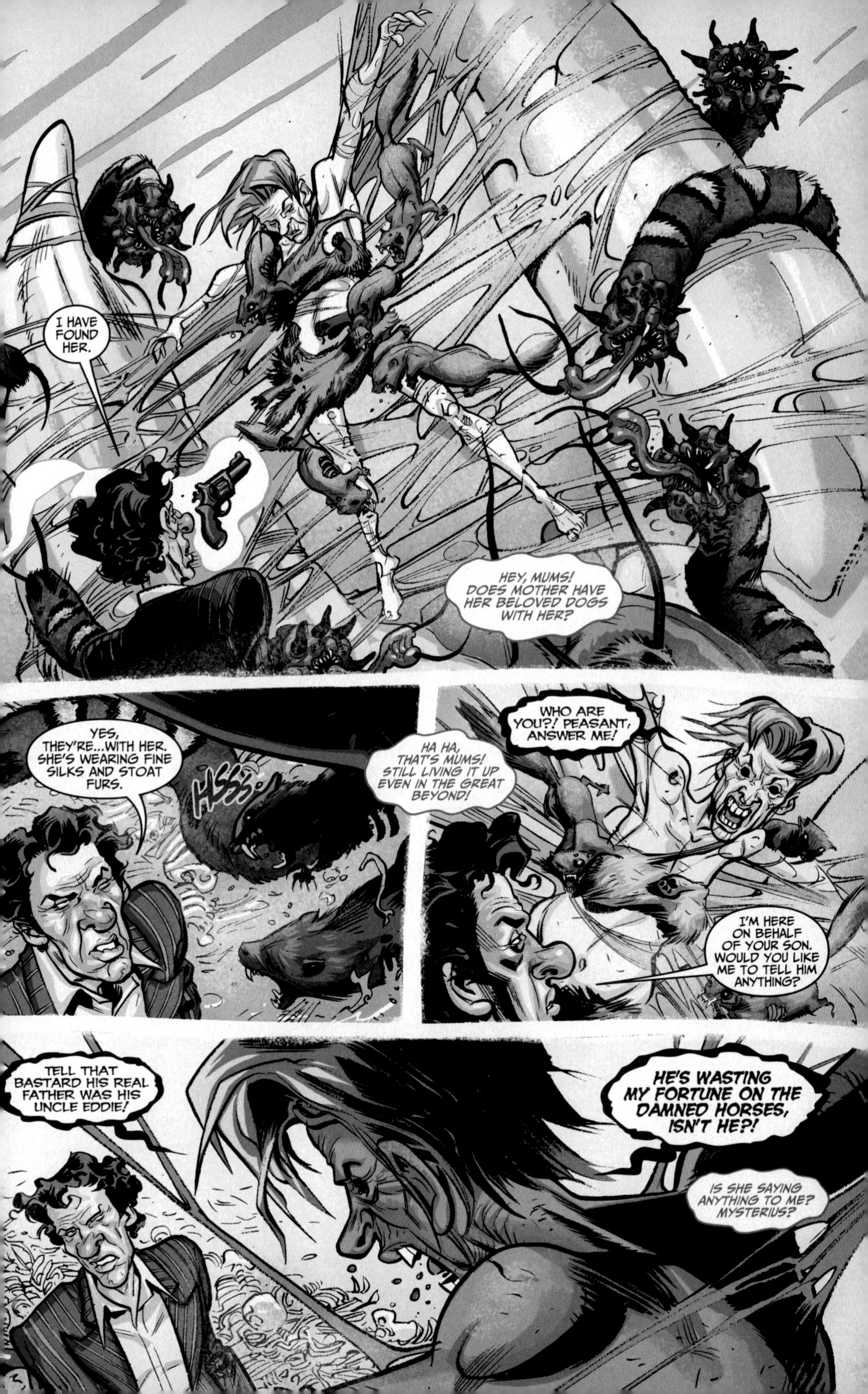
I HAVE FOUND HER.
HEY, MUMS! DOES MOTHER HAVE HER BELOVED DOGS WITH HER?
YES, THEY'RE...WITH HER. SHE'S WEARING FINE SILKS AND STOAT FURS.
HSSS
HA HA, THAT'S MUMS! STILL LIVING IT UP EVEN IN THE GREAT BEYOND!
WHO ARE YOU?! PEASANT, ANSWER ME!
I'M HERE ON BEHALF OF YOUR SON. WOULD YOU LIKE ME TO TELL HIM ANYTHING?
TELL THAT BASTARD HIS REAL FATHER WAS HIS UNCLE EDDIE!
HE'S WASTING MY FORTUNE ON THE DAMNED HORSES, ISN'T HE?!
IS SHE SAYING ANYTHING TO ME? MYSTERIUS?

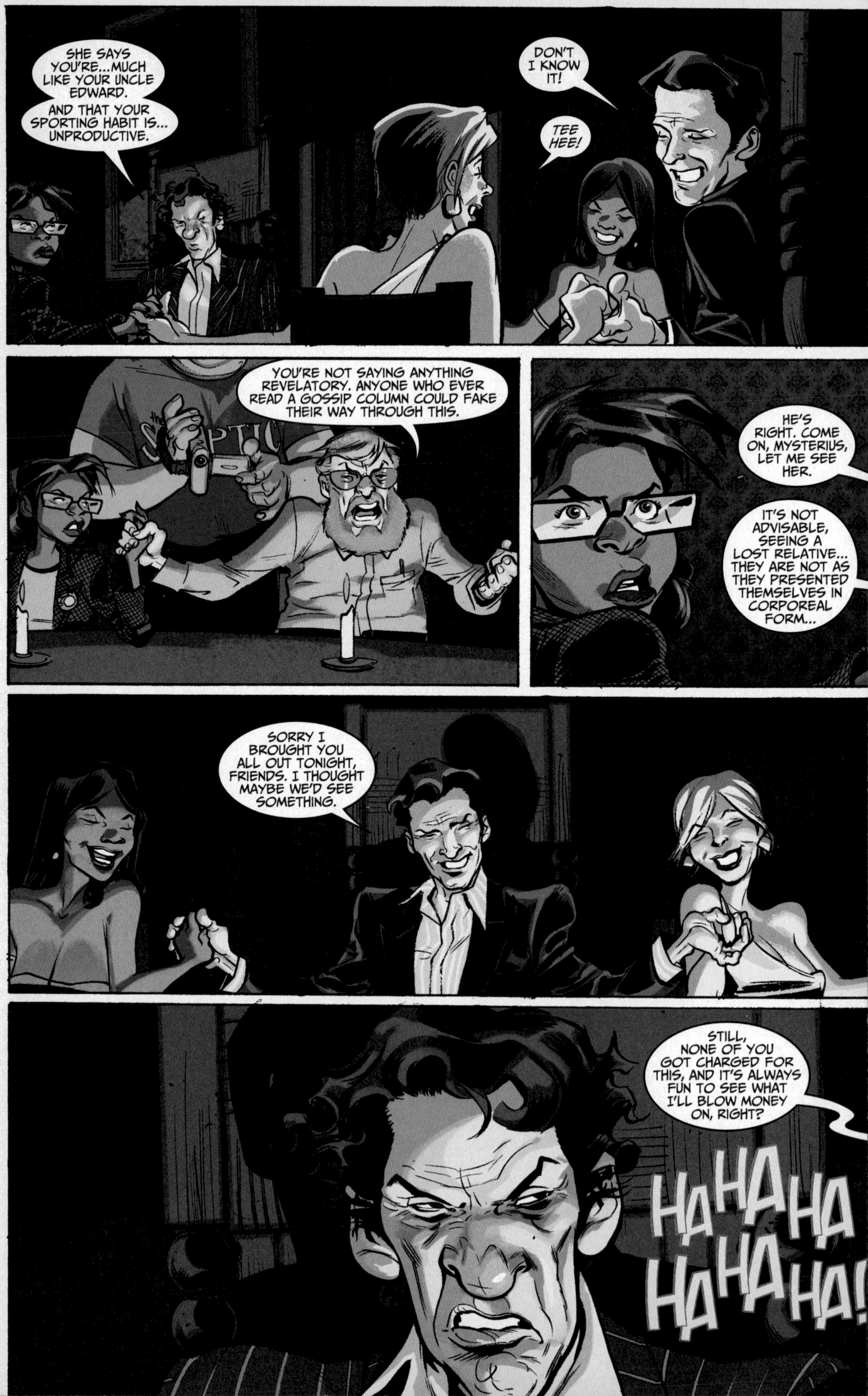
SHE SAYS YOU'RE...MUCH LIKE YOUR UNCLE EDWARD.
AND THAT YOUR SPORTING HABIT IS... UNPRODUCTIVE.
DON'T I KNOW IT!
TEE HEE!
YOU'RE NOT SAYING ANYTHING REVELATORY. ANYONE WHO EVER READ A GOSSIP COLUMN COULD FAKE THEIR WAY THROUGH THIS.
HE'S RIGHT. COME ON, MYSTERIUS, LET ME SEE HER.
IT'S NOT ADVISABLE, SEEING A LOST RELATIVE... THEY ARE NOT AS THEY PRESENTED THEMSELVES IN CORPOREAL FORM...
SORRY I BROUGHT YOU ALL OUT TONIGHT, FRIENDS. I THOUGHT MAYBE WE'D SEE SOMETHING.
STILL, NONE OF YOU GOT CHARGED FOR THIS, AND IT'S ALWAYS FUN TO SEE WHAT I'LL BLOW MONEY ON, RIGHT?
HAHAHAHA HAHAHAHA!

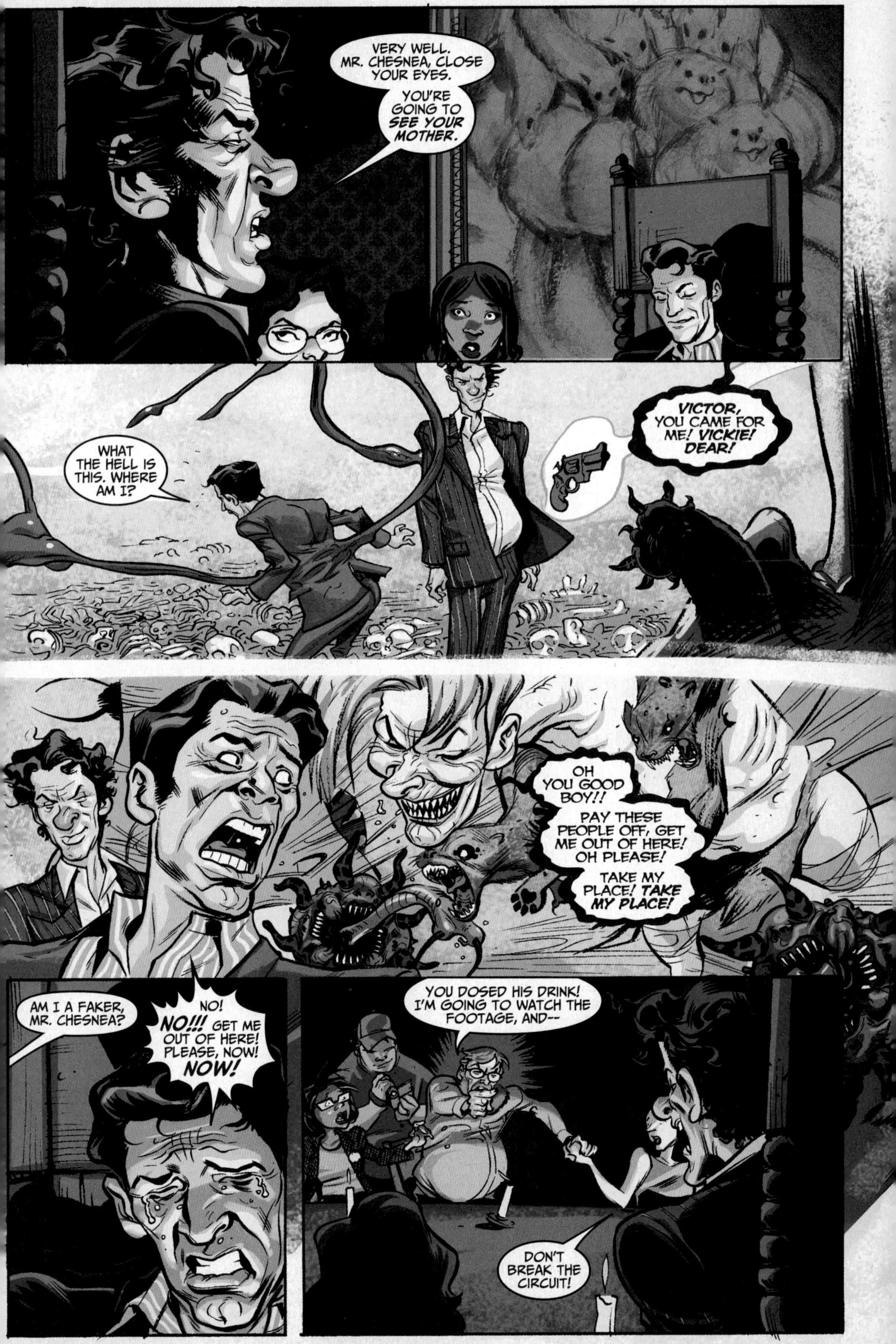
VERY WELL. MR. CHESNEA, CLOSE YOUR EYES.
YOU'RE GOING TO SEE YOUR MOTHER.
WHAT THE HELL IS THIS. WHERE AM I?
VICTOR, YOU CAME FOR ME! VICKIE! DEAR!
OH YOU GOOD BOY!!
PAY THESE PEOPLE OFF, GET ME OUT OF HERE! OH PLEASE!
TAKE MY PLACE! TAKE MY PLACE!
AM I A FAKER, MR. CHESNEA?
NO! NO!!! GET ME OUT OF HERE! PLEASE, NOW! NOW!
YOU DOSED HIS DRINK! I'M GOING TO WATCH THE FOOTAGE, AND--
DON'T BREAK THE CIRCUIT!

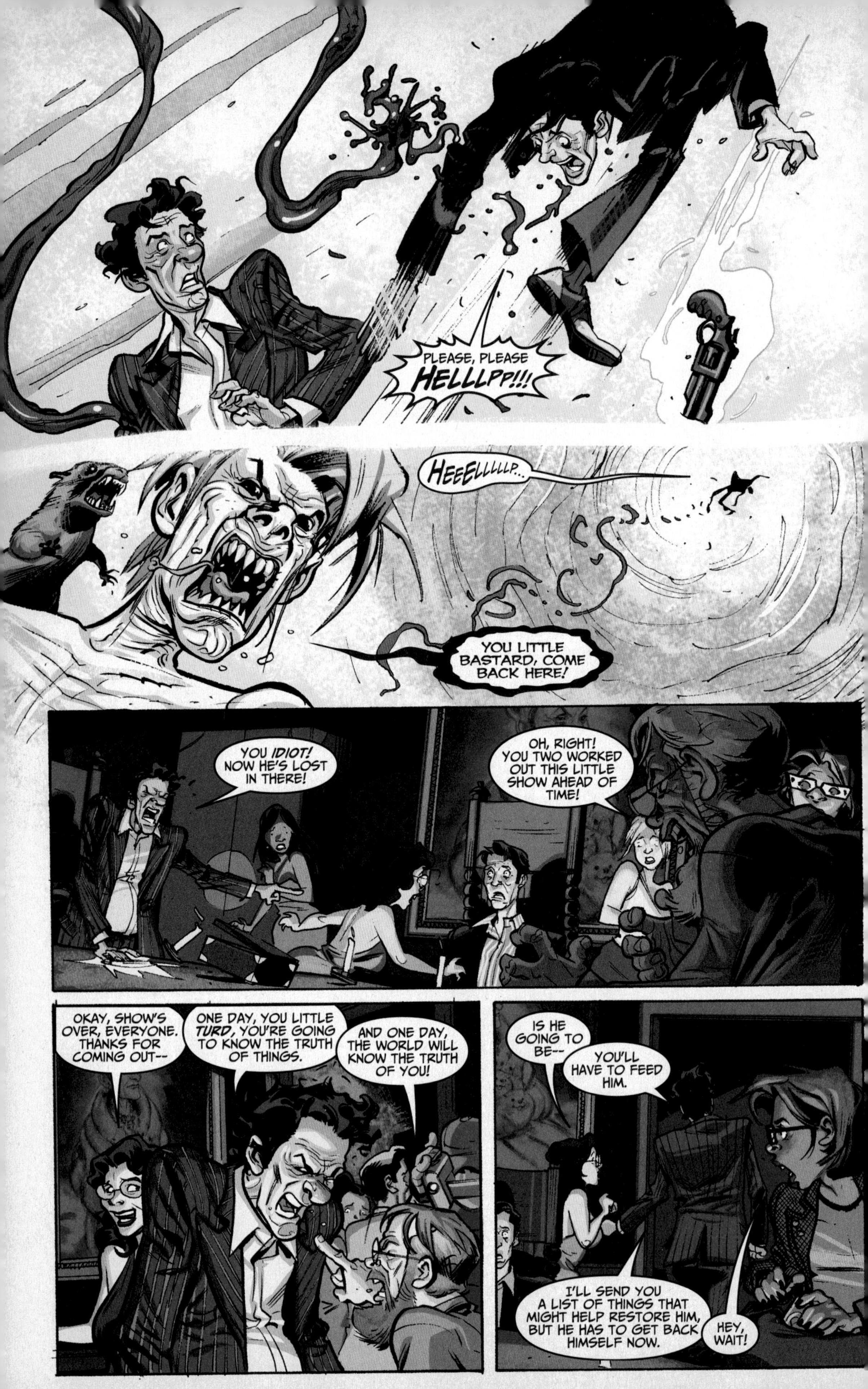
PLEASE, PLEASE HELLLPP!!!
HEEELLLLLP...
YOU LITTLE BASTARD, COME BACK HERE!
YOU IDIOT! NOW HE'S LOST IN THERE!
OH, RIGHT! YOU TWO WORKED OUT THIS LITTLE SHOW AHEAD OF TIME!
OKAY, SHOW'S OVER, EVERYONE. THANKS FOR COMING OUT--
ONE DAY, YOU LITTLE TURD, YOU'RE GOING TO KNOW THE TRUTH OF THINGS.
AND ONE DAY, THE WORLD WILL KNOW THE TRUTH OF YOU!
IS HE GOING TO BE--
YOU'LL HAVE TO FEED HIM.
I'LL SEND YOU A LIST OF THINGS THAT MIGHT HELP RESTORE HIM, BUT HE HAS TO GET BACK HIMSELF NOW.
HEY, WAIT!

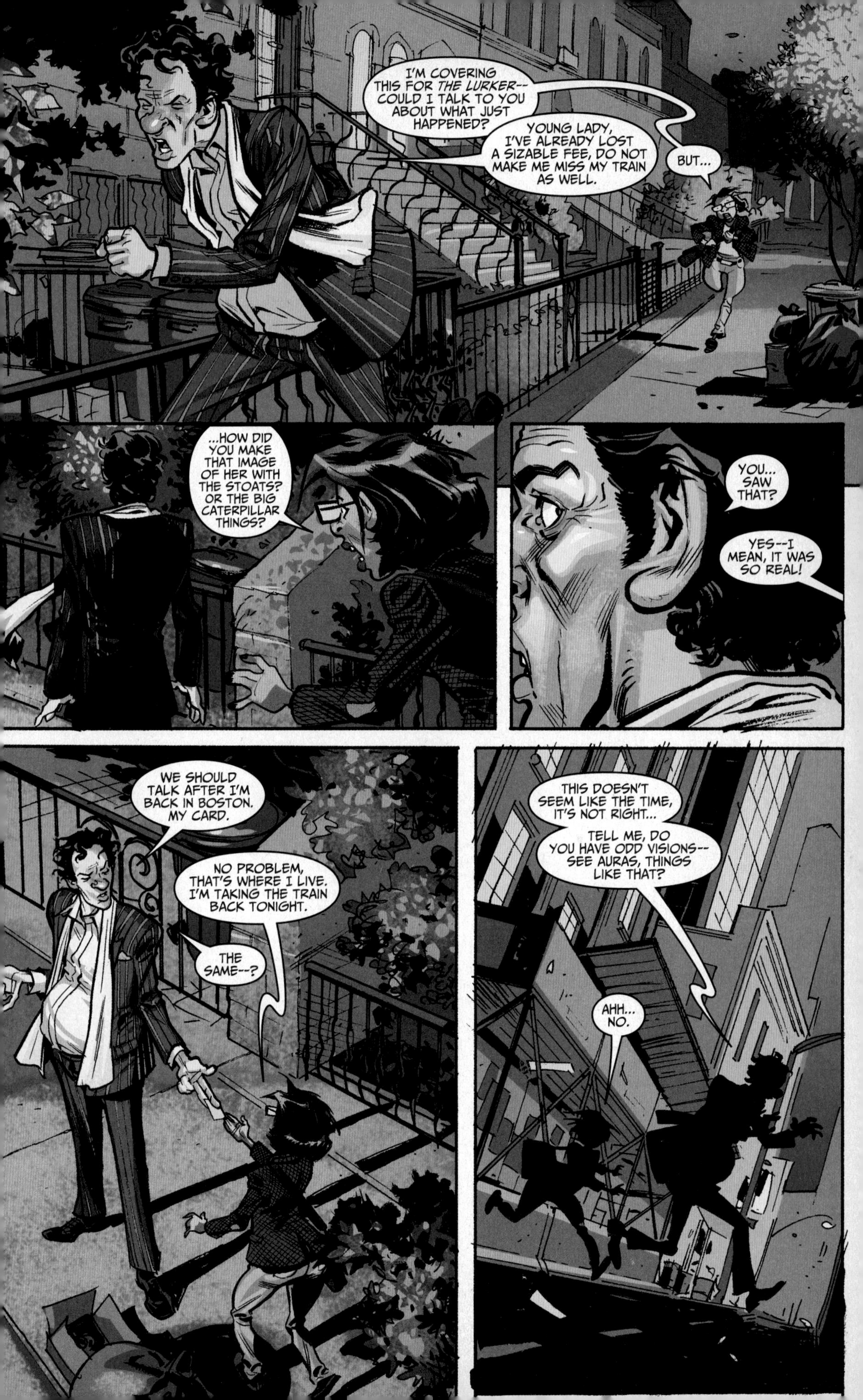

I'M COVERING THIS FOR *THE LURKER*-- COULD I TALK TO YOU ABOUT WHAT JUST HAPPENED?
YOUNG LADY, I'VE ALREADY LOST A SIZABLE FEE, DO NOT MAKE ME MISS MY TRAIN AS WELL.
BUT...
...HOW DID YOU MAKE THAT IMAGE OF HER WITH THE STOATS? OR THE BIG CATERPILLAR THINGS?
YOU... SAW THAT?
YES--I MEAN, IT WAS SO REAL!
WE SHOULD TALK AFTER I'M BACK IN BOSTON. MY CARD.
NO PROBLEM, THAT'S WHERE I LIVE. I'M TAKING THE TRAIN BACK TONIGHT.
THE SAME--?
THIS DOESN'T SEEM LIKE THE TIME, IT'S NOT RIGHT...
TELL ME, DO YOU HAVE ODD VISIONS-- SEE AURAS, THINGS LIKE THAT?
AHH... NO.

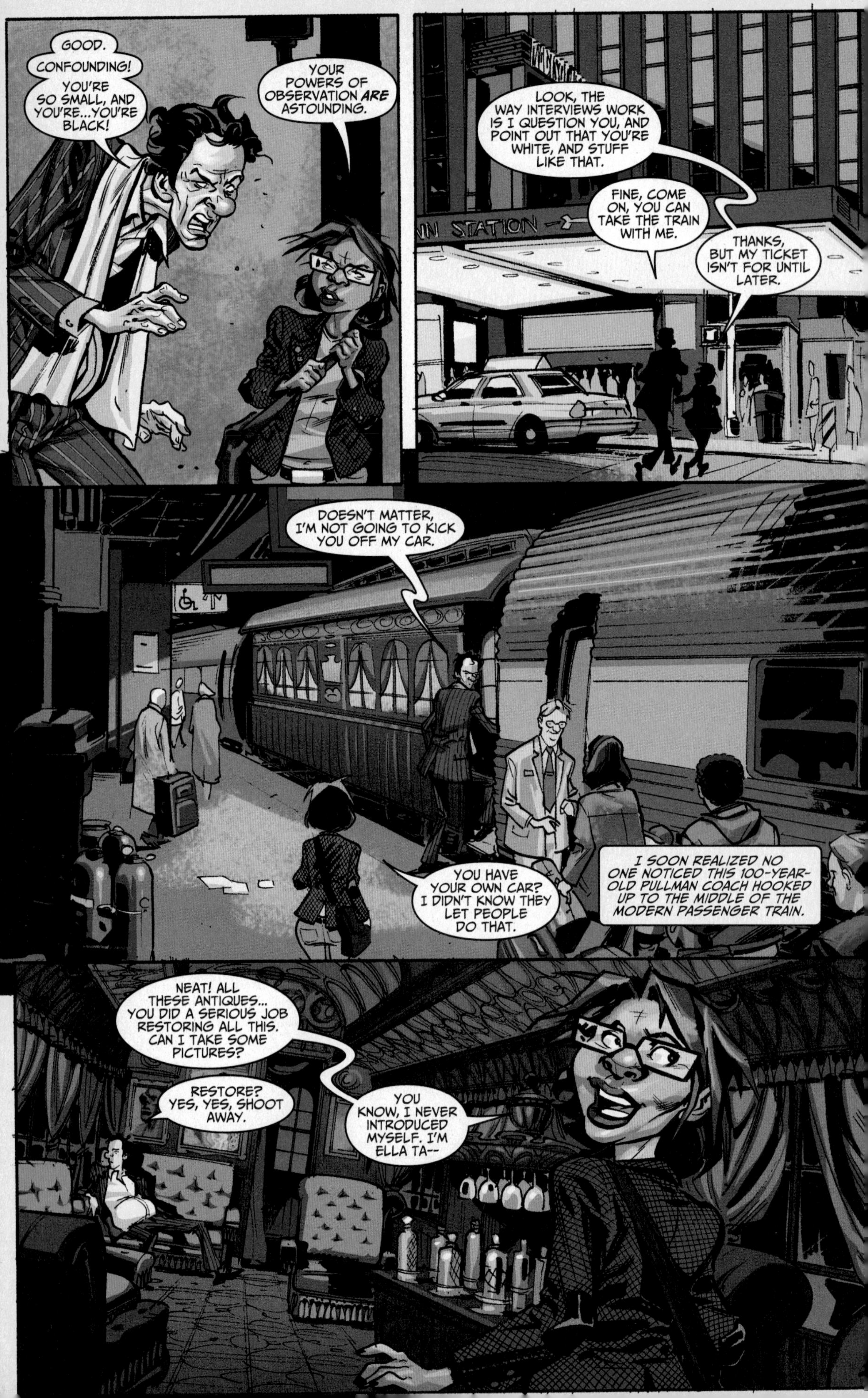
GOOD.
CONFOUNDING!
YOU'RE SO SMALL, AND YOU'RE...YOU'RE BLACK!
YOUR POWERS OF OBSERVATION ***ARE*** ASTOUNDING.
LOOK, THE WAY INTERVIEWS WORK IS I QUESTION YOU, AND POINT OUT THAT YOU'RE WHITE, AND STUFF LIKE THAT.
FINE, COME ON, YOU CAN TAKE THE TRAIN WITH ME.
THANKS, BUT MY TICKET ISN'T FOR UNTIL LATER.
DOESN'T MATTER, I'M NOT GOING TO KICK YOU OFF MY CAR.
YOU HAVE YOUR OWN CAR? I DIDN'T KNOW THEY LET PEOPLE DO THAT.
I SOON REALIZED NO ONE NOTICED THIS 100-YEAR-OLD PULLMAN COACH HOOKED UP TO THE MIDDLE OF THE MODERN PASSENGER TRAIN.
NEAT! ALL THESE ANTIQUES... YOU DID A SERIOUS JOB RESTORING ALL THIS. CAN I TAKE SOME PICTURES?
RESTORE? YES, YES, SHOOT AWAY.
YOU KNOW, I NEVER INTRODUCED MYSELF. I'M ELLA TA--

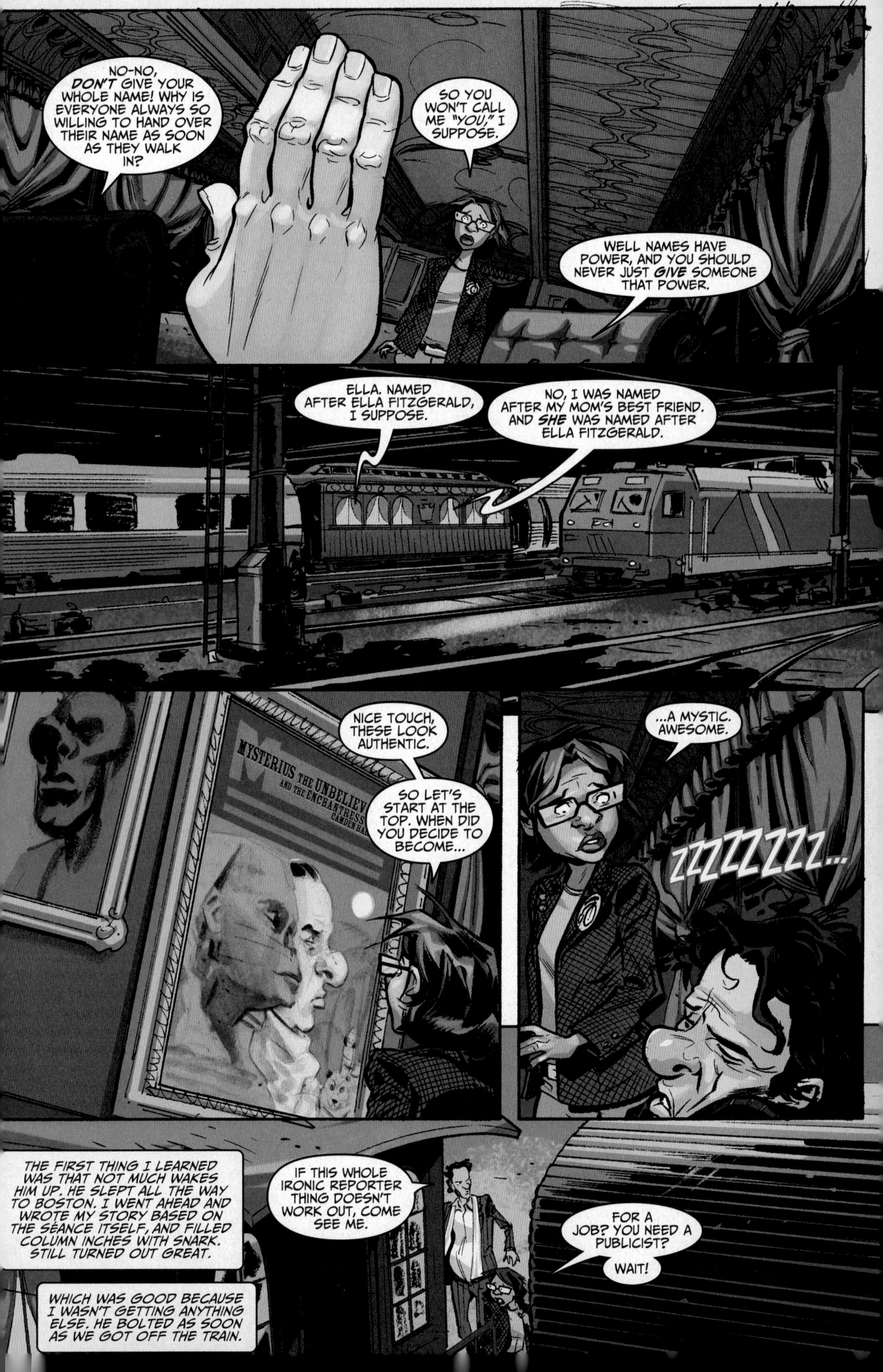

NO-NO, **DON'T** GIVE YOUR WHOLE NAME! WHY IS EVERYONE ALWAYS SO WILLING TO HAND OVER THEIR NAME AS SOON AS THEY WALK IN?
SO YOU WON'T CALL ME *"YOU,"* I SUPPOSE.
WELL NAMES HAVE POWER, AND YOU SHOULD NEVER JUST **GIVE** SOMEONE THAT POWER.
ELLA. NAMED AFTER ELLA FITZGERALD, I SUPPOSE.
NO, I WAS NAMED AFTER MY MOM'S BEST FRIEND. AND **SHE** WAS NAMED AFTER ELLA FITZGERALD.
MYSTERIUS THE UNBELIEV
AND THE ENCHANTRESS
NICE TOUCH, THESE LOOK AUTHENTIC.
SO LET'S START AT THE TOP. WHEN DID YOU DECIDE TO BECOME...
...A MYSTIC. AWESOME.
ZZZZZZZZ...
THE FIRST THING I LEARNED WAS THAT NOT MUCH WAKES HIM UP. HE SLEPT ALL THE WAY TO BOSTON. I WENT AHEAD AND WROTE MY STORY BASED ON THE SÉANCE ITSELF, AND FILLED COLUMN INCHES WITH SNARK. STILL TURNED OUT GREAT.
WHICH WAS GOOD BECAUSE I WASN'T GETTING ANYTHING ELSE. HE BOLTED AS SOON AS WE GOT OFF THE TRAIN.
IF THIS WHOLE IRONIC REPORTER THING DOESN'T WORK OUT, COME SEE ME.
FOR A JOB? YOU NEED A PUBLICIST?
WAIT!

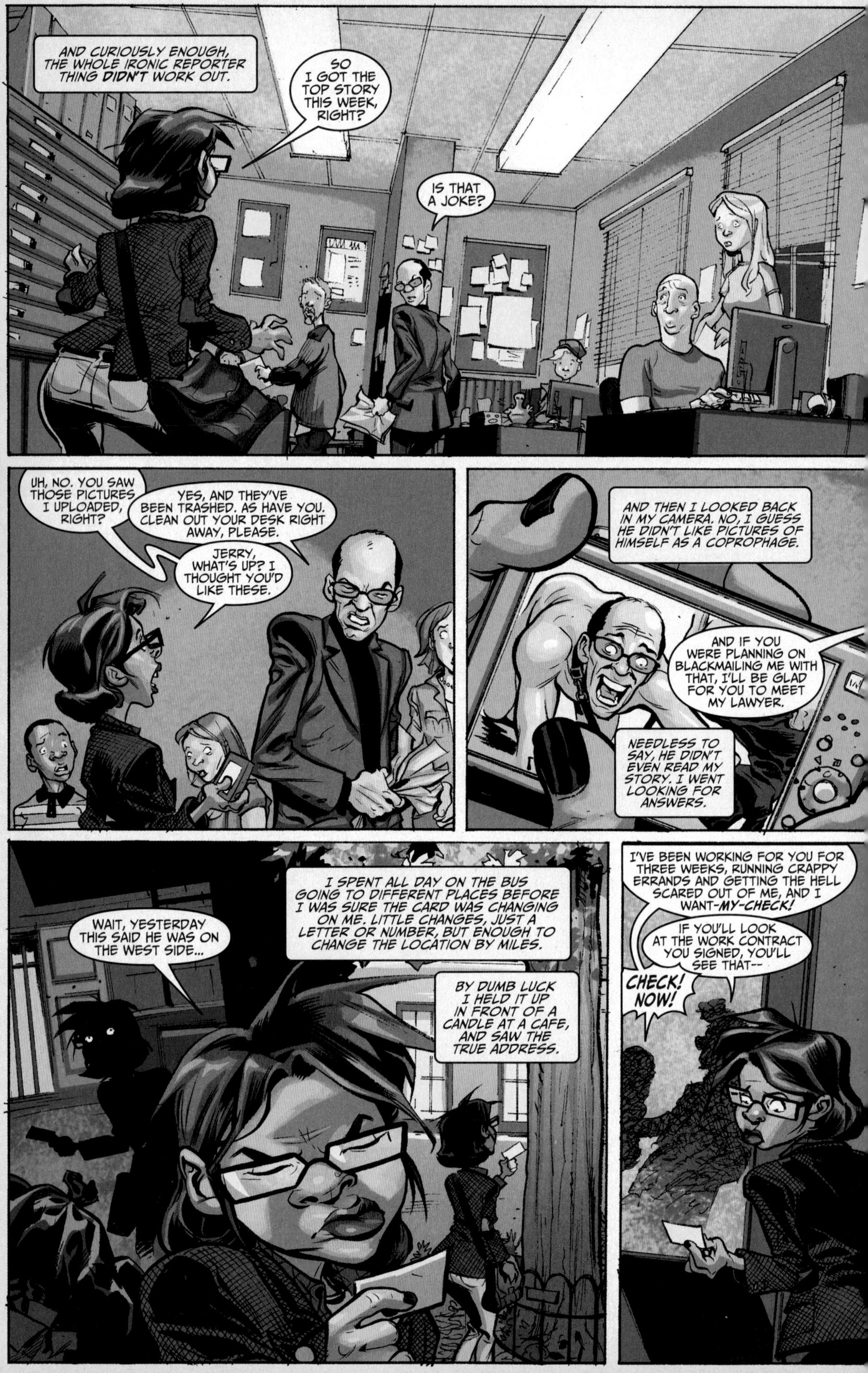
AND CURIOUSLY ENOUGH, THE WHOLE IRONIC REPORTER THING DIDN'T WORK OUT.
SO I GOT THE TOP STORY THIS WEEK, RIGHT?
IS THAT A JOKE?
UH, NO. YOU SAW THOSE PICTURES I UPLOADED, RIGHT?
YES, AND THEY'VE BEEN TRASHED. AS HAVE YOU. CLEAN OUT YOUR DESK RIGHT AWAY, PLEASE.
JERRY, WHAT'S UP? I THOUGHT YOU'D LIKE THESE.
AND THEN I LOOKED BACK IN MY CAMERA. NO, I GUESS HE DIDN'T LIKE PICTURES OF HIMSELF AS A COPROPHAGE.
AND IF YOU WERE PLANNING ON BLACKMAILING ME WITH THAT, I'LL BE GLAD FOR YOU TO MEET MY LAWYER.
NEEDLESS TO SAY, HE DIDN'T EVEN READ MY STORY. I WENT LOOKING FOR ANSWERS.
WAIT, YESTERDAY THIS SAID HE WAS ON THE WEST SIDE...
I SPENT ALL DAY ON THE BUS GOING TO DIFFERENT PLACES BEFORE I WAS SURE THE CARD WAS CHANGING ON ME. LITTLE CHANGES, JUST A LETTER OR NUMBER, BUT ENOUGH TO CHANGE THE LOCATION BY MILES.
BY DUMB LUCK I HELD IT UP IN FRONT OF A CANDLE AT A CAFE, AND SAW THE TRUE ADDRESS.
I'VE BEEN WORKING FOR YOU FOR THREE WEEKS, RUNNING CRAPPY ERRANDS AND GETTING THE HELL SCARED OUT OF ME, AND I WANT-MY-CHECK!
IF YOU'LL LOOK AT THE WORK CONTRACT YOU SIGNED, YOU'LL SEE THAT--
CHECK! NOW!

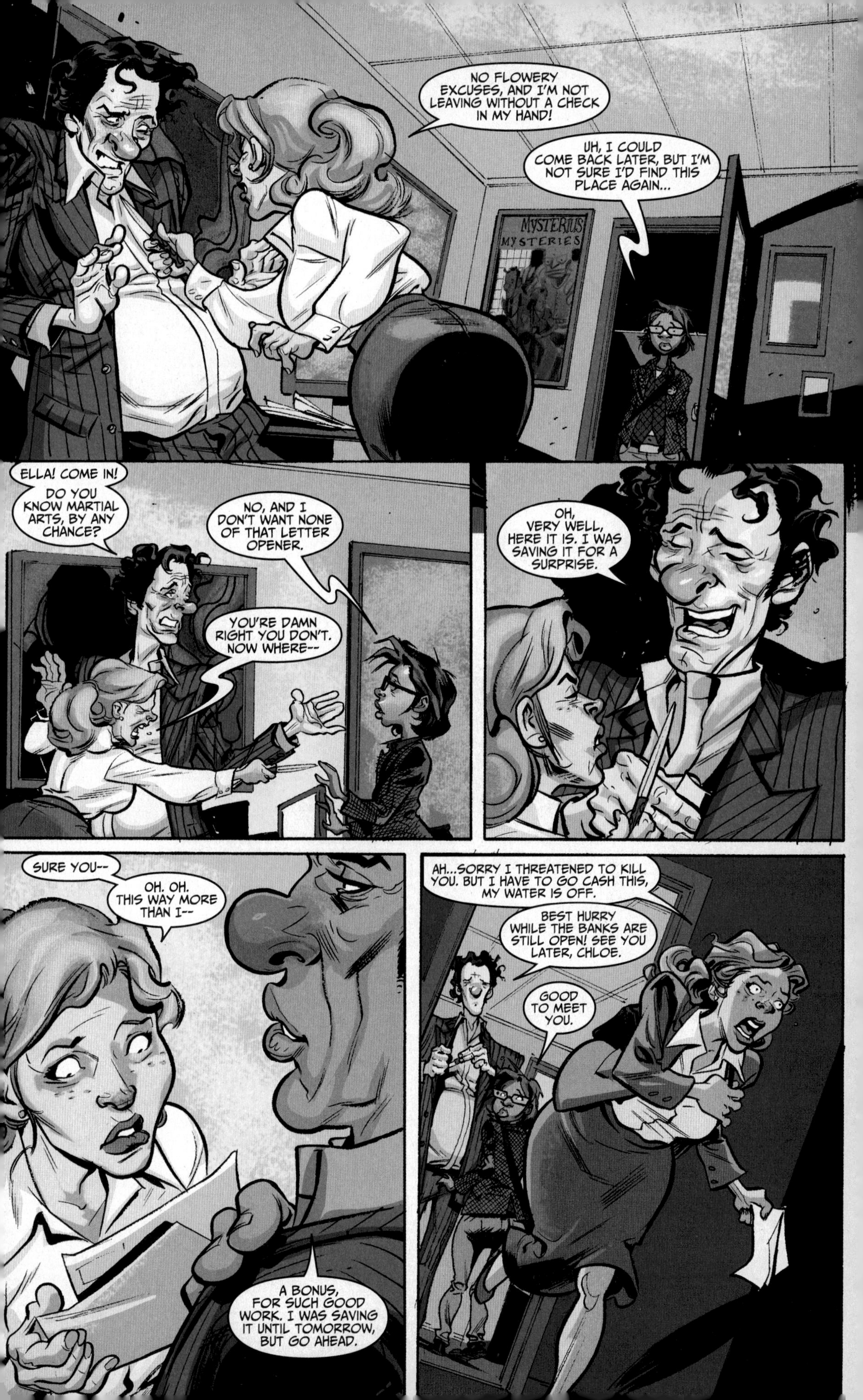
NO FLOWERY EXCUSES, AND I'M NOT LEAVING WITHOUT A CHECK IN MY HAND!
UH, I COULD COME BACK LATER, BUT I'M NOT SURE I'D FIND THIS PLACE AGAIN...
MYSTERIUS MYSTERIES
ELLA! COME IN! DO YOU KNOW MARTIAL ARTS, BY ANY CHANCE?
NO, AND I DON'T WANT NONE OF THAT LETTER OPENER.
YOU'RE DAMN RIGHT YOU DON'T. NOW WHERE--
OH, VERY WELL, HERE IT IS. I WAS SAVING IT FOR A SURPRISE.
SURE YOU--
OH. OH. THIS WAY MORE THAN I--
A BONUS, FOR SUCH GOOD WORK. I WAS SAVING IT UNTIL TOMORROW, BUT GO AHEAD.
AH...SORRY I THREATENED TO KILL YOU. BUT I HAVE TO GO CASH THIS, MY WATER IS OFF.
BEST HURRY WHILE THE BANKS ARE STILL OPEN! SEE YOU LATER, CHLOE.
GOOD TO MEET YOU.

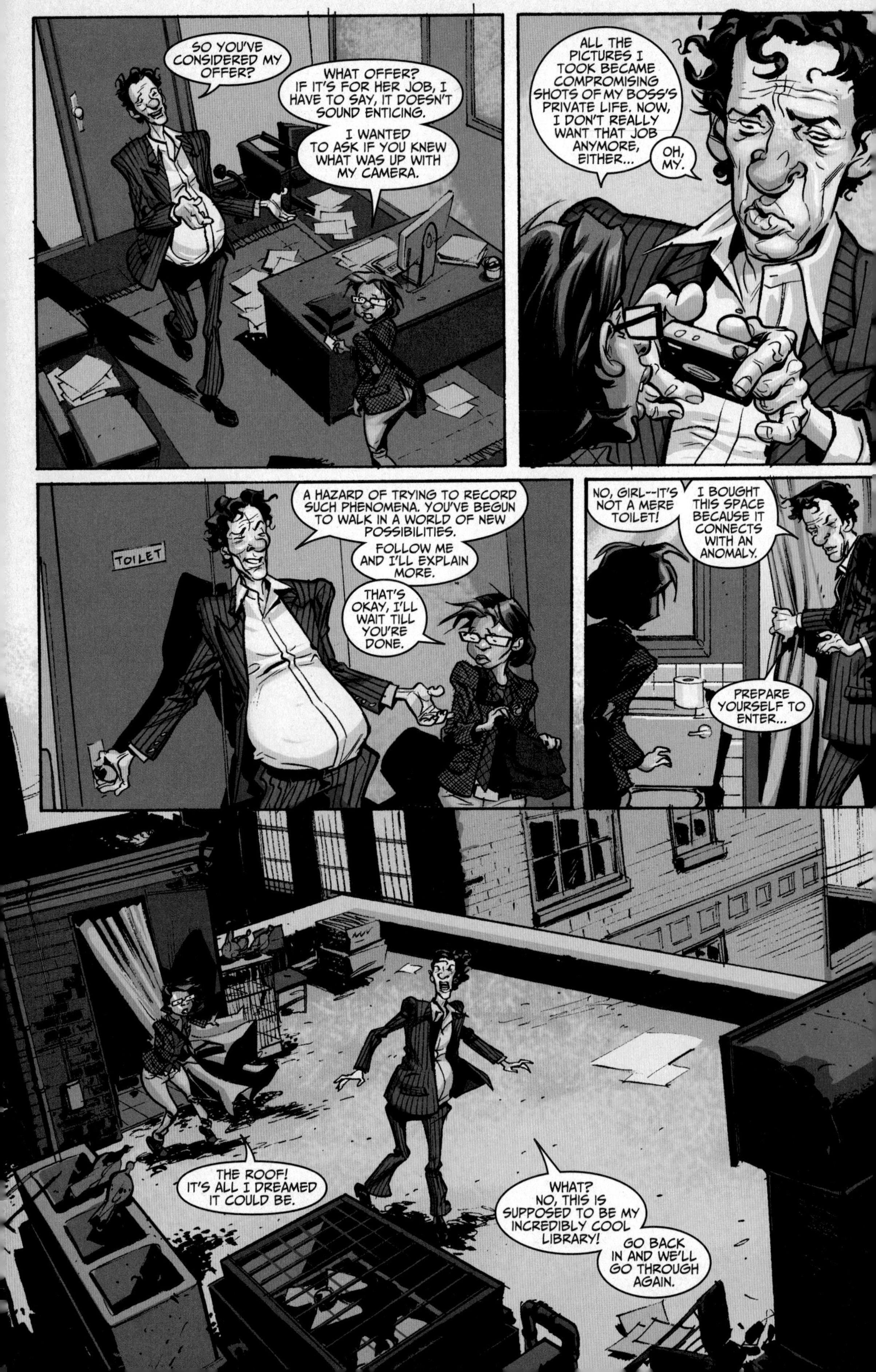
SO YOU'VE CONSIDERED MY OFFER?
WHAT OFFER? IF IT'S FOR HER JOB, I HAVE TO SAY, IT DOESN'T SOUND ENTICING.
I WANTED TO ASK IF YOU KNEW WHAT WAS UP WITH MY CAMERA.
ALL THE PICTURES I TOOK BECAME COMPROMISING SHOTS OF MY BOSS'S PRIVATE LIFE. NOW, I DON'T REALLY WANT THAT JOB ANYMORE, EITHER...
OH, MY.
TOILET
A HAZARD OF TRYING TO RECORD SUCH PHENOMENA. YOU'VE BEGUN TO WALK IN A WORLD OF NEW POSSIBILITIES.
FOLLOW ME AND I'LL EXPLAIN MORE.
THAT'S OKAY, I'LL WAIT TILL YOU'RE DONE.
NO, GIRL--IT'S NOT A MERE TOILET!
I BOUGHT THIS SPACE BECAUSE IT CONNECTS WITH AN ANOMALY.
PREPARE YOURSELF TO ENTER...
THE ROOF! IT'S ALL I DREAMED IT COULD BE.
WHAT? NO, THIS IS SUPPOSED TO BE MY INCREDIBLY COOL LIBRARY!
GO BACK IN AND WE'LL GO THROUGH AGAIN.

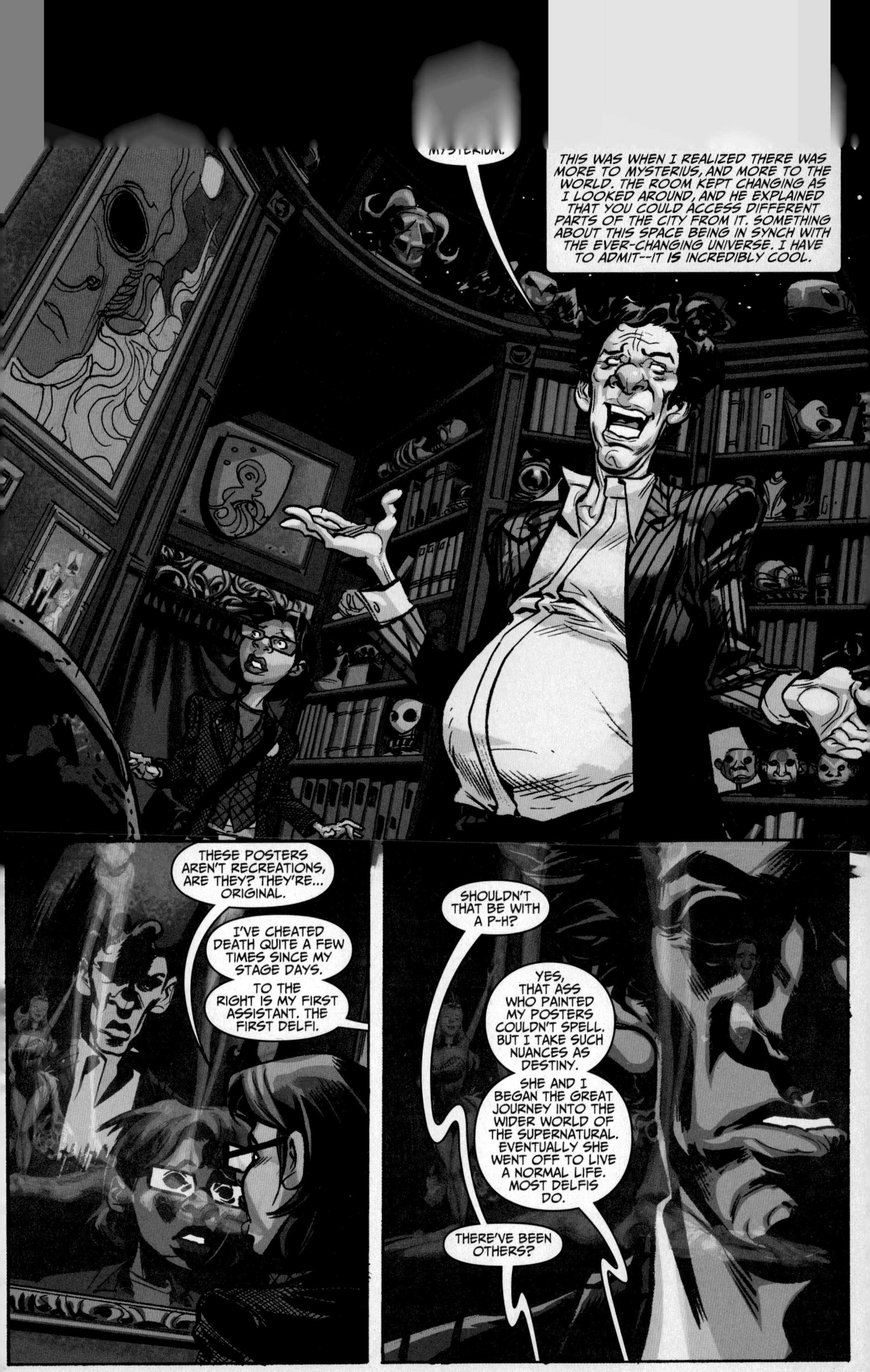
MYSTERIUM.
THIS WAS WHEN I REALIZED THERE WAS MORE TO MYSTERIUS, AND MORE TO THE WORLD. THE ROOM KEPT CHANGING AS I LOOKED AROUND, AND HE EXPLAINED THAT YOU COULD ACCESS DIFFERENT PARTS OF THE CITY FROM IT. SOMETHING ABOUT THIS SPACE BEING IN SYNCH WITH THE EVER-CHANGING UNIVERSE. I HAVE TO ADMIT--IT IS INCREDIBLY COOL.
THESE POSTERS AREN'T RECREATIONS, ARE THEY? THEY'RE... ORIGINAL.
I'VE CHEATED DEATH QUITE A FEW TIMES SINCE MY STAGE DAYS.
TO THE RIGHT IS MY FIRST ASSISTANT. THE FIRST DELFI.
SHOULDN'T THAT BE WITH A P-H?
YES, THAT ASS WHO PAINTED MY POSTERS COULDN'T SPELL. BUT I TAKE SUCH NUANCES AS DESTINY.
SHE AND I BEGAN THE GREAT JOURNEY INTO THE WIDER WORLD OF THE SUPERNATURAL. EVENTUALLY SHE WENT OFF TO LIVE A NORMAL LIFE. MOST DELFIS DO.
THERE'VE BEEN OTHERS?

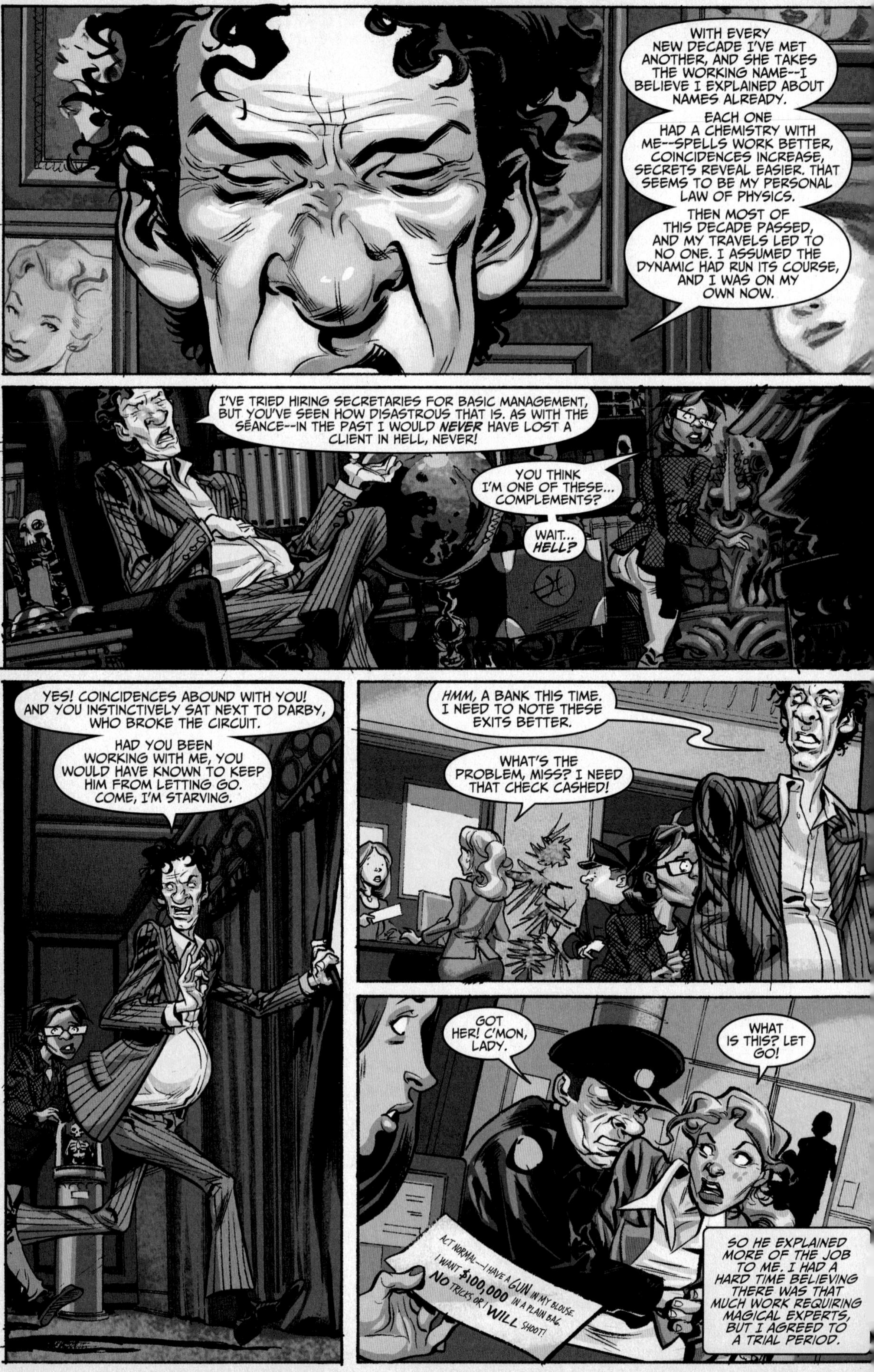
WITH EVERY NEW DECADE I'VE MET ANOTHER, AND SHE TAKES THE WORKING NAME--I BELIEVE I EXPLAINED ABOUT NAMES ALREADY.
EACH ONE HAD A CHEMISTRY WITH ME--SPELLS WORK BETTER, COINCIDENCES INCREASE, SECRETS REVEAL EASIER. THAT SEEMS TO BE MY PERSONAL LAW OF PHYSICS.
THEN MOST OF THIS DECADE PASSED, AND MY TRAVELS LED TO NO ONE. I ASSUMED THE DYNAMIC HAD RUN ITS COURSE, AND I WAS ON MY OWN NOW.
I'VE TRIED HIRING SECRETARIES FOR BASIC MANAGEMENT, BUT YOU'VE SEEN HOW DISASTROUS THAT IS. AS WITH THE SÉANCE--IN THE PAST I WOULD NEVER HAVE LOST A CLIENT IN HELL, NEVER!
YOU THINK I'M ONE OF THESE... COMPLEMENTS?
WAIT... HELL?
YES! COINCIDENCES ABOUND WITH YOU! AND YOU INSTINCTIVELY SAT NEXT TO DARBY, WHO BROKE THE CIRCUIT.
HAD YOU BEEN WORKING WITH ME, YOU WOULD HAVE KNOWN TO KEEP HIM FROM LETTING GO. COME, I'M STARVING.
HMM, A BANK THIS TIME. I NEED TO NOTE THESE EXITS BETTER.
WHAT'S THE PROBLEM, MISS? I NEED THAT CHECK CASHED!
GOT HER! C'MON, LADY.
WHAT IS THIS? LET GO!
ACT NORMAL—I HAVE A GUN IN MY BLOUSE. I WANT $100,000 IN A PLAIN BAG. NO TRICKS OR I WILL SHOOT!
SO HE EXPLAINED MORE OF THE JOB TO ME. I HAD A HARD TIME BELIEVING THERE WAS THAT MUCH WORK REQUIRING MAGICAL EXPERTS, BUT I AGREED TO A TRIAL PERIOD.

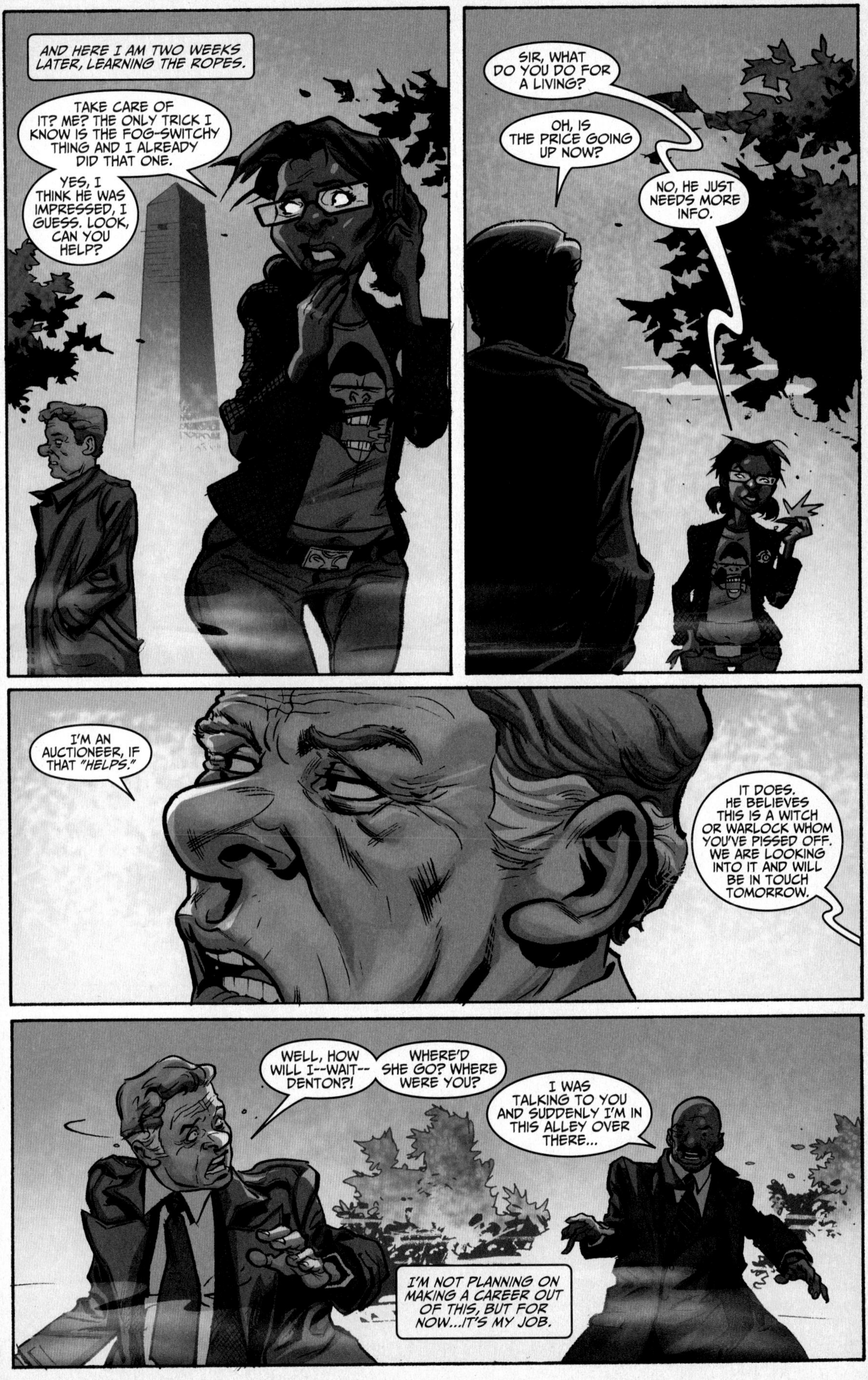
AND HERE I AM TWO WEEKS LATER, LEARNING THE ROPES.
TAKE CARE OF IT? ME? THE ONLY TRICK I KNOW IS THE FOG-SWITCHY THING AND I ALREADY DID THAT ONE.
YES, I THINK HE WAS IMPRESSED, I GUESS. LOOK, CAN YOU HELP?
SIR, WHAT DO YOU DO FOR A LIVING?
OH, IS THE PRICE GOING UP NOW?
NO, HE JUST NEEDS MORE INFO.
I'M AN AUCTIONEER, IF THAT "HELPS."
IT DOES. HE BELIEVES THIS IS A WITCH OR WARLOCK WHOM YOU'VE PISSED OFF. WE ARE LOOKING INTO IT AND WILL BE IN TOUCH TOMORROW.
WELL, HOW WILL I--WAIT-- DENTON?!
WHERE'D SHE GO? WHERE WERE YOU?
I WAS TALKING TO YOU AND SUDDENLY I'M IN THIS ALLEY OVER THERE...
I'M NOT PLANNING ON MAKING A CAREER OUT OF THIS, BUT FOR NOW...IT'S MY JOB.

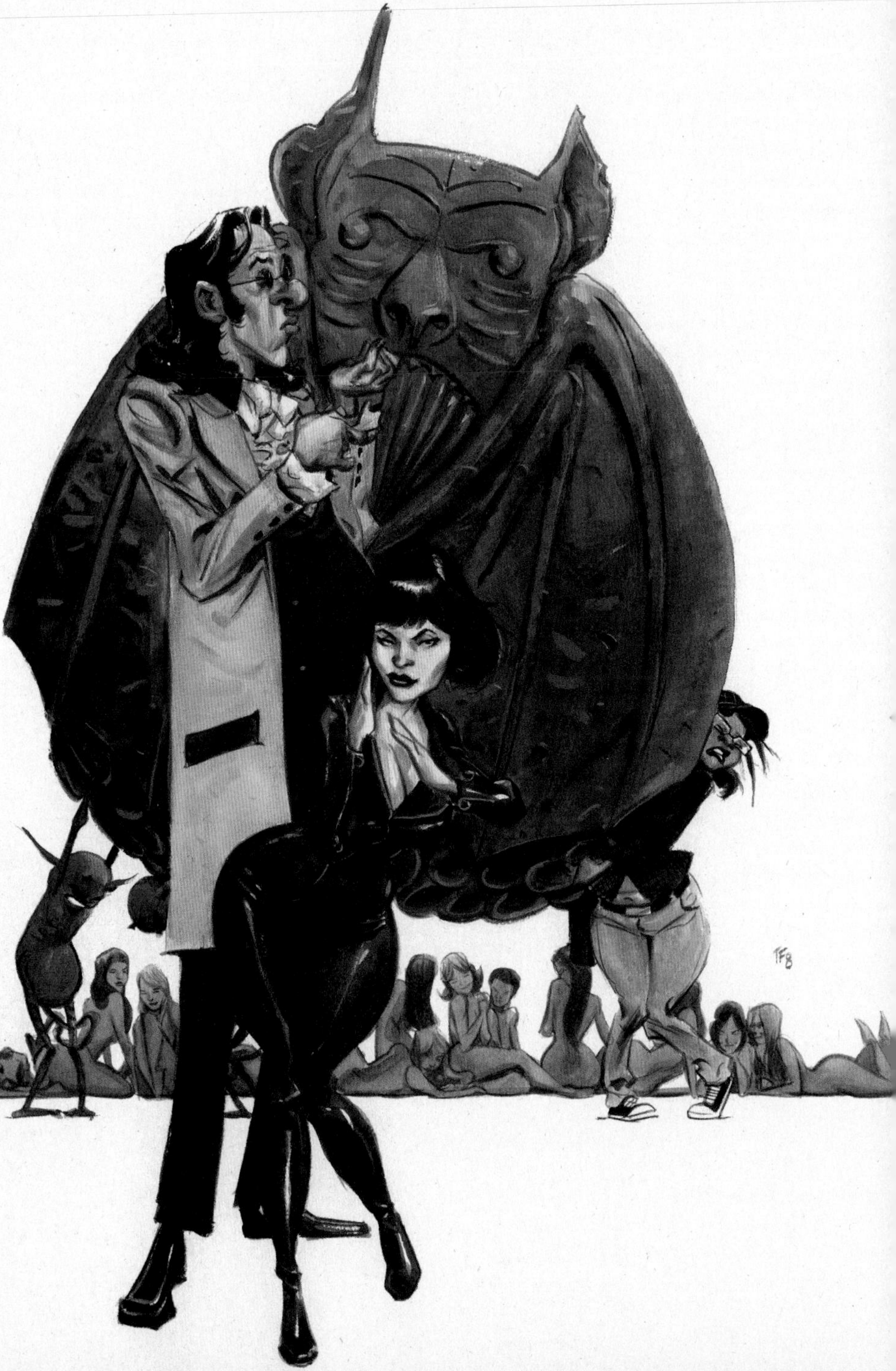

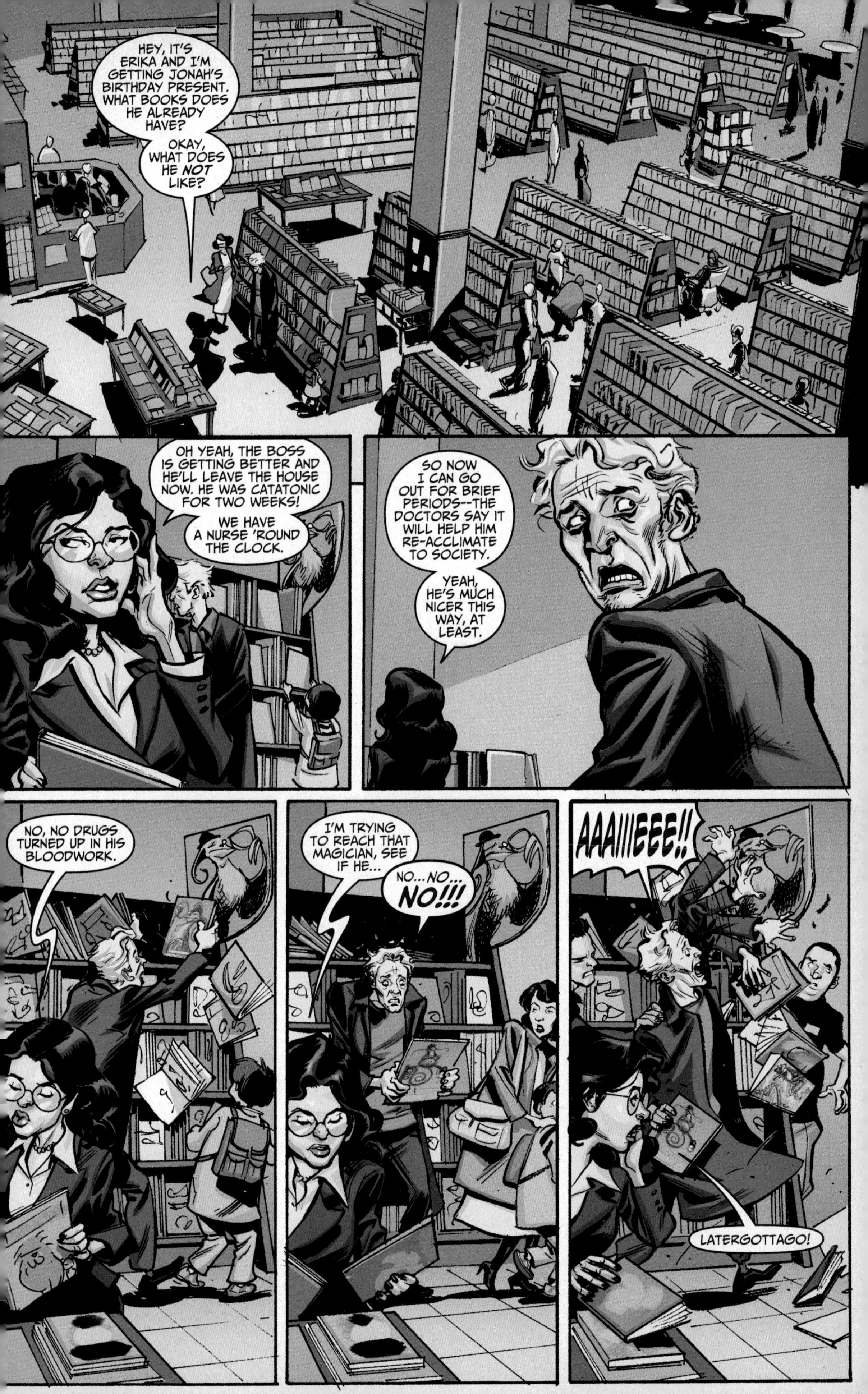
HEY, IT'S ERIKA AND I'M GETTING JONAH'S BIRTHDAY PRESENT. WHAT BOOKS DOES HE ALREADY HAVE?
OKAY, WHAT DOES HE NOT LIKE?
OH YEAH, THE BOSS IS GETTING BETTER AND HE'LL LEAVE THE HOUSE NOW. HE WAS CATATONIC FOR TWO WEEKS!
WE HAVE A NURSE 'ROUND THE CLOCK.
SO NOW I CAN GO OUT FOR BRIEF PERIODS--THE DOCTORS SAY IT WILL HELP HIM RE-ACCLIMATE TO SOCIETY.
YEAH, HE'S MUCH NICER THIS WAY, AT LEAST.
NO, NO DRUGS TURNED UP IN HIS BLOODWORK.
I'M TRYING TO REACH THAT MAGICIAN, SEE IF HE...
NO...NO... NO!!!
AAAIIIIEEE!!
LATERGOTTAGO!

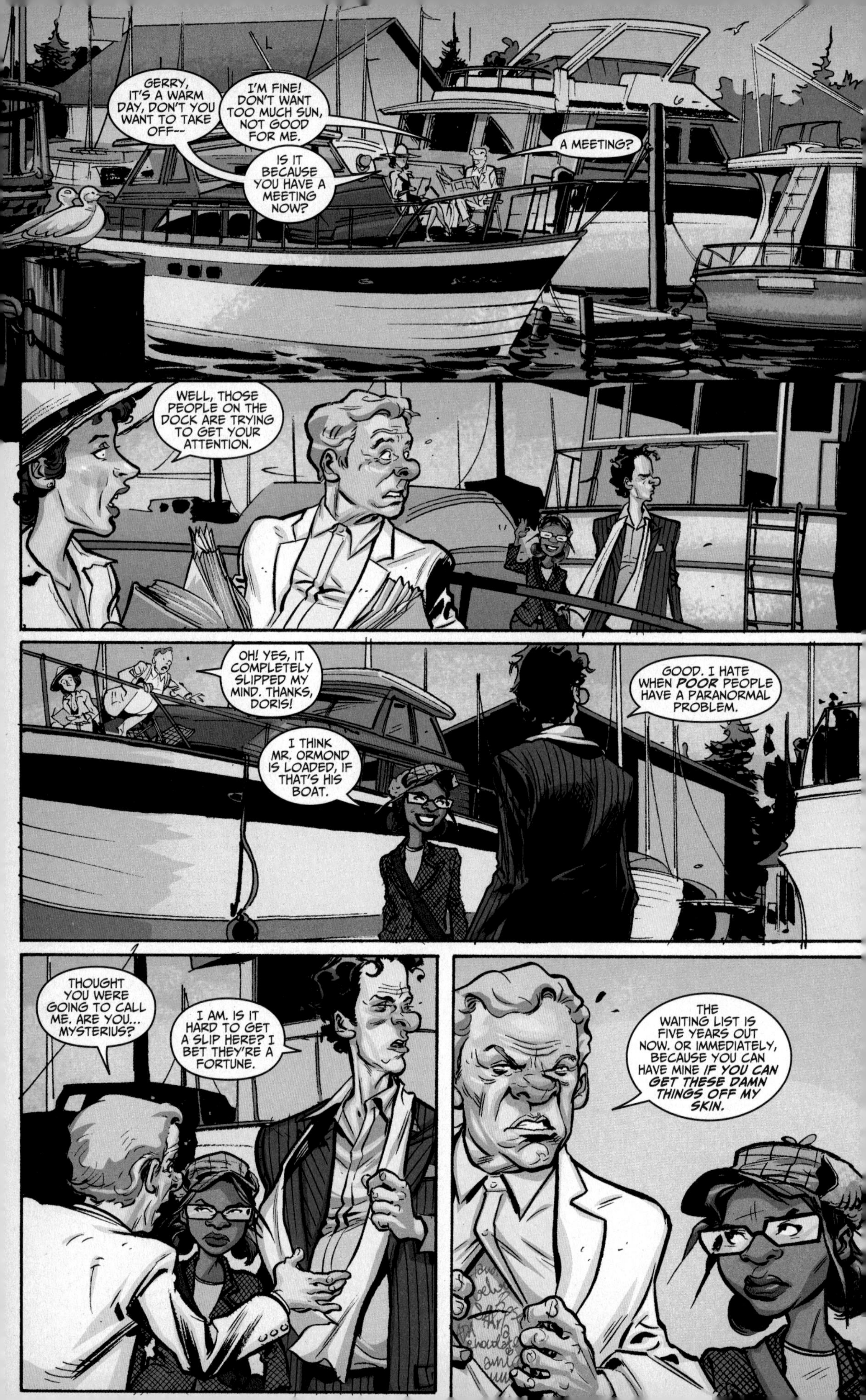
GERRY, IT'S A WARM DAY, DON'T YOU WANT TO TAKE OFF--
I'M FINE! DON'T WANT TOO MUCH SUN, NOT GOOD FOR ME.
IS IT BECAUSE YOU HAVE A MEETING NOW?
A MEETING?
WELL, THOSE PEOPLE ON THE DOCK ARE TRYING TO GET YOUR ATTENTION.
OH! YES, IT COMPLETELY SLIPPED MY MIND. THANKS, DORIS!
I THINK MR. ORMOND IS LOADED, IF THAT'S HIS BOAT.
GOOD. I HATE WHEN POOR PEOPLE HAVE A PARANORMAL PROBLEM.
THOUGHT YOU WERE GOING TO CALL ME. ARE YOU... MYSTERIUS?
I AM. IS IT HARD TO GET A SLIP HERE? I BET THEY'RE A FORTUNE.
THE WAITING LIST IS FIVE YEARS OUT NOW. OR IMMEDIATELY, BECAUSE YOU CAN HAVE MINE IF YOU CAN GET THESE DAMN THINGS OFF MY SKIN.

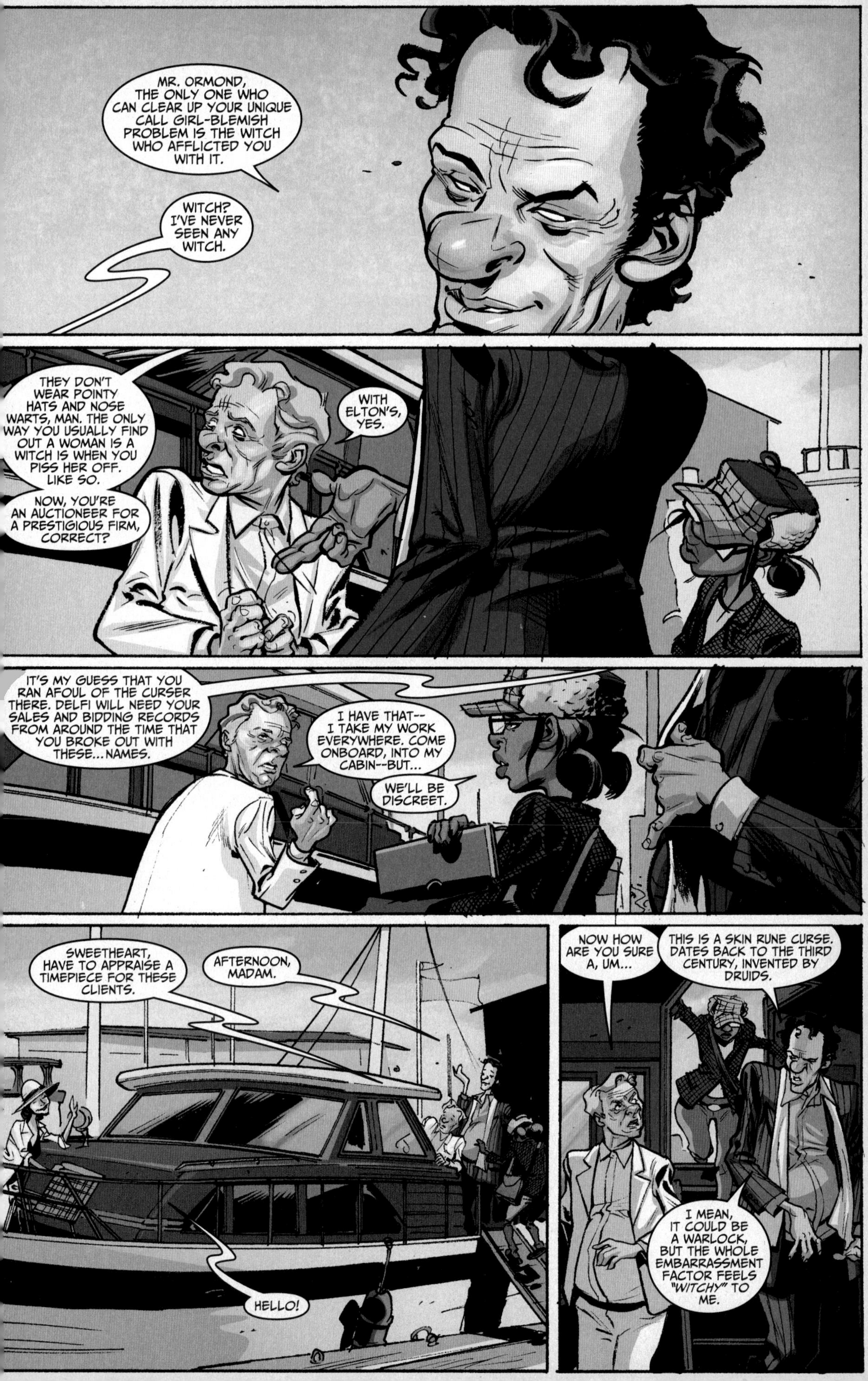
MR. ORMOND, THE ONLY ONE WHO CAN CLEAR UP YOUR UNIQUE CALL GIRL-BLEMISH PROBLEM IS THE WITCH WHO AFFLICTED YOU WITH IT.
WITCH? I'VE NEVER SEEN ANY WITCH.
THEY DON'T WEAR POINTY HATS AND NOSE WARTS, MAN. THE ONLY WAY YOU USUALLY FIND OUT A WOMAN IS A WITCH IS WHEN YOU PISS HER OFF. LIKE SO.
NOW, YOU'RE AN AUCTIONEER FOR A PRESTIGIOUS FIRM, CORRECT?
WITH ELTON'S, YES.
IT'S MY GUESS THAT YOU RAN AFOUL OF THE CURSER THERE. DELFI WILL NEED YOUR SALES AND BIDDING RECORDS FROM AROUND THE TIME THAT YOU BROKE OUT WITH THESE...NAMES.
I HAVE THAT-- I TAKE MY WORK EVERYWHERE. COME ONBOARD, INTO MY CABIN--BUT...
WE'LL BE DISCREET.
SWEETHEART, HAVE TO APPRAISE A TIMEPIECE FOR THESE CLIENTS.
AFTERNOON, MADAM.
HELLO!
NOW HOW ARE YOU SURE A, UM...
THIS IS A SKIN RUNE CURSE. DATES BACK TO THE THIRD CENTURY, INVENTED BY DRUIDS.
I MEAN, IT COULD BE A WARLOCK, BUT THE WHOLE EMBARRASSMENT FACTOR FEELS "WITCHY" TO ME.

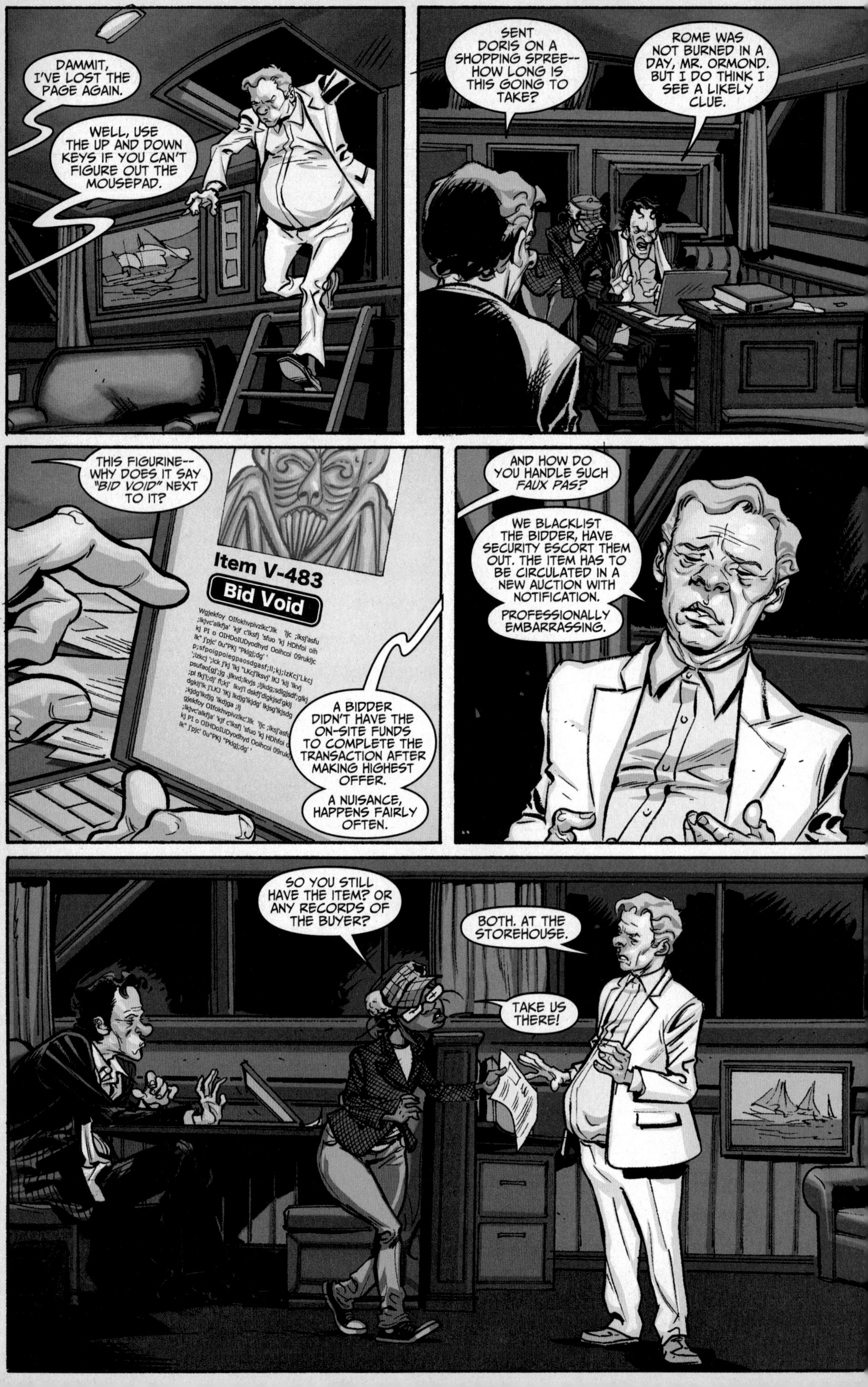

DAMMIT, I'VE LOST THE PAGE AGAIN.
WELL, USE THE UP AND DOWN KEYS IF YOU CAN'T FIGURE OUT THE MOUSEPAD.
SENT DORIS ON A SHOPPING SPREE-- HOW LONG IS THIS GOING TO TAKE?
ROME WAS NOT BURNED IN A DAY, MR. ORMOND. BUT I DO THINK I SEE A LIKELY CLUE.
THIS FIGURINE-- WHY DOES IT SAY "BID VOID" NEXT TO IT?
Item V-483
Bid Void
A BIDDER DIDN'T HAVE THE ON-SITE FUNDS TO COMPLETE THE TRANSACTION AFTER MAKING HIGHEST OFFER.
A NUISANCE, HAPPENS FAIRLY OFTEN.
AND HOW DO YOU HANDLE SUCH FAUX PAS?
WE BLACKLIST THE BIDDER, HAVE SECURITY ESCORT THEM OUT. THE ITEM HAS TO BE CIRCULATED IN A NEW AUCTION WITH NOTIFICATION.
PROFESSIONALLY EMBARRASSING.
SO YOU STILL HAVE THE ITEM? OR ANY RECORDS OF THE BUYER?
BOTH. AT THE STOREHOUSE.
TAKE US THERE!

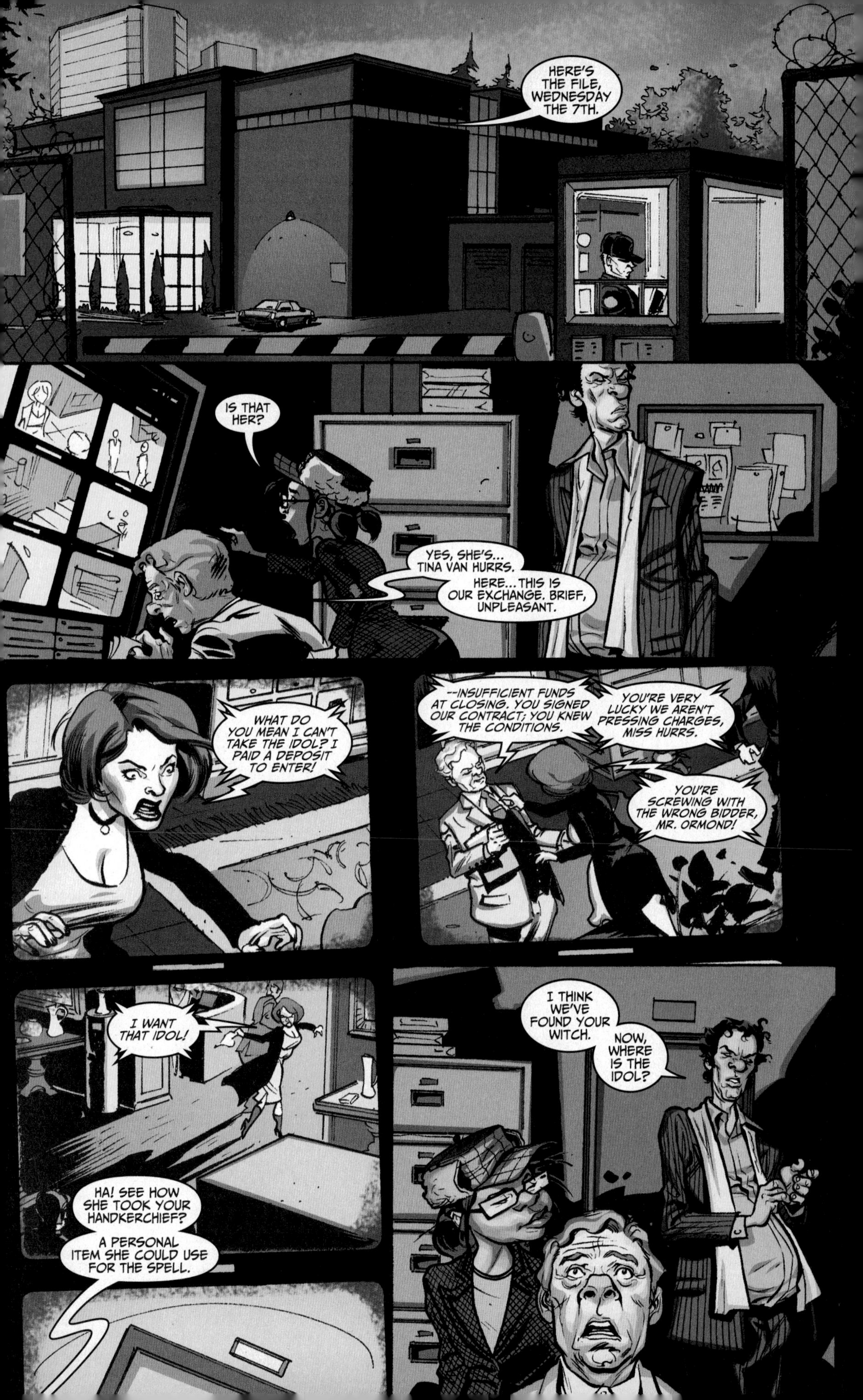
HERE'S THE FILE, WEDNESDAY THE 7TH.
IS THAT HER?
YES, SHE'S... TINA VAN HURRS.
HERE... THIS IS OUR EXCHANGE. BRIEF, UNPLEASANT.
WHAT DO YOU MEAN I CAN'T TAKE THE IDOL? I PAID A DEPOSIT TO ENTER!
--INSUFFICIENT FUNDS AT CLOSING. YOU SIGNED OUR CONTRACT; YOU KNEW THE CONDITIONS.
YOU'RE VERY LUCKY WE AREN'T PRESSING CHARGES, MISS HURRS.
YOU'RE SCREWING WITH THE WRONG BIDDER, MR. ORMOND!
I WANT THAT IDOL!
HA! SEE HOW SHE TOOK YOUR HANDKERCHIEF?
A PERSONAL ITEM SHE COULD USE FOR THE SPELL.
I THINK WE'VE FOUND YOUR WITCH.
NOW, WHERE IS THE IDOL?

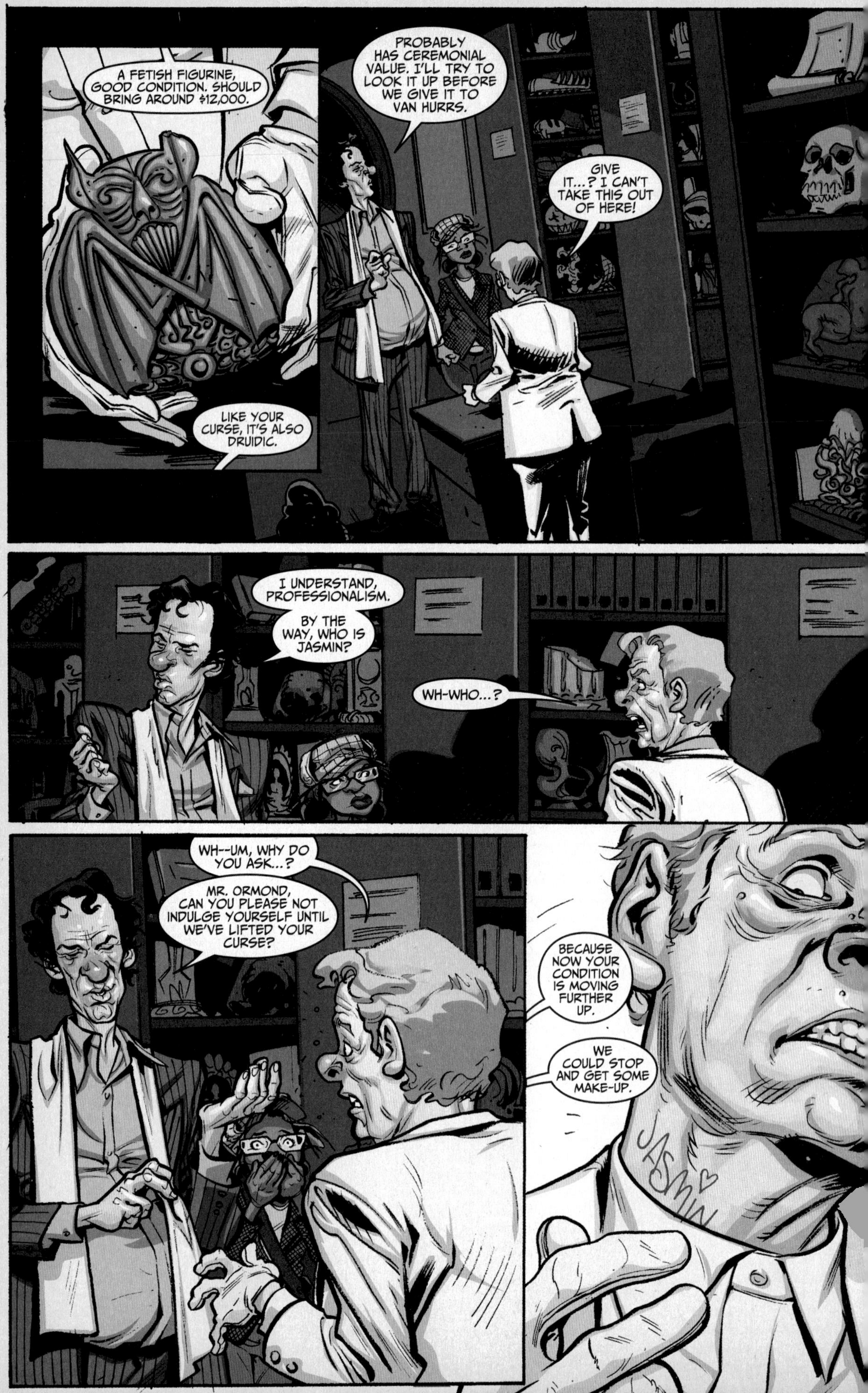

A FETISH FIGURINE, GOOD CONDITION. SHOULD BRING AROUND $12,000.
LIKE YOUR CURSE, IT'S ALSO DRUIDIC.
PROBABLY HAS CEREMONIAL VALUE. I'LL TRY TO LOOK IT UP BEFORE WE GIVE IT TO VAN HURRS.
GIVE IT...? I CAN'T TAKE THIS OUT OF HERE!
I UNDERSTAND, PROFESSIONALISM.
BY THE WAY, WHO IS JASMIN?
WH-WHO...?
WH--UM, WHY DO YOU ASK...?
MR. ORMOND, CAN YOU PLEASE NOT INDULGE YOURSELF UNTIL WE'VE LIFTED YOUR CURSE?
BECAUSE NOW YOUR CONDITION IS MOVING FURTHER UP.
WE COULD STOP AND GET SOME MAKE-UP.
JASMIN

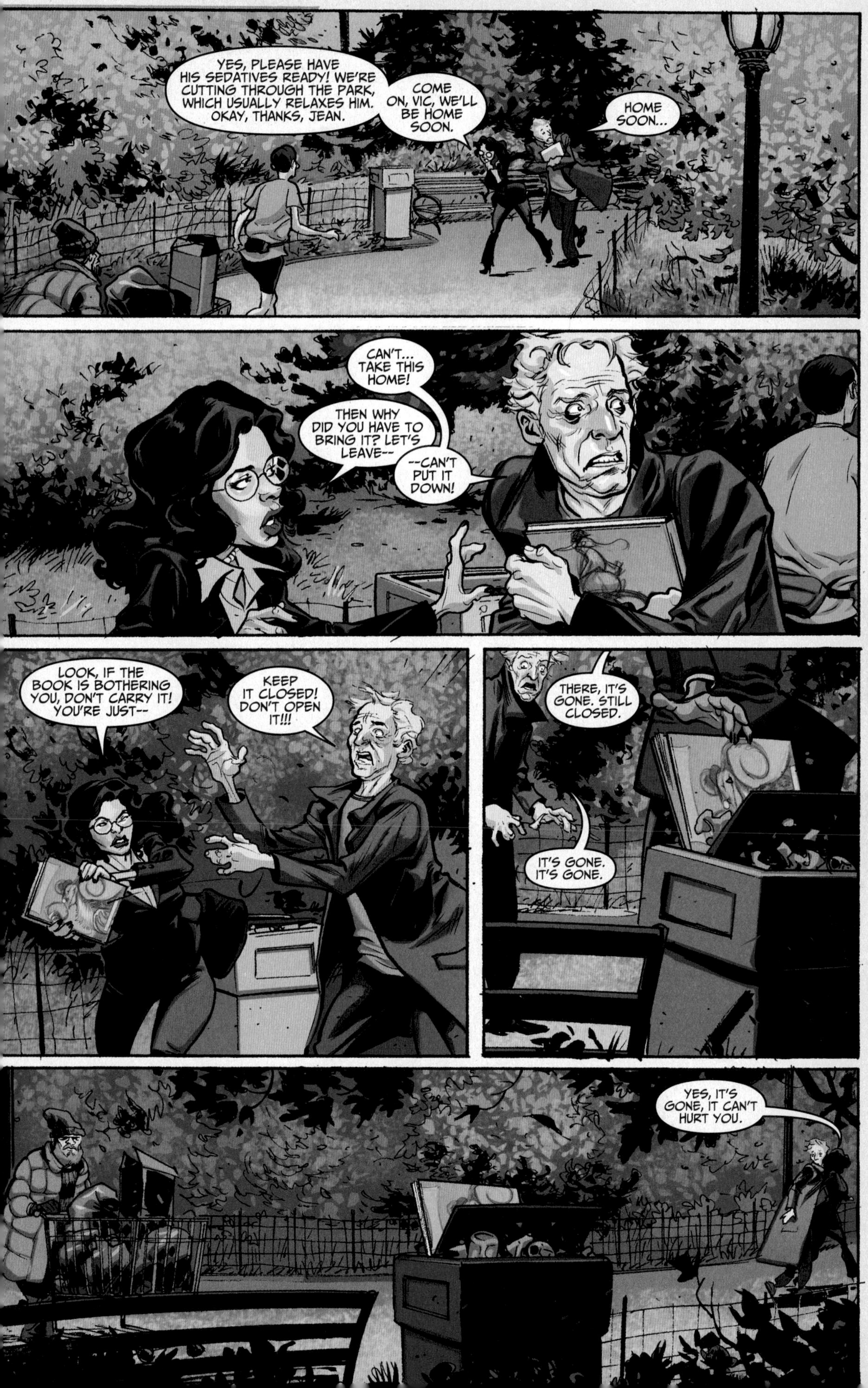
YES, PLEASE HAVE HIS SEDATIVES READY! WE'RE CUTTING THROUGH THE PARK, WHICH USUALLY RELAXES HIM. OKAY, THANKS, JEAN.
COME ON, VIC, WE'LL BE HOME SOON.
HOME SOON...
CAN'T... TAKE THIS HOME!
THEN WHY DID YOU HAVE TO BRING IT? LET'S LEAVE--
--CAN'T PUT IT DOWN!
LOOK, IF THE BOOK IS BOTHERING YOU, DON'T CARRY IT! YOU'RE JUST--
KEEP IT CLOSED! DON'T OPEN IT!!!
THERE, IT'S GONE. STILL CLOSED.
IT'S GONE. IT'S GONE.
YES, IT'S GONE, IT CAN'T HURT YOU.

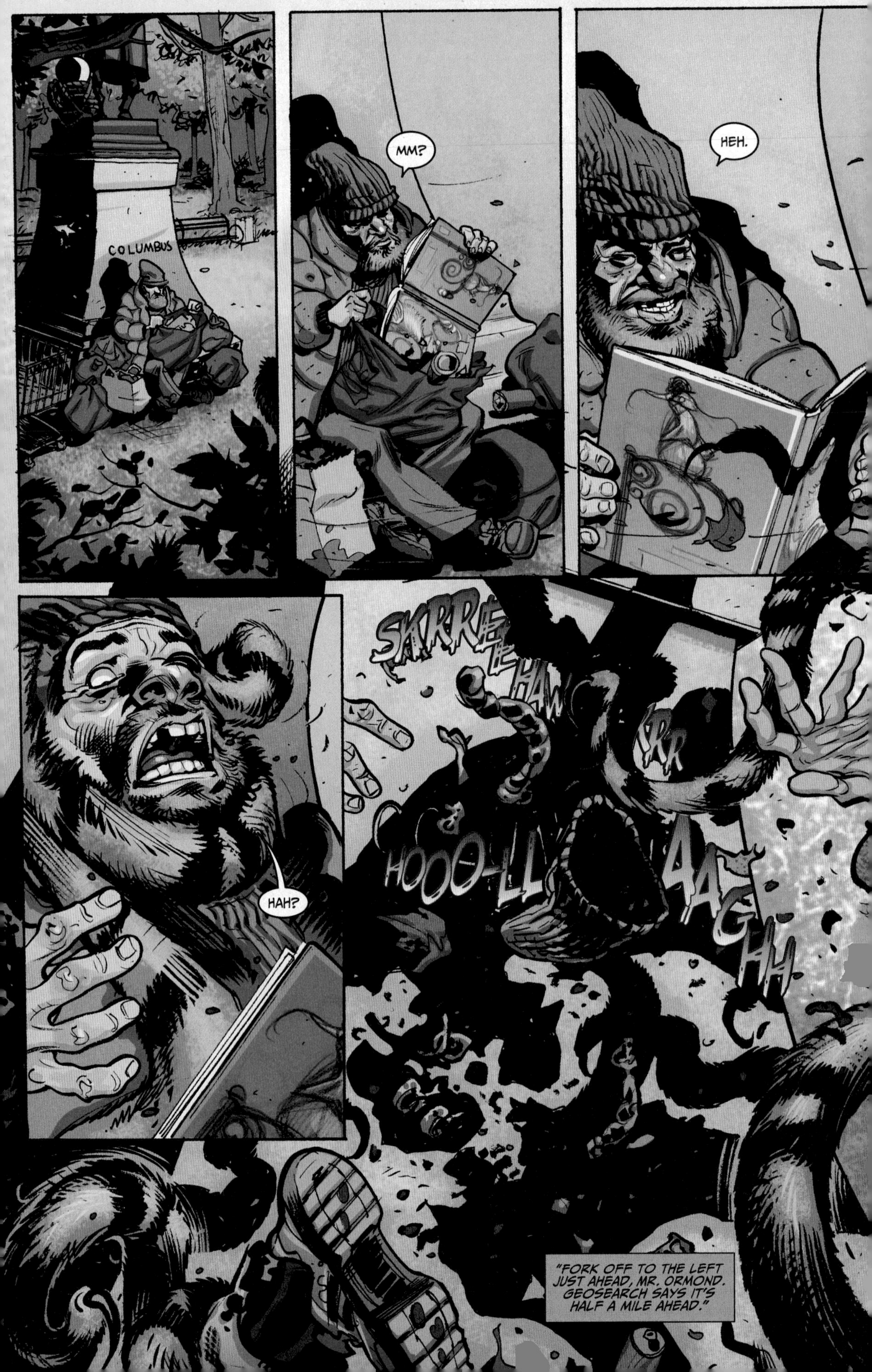
COLUMBUS
MM?
HEH.
HAH?
SKRREE
HAW
HOOO-LL
RRR
AAGHH
"FORK OFF TO THE LEFT JUST AHEAD, MR. ORMOND. GEOSEARCH SAYS IT'S HALF A MILE AHEAD."

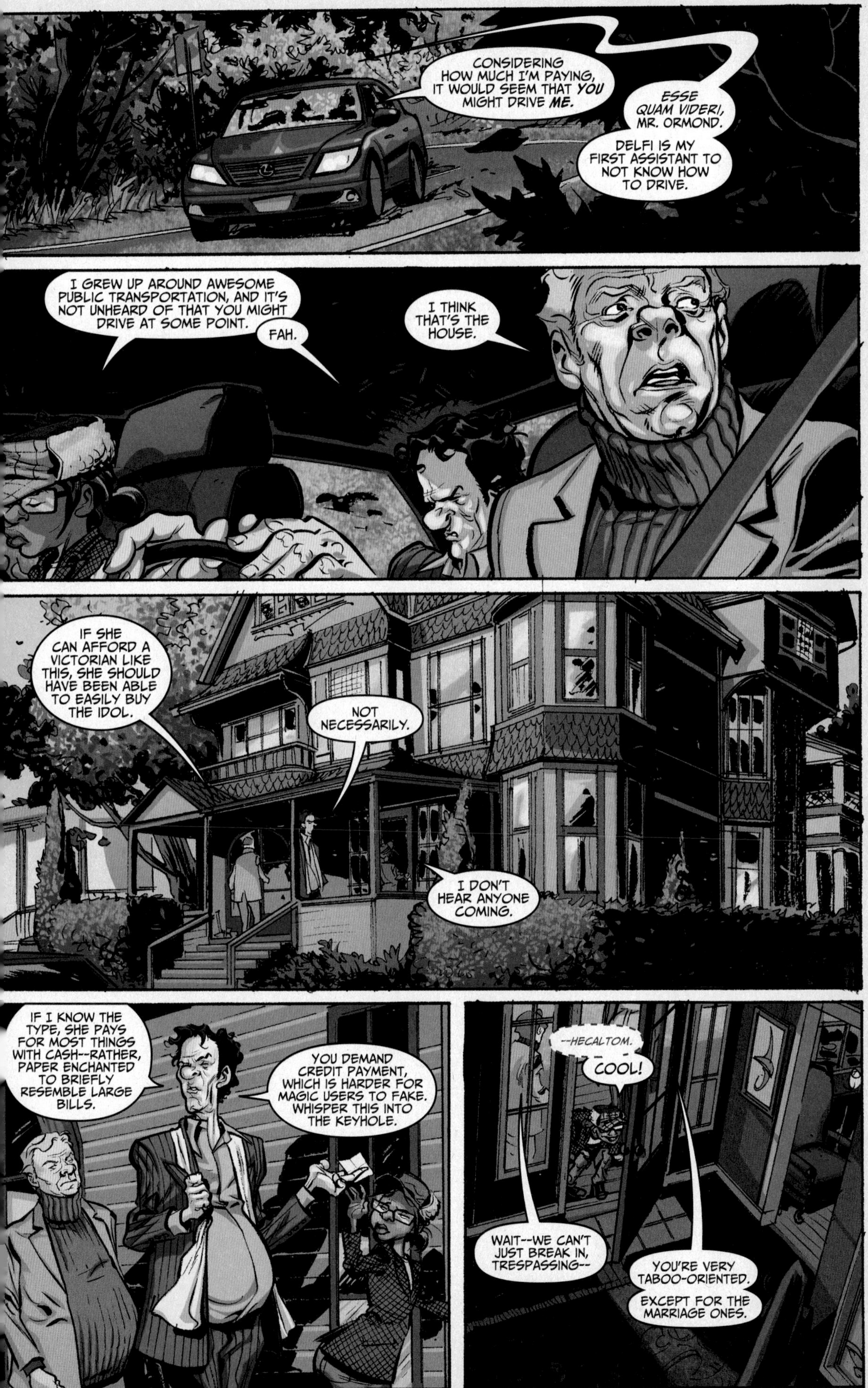
CONSIDERING HOW MUCH I'M PAYING, IT WOULD SEEM THAT *YOU* MIGHT DRIVE *ME.*
ESSE QUAM VIDERI, MR. ORMOND.
DELFI IS MY FIRST ASSISTANT TO NOT KNOW HOW TO DRIVE.
I GREW UP AROUND AWESOME PUBLIC TRANSPORTATION, AND IT'S NOT UNHEARD OF THAT YOU MIGHT DRIVE AT SOME POINT.
FAH.
I THINK THAT'S THE HOUSE.
IF SHE CAN AFFORD A VICTORIAN LIKE THIS, SHE SHOULD HAVE BEEN ABLE TO EASILY BUY THE IDOL.
NOT NECESSARILY.
I DON'T HEAR ANYONE COMING.
IF I KNOW THE TYPE, SHE PAYS FOR MOST THINGS WITH CASH--RATHER, PAPER ENCHANTED TO BRIEFLY RESEMBLE LARGE BILLS.
YOU DEMAND CREDIT PAYMENT, WHICH IS HARDER FOR MAGIC USERS TO FAKE. WHISPER THIS INTO THE KEYHOLE.
--HECALTOM.
COOL!
WAIT--WE CAN'T JUST BREAK IN, TRESPASSING--
YOU'RE VERY TABOO-ORIENTED.
EXCEPT FOR THE MARRIAGE ONES.

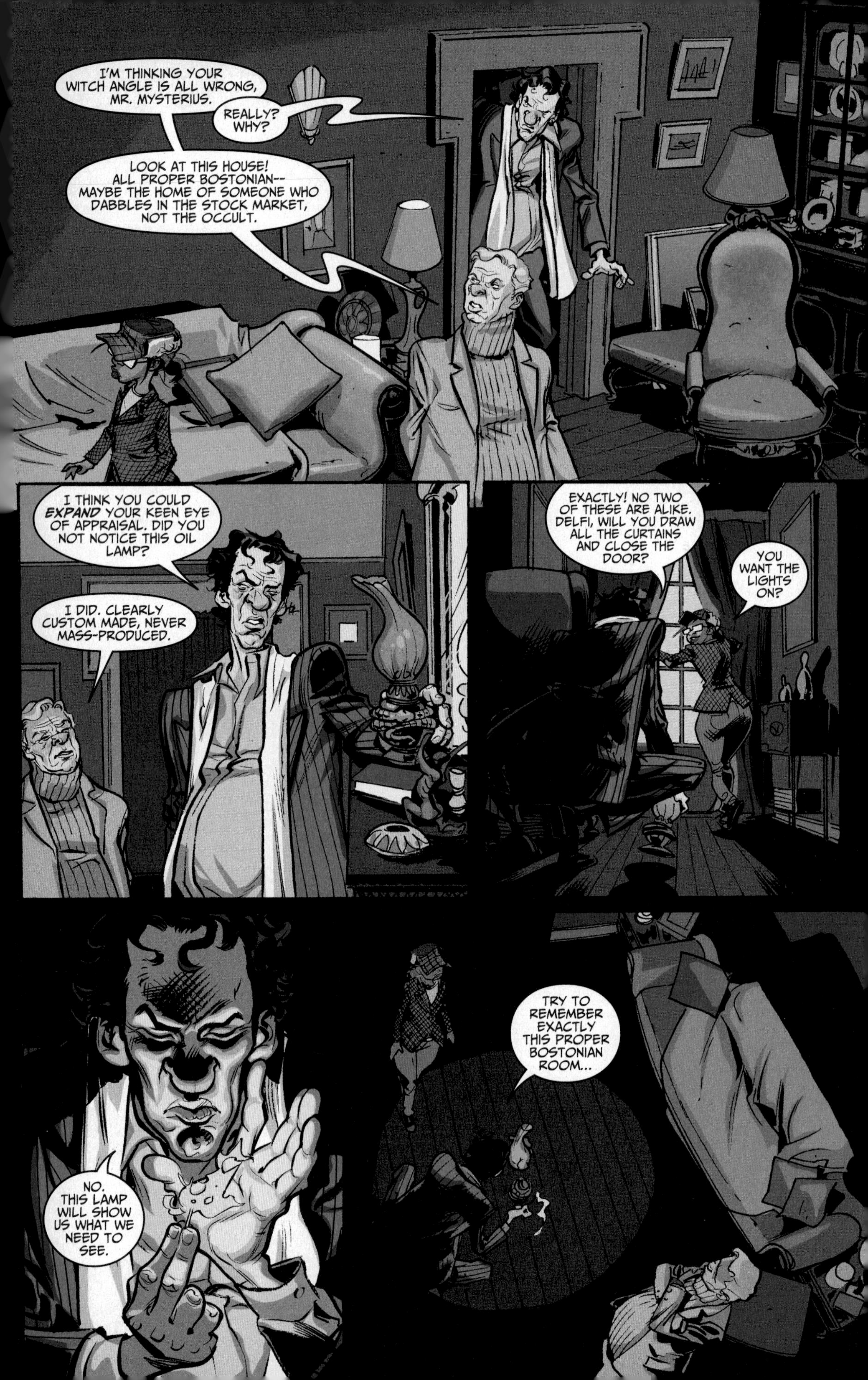
I'M THINKING YOUR WITCH ANGLE IS ALL WRONG, MR. MYSTERIUS.
REALLY? WHY?
LOOK AT THIS HOUSE! ALL PROPER BOSTONIAN-- MAYBE THE HOME OF SOMEONE WHO DABBLES IN THE STOCK MARKET, NOT THE OCCULT.
I THINK YOU COULD *EXPAND* YOUR KEEN EYE OF APPRAISAL. DID YOU NOT NOTICE THIS OIL LAMP?
I DID. CLEARLY CUSTOM MADE, NEVER MASS-PRODUCED.
EXACTLY! NO TWO OF THESE ARE ALIKE. DELFI, WILL YOU DRAW ALL THE CURTAINS AND CLOSE THE DOOR?
YOU WANT THE LIGHTS ON?
NO. THIS LAMP WILL SHOW US WHAT WE NEED TO SEE.
TRY TO REMEMBER EXACTLY THIS PROPER BOSTONIAN ROOM...

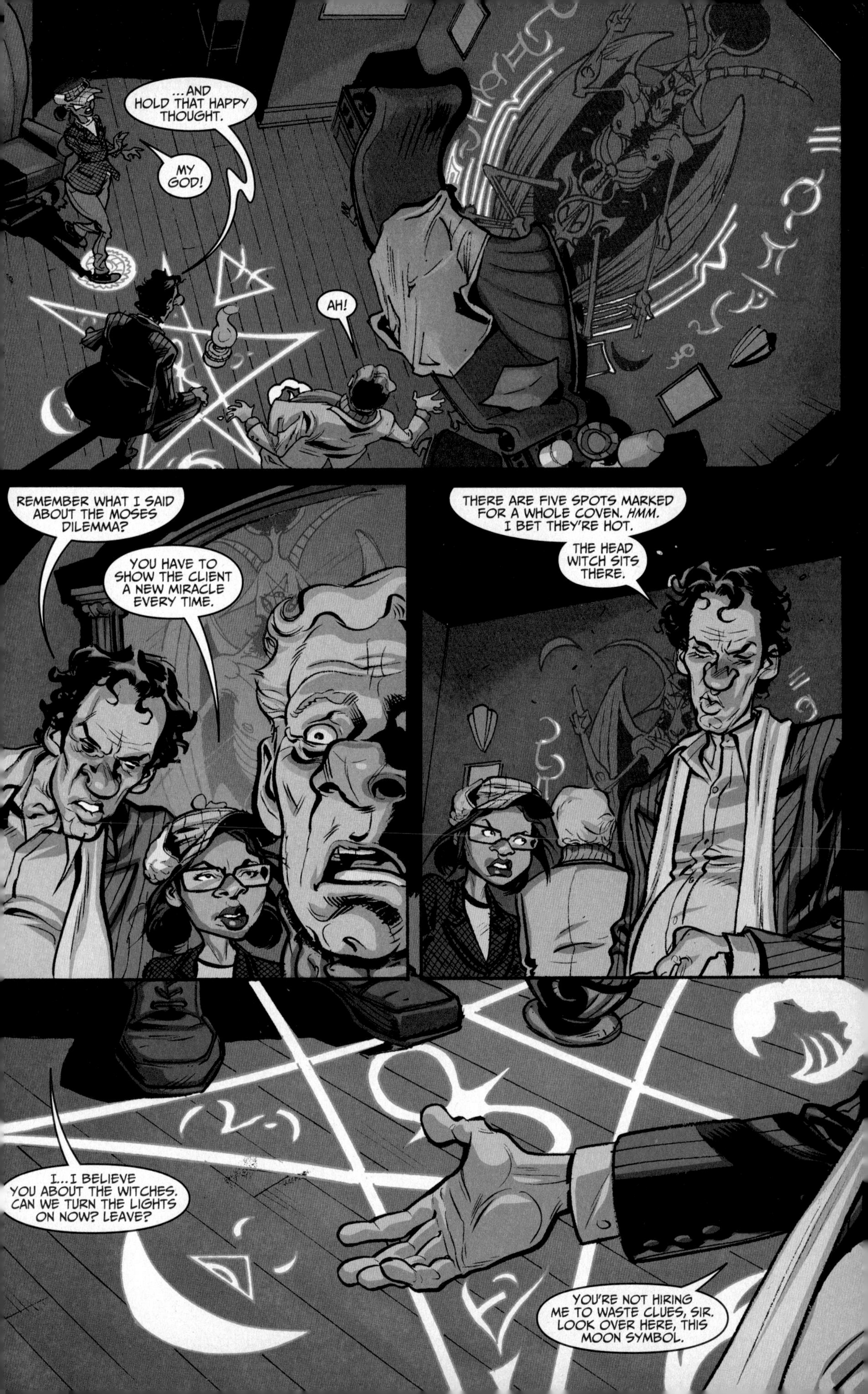
...AND HOLD THAT HAPPY THOUGHT.
MY GOD!
AH!
REMEMBER WHAT I SAID ABOUT THE MOSES DILEMMA?
YOU HAVE TO SHOW THE CLIENT A NEW MIRACLE EVERY TIME.
THERE ARE FIVE SPOTS MARKED FOR A WHOLE COVEN. *HMM.* I BET THEY'RE HOT.
THE HEAD WITCH SITS THERE.
I...I BELIEVE YOU ABOUT THE WITCHES. CAN WE TURN THE LIGHTS ON NOW? LEAVE?
YOU'RE NOT HIRING ME TO WASTE CLUES, SIR. LOOK OVER HERE, THIS MOON SYMBOL.

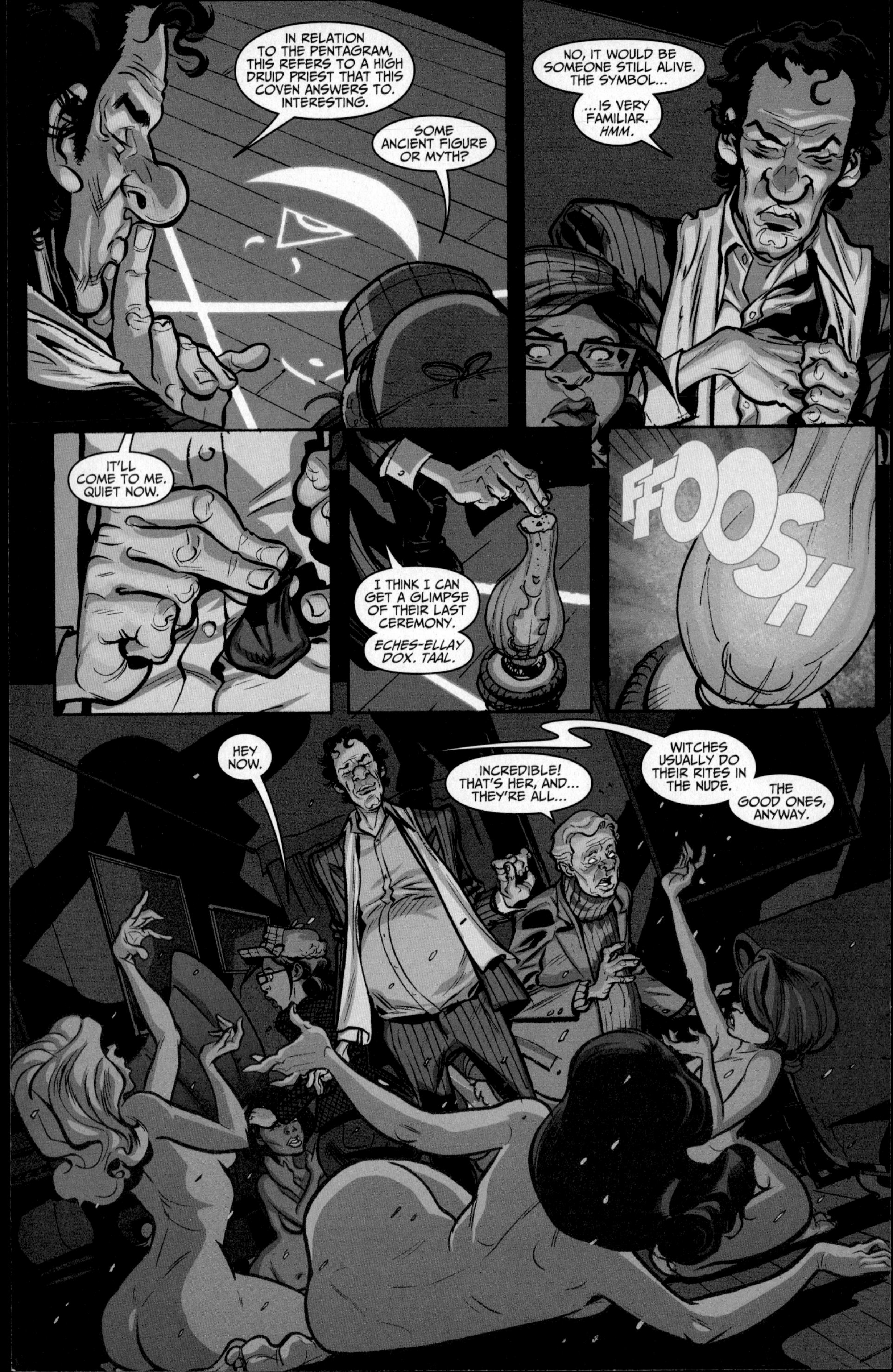
IN RELATION TO THE PENTAGRAM, THIS REFERS TO A HIGH DRUID PRIEST THAT THIS COVEN ANSWERS TO. INTERESTING.
SOME ANCIENT FIGURE OR MYTH?
NO, IT WOULD BE SOMEONE STILL ALIVE. THE SYMBOL...
...IS VERY FAMILIAR. *HMM.*
IT'LL COME TO ME. QUIET NOW.
I THINK I CAN GET A GLIMPSE OF THEIR LAST CEREMONY.
ECHES-ELLAY DOX. TAAL.
FFOOSH
HEY NOW.
INCREDIBLE! THAT'S HER, AND... THEY'RE ALL...
WITCHES USUALLY DO THEIR RITES IN THE NUDE.
THE GOOD ONES, ANYWAY.

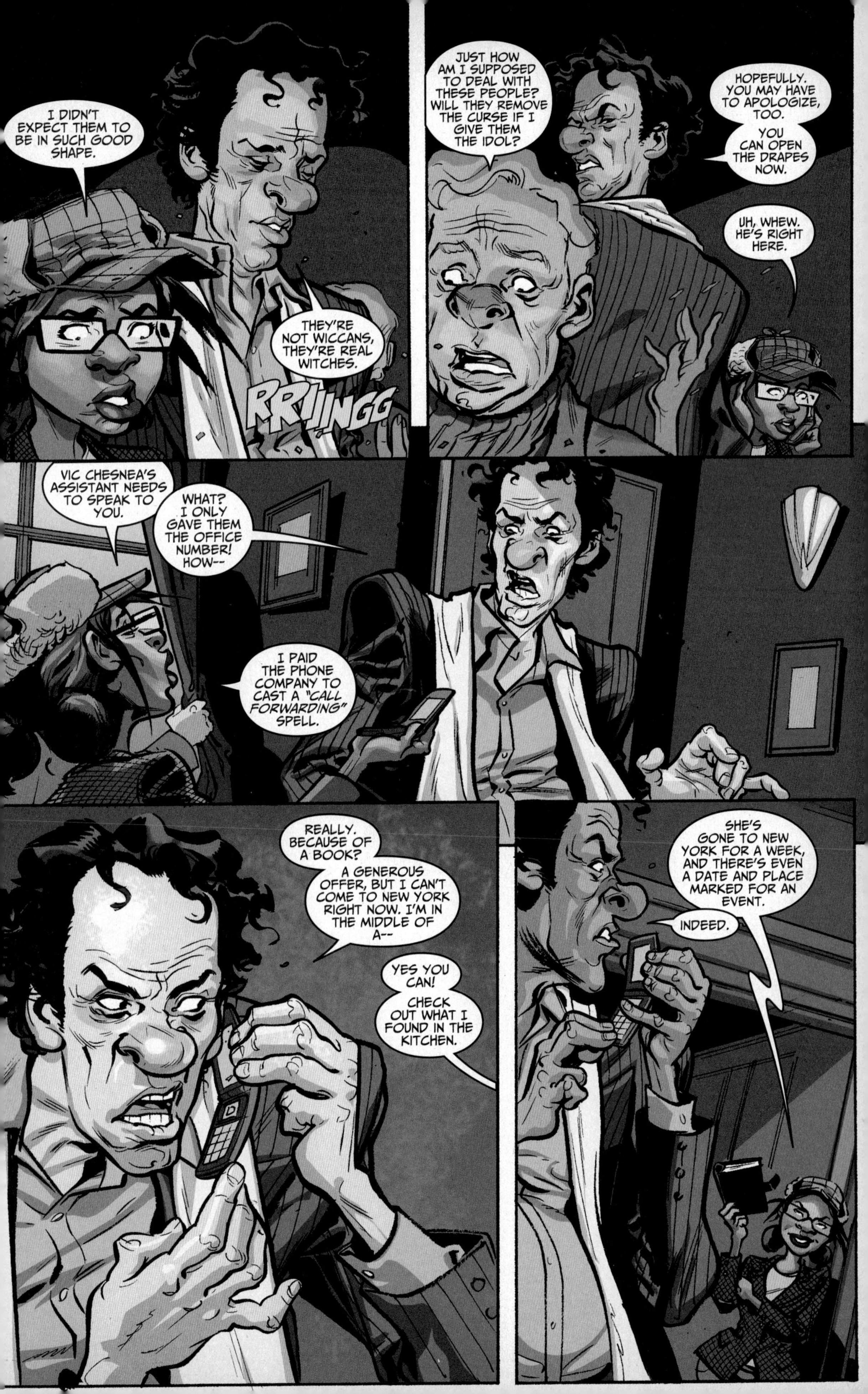
I DIDN'T EXPECT THEM TO BE IN SUCH GOOD SHAPE.
THEY'RE NOT WICCANS, THEY'RE REAL WITCHES.
RRIIINGG
JUST HOW AM I SUPPOSED TO DEAL WITH THESE PEOPLE? WILL THEY REMOVE THE CURSE IF I GIVE THEM THE IDOL?
HOPEFULLY. YOU MAY HAVE TO APOLOGIZE, TOO.
YOU CAN OPEN THE DRAPES NOW.
UH, WHEW. HE'S RIGHT HERE.
VIC CHESNEA'S ASSISTANT NEEDS TO SPEAK TO YOU.
WHAT? I ONLY GAVE THEM THE OFFICE NUMBER! HOW--
I PAID THE PHONE COMPANY TO CAST A "CALL FORWARDING" SPELL.
REALLY. BECAUSE OF A BOOK?
A GENEROUS OFFER, BUT I CAN'T COME TO NEW YORK RIGHT NOW. I'M IN THE MIDDLE OF A--
YES YOU CAN!
CHECK OUT WHAT I FOUND IN THE KITCHEN.
SHE'S GONE TO NEW YORK FOR A WEEK, AND THERE'S EVEN A DATE AND PLACE MARKED FOR AN EVENT.
INDEED.

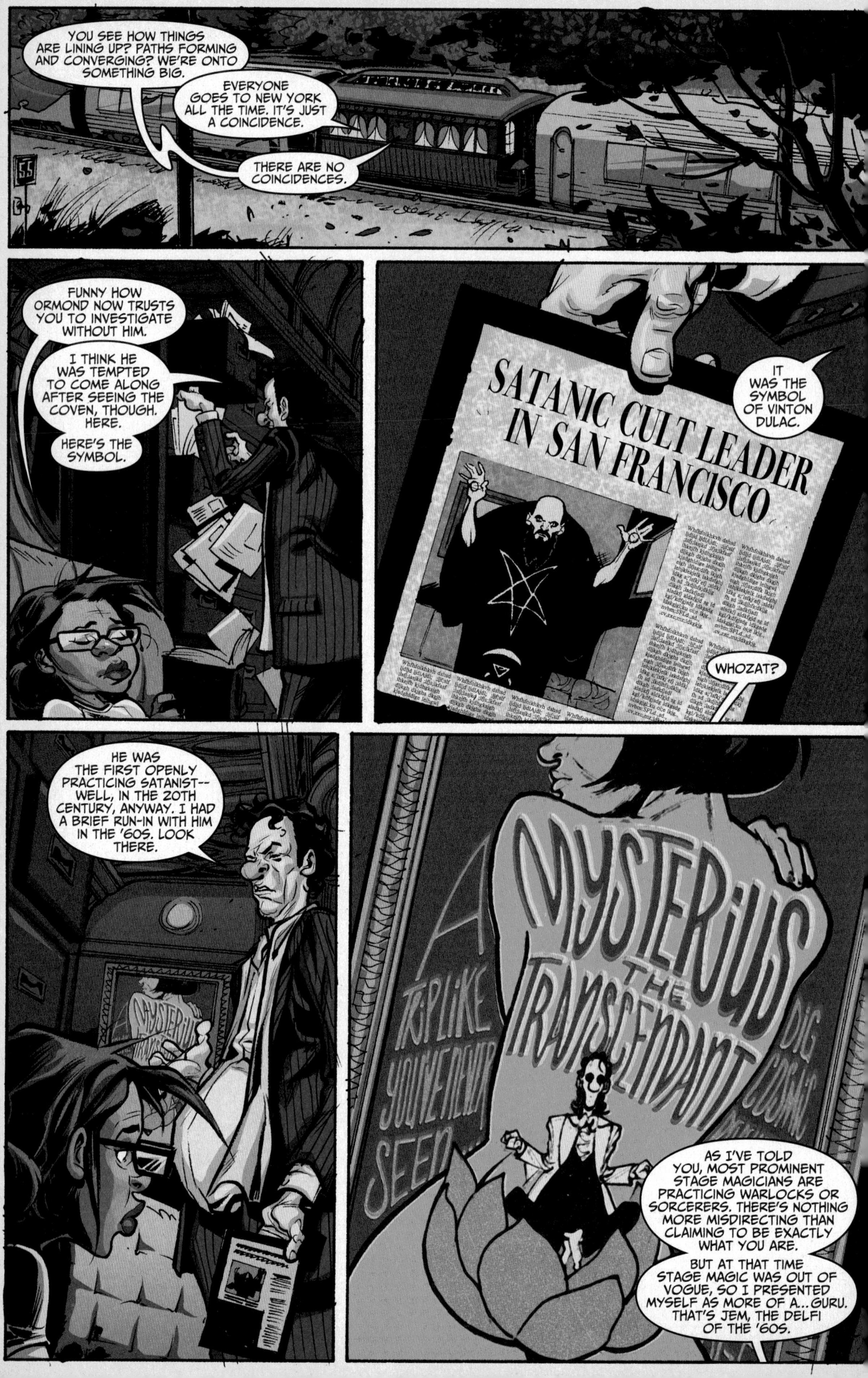
YOU SEE HOW THINGS ARE LINING UP? PATHS FORMING AND CONVERGING? WE'RE ONTO SOMETHING BIG.
EVERYONE GOES TO NEW YORK ALL THE TIME. IT'S JUST A COINCIDENCE.
THERE ARE NO COINCIDENCES.
55
FUNNY HOW ORMOND NOW TRUSTS YOU TO INVESTIGATE WITHOUT HIM.
I THINK HE WAS TEMPTED TO COME ALONG AFTER SEEING THE COVEN, THOUGH. HERE.
HERE'S THE SYMBOL.
SATANIC CULT LEADER IN SAN FRANCISCO
IT WAS THE SYMBOL OF VINTON DULAC.
WHOZAT?
HE WAS THE FIRST OPENLY PRACTICING SATANIST--WELL, IN THE 20TH CENTURY, ANYWAY. I HAD A BRIEF RUN-IN WITH HIM IN THE '60S. LOOK THERE.
A MYSTERIUS THE TRANSCENDANT
TRIP LIKE YOU'VE NEVER SEEN
AS I'VE TOLD YOU, MOST PROMINENT STAGE MAGICIANS ARE PRACTICING WARLOCKS OR SORCERERS. THERE'S NOTHING MORE MISDIRECTING THAN CLAIMING TO BE EXACTLY WHAT YOU ARE.
BUT AT THAT TIME STAGE MAGIC WAS OUT OF VOGUE, SO I PRESENTED MYSELF AS MORE OF A...GURU. THAT'S JEM, THE DELFI OF THE '60S.

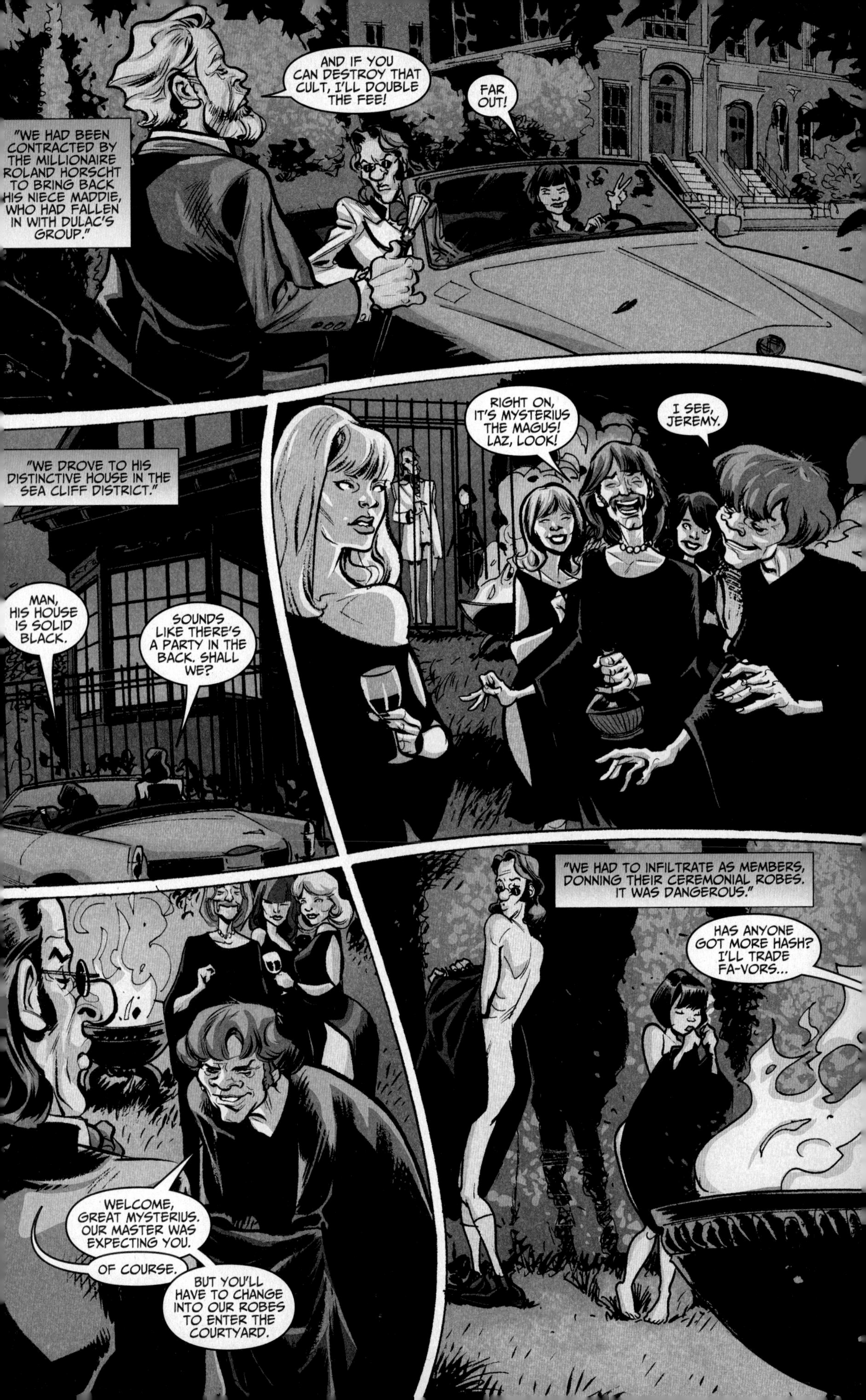
"WE HAD BEEN CONTRACTED BY THE MILLIONAIRE ROLAND HORSCHT TO BRING BACK HIS NIECE MADDIE, WHO HAD FALLEN IN WITH DULAC'S GROUP."
AND IF YOU CAN DESTROY THAT CULT, I'LL DOUBLE THE FEE!
FAR OUT!
"WE DROVE TO HIS DISTINCTIVE HOUSE IN THE SEA CLIFF DISTRICT."
MAN, HIS HOUSE IS SOLID BLACK.
SOUNDS LIKE THERE'S A PARTY IN THE BACK. SHALL WE?
RIGHT ON, IT'S MYSTERIUS THE MAGUS! LAZ, LOOK!
I SEE, JEREMY.
WELCOME, GREAT MYSTERIUS. OUR MASTER WAS EXPECTING YOU.
OF COURSE.
BUT YOU'LL HAVE TO CHANGE INTO OUR ROBES TO ENTER THE COURTYARD.
"WE HAD TO INFILTRATE AS MEMBERS, DONNING THEIR CEREMONIAL ROBES. IT WAS DANGEROUS."
HAS ANYONE GOT MORE HASH? I'LL TRADE FA-VORS...

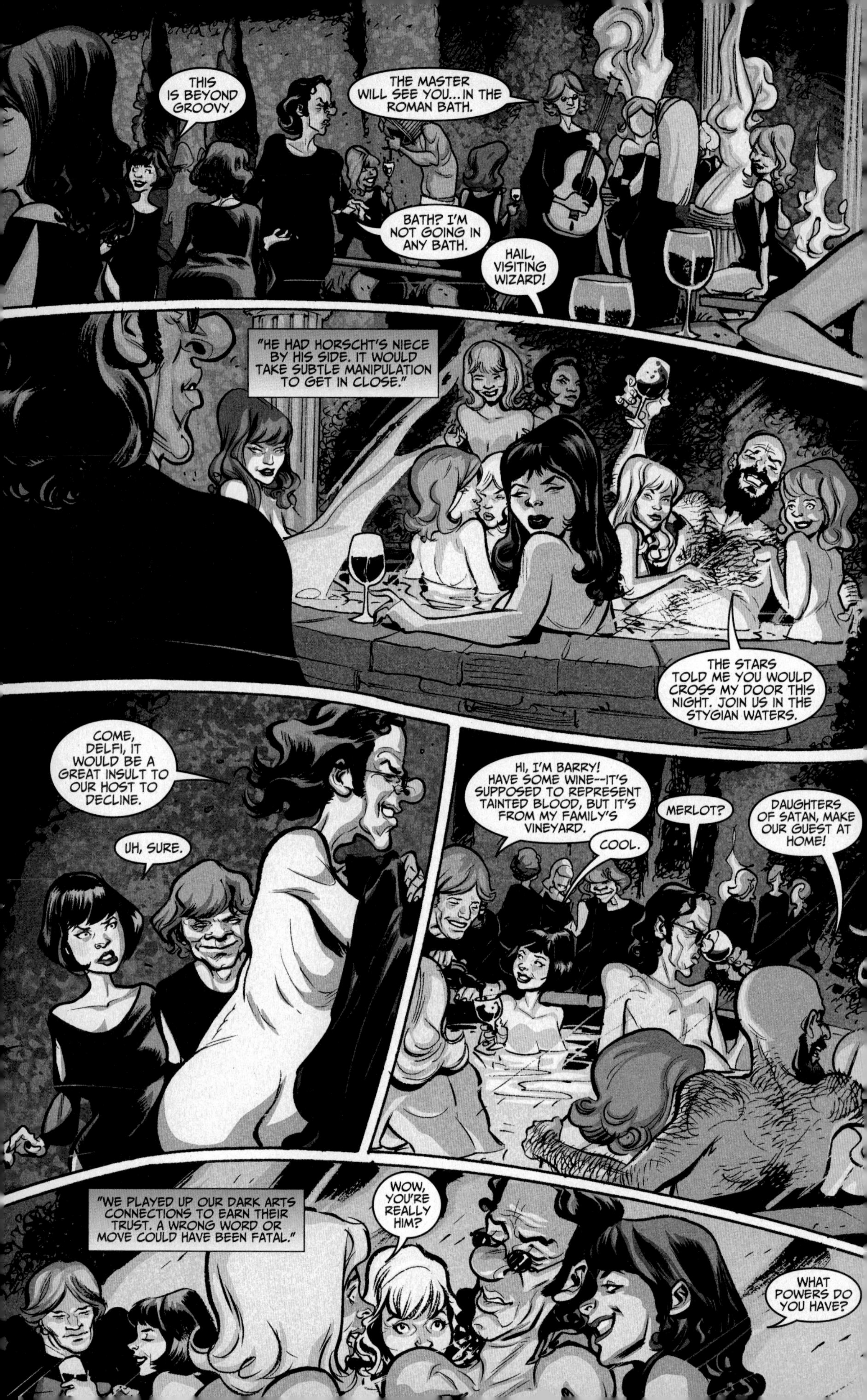
THIS IS BEYOND GROOVY.
THE MASTER WILL SEE YOU... IN THE ROMAN BATH.
BATH? I'M NOT GOING IN ANY BATH.
HAIL, VISITING WIZARD!
"HE HAD HORSCHT'S NIECE BY HIS SIDE. IT WOULD TAKE SUBTLE MANIPULATION TO GET IN CLOSE."
THE STARS TOLD ME YOU WOULD CROSS MY DOOR THIS NIGHT. JOIN US IN THE STYGIAN WATERS.
COME, DELFI, IT WOULD BE A GREAT INSULT TO OUR HOST TO DECLINE.
UH, SURE.
HI, I'M BARRY! HAVE SOME WINE--IT'S SUPPOSED TO REPRESENT TAINTED BLOOD, BUT IT'S FROM MY FAMILY'S VINEYARD.
MERLOT?
COOL.
DAUGHTERS OF SATAN, MAKE OUR GUEST AT HOME!
"WE PLAYED UP OUR DARK ARTS CONNECTIONS TO EARN THEIR TRUST. A WRONG WORD OR MOVE COULD HAVE BEEN FATAL."
WOW, YOU'RE REALLY HIM?
WHAT POWERS DO YOU HAVE?

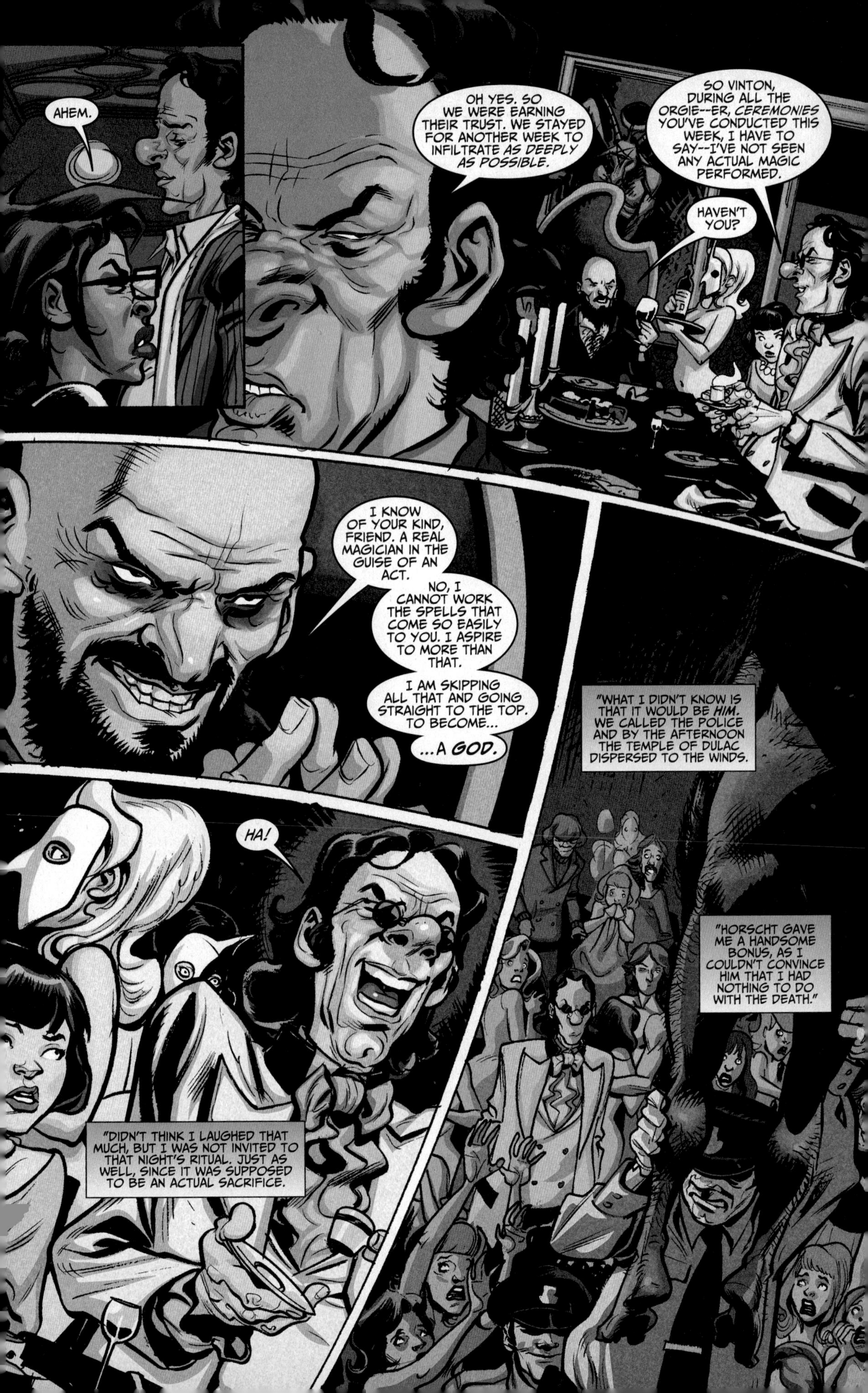
AHEM.
OH YES. SO WE WERE EARNING THEIR TRUST. WE STAYED FOR ANOTHER WEEK TO INFILTRATE AS DEEPLY AS POSSIBLE.
SO VINTON, DURING ALL THE ORGIE--ER, CEREMONIES YOU'VE CONDUCTED THIS WEEK, I HAVE TO SAY--I'VE NOT SEEN ANY ACTUAL MAGIC PERFORMED.
HAVEN'T YOU?
I KNOW OF YOUR KIND, FRIEND. A REAL MAGICIAN IN THE GUISE OF AN ACT.
NO, I CANNOT WORK THE SPELLS THAT COME SO EASILY TO YOU. I ASPIRE TO MORE THAN THAT.
I AM SKIPPING ALL THAT AND GOING STRAIGHT TO THE TOP. TO BECOME...
...A GOD.
HA!
"DIDN'T THINK I LAUGHED THAT MUCH, BUT I WAS NOT INVITED TO THAT NIGHT'S RITUAL. JUST AS WELL, SINCE IT WAS SUPPOSED TO BE AN ACTUAL SACRIFICE.
"WHAT I DIDN'T KNOW IS THAT IT WOULD BE HIM. WE CALLED THE POLICE AND BY THE AFTERNOON THE TEMPLE OF DULAC DISPERSED TO THE WINDS.
"HORSCHT GAVE ME A HANDSOME BONUS, AS I COULDN'T CONVINCE HIM THAT I HAD NOTHING TO DO WITH THE DEATH."

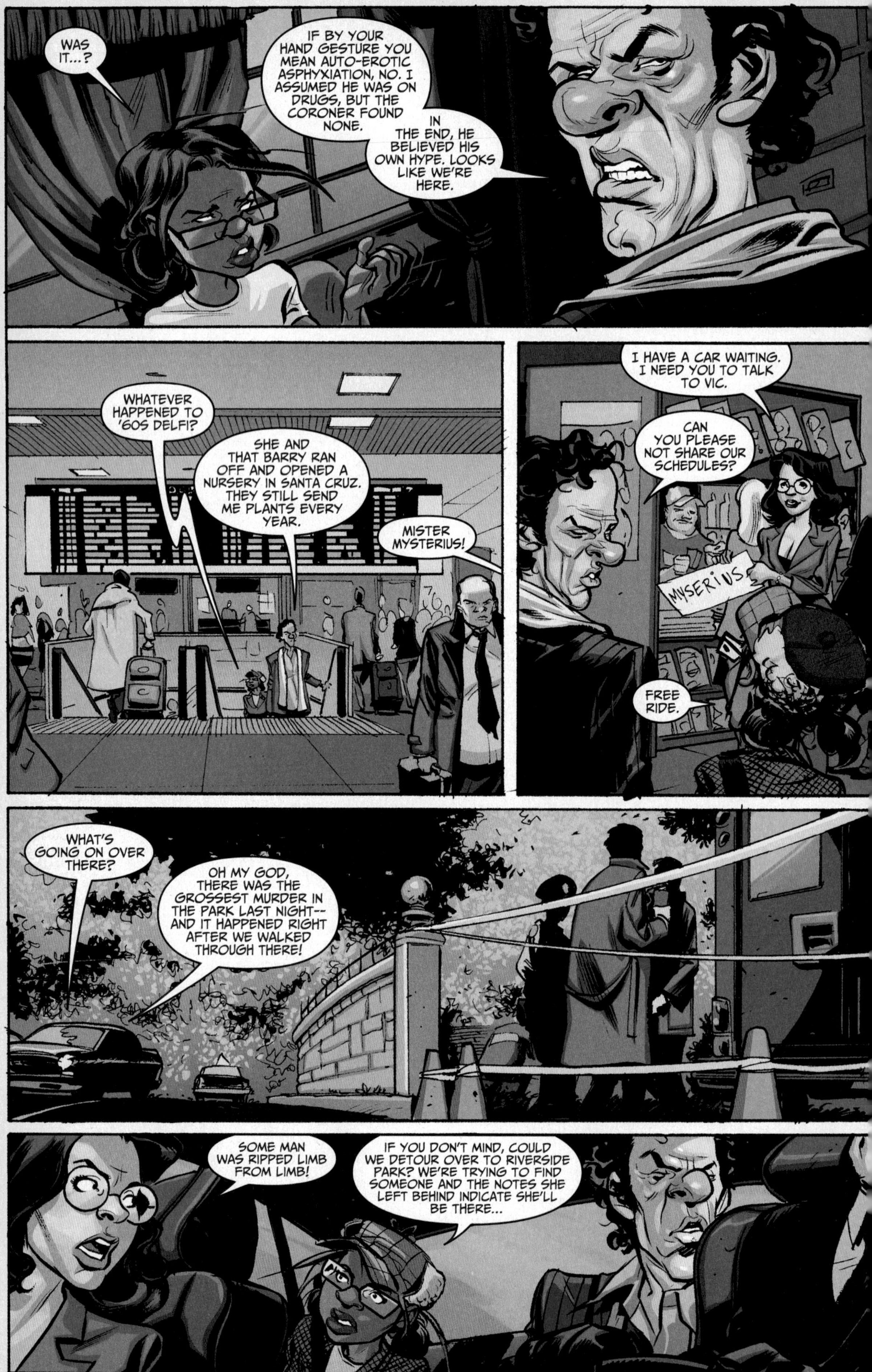
WAS IT...?
IF BY YOUR HAND GESTURE YOU MEAN AUTO-EROTIC ASPHYXIATION, NO. I ASSUMED HE WAS ON DRUGS, BUT THE CORONER FOUND NONE.
IN THE END, HE BELIEVED HIS OWN HYPE. LOOKS LIKE WE'RE HERE.
WHATEVER HAPPENED TO '60S DELFI?
SHE AND THAT BARRY RAN OFF AND OPENED A NURSERY IN SANTA CRUZ. THEY STILL SEND ME PLANTS EVERY YEAR.
MISTER MYSTERIUS!
I HAVE A CAR WAITING. I NEED YOU TO TALK TO VIC.
CAN YOU PLEASE NOT SHARE OUR SCHEDULES?
MYSERIUS
FREE RIDE.
WHAT'S GOING ON OVER THERE?
OH MY GOD, THERE WAS THE GROSSEST MURDER IN THE PARK LAST NIGHT-- AND IT HAPPENED RIGHT AFTER WE WALKED THROUGH THERE!
SOME MAN WAS RIPPED LIMB FROM LIMB!
IF YOU DON'T MIND, COULD WE DETOUR OVER TO RIVERSIDE PARK? WE'RE TRYING TO FIND SOMEONE AND THE NOTES SHE LEFT BEHIND INDICATE SHE'LL BE THERE...

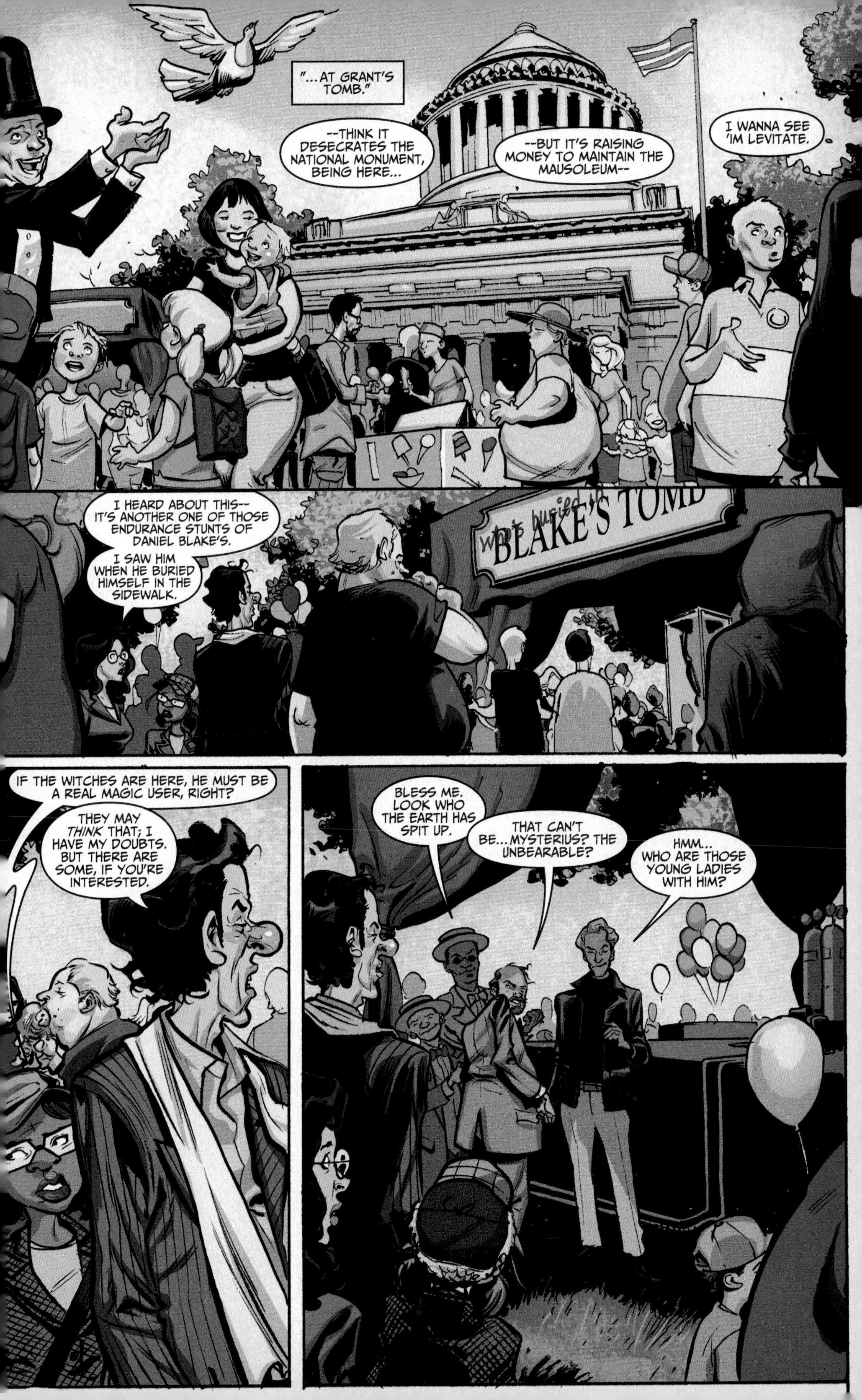
"...AT GRANT'S TOMB."
--THINK IT DESECRATES THE NATIONAL MONUMENT, BEING HERE...
--BUT IT'S RAISING MONEY TO MAINTAIN THE MAUSOLEUM--
I WANNA SEE 'IM LEVITATE.
I HEARD ABOUT THIS-- IT'S ANOTHER ONE OF THOSE ENDURANCE STUNTS OF DANIEL BLAKE'S.
I SAW HIM WHEN HE BURIED HIMSELF IN THE SIDEWALK.
BLAKE'S TOMB
IF THE WITCHES ARE HERE, HE MUST BE A REAL MAGIC USER, RIGHT?
THEY MAY *THINK* THAT; I HAVE MY DOUBTS. BUT THERE ARE SOME, IF YOU'RE INTERESTED.
BLESS ME. LOOK WHO THE EARTH HAS SPIT UP.
THAT CAN'T BE...MYSTERIUS? THE UNBEARABLE?
HMM... WHO ARE THOSE YOUNG LADIES WITH HIM?

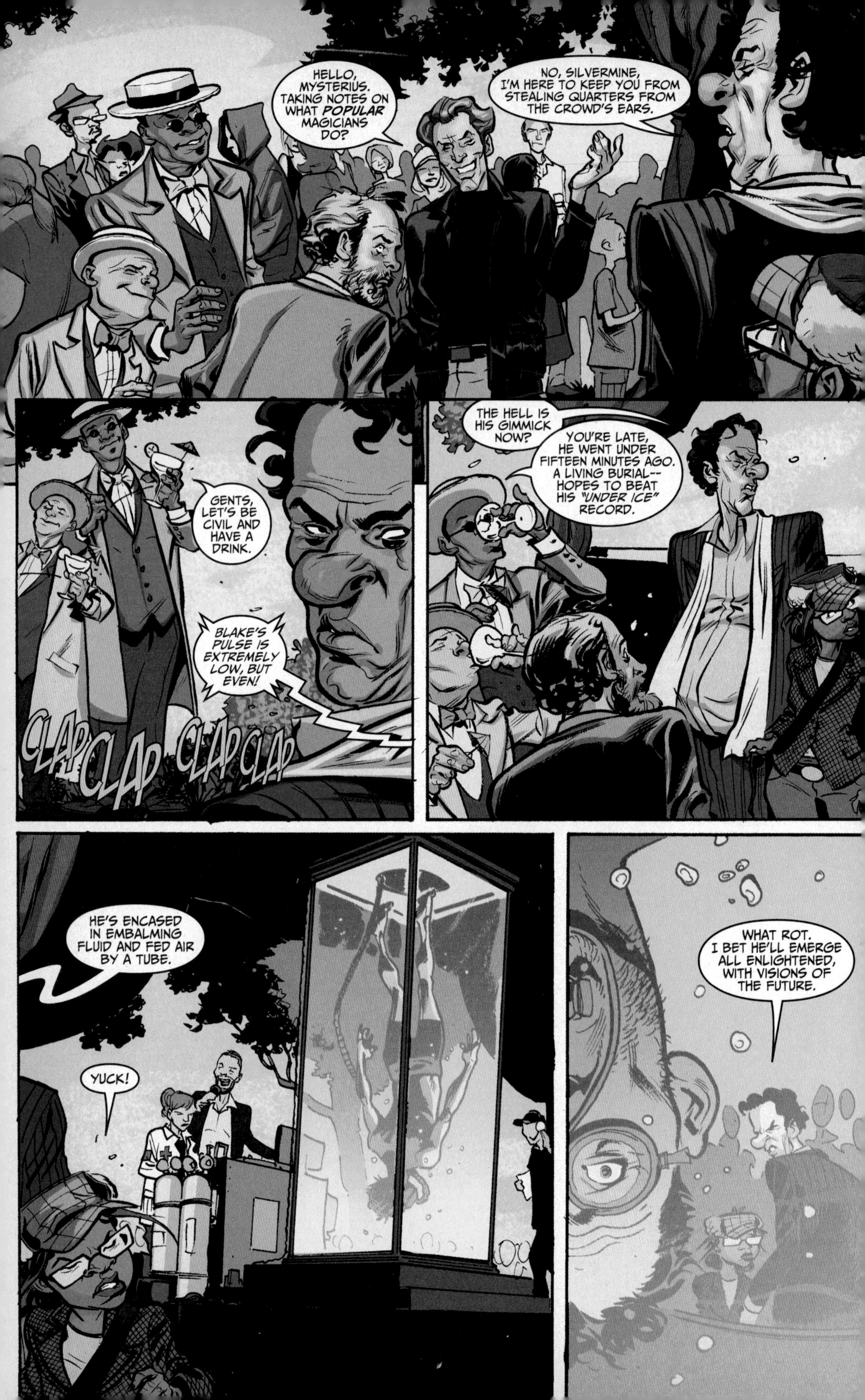
HELLO, MYSTERIUS. TAKING NOTES ON WHAT POPULAR MAGICIANS DO?
NO, SILVERMINE, I'M HERE TO KEEP YOU FROM STEALING QUARTERS FROM THE CROWD'S EARS.
GENTS, LET'S BE CIVIL AND HAVE A DRINK.
BLAKE'S PULSE IS EXTREMELY LOW, BUT EVEN!
CLAP CLAP CLAP CLAP
THE HELL IS HIS GIMMICK NOW?
YOU'RE LATE, HE WENT UNDER FIFTEEN MINUTES AGO. A LIVING BURIAL-- HOPES TO BEAT HIS "UNDER ICE" RECORD.
HE'S ENCASED IN EMBALMING FLUID AND FED AIR BY A TUBE.
YUCK!
WHAT ROT. I BET HE'LL EMERGE ALL ENLIGHTENED, WITH VISIONS OF THE FUTURE.

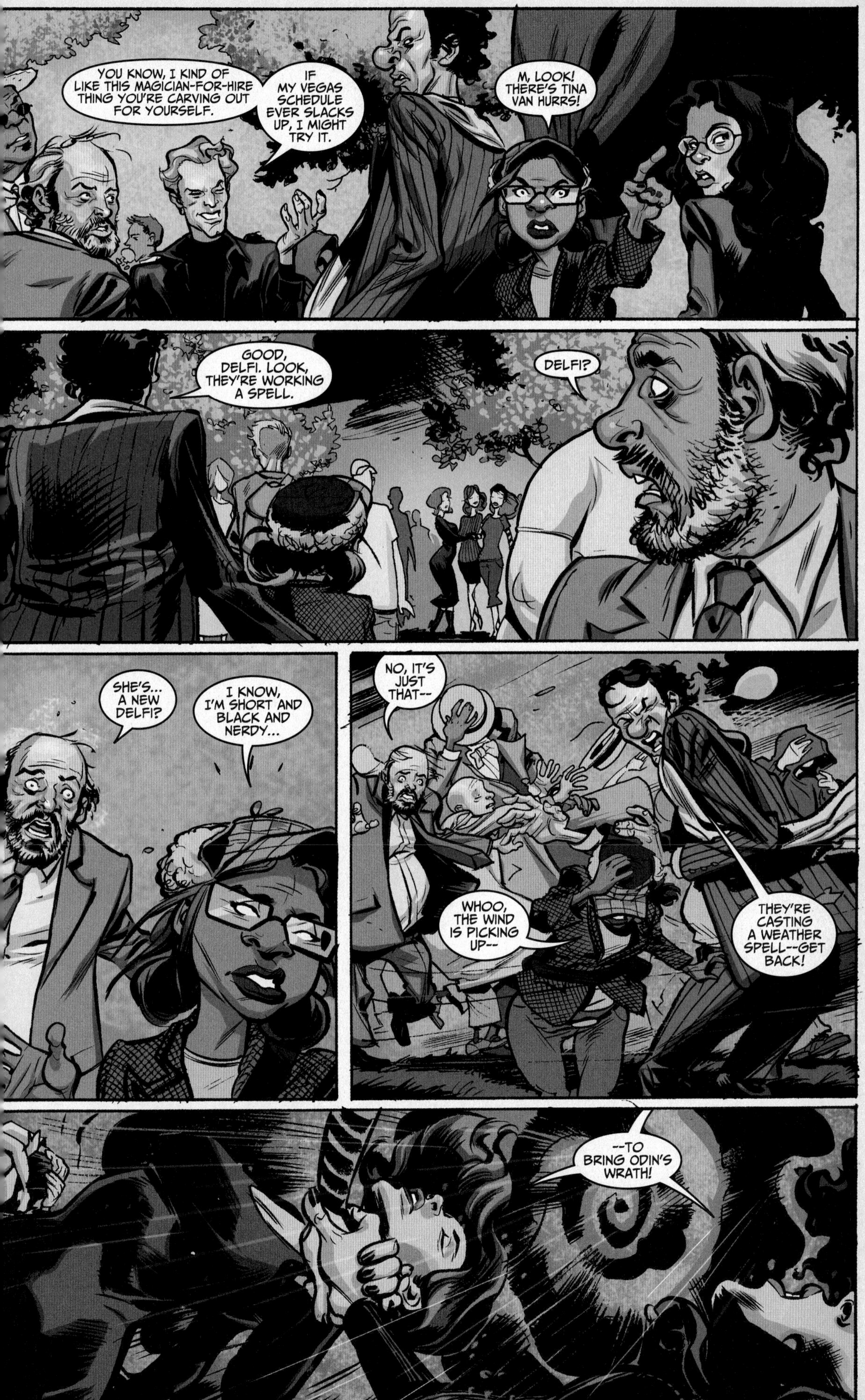
YOU KNOW, I KIND OF LIKE THIS MAGICIAN-FOR-HIRE THING YOU'RE CARVING OUT FOR YOURSELF.
IF MY VEGAS SCHEDULE EVER SLACKS UP, I MIGHT TRY IT.
M, LOOK! THERE'S TINA VAN HURRS!
GOOD, DELFI. LOOK, THEY'RE WORKING A SPELL.
DELFI?
SHE'S... A NEW DELFI?
I KNOW, I'M SHORT AND BLACK AND NERDY...
NO, IT'S JUST THAT--
WHOO, THE WIND IS PICKING UP--
THEY'RE CASTING A WEATHER SPELL--GET BACK!
--TO BRING ODIN'S WRATH!

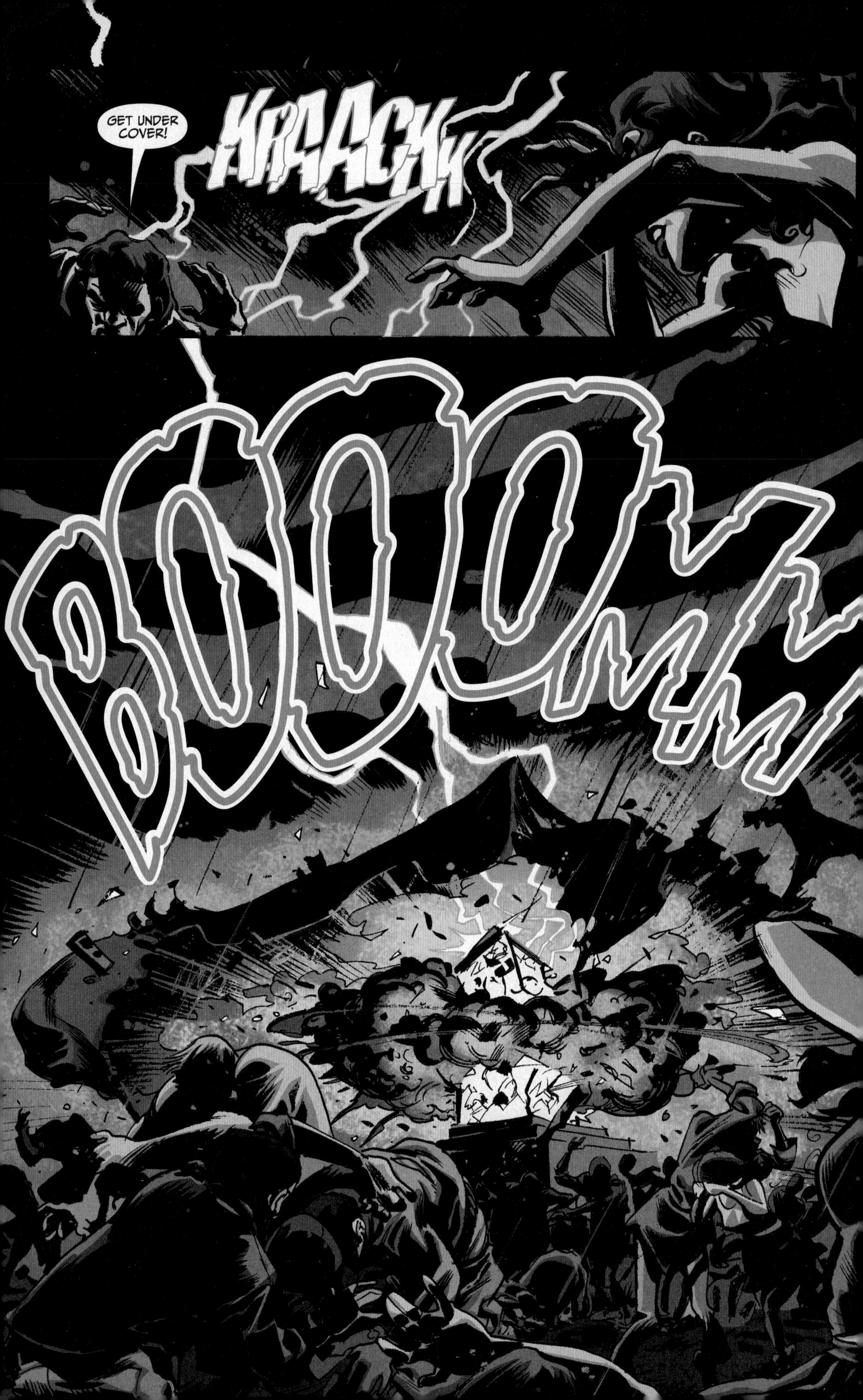

GET UNDER COVER!
KRAACKK
BOOOMM

MYSTERIUS AND THE MISSING DIVA

A nearly complete tale from the popular pulp *Diabolic Tales*, March 1935

The tires of the cab turned slowly, crunching in the fresh snow as the vehicle came to a stop in front of the theatre.

"Mammoth Hall," announced the cabbie in purest East Boston dialect.

He looked back at the couple he had just ferried. The petite young woman smiled sheepishly as the tall man next to her remained seated, looking out the window. At last the driver realized that this was one of those fares, and hopped out to open the man's door. "Opera lovers, eh?"

The tall man kept his eyes on the building itself as he produced a dollar out of the air. The driver's eyes flashed. "Thankyasir!" As he went back to steering his car out of the short snowdrift, the young lady marched in place and waited for her boss to move. Instead, the tall man kept staring up at the building.

"M, can we go inside already?" she asked while batting away snowflakes that seemed drawn to her face. "Look at the masonry around the top of the theatre," he said, pointing around. "Those busts—are they supposed to be the Ages of Man?" He turned to see no one standing by to answer, and looked down to see footprints that led over to the door by the box office. His stalwart assistant Delfi was going inside.

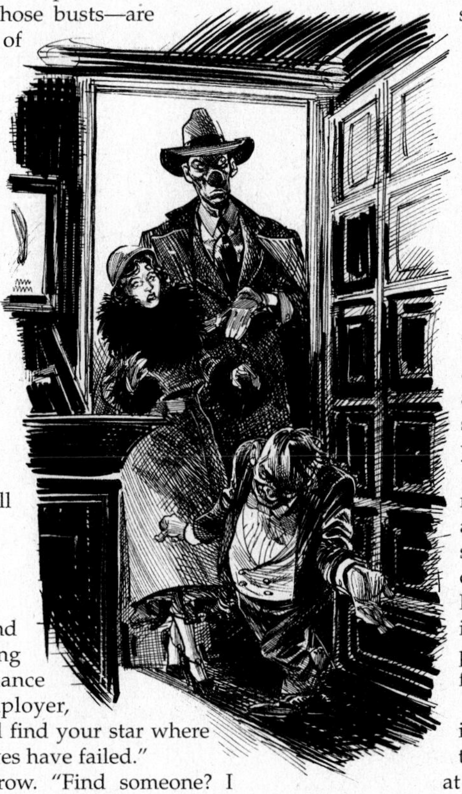

"Rude," mumbled Mysterius, following her into the theatre. He barely heard the wet squeal of brakes down the street where the cabbie was puzzling over a laundry ticket in his hand in place of a dollar.

"I was expecting you much earlier," said the older gentleman to Delfi. "Our patrons will be arriving soon for the seven o'clock performance. And where is this…magician I was badgered into hiring?"

Delfi waved out her arm, and realized that she was lapsing into her old stage performance manner. "This is my employer, Mysterius the Arcane. He will find your star where the police and private detectives have failed."

Mysterius raised an eyebrow. "Find someone? I thought we were being given tickets to a show." Delfi dragged her palm across her face, uncertain how to recover. "Boss, I explained that this was a missing person case," she spoke quietly.

The theatre manager's face turned flush and then Mysterius interjected. "Well, of course. But I am a firm believer in culprits revisiting their crimes—the abduction did occur in the middle of a performance, did it not?"

The Manager, Wendell Garland, relaxed a bit. "Yes." Delfi felt Mysterius' triumphant smile at what must have been a lucky bluff. "Come, I'll show you where it happened, I'm getting good at it."

The three soon were walking around on the large stage, Delfi agape at the scale of everything. "Wow, we never worked a hall like this in the traveling show."

The manager snorted. "An august venue like The Mammoth hosts orchestra and opera, we do not feature women being sawed in two or hats manifesting hares." Mysterius smiled. "Nor did we resort to such tired old routines in our shows. But it sounds like magic did happen on this stage, Mr. Garland. When your opera singer vanished, were there any accompanying phenomena? Flames, steam, things like that?"

"There was a tower of smoke, but that is part of the show." Garland stepped over to a depression in the wooden floor. "When Greta summons the Valkyries with her song, a propmaster issues smoke from this trap door. Last night, much more rolled out than usual, enveloping the stage. When we had cleared it away with fans, Greta was gone."

Mysterius slid open the trap door to view the understage, which was the usual collection of ropes, blocks and props spaced among support posts on a much rougher wooden deck. "Where is the propmaster from last night?"

Garland was stepping down into the orchestra pit. "He is in Greta's dressing room, still recovering from a fall or perhaps alcohol poisoning. His testimony hasn't been of use yet, but you can speak with him. I have to go to the front and prepare, so Belgand will take you to him."

"Belgand?" Mysterius frowned. Delfi felt hot breath on her, low and from behind. She spun around to see a dwarf in tuxedo, smiling through a bend of blocky yellow teeth.

"I take you to Wallace." Belgand noisily sucked in a large volume of air through his vaguely boar-like snout, and shambled behind the curtains. Delfi looked accusingly at Mysterius, who was still absorbed in studying the stage. Finally she pulled him along by his sleeve to follow the little man.

"I didn't fall and I wasn't drinking!" Wallace blurted, immediately touching a steak to his swollen face at the resulting shock of pain. "I was starting the smoker when I heard something growl like a dog behind me. I turned around and everything went black." Wallace leaned back on the divan, dizzy from his brief time sitting up. Delfi was seated at the make-up table, admiring a silver handled brush. She started to pull it through her own hair and then stopped, noticing the rust red and pale blonde strands that would certainly mix with her own chestnut locks.

Mysterius leaned back in a chair. "There are lots of wood beams under the stage, you likely ran afoul of them. Heard the growl, were startled and knocked into a support." At this Delfi spun around, still sniffing an atomizer of perfume.

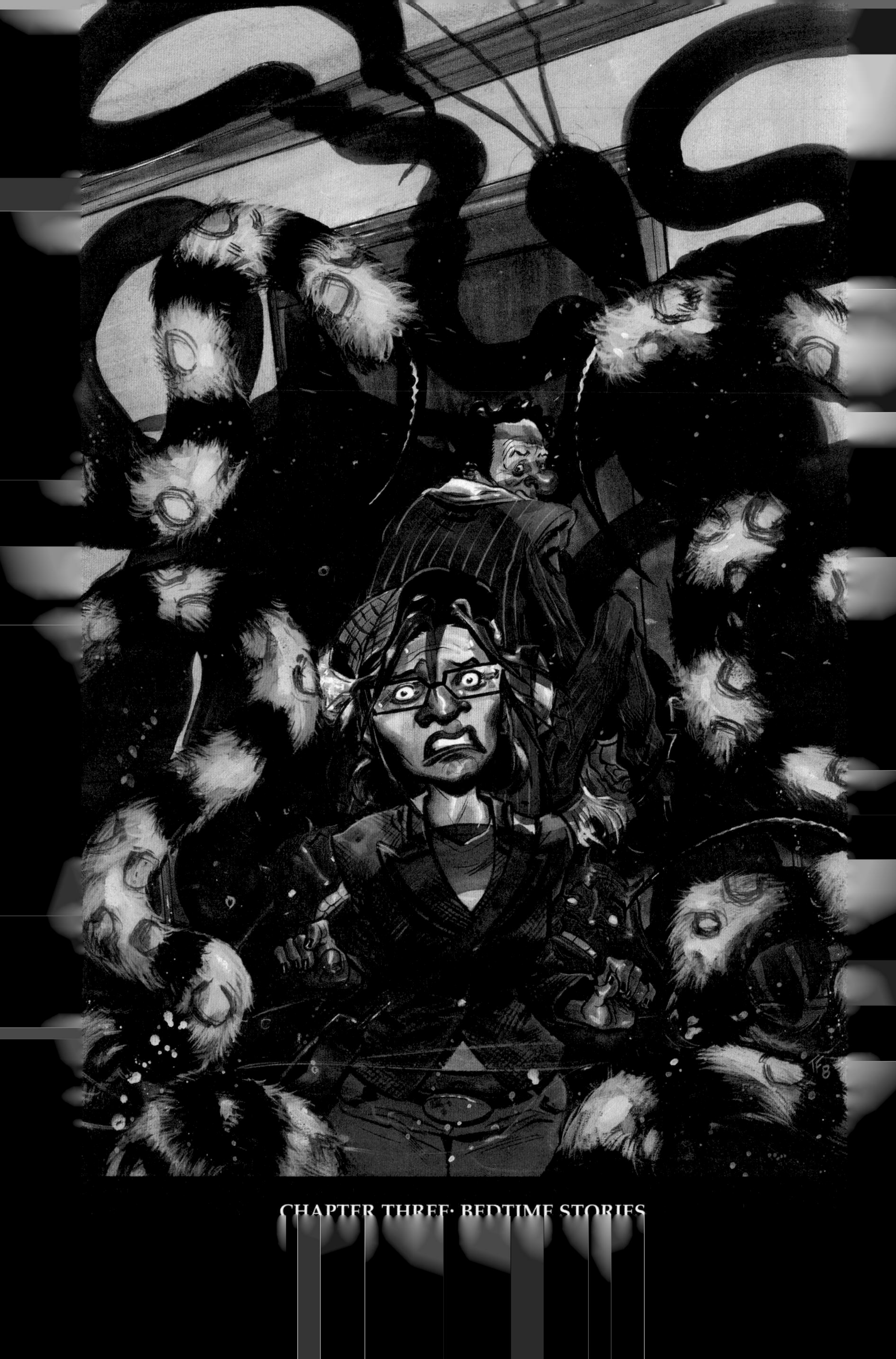

CHAPTER THREE: BEDTIME STORIES

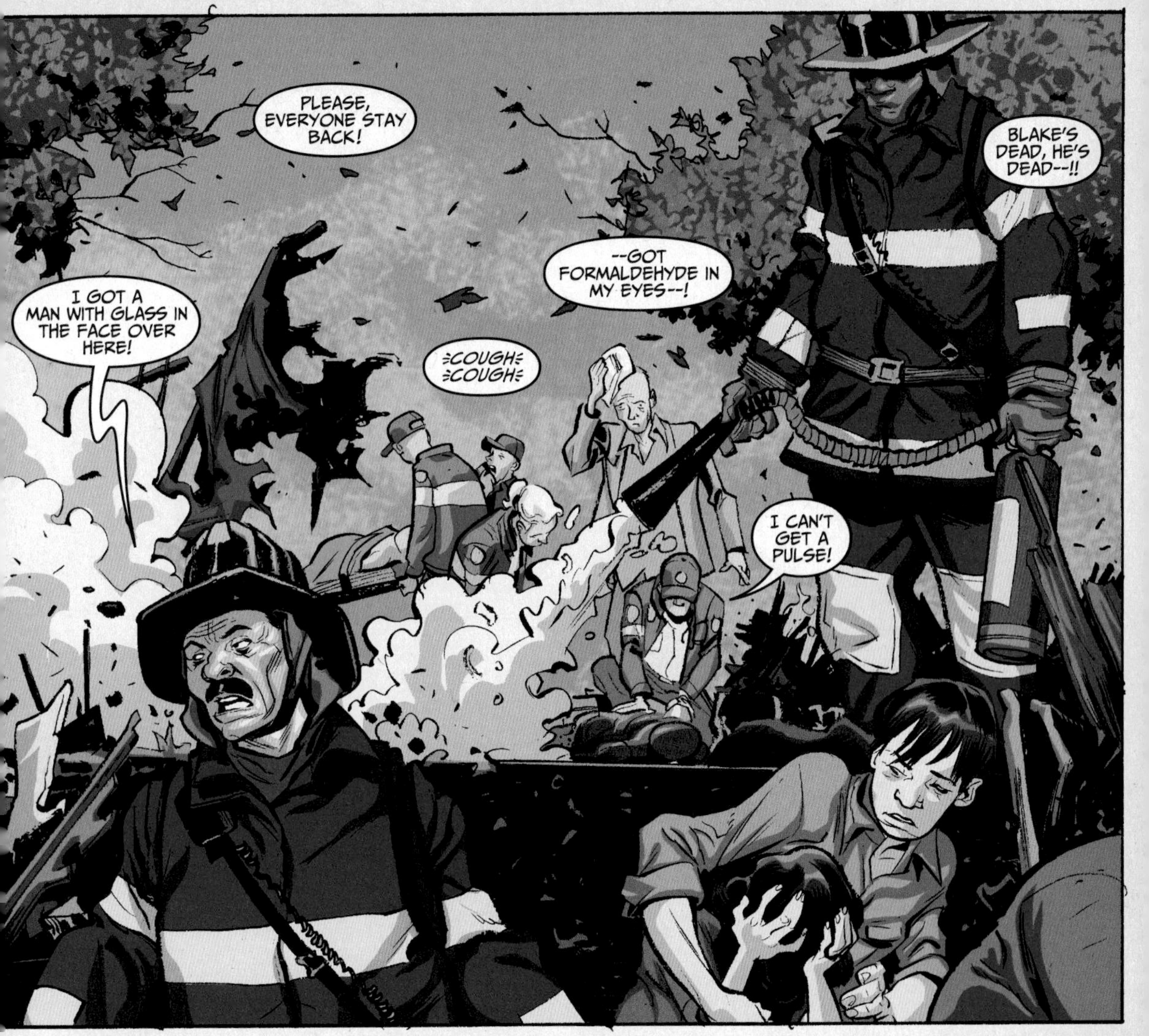
PLEASE, EVERYONE STAY BACK!
BLAKE'S DEAD, HE'S DEAD--!!
I GOT A MAN WITH GLASS IN THE FACE OVER HERE!
--GOT FORMALDEHYDE IN MY EYES--!
COUGH COUGH
I CAN'T GET A PULSE!

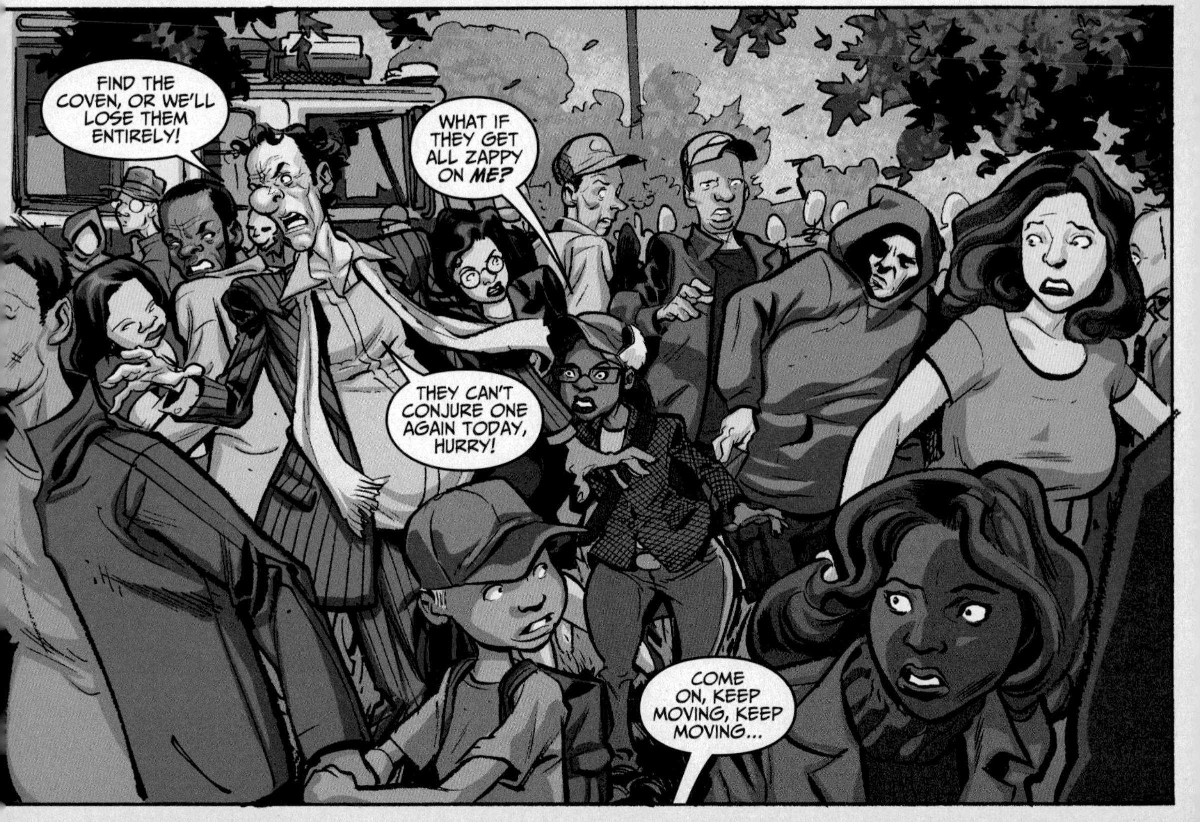
FIND THE COVEN, OR WE'LL LOSE THEM ENTIRELY!
WHAT IF THEY GET ALL ZAPPY ON *ME?*
THEY CAN'T CONJURE ONE AGAIN TODAY, HURRY!
COME ON, KEEP MOVING, KEEP MOVING...

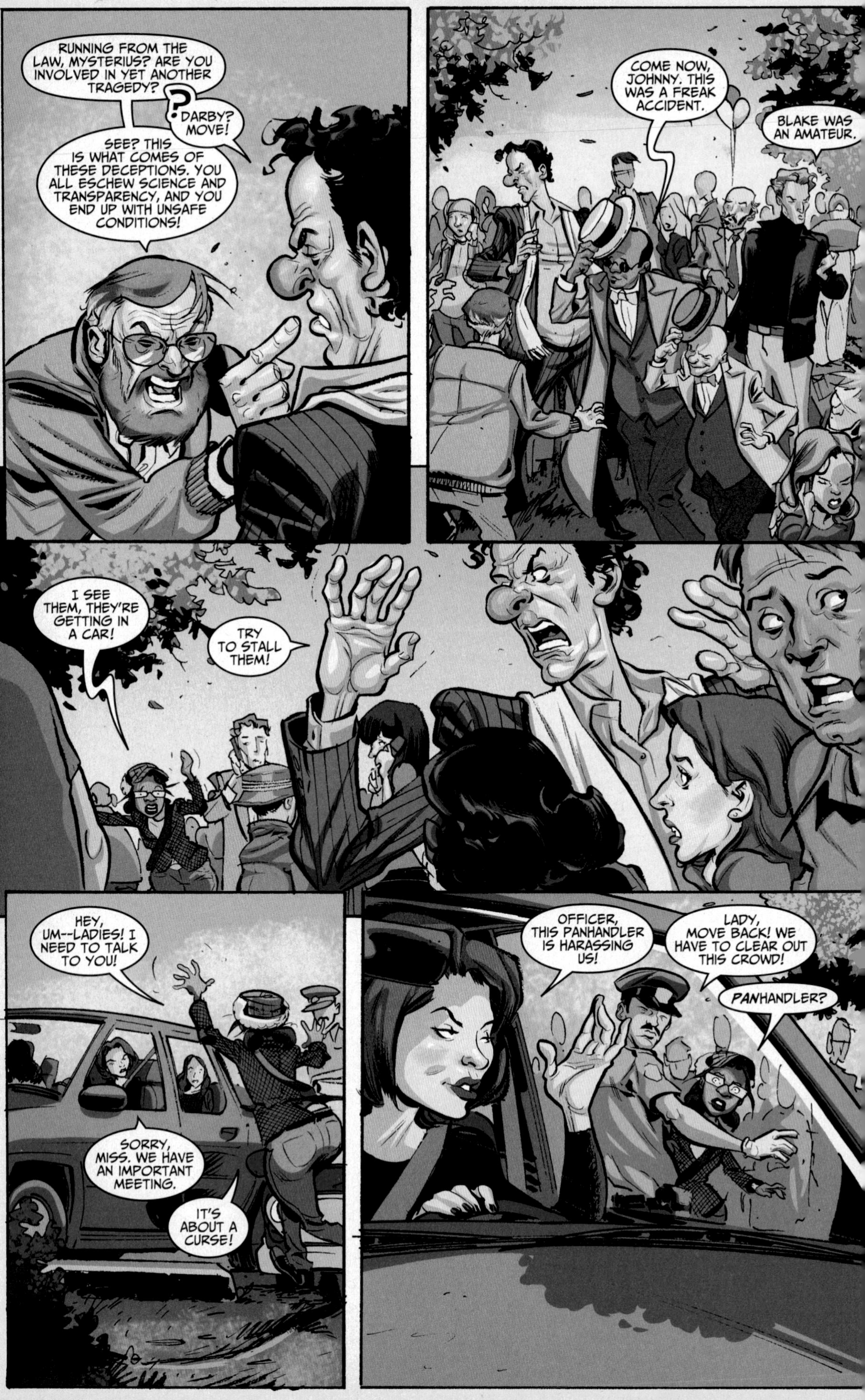
RUNNING FROM THE LAW, MYSTERIUS? ARE YOU INVOLVED IN YET ANOTHER TRAGEDY?
?
DARBY? MOVE!
SEE? THIS IS WHAT COMES OF THESE DECEPTIONS. YOU ALL ESCHEW SCIENCE AND TRANSPARENCY, AND YOU END UP WITH UNSAFE CONDITIONS!
COME NOW, JOHNNY. THIS WAS A FREAK ACCIDENT.
BLAKE WAS AN AMATEUR.
I SEE THEM, THEY'RE GETTING IN A CAR!
TRY TO STALL THEM!
HEY, UM--LADIES! I NEED TO TALK TO YOU!
SORRY, MISS. WE HAVE AN IMPORTANT MEETING.
IT'S ABOUT A CURSE!
OFFICER, THIS PANHANDLER IS HARASSING US!
LADY, MOVE BACK! WE HAVE TO CLEAR OUT THIS CROWD!
PANHANDLER?

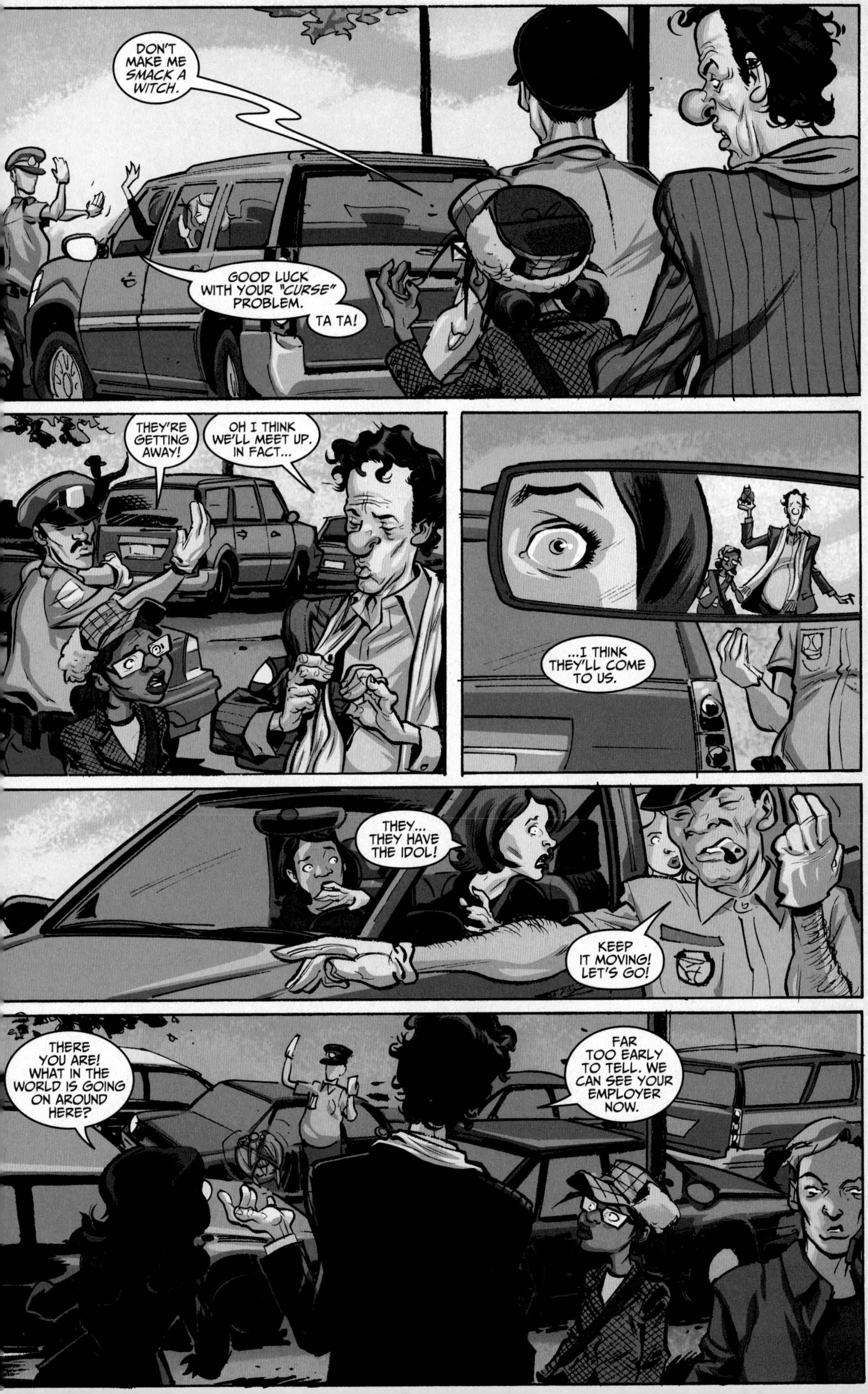
DON'T MAKE ME SMACK A WITCH.
GOOD LUCK WITH YOUR "CURSE" PROBLEM.
TA TA!
THEY'RE GETTING AWAY!
OH I THINK WE'LL MEET UP. IN FACT...
...I THINK THEY'LL COME TO US.
THEY... THEY HAVE THE IDOL!
KEEP IT MOVING! LET'S GO!
THERE YOU ARE! WHAT IN THE WORLD IS GOING ON AROUND HERE?
FAR TOO EARLY TO TELL. WE CAN SEE YOUR EMPLOYER NOW.

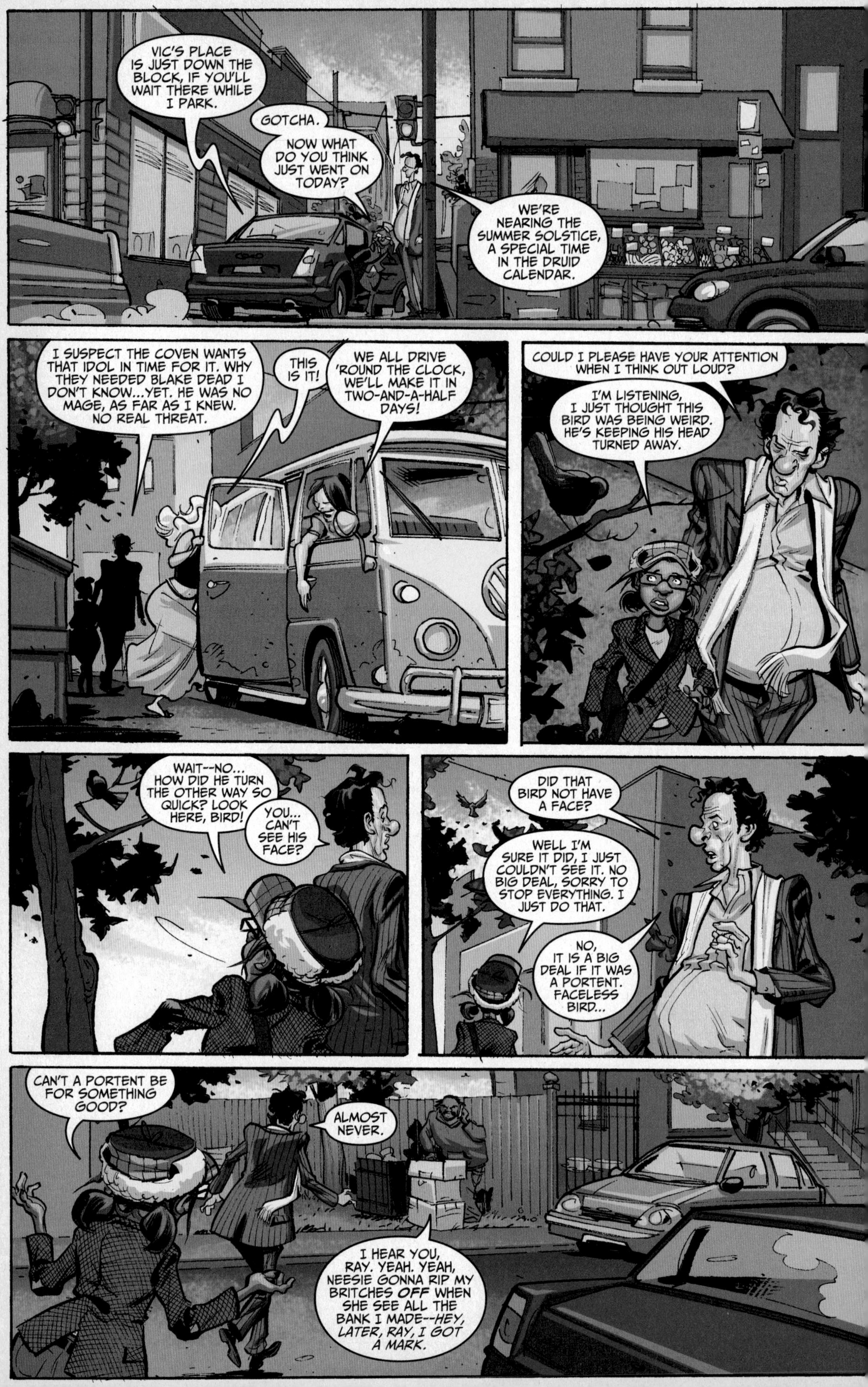
VIC'S PLACE IS JUST DOWN THE BLOCK, IF YOU'LL WAIT THERE WHILE I PARK.
GOTCHA.
NOW WHAT DO YOU THINK JUST WENT ON TODAY?
WE'RE NEARING THE SUMMER SOLSTICE, A SPECIAL TIME IN THE DRUID CALENDAR.
I SUSPECT THE COVEN WANTS THAT IDOL IN TIME FOR IT. WHY THEY NEEDED BLAKE DEAD I DON'T KNOW...YET. HE WAS NO MAGE, AS FAR AS I KNEW. NO REAL THREAT.
THIS IS IT!
WE ALL DRIVE 'ROUND THE CLOCK, WE'LL MAKE IT IN TWO-AND-A-HALF DAYS!
COULD I PLEASE HAVE YOUR ATTENTION WHEN I THINK OUT LOUD?
I'M LISTENING, I JUST THOUGHT THIS BIRD WAS BEING WEIRD. HE'S KEEPING HIS HEAD TURNED AWAY.
WAIT--NO... HOW DID HE TURN THE OTHER WAY SO QUICK? LOOK HERE, BIRD!
YOU... CAN'T SEE HIS FACE?
DID THAT BIRD NOT HAVE A FACE?
WELL I'M SURE IT DID, I JUST COULDN'T SEE IT. NO BIG DEAL, SORRY TO STOP EVERYTHING. I JUST DO THAT.
NO, IT IS A BIG DEAL IF IT WAS A PORTENT. FACELESS BIRD...
CAN'T A PORTENT BE FOR SOMETHING GOOD?
ALMOST NEVER.
I HEAR YOU, RAY. YEAH. YEAH, NEESIE GONNA RIP MY BRITCHES *OFF* WHEN SHE SEE ALL THE BANK I MADE--*HEY, LATER, RAY, I GOT A MARK.*

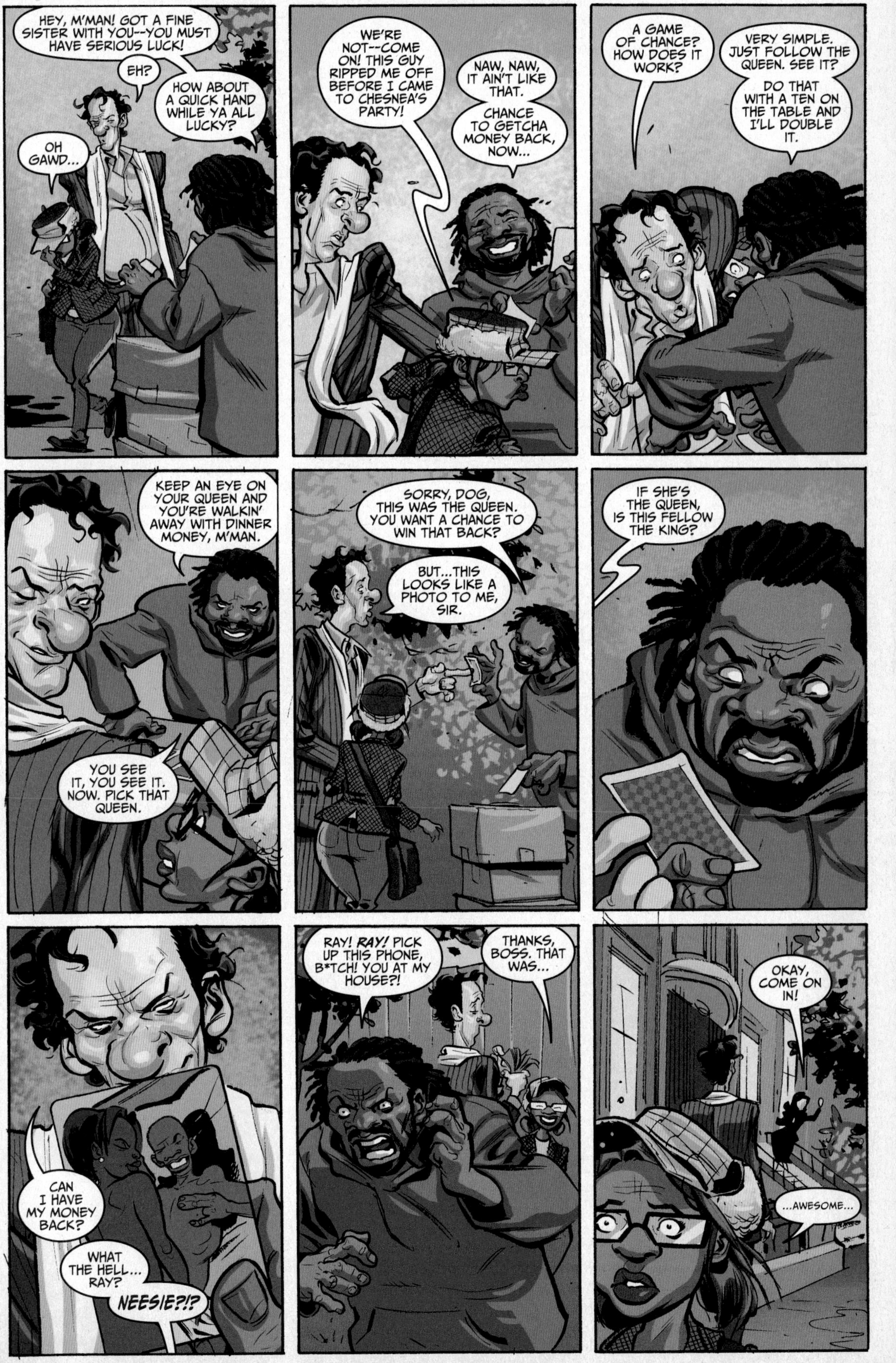
HEY, M'MAN! GOT A FINE SISTER WITH YOU--YOU MUST HAVE SERIOUS LUCK!
EH?
HOW ABOUT A QUICK HAND WHILE YA ALL LUCKY?
OH GAWD...
WE'RE NOT--COME ON! THIS GUY RIPPED ME OFF BEFORE I CAME TO CHESNEA'S PARTY!
NAW, NAW, IT AIN'T LIKE THAT.
CHANCE TO GETCHA MONEY BACK, NOW...
A GAME OF CHANCE? HOW DOES IT WORK?
VERY SIMPLE. JUST FOLLOW THE QUEEN. SEE IT?
DO THAT WITH A TEN ON THE TABLE AND I'LL DOUBLE IT.
KEEP AN EYE ON YOUR QUEEN AND YOU'RE WALKIN' AWAY WITH DINNER MONEY, M'MAN.
YOU SEE IT, YOU SEE IT. NOW. PICK THAT QUEEN.
SORRY, DOG, THIS WAS THE QUEEN. YOU WANT A CHANCE TO WIN THAT BACK?
BUT...THIS LOOKS LIKE A PHOTO TO ME, SIR.
IF SHE'S THE QUEEN, IS THIS FELLOW THE KING?
CAN I HAVE MY MONEY BACK?
WHAT THE HELL... RAY?
NEESIE?!?
RAY! RAY! PICK UP THIS PHONE, B*TCH! YOU AT MY HOUSE?!
THANKS, BOSS. THAT WAS...
OKAY, COME ON IN!
...AWESOME...

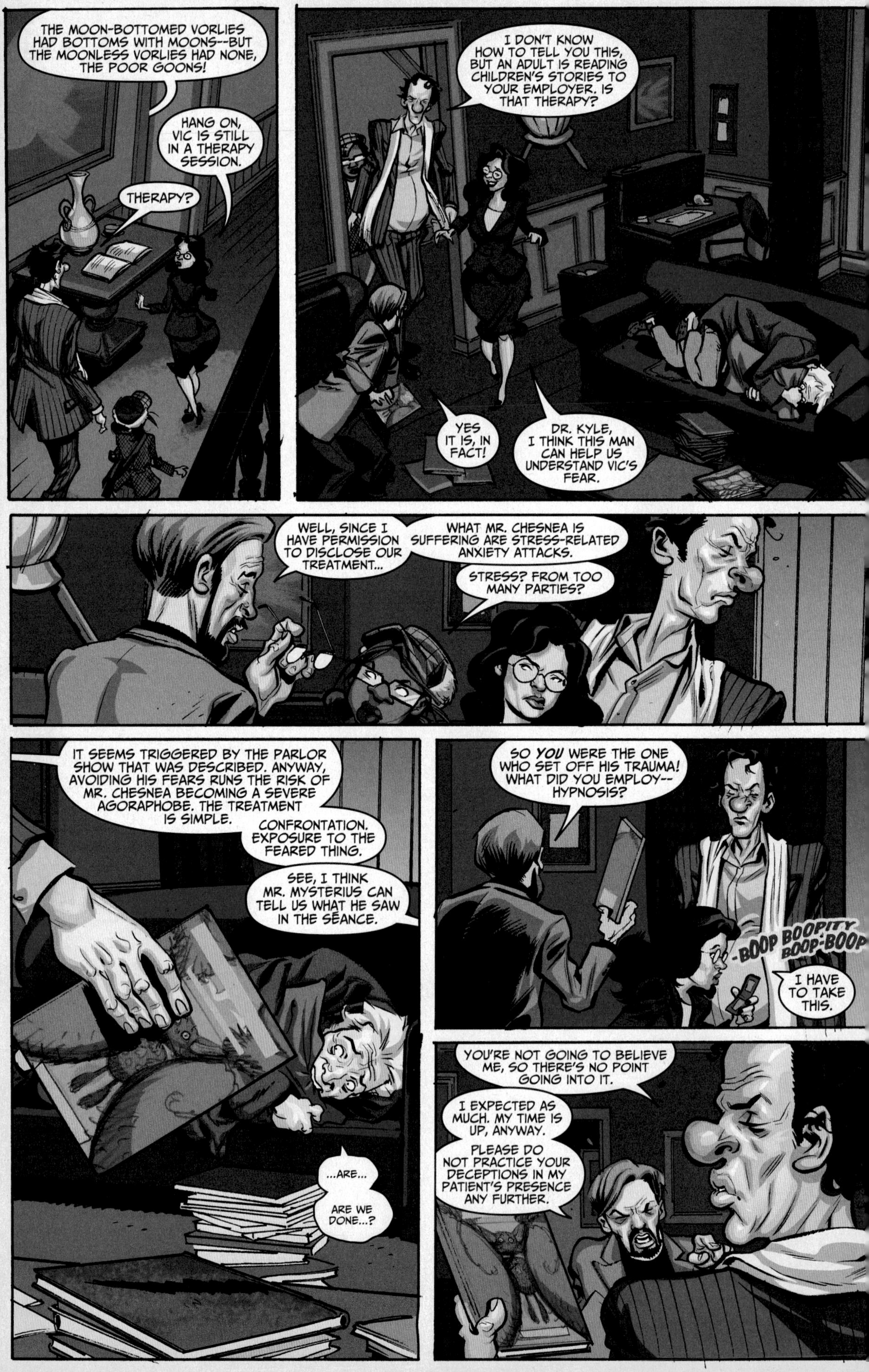
THE MOON-BOTTOMED VORLIES HAD BOTTOMS WITH MOONS--BUT THE MOONLESS VORLIES HAD NONE, THE POOR GOONS!
HANG ON, VIC IS STILL IN A THERAPY SESSION.
THERAPY?
I DON'T KNOW HOW TO TELL YOU THIS, BUT AN ADULT IS READING CHILDREN'S STORIES TO YOUR EMPLOYER. IS THAT THERAPY?
YES IT IS, IN FACT!
DR. KYLE, I THINK THIS MAN CAN HELP US UNDERSTAND VIC'S FEAR.
WELL, SINCE I HAVE PERMISSION TO DISCLOSE OUR TREATMENT...
WHAT MR. CHESNEA IS SUFFERING ARE STRESS-RELATED ANXIETY ATTACKS.
STRESS? FROM TOO MANY PARTIES?
IT SEEMS TRIGGERED BY THE PARLOR SHOW THAT WAS DESCRIBED. ANYWAY, AVOIDING HIS FEARS RUNS THE RISK OF MR. CHESNEA BECOMING A SEVERE AGORAPHOBE. THE TREATMENT IS SIMPLE.
CONFRONTATION. EXPOSURE TO THE FEARED THING.
SEE, I THINK MR. MYSTERIUS CAN TELL US WHAT HE SAW IN THE SÉANCE.
...ARE...
ARE WE DONE...?
SO *YOU* WERE THE ONE WHO SET OFF HIS TRAUMA! WHAT DID YOU EMPLOY-- HYPNOSIS?
-BOOP BOOPITY BOOP-BOOP
I HAVE TO TAKE THIS.
YOU'RE NOT GOING TO BELIEVE ME, SO THERE'S NO POINT GOING INTO IT.
I EXPECTED AS MUCH. MY TIME IS UP, ANYWAY.
PLEASE DO NOT PRACTICE YOUR DECEPTIONS IN MY PATIENT'S PRESENCE ANY FURTHER.

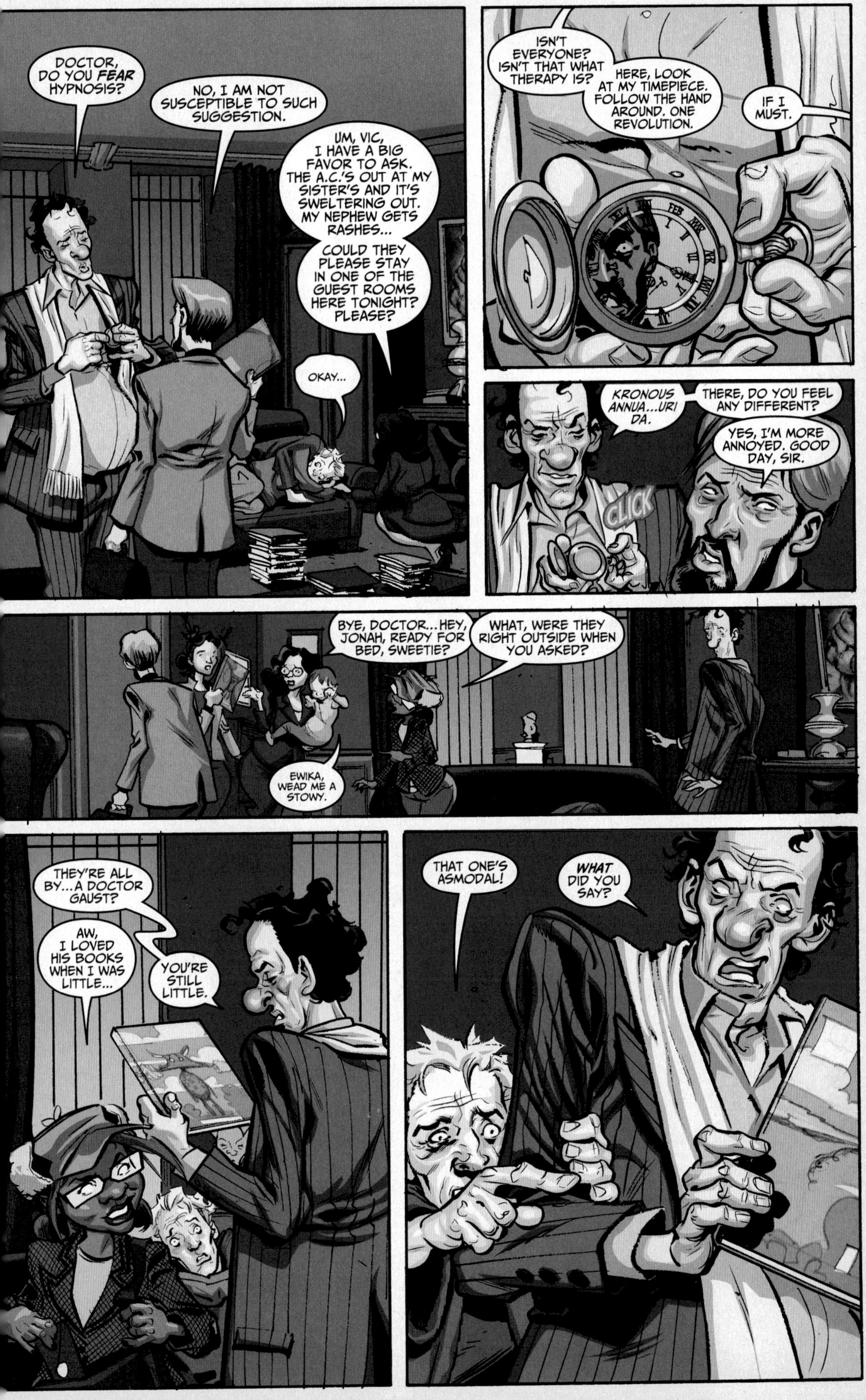
DOCTOR, DO YOU FEAR HYPNOSIS?
NO, I AM NOT SUSCEPTIBLE TO SUCH SUGGESTION.
UM, VIC, I HAVE A BIG FAVOR TO ASK. THE A.C.'S OUT AT MY SISTER'S AND IT'S SWELTERING OUT. MY NEPHEW GETS RASHES...
COULD THEY PLEASE STAY IN ONE OF THE GUEST ROOMS HERE TONIGHT? PLEASE?
OKAY...
ISN'T EVERYONE? ISN'T THAT WHAT THERAPY IS?
HERE, LOOK AT MY TIMEPIECE. FOLLOW THE HAND AROUND. ONE REVOLUTION.
IF I MUST.
KRONOUS ANNUA...URI DA.
THERE, DO YOU FEEL ANY DIFFERENT?
YES, I'M MORE ANNOYED. GOOD DAY, SIR.
CLICK
BYE, DOCTOR...HEY, JONAH, READY FOR BED, SWEETIE?
WHAT, WERE THEY RIGHT OUTSIDE WHEN YOU ASKED?
EWIKA, WEAD ME A STOWY.
THEY'RE ALL BY...A DOCTOR GAUST?
AW, I LOVED HIS BOOKS WHEN I WAS LITTLE...
YOU'RE STILL LITTLE.
THAT ONE'S ASMODAL!
WHAT DID YOU SAY?

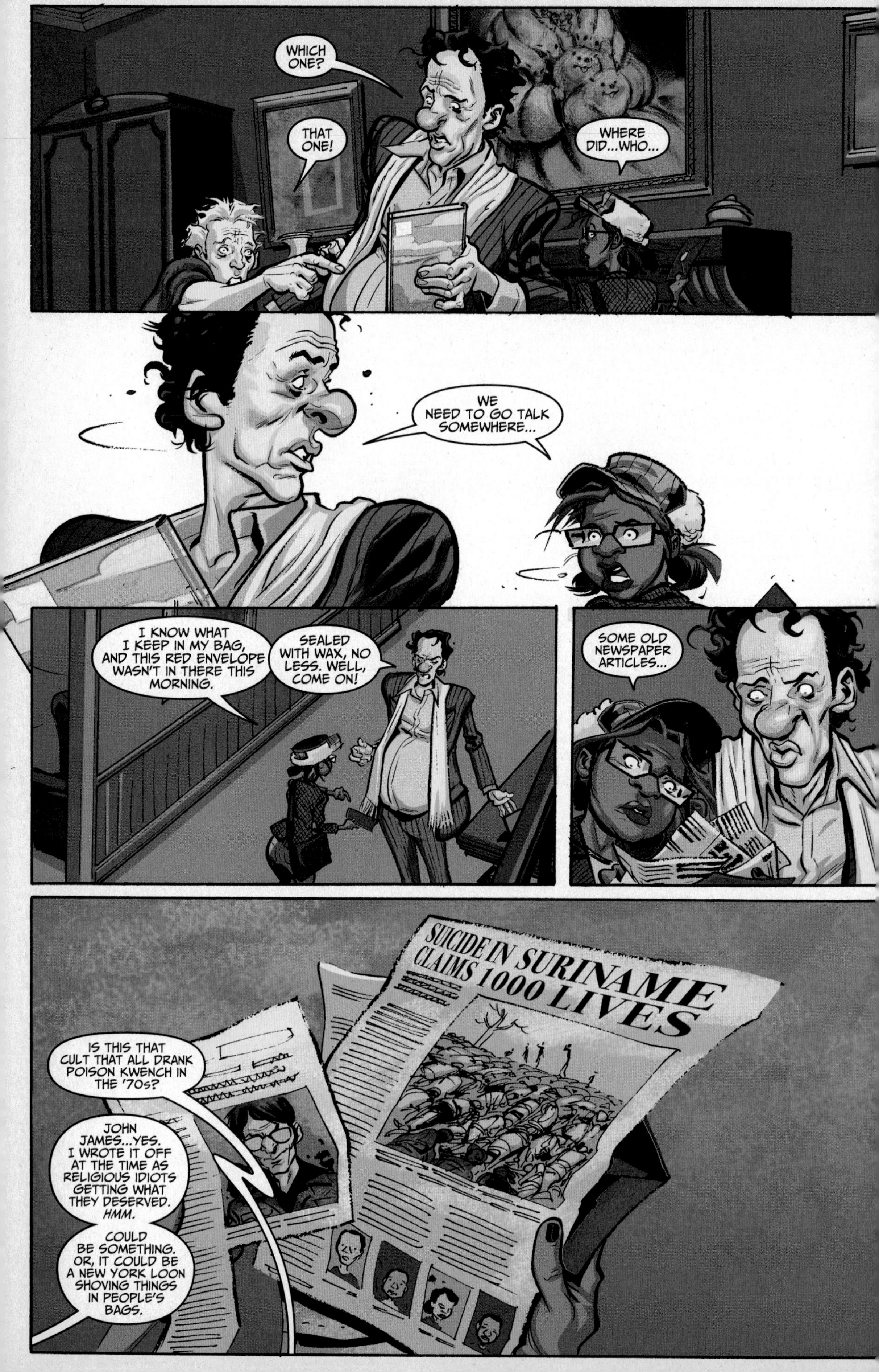
WHICH ONE?
THAT ONE!
WHERE DID...WHO...
WE NEED TO GO TALK SOMEWHERE...
I KNOW WHAT I KEEP IN MY BAG, AND THIS RED ENVELOPE WASN'T IN THERE THIS MORNING.
SEALED WITH WAX, NO LESS. WELL, COME ON!
SOME OLD NEWSPAPER ARTICLES...
SUICIDE IN SURINAME CLAIMS 1000 LIVES
IS THIS THAT CULT THAT ALL DRANK POISON KWENCH IN THE '70s?
JOHN JAMES...YES. I WROTE IT OFF AT THE TIME AS RELIGIOUS IDIOTS GETTING WHAT THEY DESERVED. *HMM.*
COULD BE SOMETHING. OR, IT COULD BE A NEW YORK LOON SHOVING THINGS IN PEOPLE'S BAGS.

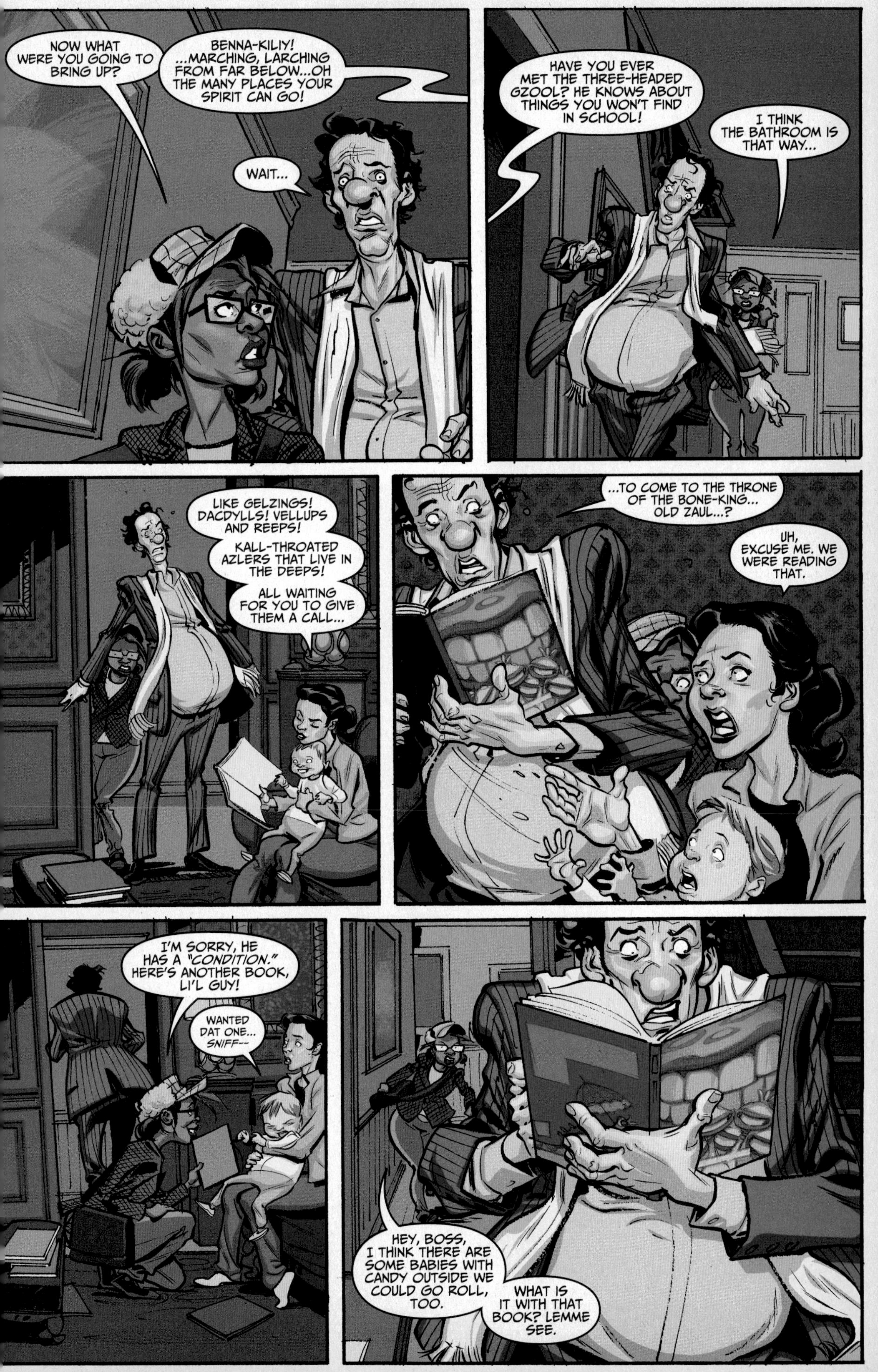
NOW WHAT WERE YOU GOING TO BRING UP?
BENNA-KILIY! ...MARCHING, LARCHING FROM FAR BELOW...OH THE MANY PLACES YOUR SPIRIT CAN GO!
WAIT...
HAVE YOU EVER MET THE THREE-HEADED GZOOL? HE KNOWS ABOUT THINGS YOU WON'T FIND IN SCHOOL!
I THINK THE BATHROOM IS THAT WAY...
LIKE GELZINGS! DACDYLLS! VELLUPS AND REEPS!
KALL-THROATED AZLERS THAT LIVE IN THE DEEPS!
ALL WAITING FOR YOU TO GIVE THEM A CALL...
...TO COME TO THE THRONE OF THE BONE-KING... OLD ZAUL...?
UH, EXCUSE ME. WE WERE READING THAT.
I'M SORRY, HE HAS A "CONDITION." HERE'S ANOTHER BOOK, LI'L GUY!
WANTED DAT ONE... SNIFF--
HEY, BOSS, I THINK THERE ARE SOME BABIES WITH CANDY OUTSIDE WE COULD GO ROLL, TOO.
WHAT IS IT WITH THAT BOOK? LEMME SEE.

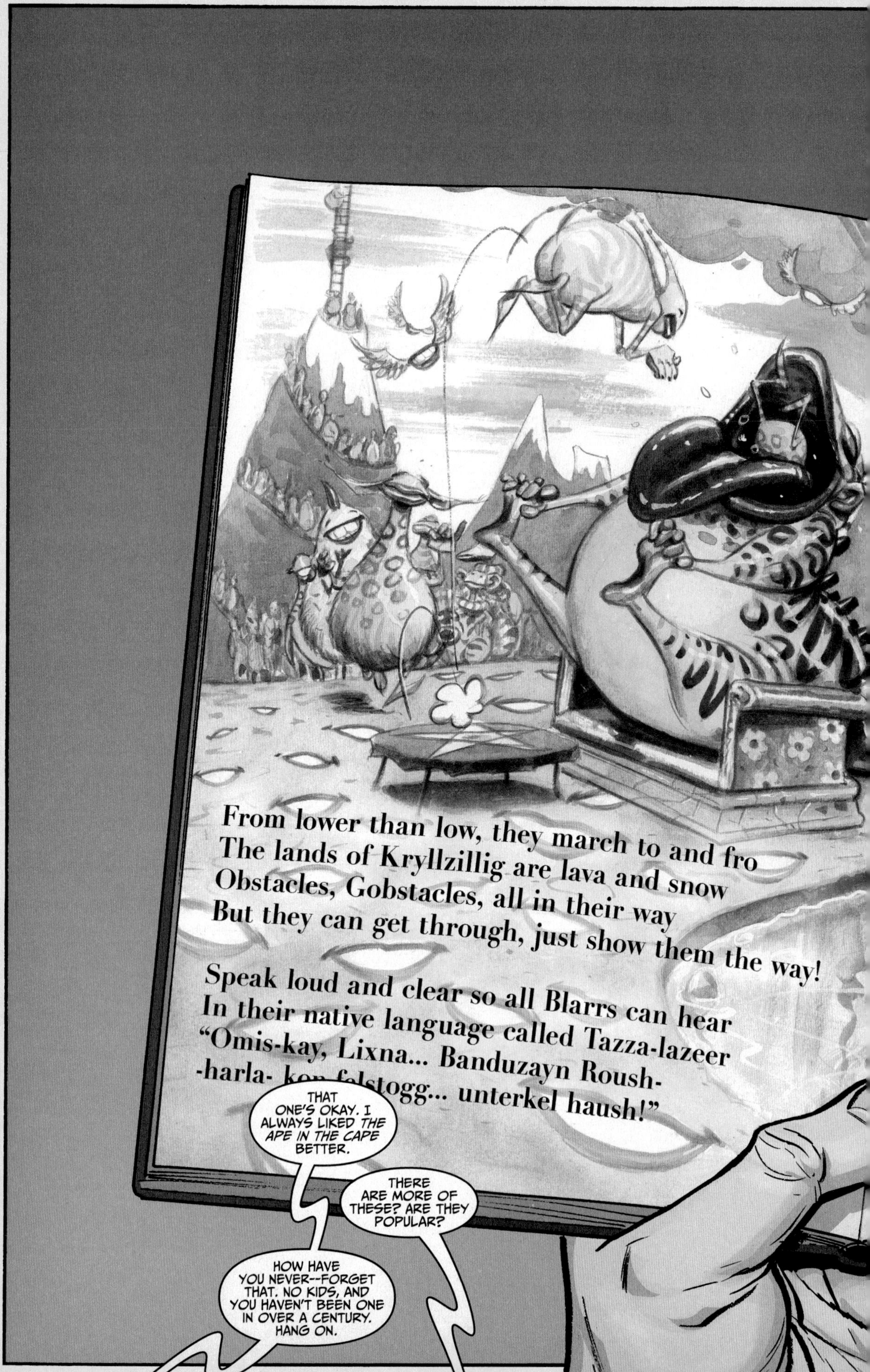
From lower than low, they march to and fro
The lands of Kryllzillig are lava and snow
Obstacles, Gobstacles, all in their way
But they can get through, just show them the way!
Speak loud and clear so all Blarrs can hear
In their native language called Tazza-lazeer
“Omis-kay, Lixna... Banduzayn Roush-
-harla- ...togg... unterkel haush!”
THAT ONE'S OKAY. I ALWAYS LIKED *THE APE IN THE CAPE* BETTER.
THERE ARE MORE OF THESE? ARE THEY POPULAR?
HOW HAVE YOU NEVER--FORGET THAT. NO KIDS, AND YOU HAVEN'T BEEN ONE IN OVER A CENTURY. HANG ON.

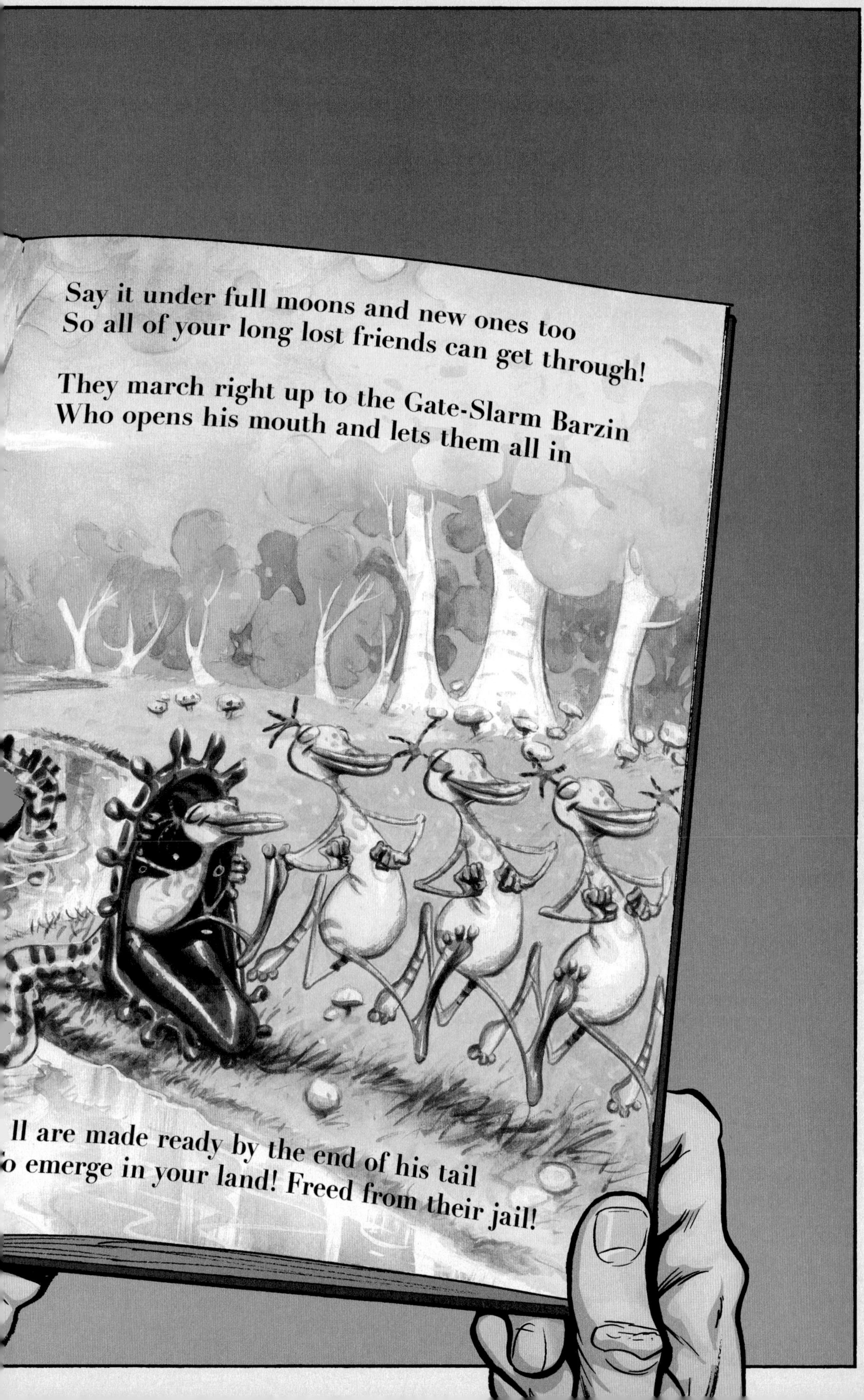
Say it under full moons and new ones too
So all of your long lost friends can get through!
They march right up to the Gate-Slarm Barzin
Who opens his mouth and lets them all in
ll are made ready by the end of his tail
o emerge in your land! Freed from their jail!

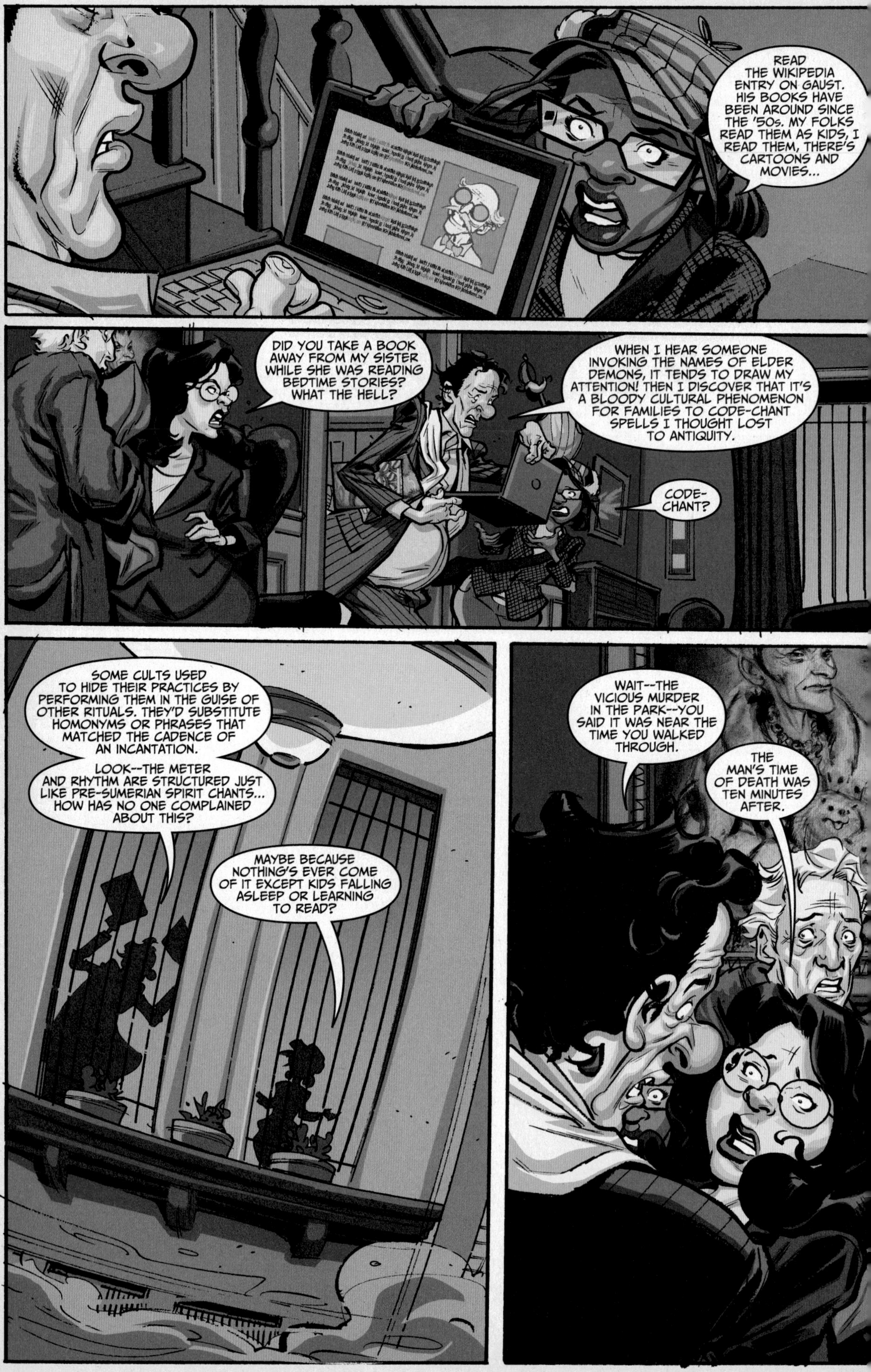
READ THE WIKIPEDIA ENTRY ON GAUST. HIS BOOKS HAVE BEEN AROUND SINCE THE '50s. MY FOLKS READ THEM AS KIDS, I READ THEM, THERE'S CARTOONS AND MOVIES...
DID YOU TAKE A BOOK AWAY FROM MY SISTER WHILE SHE WAS READING BEDTIME STORIES? WHAT THE HELL?
WHEN I HEAR SOMEONE INVOKING THE NAMES OF ELDER DEMONS, IT TENDS TO DRAW MY ATTENTION! THEN I DISCOVER THAT IT'S A BLOODY CULTURAL PHENOMENON FOR FAMILIES TO CODE-CHANT SPELLS I THOUGHT LOST TO ANTIQUITY.
CODE-CHANT?
SOME CULTS USED TO HIDE THEIR PRACTICES BY PERFORMING THEM IN THE GUISE OF OTHER RITUALS. THEY'D SUBSTITUTE HOMONYMS OR PHRASES THAT MATCHED THE CADENCE OF AN INCANTATION.
LOOK--THE METER AND RHYTHM ARE STRUCTURED JUST LIKE PRE-SUMERIAN SPIRIT CHANTS... HOW HAS NO ONE COMPLAINED ABOUT THIS?
MAYBE BECAUSE NOTHING'S EVER COME OF IT EXCEPT KIDS FALLING ASLEEP OR LEARNING TO READ?
WAIT--THE VICIOUS MURDER IN THE PARK--YOU SAID IT WAS NEAR THE TIME YOU WALKED THROUGH.
THE MAN'S TIME OF DEATH WAS TEN MINUTES AFTER.

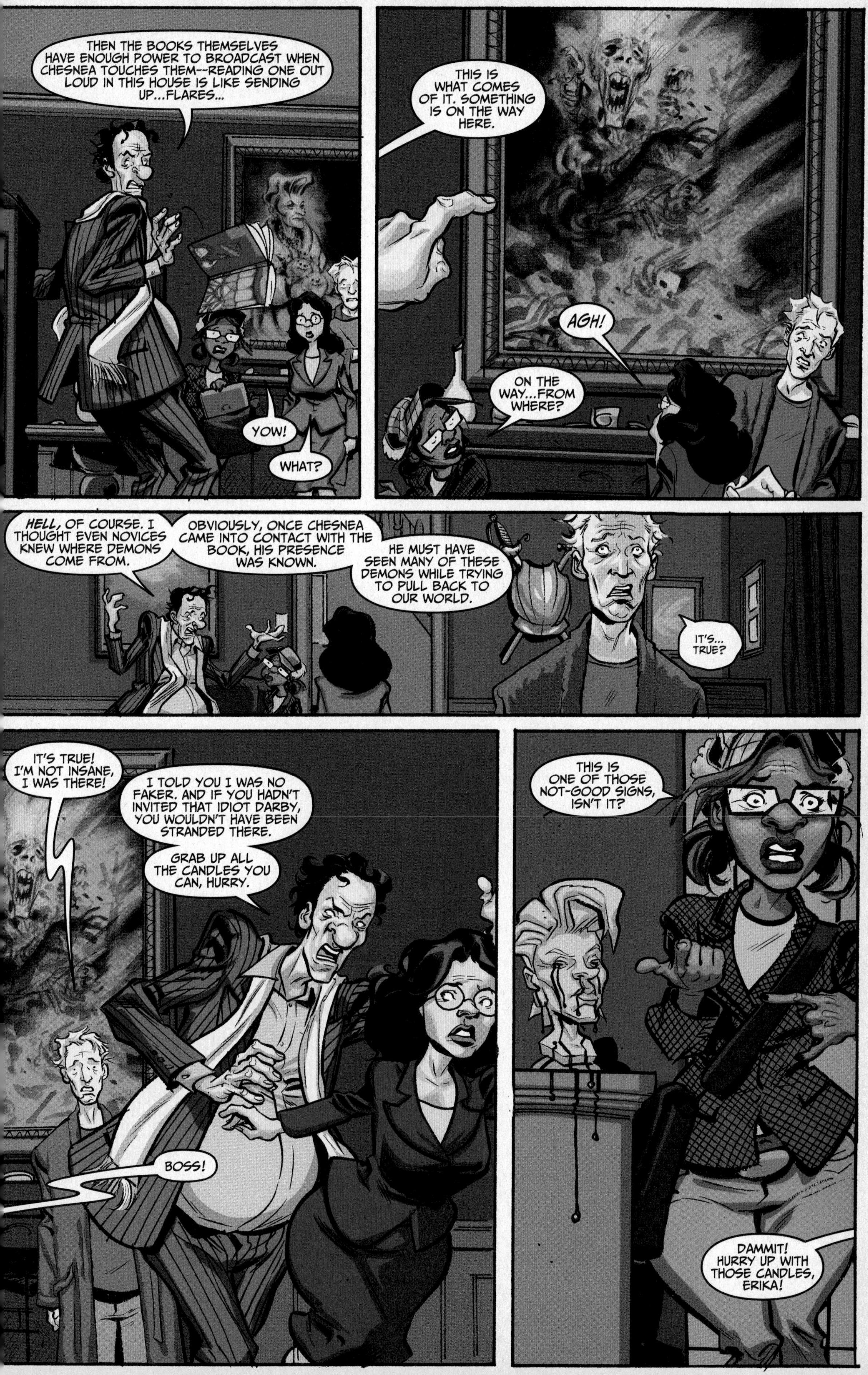
THEN THE BOOKS THEMSELVES HAVE ENOUGH POWER TO BROADCAST WHEN CHESNEA TOUCHES THEM--READING ONE OUT LOUD IN THIS HOUSE IS LIKE SENDING UP...FLARES...
YOW!
WHAT?
THIS IS WHAT COMES OF IT. SOMETHING IS ON THE WAY HERE.
AGH!
ON THE WAY...FROM WHERE?
HELL, OF COURSE. I THOUGHT EVEN NOVICES KNEW WHERE DEMONS COME FROM.
OBVIOUSLY, ONCE CHESNEA CAME INTO CONTACT WITH THE BOOK, HIS PRESENCE WAS KNOWN.
HE MUST HAVE SEEN MANY OF THESE DEMONS WHILE TRYING TO PULL BACK TO OUR WORLD.
IT'S... TRUE?
IT'S TRUE! I'M NOT INSANE, I WAS THERE!
I TOLD YOU I WAS NO FAKER. AND IF YOU HADN'T INVITED THAT IDIOT DARBY, YOU WOULDN'T HAVE BEEN STRANDED THERE.
GRAB UP ALL THE CANDLES YOU CAN, HURRY.
BOSS!
THIS IS ONE OF THOSE NOT-GOOD SIGNS, ISN'T IT?
DAMMIT! HURRY UP WITH THOSE CANDLES, ERIKA!

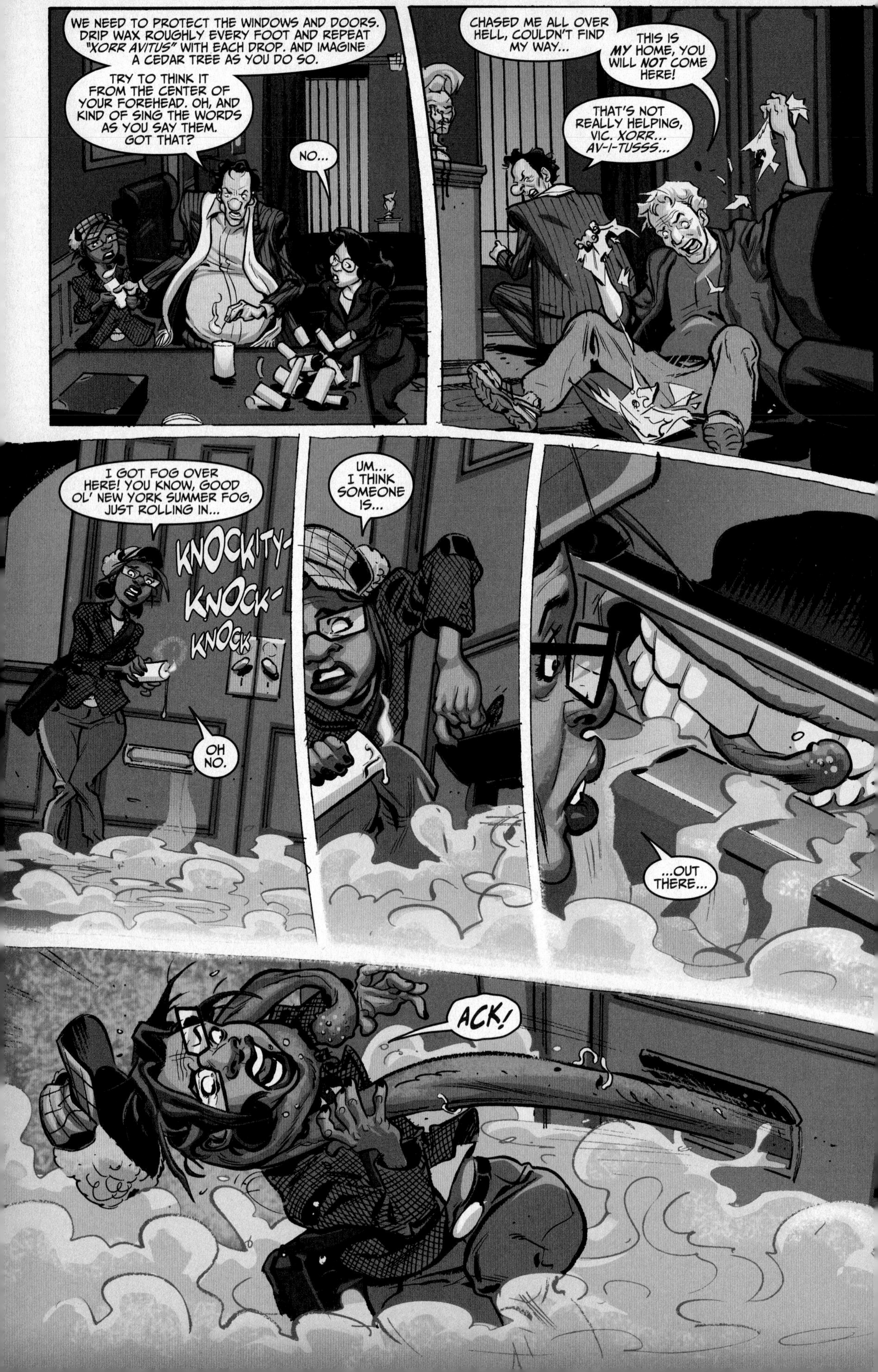
WE NEED TO PROTECT THE WINDOWS AND DOORS. DRIP WAX ROUGHLY EVERY FOOT AND REPEAT "XORR AVITUS" WITH EACH DROP. AND IMAGINE A CEDAR TREE AS YOU DO SO.
TRY TO THINK IT FROM THE CENTER OF YOUR FOREHEAD. OH, AND KIND OF SING THE WORDS AS YOU SAY THEM. GOT THAT?
NO...
CHASED ME ALL OVER HELL, COULDN'T FIND MY WAY...
THIS IS MY HOME, YOU WILL NOT COME HERE!
THAT'S NOT REALLY HELPING, VIC. XORR... AV-I-TUSSS...
I GOT FOG OVER HERE! YOU KNOW, GOOD OL' NEW YORK SUMMER FOG, JUST ROLLING IN...
KNOCKITY-KNOCK-KNOCK
OH NO.
UM... I THINK SOMEONE IS...
...OUT THERE...
ACK!

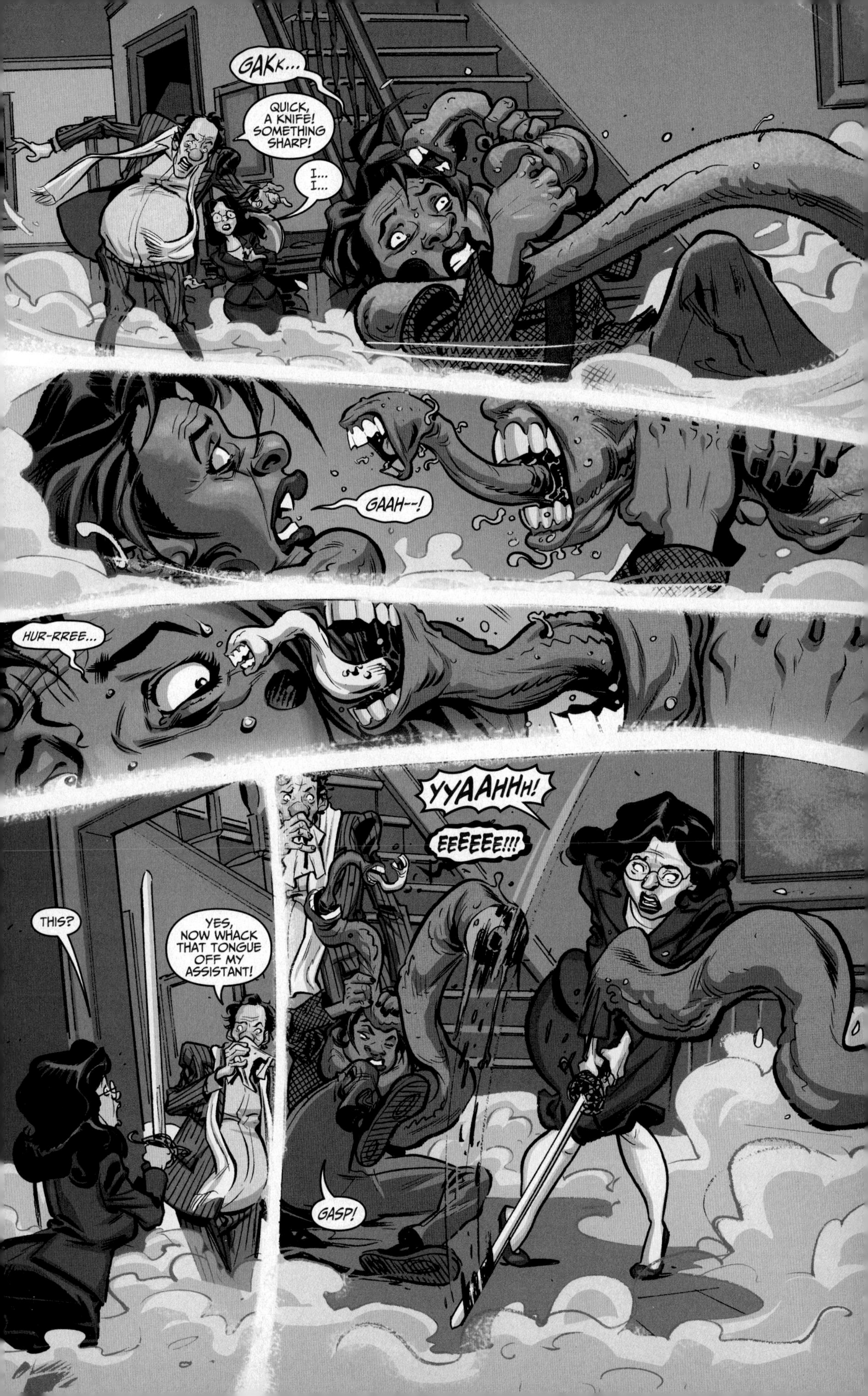
GAKK...
QUICK, A KNIFE! SOMETHING SHARP!
I... I...
GAAH--!
HUR-RREE...
YYAAHHH!
EEEEEE!!!
THIS?
YES, NOW WHACK THAT TONGUE OFF MY ASSISTANT!
GASP!

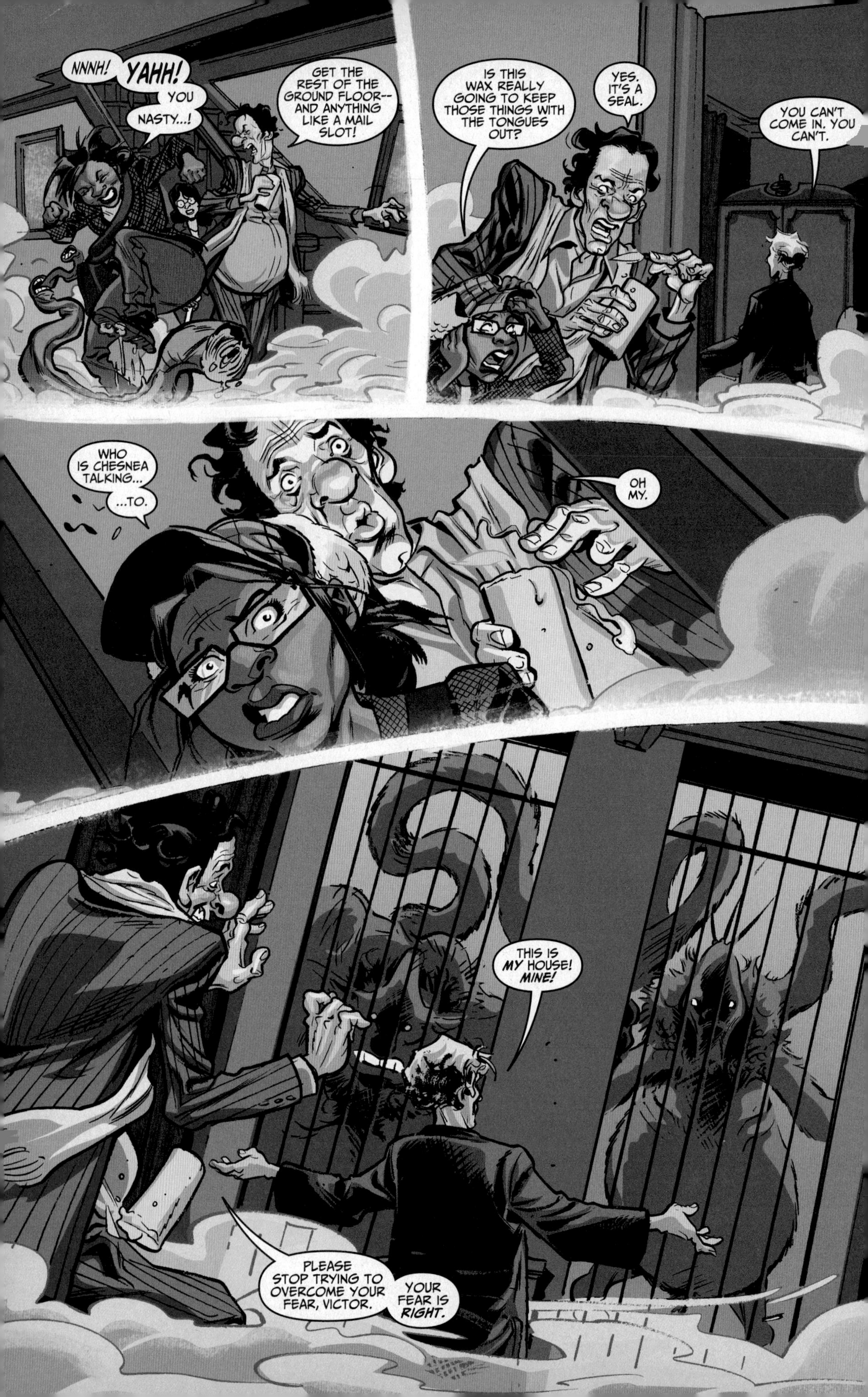
NNNH!
YAHH!
YOU NASTY...!
GET THE REST OF THE GROUND FLOOR-- AND ANYTHING LIKE A MAIL SLOT!
IS THIS WAX REALLY GOING TO KEEP THOSE THINGS WITH THE TONGUES OUT?
YES. IT'S A SEAL.
YOU CAN'T COME IN. YOU CAN'T.
WHO IS CHESNEA TALKING...
...TO.
OH MY.
THIS IS MY HOUSE! MINE!
PLEASE STOP TRYING TO OVERCOME YOUR FEAR, VICTOR.
YOUR FEAR IS RIGHT.

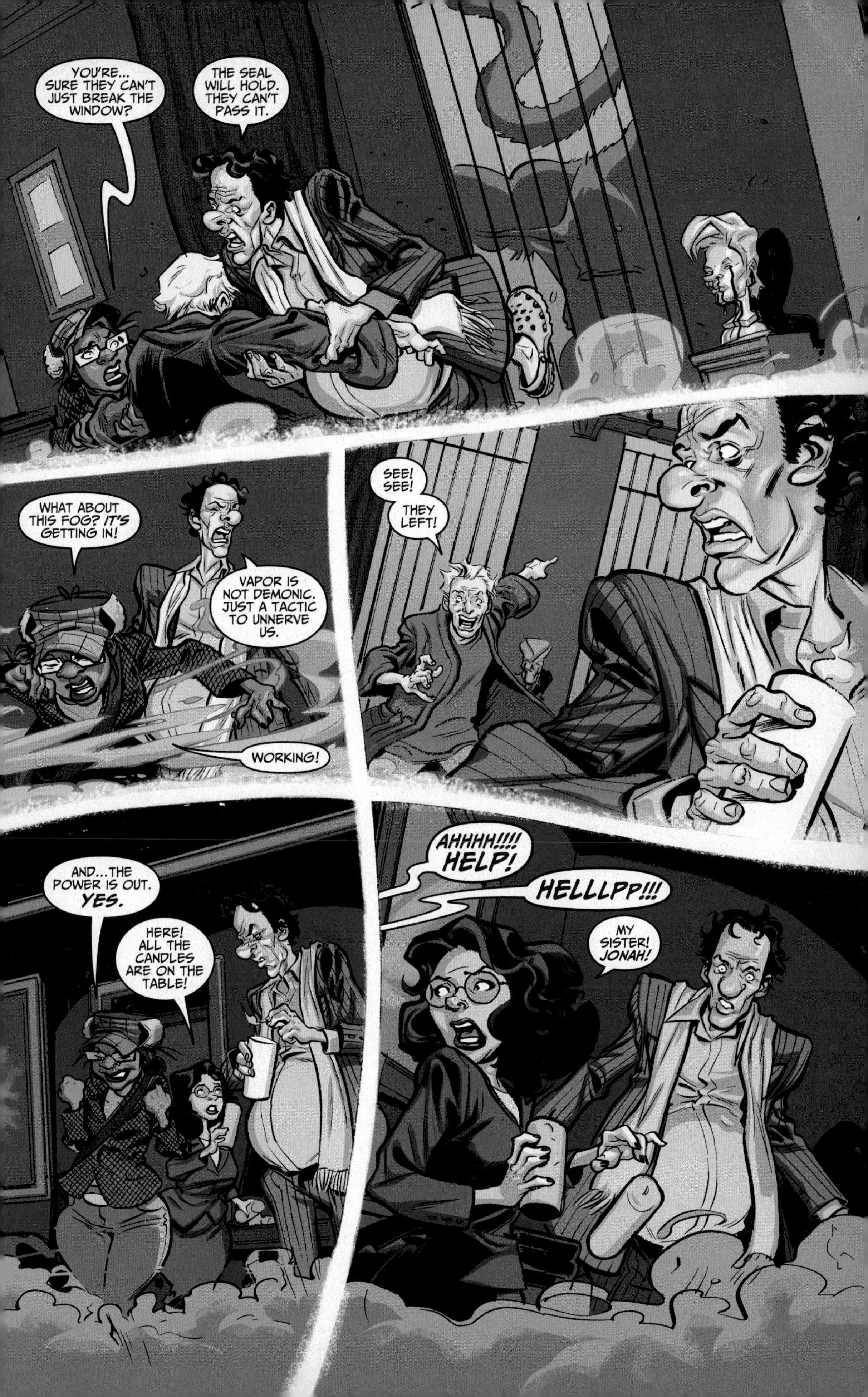
YOU'RE... SURE THEY CAN'T JUST BREAK THE WINDOW?
THE SEAL WILL HOLD. THEY CAN'T PASS IT.
WHAT ABOUT THIS FOG? IT'S GETTING IN!
VAPOR IS NOT DEMONIC. JUST A TACTIC TO UNNERVE US.
WORKING!
SEE! SEE!
THEY LEFT!
AND...THE POWER IS OUT. YES.
HERE! ALL THE CANDLES ARE ON THE TABLE!
AHHHH!!!! HELP!
HELLLPP!!!
MY SISTER! JONAH!

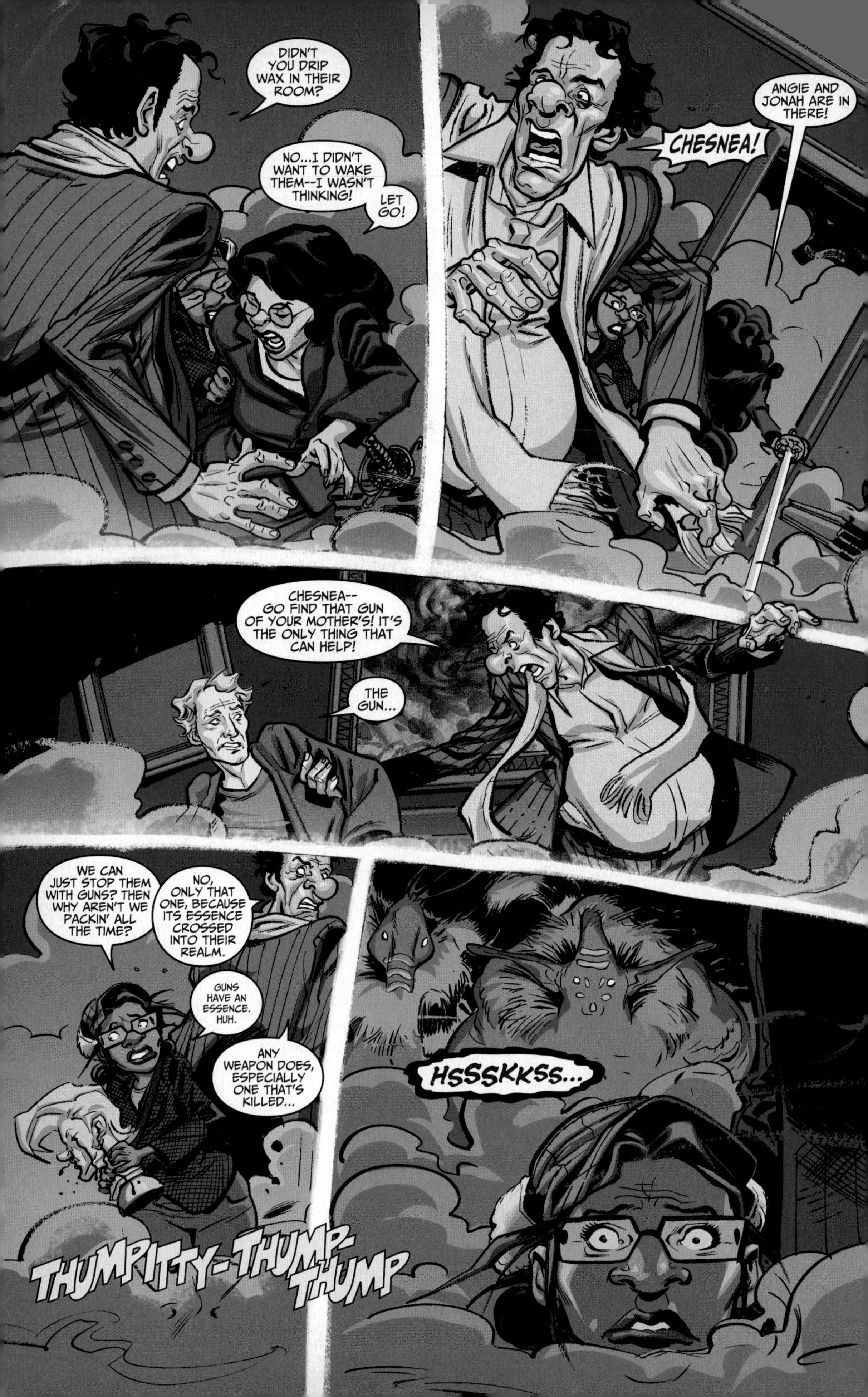
DIDN'T YOU DRIP WAX IN THEIR ROOM?
NO...I DIDN'T WANT TO WAKE THEM--I WASN'T THINKING!
LET GO!
CHESNEA!
ANGIE AND JONAH ARE IN THERE!
CHESNEA-- GO FIND THAT GUN OF YOUR MOTHER'S! IT'S THE ONLY THING THAT CAN HELP!
THE GUN...
WE CAN JUST STOP THEM WITH GUNS? THEN WHY AREN'T WE PACKIN' ALL THE TIME?
NO, ONLY THAT ONE, BECAUSE ITS ESSENCE CROSSED INTO THEIR REALM.
GUNS HAVE AN ESSENCE. HUH.
ANY WEAPON DOES, ESPECIALLY ONE THAT'S KILLED...
THUMPITTY-THUMP-THUMP
HSSSKKSS...

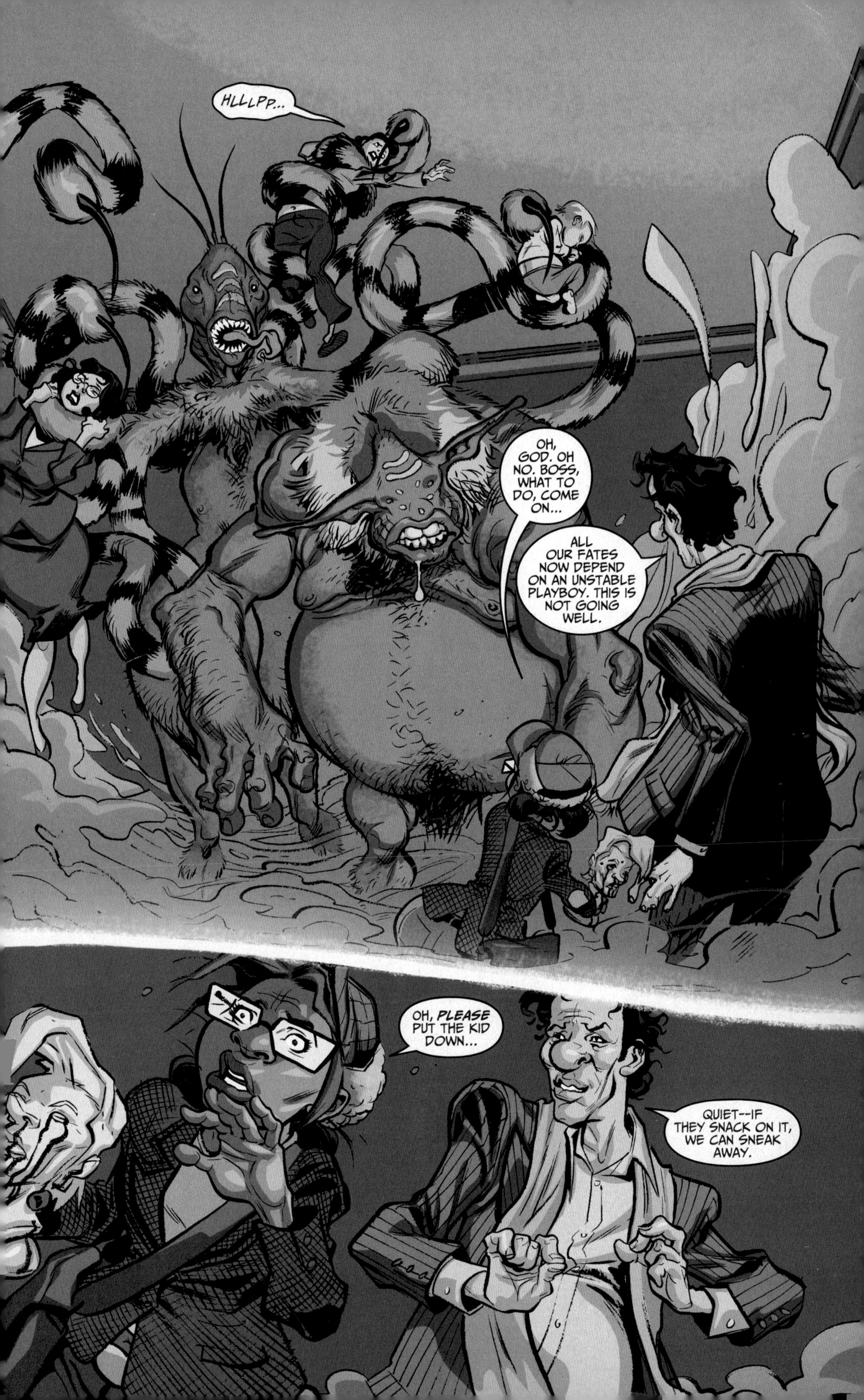
HLLLPP...
OH, GOD. OH NO. BOSS, WHAT TO DO, COME ON...
ALL OUR FATES NOW DEPEND ON AN UNSTABLE PLAYBOY. THIS IS NOT GOING WELL.
OH, *PLEASE* PUT THE KID DOWN...
QUIET--IF THEY SNACK ON IT, WE CAN SNEAK AWAY.

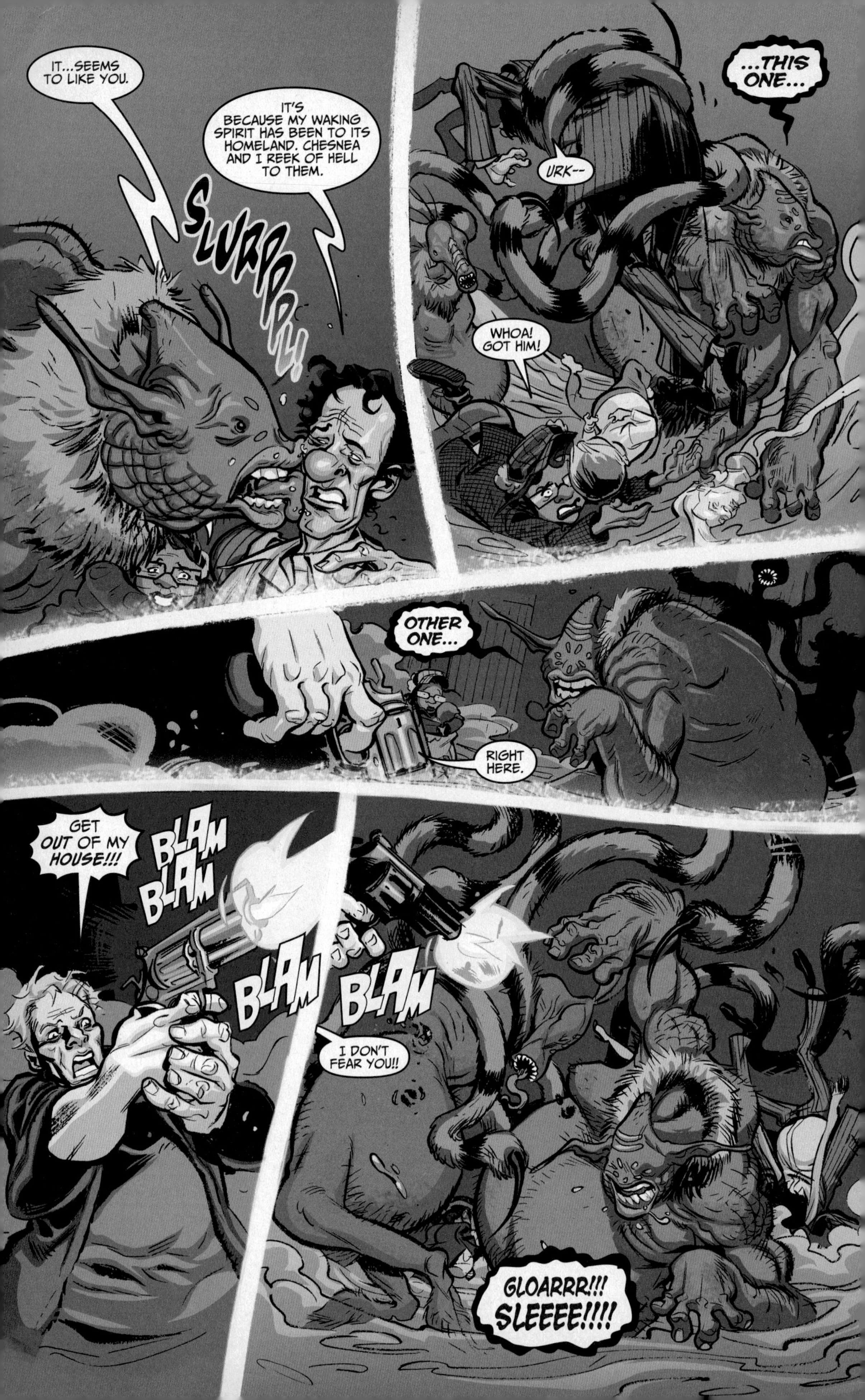
IT...SEEMS TO LIKE YOU.
IT'S BECAUSE MY WAKING SPIRIT HAS BEEN TO ITS HOMELAND. CHESNEA AND I REEK OF HELL TO THEM.
SLURPPP!
...THIS ONE...
URK--
WHOA! GOT HIM!
OTHER ONE...
RIGHT HERE.
GET OUT OF MY HOUSE!!!
BLAM BLAM
BLAM
BLAM
I DON'T FEAR YOU!!
GLOARRR!!! SLEEEE!!!!

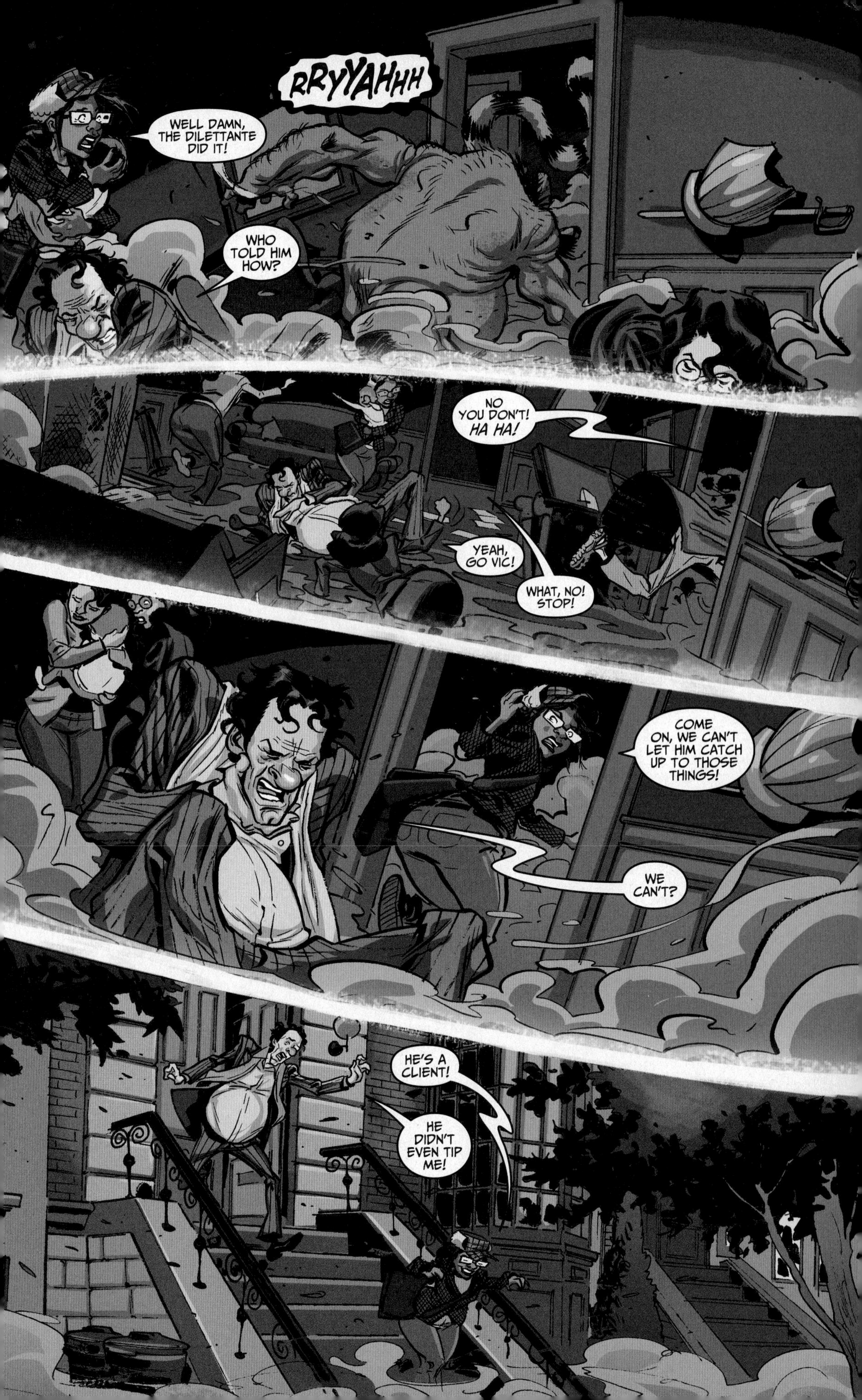
RRYYAHHH
WELL DAMN, THE DILETTANTE DID IT!
WHO TOLD HIM HOW?
NO YOU DON'T! HA HA!
YEAH, GO VIC!
WHAT, NO! STOP!
COME ON, WE CAN'T LET HIM CATCH UP TO THOSE THINGS!
WE CAN'T?
HE'S A CLIENT!
HE DIDN'T EVEN TIP ME!

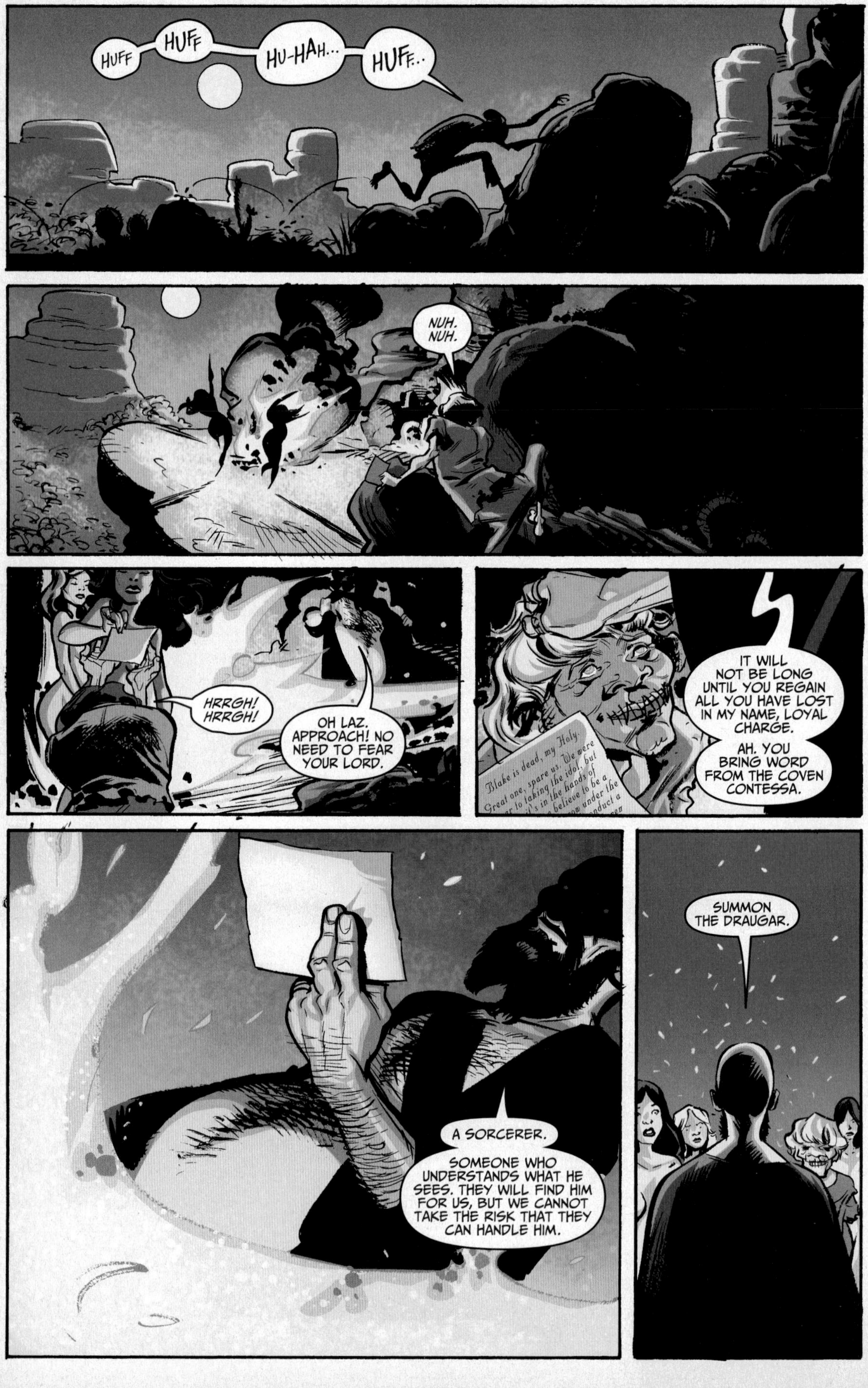
HUFF
HUFF
HU-HAH...
HUFF...
NUH. NUH.
HRRGH! HRRGH!
OH LAZ. APPROACH! NO NEED TO FEAR YOUR LORD.
Blake is dead, my Holy.
IT WILL NOT BE LONG UNTIL YOU REGAIN ALL YOU HAVE LOST IN MY NAME, LOYAL CHARGE.
AH. YOU BRING WORD FROM THE COVEN CONTESSA.
A SORCERER.
SOMEONE WHO UNDERSTANDS WHAT HE SEES. THEY WILL FIND HIM FOR US, BUT WE CANNOT TAKE THE RISK THAT THEY CAN HANDLE HIM.
SUMMON THE DRAUGAR.

"Oh come on, he was clearly decked—the side of his face looks like a palooka who just got hammered in the ring." She sprayed a large puff of the scent, and wrinkled her nose. "I guess that's so the back row can smell her. Ugh, I have to wash this off." Delfi excused herself to the bathroom across the hall.

"What about this?!" The voice was the scratchy rasp of Belgand, who had just grabbed something from a bookcase and was now bouncing down to Mysterius. The magician looked down to see the dwarf splay out a deck of cards. "A clue?" asked Mysterius.

Belgand flipped the deck face up, then back down, and pulled out a card that revealed itself as the 4 of Hearts. He then shuffled the deck in a manner that was unlikely for such thick, contorted hands. He then fanned the deck out to Mysterius and looked up eagerly. "Pick two."

"You...want to show me a card trick? Saturn's hooves! I was brought here to find a missing woman, you imp!"

"I know—I tell brother Wendell to call you! I see five of your shows!"

Mysterius slumped back in his chair and closed his eyes. "The real reason we were summoned was because you wanted to show your magic? The diva is just off somewhere having hysterics, isn't she?"

"Not know. Pull two!"

Almost by force of habit the magician's hand went out and deftly grabbed two cards from opposite ends of the deck. Belgand began to bounce slightly. "Turn over!" Mysterius flipped the cards and started to look around the room when his eyes pulled back to the table. He had pulled the 3 and 5 of Hearts.

"The deuce...how did you—?" A scream interrupted his professional courtesy. Delfi's scream.

Mysterius and Belgand raced into the dark hallway to see a large figure turn the corner, Delfi draped over his shoulder. "Stop!" Mysterius' long legs carried him much faster down the hall than Belgand, but upon realizing he was in front, the magician slowed to let the dwarf catch up.

"For encouragement," mumbled Mysterius.

As the uneven pursuers reached the antechamber near backstage, they saw the fleeing figure stop under a high window. A shaft of light poured in with great intensity from the snow reflecting moonlight. A large framed man now easily held up Delfi into the beam at his considerable arms' length. She restrained sounds of terror by biting her lip. The big shape craned its neck forward almost into the light, and sniffed twice. The

long arms then tossed Delfi aside casually and the man scrambled away.

"And never dare touch her again, miscreant!" shouted Mysterius, shaking his fist once the loping figure was gone. "That was horrid!" blurted Delfi, massaging her sore hip. "Why did the brute cast me off like that? Not that I wanted to go with him. Oh!" A rustling from the shadows made the three spring to position, expecting the bulky kidnapper's return. Out stepped Mr. Garland.

"Belgand, stop messing about with them—I need you to rig the pulleys, the show will be starting in an hour!" The manager then seemed to notice the investigators as well. "So. Did you like Belgand's trick? Do you think he could work in a...sideshow or something?"

Delfi pushed her hair back in place. "I was trying to get free of the man who likely took your star performer."

Garland straightened up slightly. "Really? Hm. Well, her understudy is set to go, so no need for all that trouble. Here, expose yourself to the finer ends of culture tonight." He handed Mysterius and Delfi two tickets to the opera and made his way back through the curtains. The two regarded the tickets much as their cab driver had done the laundry ticket.

Delfi was surprised to find herself enjoying the opera. The sets were majestic, the lighting evocative, and the singing powerful, though she understood none of it. The understudy's voice boomed and the stage seemed to shake. Brightly colored smoke erupted from beneath as the story built to its climax.

Then a caveman jumped out of the floor and grabbed the diva.

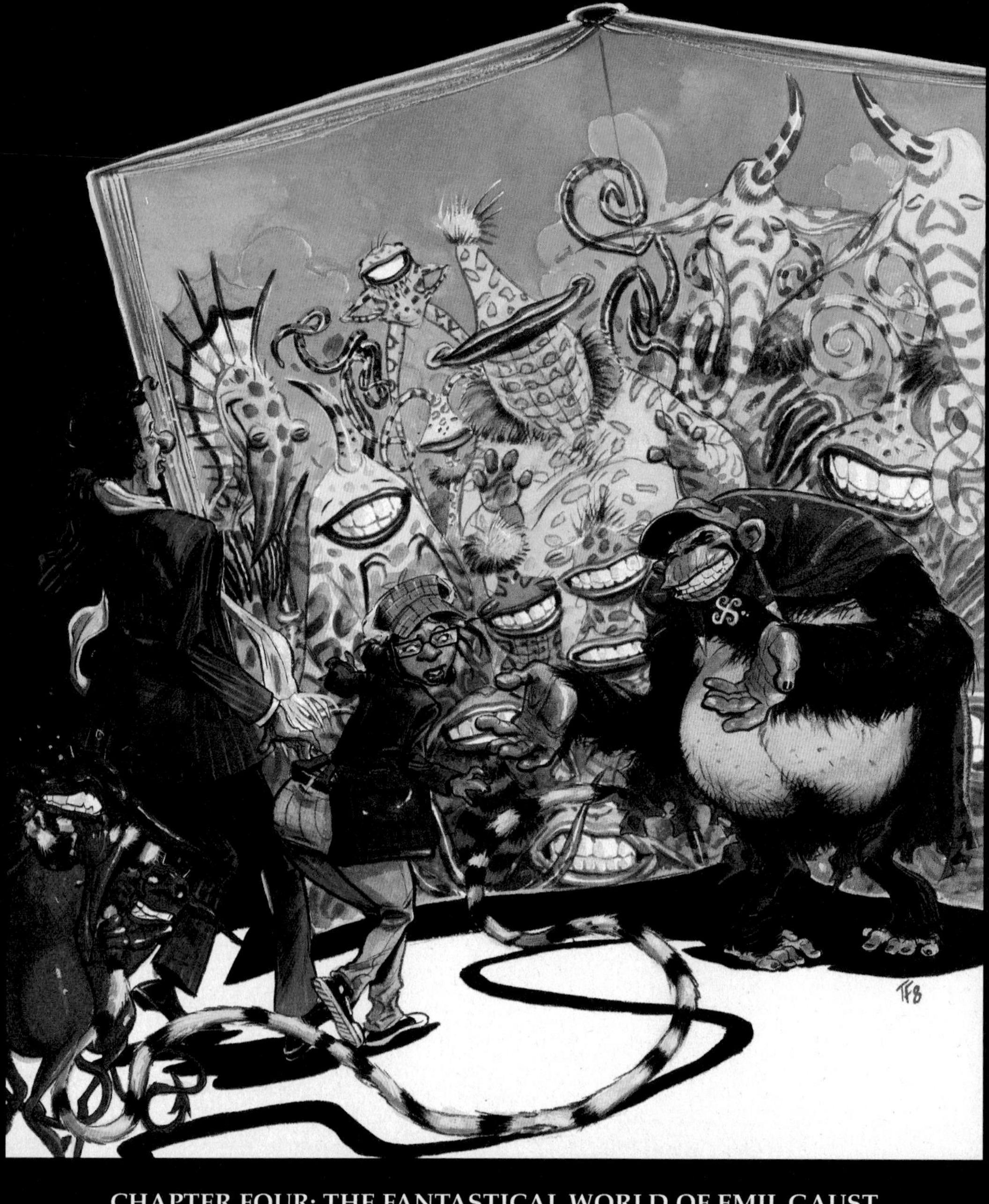

CHAPTER FOUR: THE FANTASTICAL WORLD OF EMIL GAUST

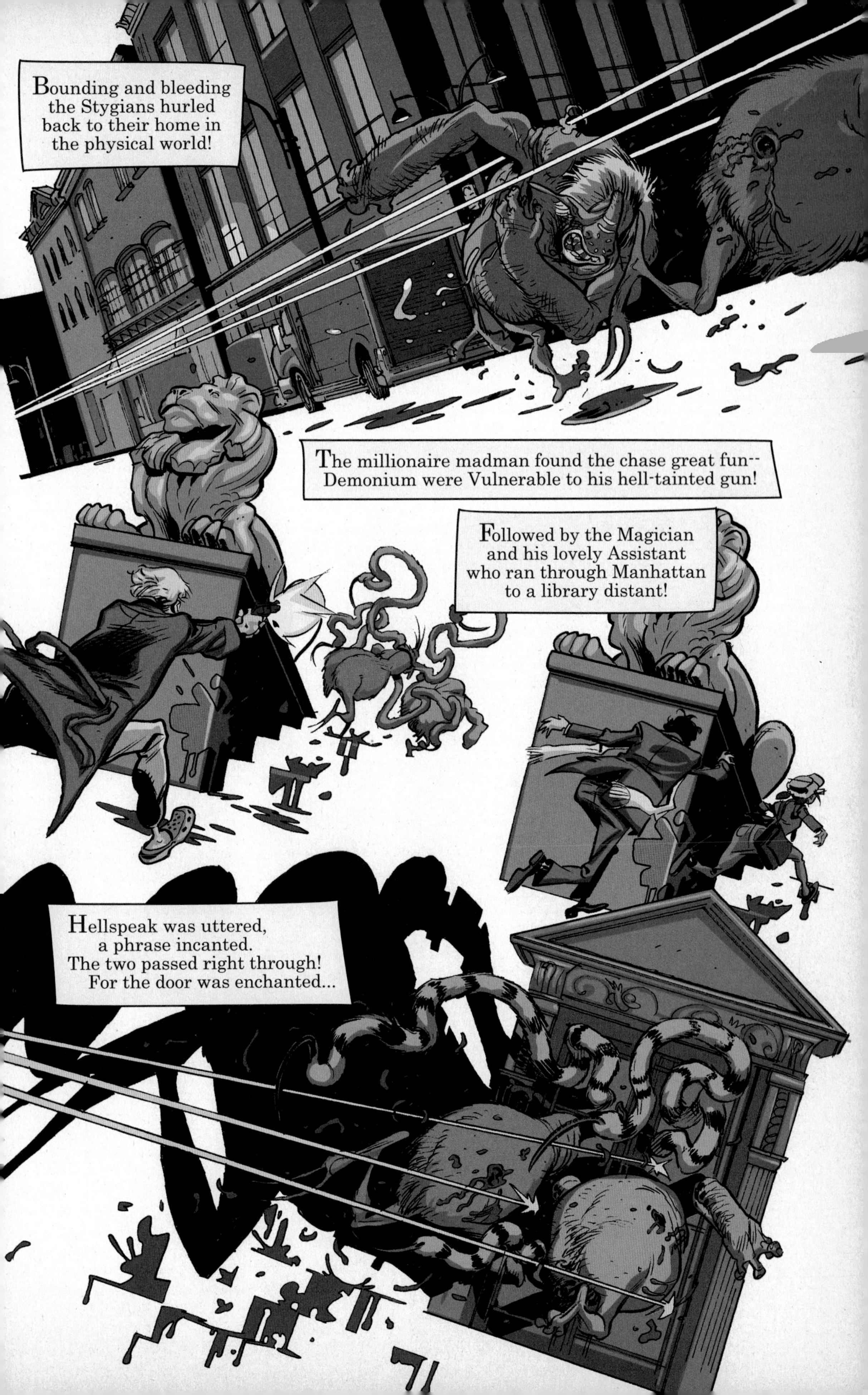
Bounding and bleeding the Stygians hurled back to their home in the physical world!
The millionaire madman found the chase great fun-- Demonium were Vulnerable to his hell-tainted gun!
Followed by the Magician and his lovely Assistant who ran through Manhattan to a library distant!
Hellspeak was uttered, a phrase incanted. The two passed right through! For the door was enchanted...

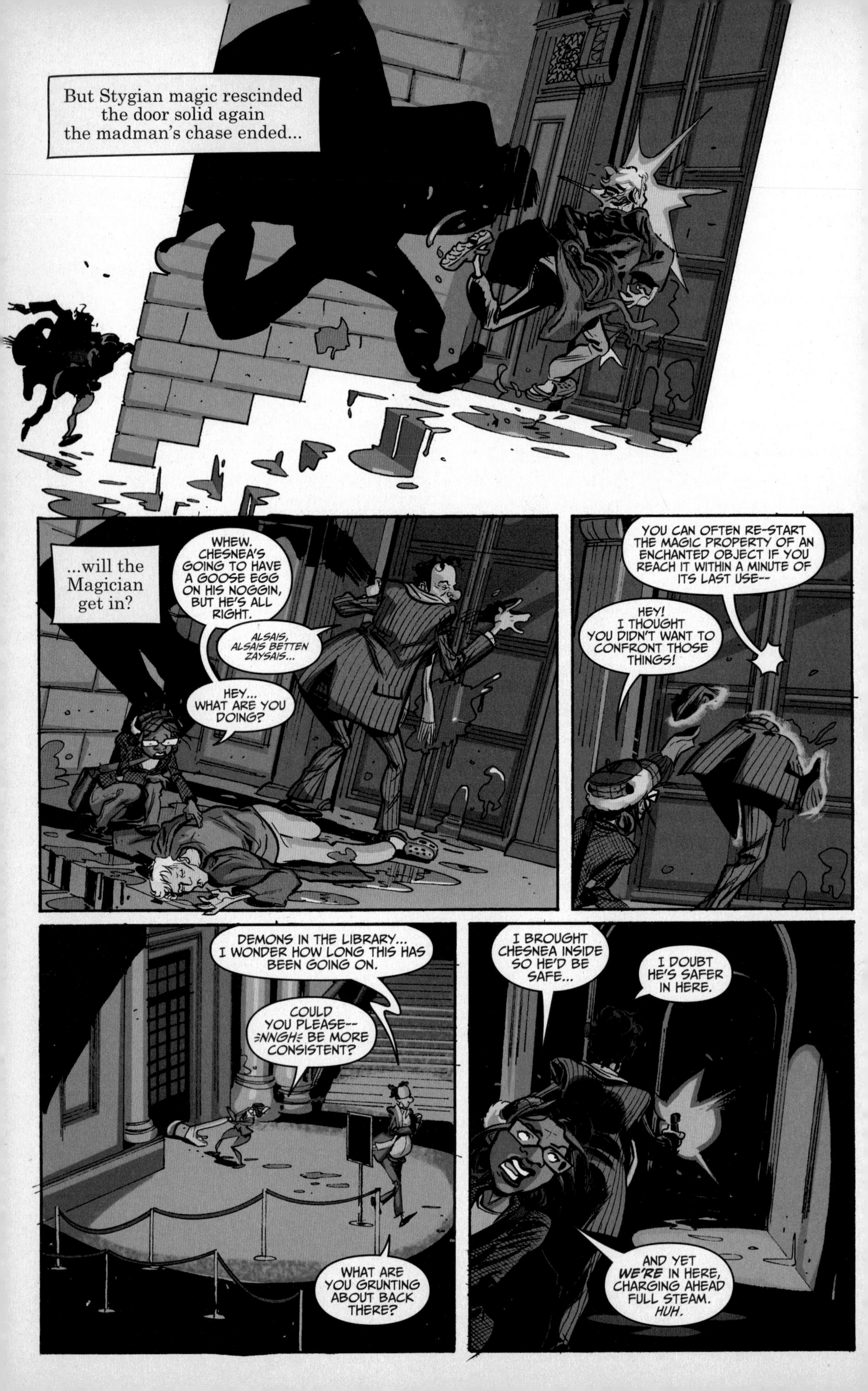
But Stygian magic rescinded the door solid again the madman's chase ended...
...will the Magician get in?
WHEW. CHESNEA'S GOING TO HAVE A GOOSE EGG ON HIS NOGGIN, BUT HE'S ALL RIGHT.
ALSAIS, ALSAIS BETTEN ZAYSAIS...
HEY... WHAT ARE YOU DOING?
YOU CAN OFTEN RE-START THE MAGIC PROPERTY OF AN ENCHANTED OBJECT IF YOU REACH IT WITHIN A MINUTE OF ITS LAST USE--
HEY! I THOUGHT YOU DIDN'T WANT TO CONFRONT THOSE THINGS!
DEMONS IN THE LIBRARY... I WONDER HOW LONG THIS HAS BEEN GOING ON.
COULD YOU PLEASE-- NNGH BE MORE CONSISTENT?
WHAT ARE YOU GRUNTING ABOUT BACK THERE?
I BROUGHT CHESNEA INSIDE SO HE'D BE SAFE...
I DOUBT HE'S SAFER IN HERE.
AND YET WE'RE IN HERE, CHARGING AHEAD FULL STEAM. HUH.

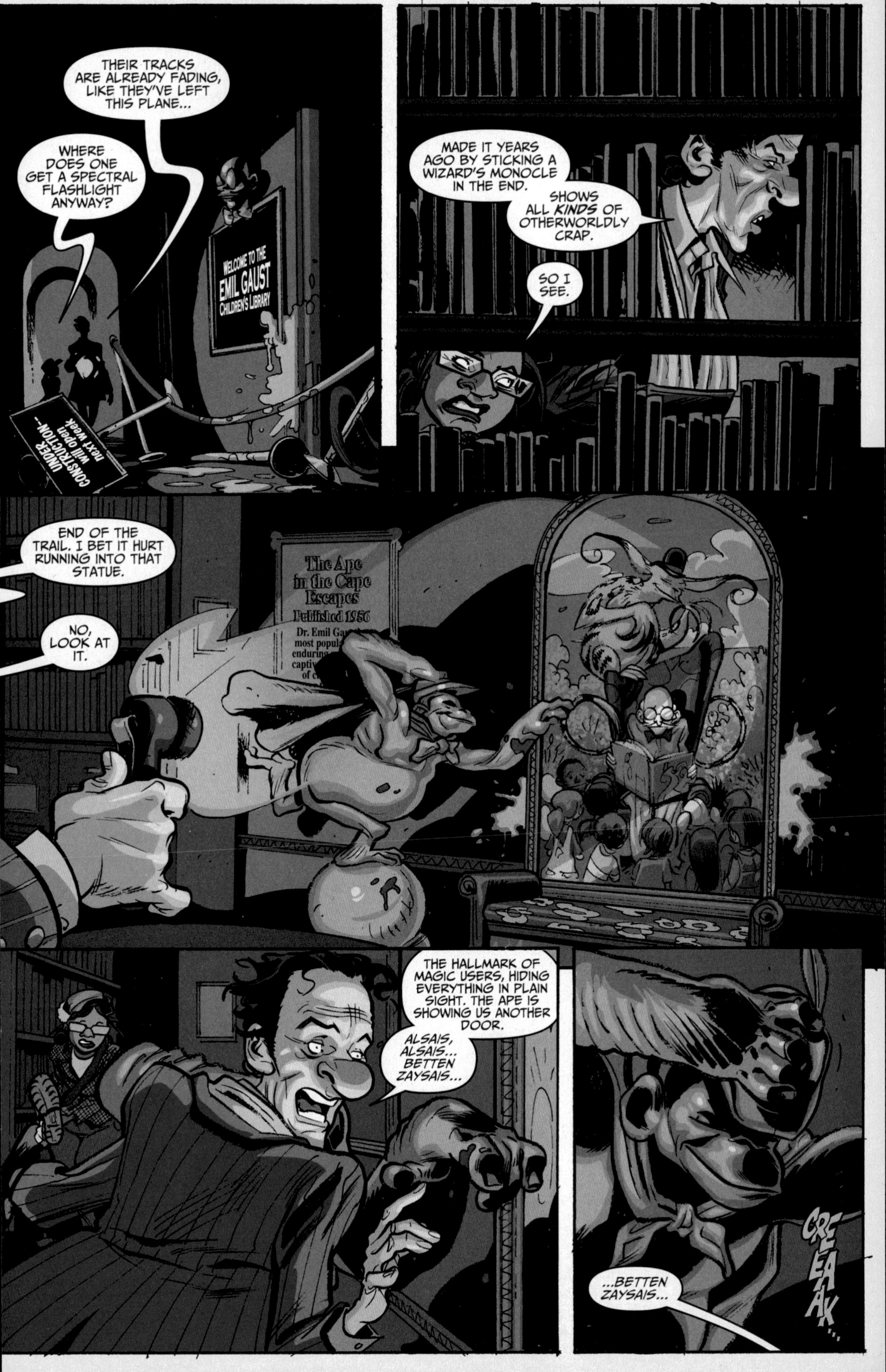
THEIR TRACKS ARE ALREADY FADING, LIKE THEY'VE LEFT THIS PLANE...
WHERE DOES ONE GET A SPECTRAL FLASHLIGHT ANYWAY?
WELCOME TO THE EMIL GAUST CHILDREN'S LIBRARY
UNDER CONSTRUCTION-- will open next week
MADE IT YEARS AGO BY STICKING A WIZARD'S MONOCLE IN THE END.
SHOWS ALL KINDS OF OTHERWORLDLY CRAP.
SO I SEE.
END OF THE TRAIL. I BET IT HURT RUNNING INTO THAT STATUE.
NO, LOOK AT IT.
The Ape in the Cape Escapes
Published 1956
THE HALLMARK OF MAGIC USERS, HIDING EVERYTHING IN PLAIN SIGHT. THE APE IS SHOWING US ANOTHER DOOR.
ALSAIS, ALSAIS... BETTEN ZAYSAIS...
CREEAAK...
...BETTEN ZAYSAIS...

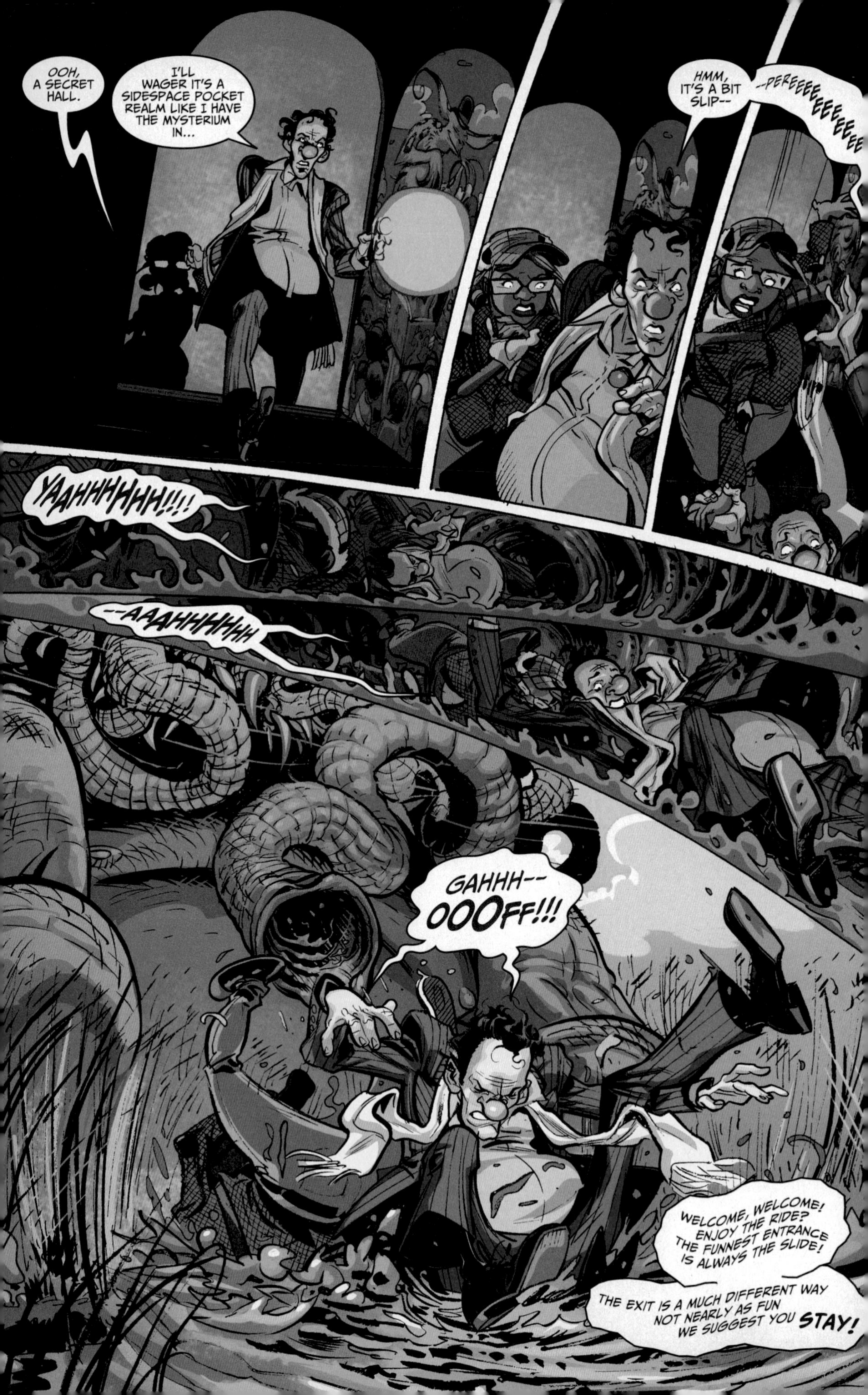
OOH, A SECRET HALL.
I'LL WAGER IT'S A SIDESPACE POCKET REALM LIKE I HAVE THE MYSTERIUM IN...
HMM, IT'S A BIT SLIP--
--PEREEEEEEEEEEEE
YAAHHHHHH!!!!
--AAAHHHHHH
GAHHH-- OOOFF!!!
WELCOME, WELCOME! ENJOY THE RIDE? THE FUNNEST ENTRANCE IS ALWAYS THE SLIDE!
THE EXIT IS A MUCH DIFFERENT WAY NOT NEARLY AS FUN WE SUGGEST YOU STAY!

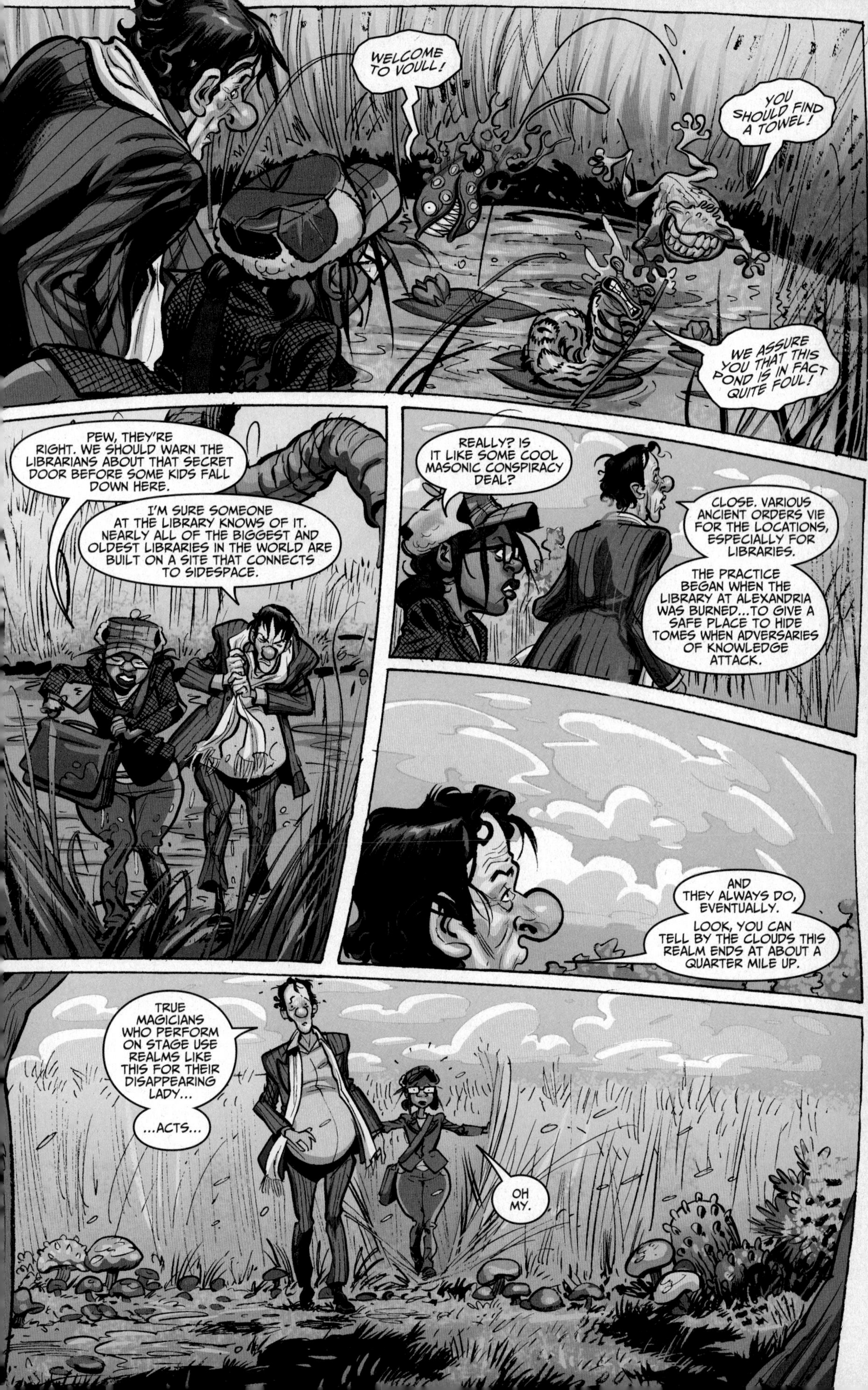
WELCOME TO VOULL!
YOU SHOULD FIND A TOWEL!
WE ASSURE YOU THAT THIS POND IS IN FACT QUITE FOUL!
PEW, THEY'RE RIGHT. WE SHOULD WARN THE LIBRARIANS ABOUT THAT SECRET DOOR BEFORE SOME KIDS FALL DOWN HERE.
I'M SURE SOMEONE AT THE LIBRARY KNOWS OF IT. NEARLY ALL OF THE BIGGEST AND OLDEST LIBRARIES IN THE WORLD ARE BUILT ON A SITE THAT CONNECTS TO SIDESPACE.
REALLY? IS IT LIKE SOME COOL MASONIC CONSPIRACY DEAL?
CLOSE. VARIOUS ANCIENT ORDERS VIE FOR THE LOCATIONS, ESPECIALLY FOR LIBRARIES.
THE PRACTICE BEGAN WHEN THE LIBRARY AT ALEXANDRIA WAS BURNED...TO GIVE A SAFE PLACE TO HIDE TOMES WHEN ADVERSARIES OF KNOWLEDGE ATTACK.
AND THEY ALWAYS DO, EVENTUALLY.
LOOK, YOU CAN TELL BY THE CLOUDS THIS REALM ENDS AT ABOUT A QUARTER MILE UP.
TRUE MAGICIANS WHO PERFORM ON STAGE USE REALMS LIKE THIS FOR THEIR DISAPPEARING LADY...
...ACTS...
OH MY.

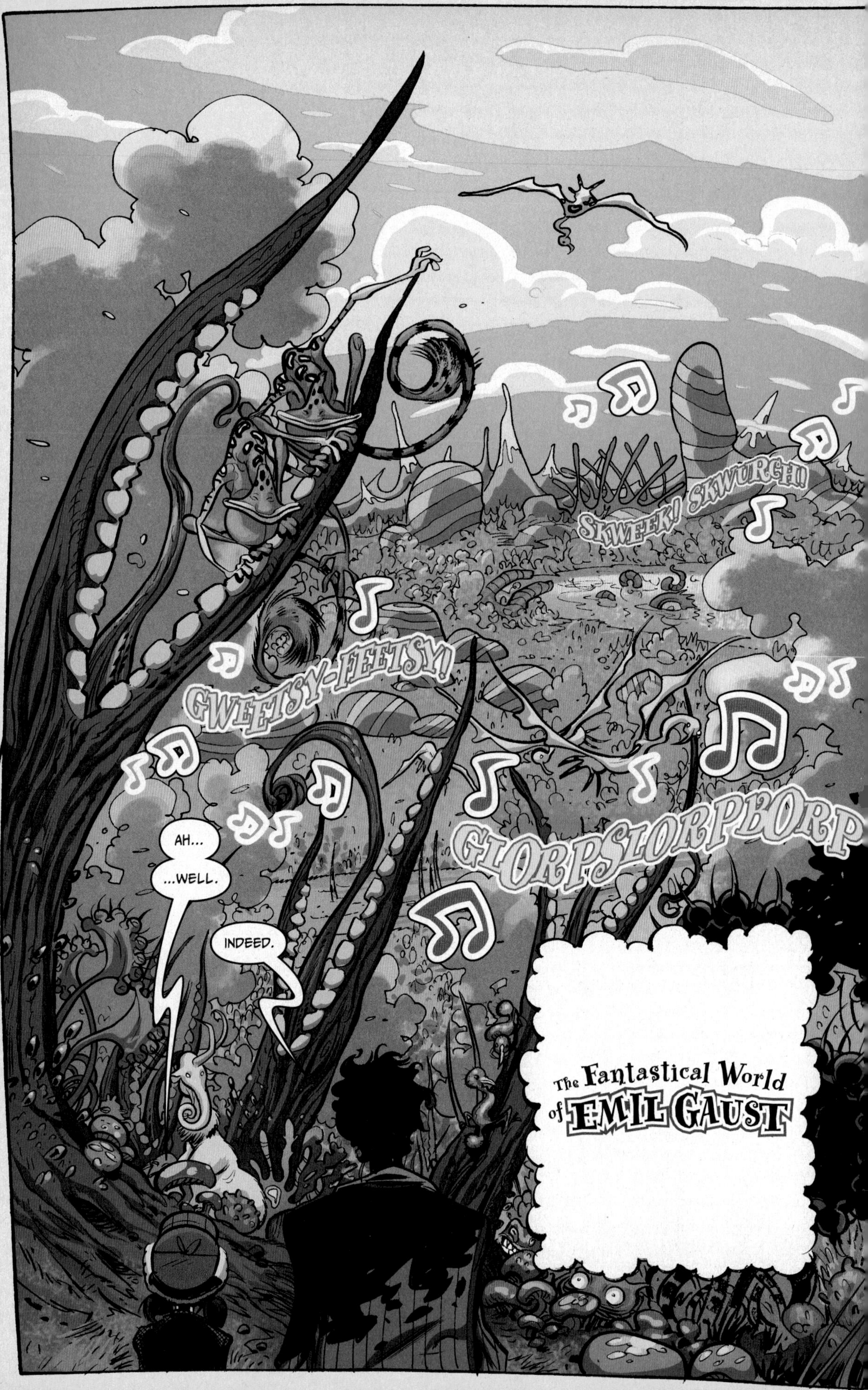
SKWEEK! SKWURCH!
GWEETSY-FEETSY!
GLORPSLORPBORP
AH...
...WELL.
INDEED.
The Fantastical World of EMIL GAUST

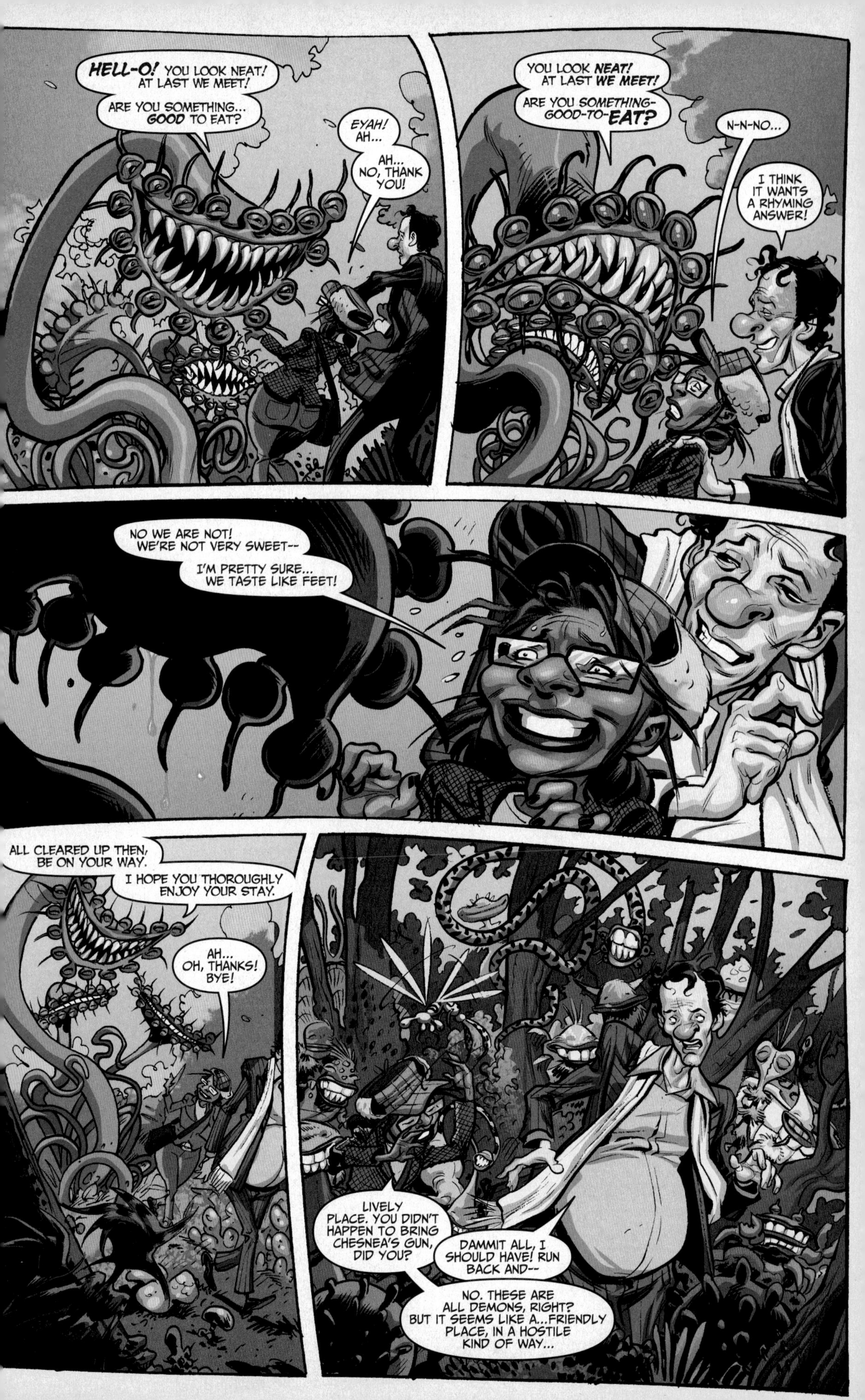

HELL-O! YOU LOOK NEAT! AT LAST WE MEET!
ARE YOU SOMETHING... GOOD TO EAT?
EYAH! AH...
AH... NO, THANK YOU!
YOU LOOK NEAT! AT LAST WE MEET!
ARE YOU SOMETHING-GOOD-TO-EAT?
N-N-NO...
I THINK IT WANTS A RHYMING ANSWER!
NO WE ARE NOT! WE'RE NOT VERY SWEET--
I'M PRETTY SURE... WE TASTE LIKE FEET!
ALL CLEARED UP THEN, BE ON YOUR WAY.
I HOPE YOU THOROUGHLY ENJOY YOUR STAY.
AH... OH, THANKS! BYE!
LIVELY PLACE. YOU DIDN'T HAPPEN TO BRING CHESNEA'S GUN, DID YOU?
DAMMIT ALL, I SHOULD HAVE! RUN BACK AND--
NO. THESE ARE ALL DEMONS, RIGHT? BUT IT SEEMS LIKE A...FRIENDLY PLACE, IN A HOSTILE KIND OF WAY...

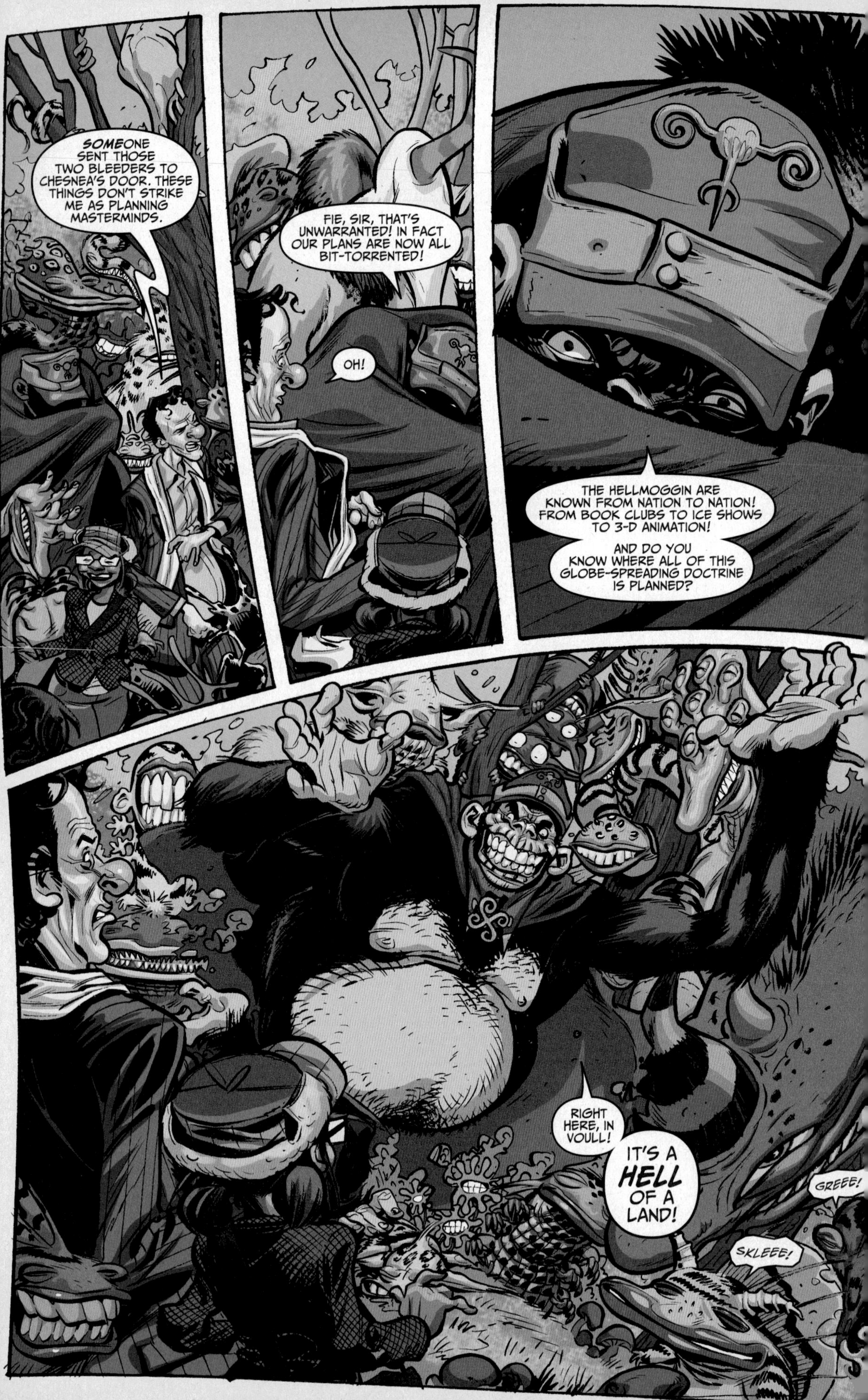
SOMEONE SENT THOSE TWO BLEEDERS TO CHESNEA'S DOOR. THESE THINGS DON'T STRIKE ME AS PLANNING MASTERMINDS.
FIE, SIR, THAT'S UNWARRANTED! IN FACT OUR PLANS ARE NOW ALL BIT-TORRENTED!
OH!
THE HELLMOGGIN ARE KNOWN FROM NATION TO NATION! FROM BOOK CLUBS TO ICE SHOWS TO 3-D ANIMATION!
AND DO YOU KNOW WHERE ALL OF THIS GLOBE-SPREADING DOCTRINE IS PLANNED?
RIGHT HERE, IN VOULL!
IT'S A HELL OF A LAND!
GREEE!
SKLEEE!

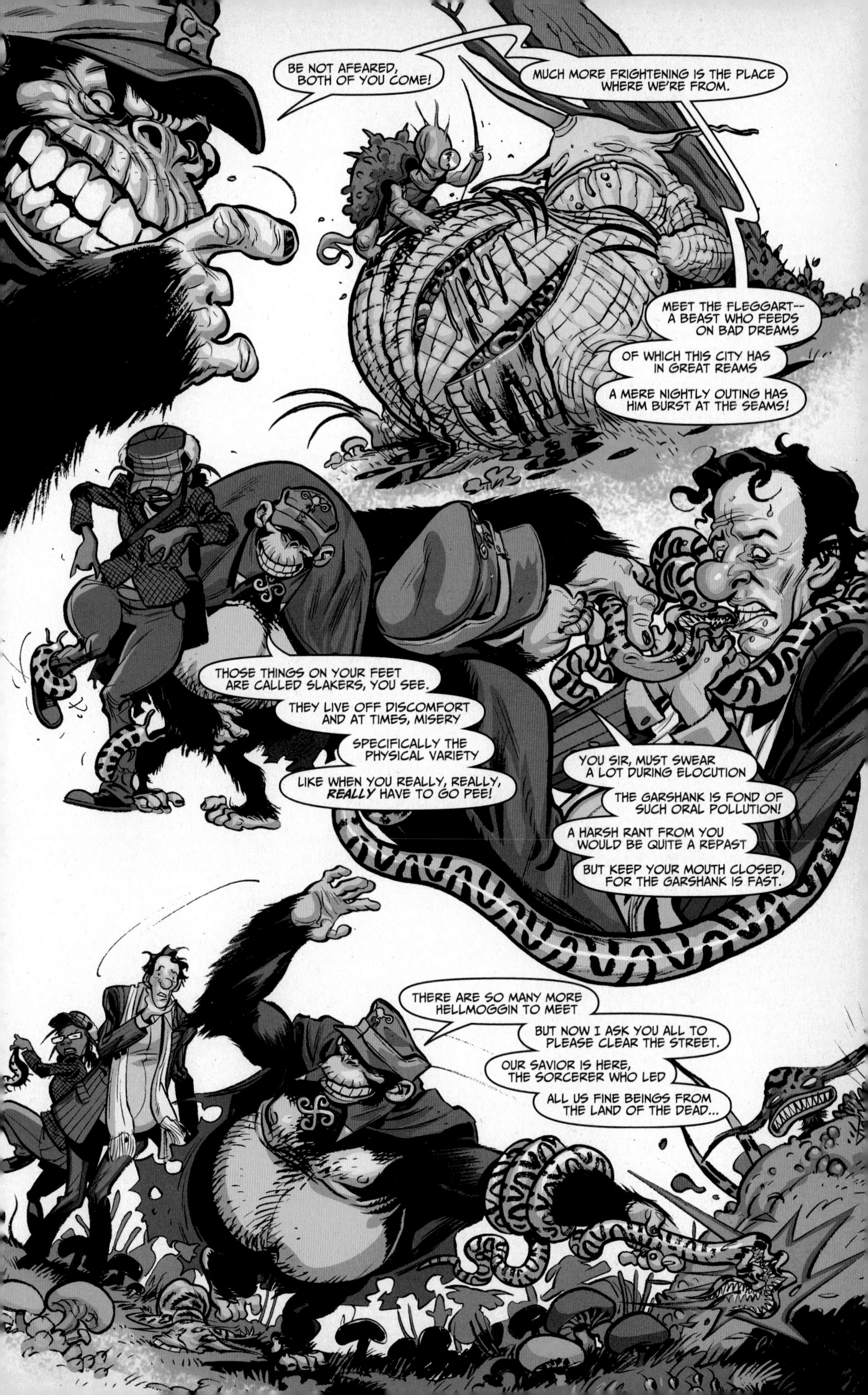
BE NOT AFEARED, BOTH OF YOU COME!
MUCH MORE FRIGHTENING IS THE PLACE WHERE WE'RE FROM.
MEET THE FLEGGART-- A BEAST WHO FEEDS ON BAD DREAMS
OF WHICH THIS CITY HAS IN GREAT REAMS
A MERE NIGHTLY OUTING HAS HIM BURST AT THE SEAMS!
THOSE THINGS ON YOUR FEET ARE CALLED SLAKERS, YOU SEE.
THEY LIVE OFF DISCOMFORT AND AT TIMES, MISERY
SPECIFICALLY THE PHYSICAL VARIETY
LIKE WHEN YOU REALLY, REALLY, ***REALLY*** HAVE TO GO PEE!
YOU SIR, MUST SWEAR A LOT DURING ELOCUTION
THE GARSHANK IS FOND OF SUCH ORAL POLLUTION!
A HARSH RANT FROM YOU WOULD BE QUITE A REPAST
BUT KEEP YOUR MOUTH CLOSED, FOR THE GARSHANK IS FAST.
THERE ARE SO MANY MORE HELLMOGGIN TO MEET
BUT NOW I ASK YOU ALL TO PLEASE CLEAR THE STREET.
OUR SAVIOR IS HERE, THE SORCERER WHO LED
ALL US FINE BEINGS FROM THE LAND OF THE DEAD...

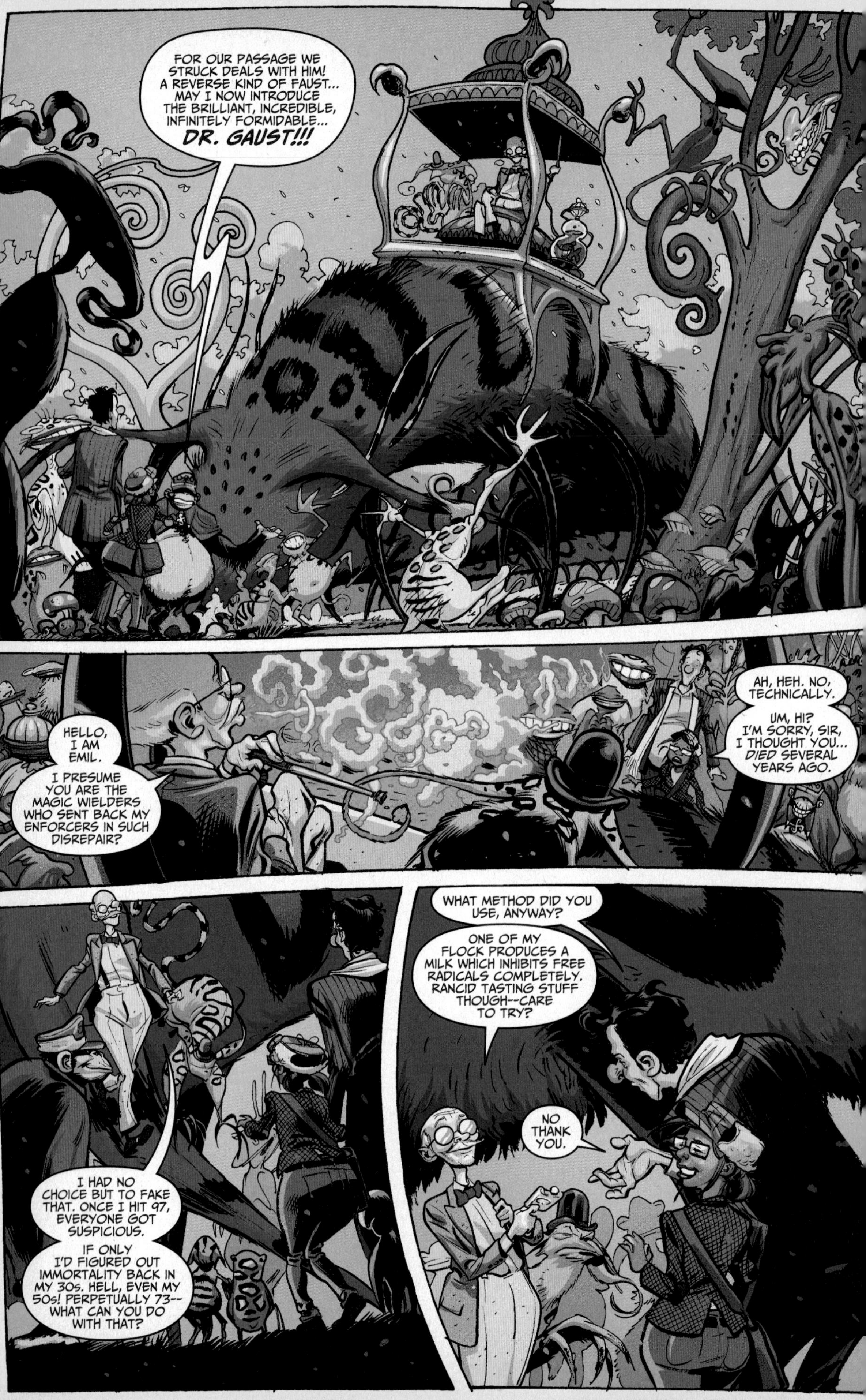
FOR OUR PASSAGE WE STRUCK DEALS WITH HIM! A REVERSE KIND OF FAUST... MAY I NOW INTRODUCE THE BRILLIANT, INCREDIBLE, INFINITELY FORMIDABLE... **DR. GAUST!!!**
HELLO, I AM EMIL.
I PRESUME YOU ARE THE MAGIC WIELDERS WHO SENT BACK MY ENFORCERS IN SUCH DISREPAIR?
AH, HEH. NO, TECHNICALLY.
UM, HI? I'M SORRY, SIR, I THOUGHT YOU... *DIED* SEVERAL YEARS AGO.
I HAD NO CHOICE BUT TO FAKE THAT. ONCE I HIT 97, EVERYONE GOT SUSPICIOUS.
IF ONLY I'D FIGURED OUT IMMORTALITY BACK IN MY 30s. HELL, EVEN MY 50s! PERPETUALLY 73-- WHAT CAN YOU DO WITH THAT?
WHAT METHOD DID YOU USE, ANYWAY?
ONE OF MY FLOCK PRODUCES A MILK WHICH INHIBITS FREE RADICALS COMPLETELY. RANCID TASTING STUFF THOUGH--CARE TO TRY?
NO THANK YOU.

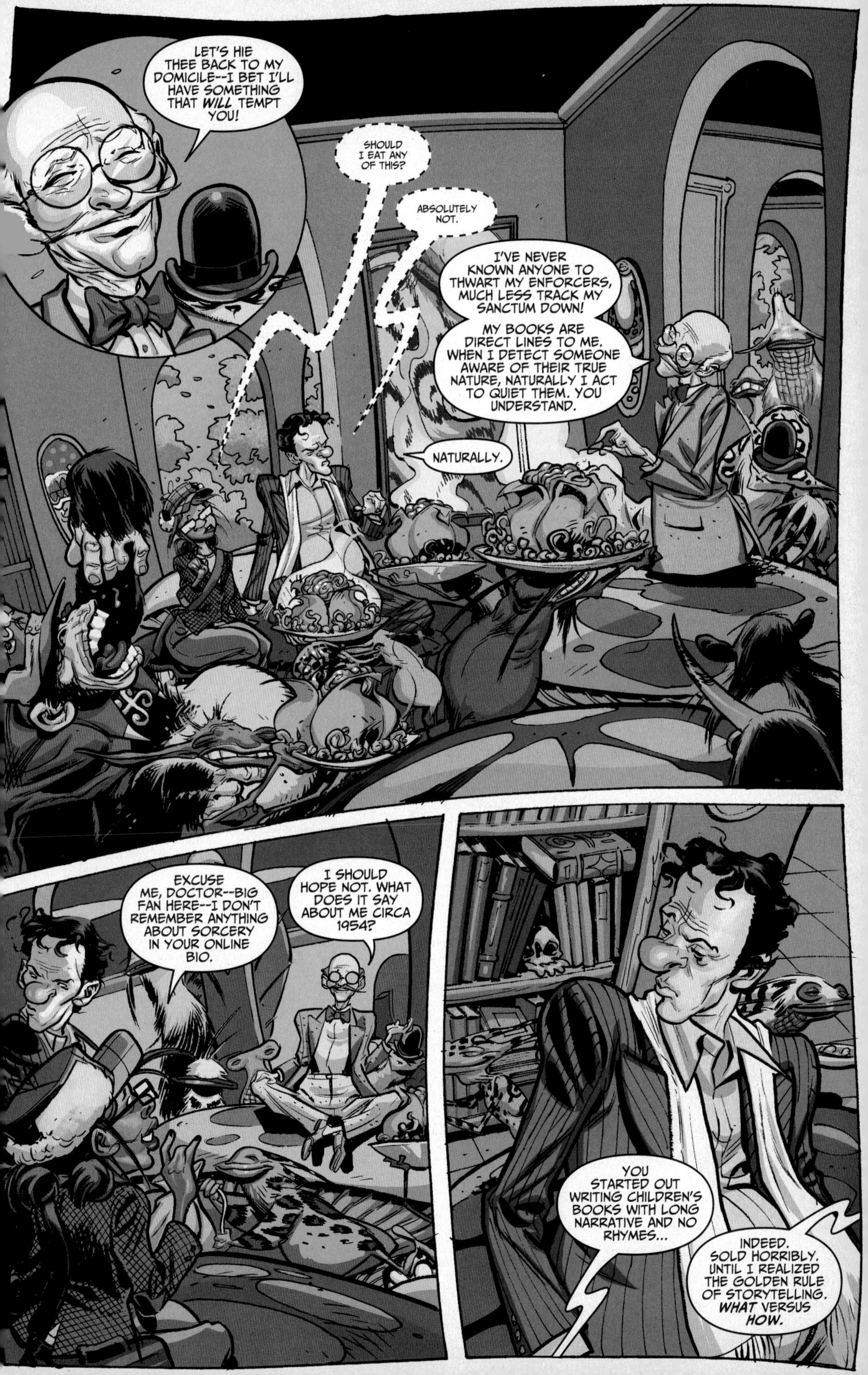
LET'S HIE THEE BACK TO MY DOMICILE--I BET I'LL HAVE SOMETHING THAT *WILL* TEMPT YOU!
SHOULD I EAT ANY OF THIS?
ABSOLUTELY NOT.
I'VE NEVER KNOWN ANYONE TO THWART MY ENFORCERS, MUCH LESS TRACK MY SANCTUM DOWN!
MY BOOKS ARE DIRECT LINES TO ME. WHEN I DETECT SOMEONE AWARE OF THEIR TRUE NATURE, NATURALLY I ACT TO QUIET THEM. YOU UNDERSTAND.
NATURALLY.
EXCUSE ME, DOCTOR--BIG FAN HERE--I DON'T REMEMBER ANYTHING ABOUT SORCERY IN YOUR ONLINE BIO.
I SHOULD HOPE NOT. WHAT DOES IT SAY ABOUT ME CIRCA 1954?
YOU STARTED OUT WRITING CHILDREN'S BOOKS WITH LONG NARRATIVE AND NO RHYMES...
INDEED. SOLD HORRIBLY. UNTIL I REALIZED THE GOLDEN RULE OF STORYTELLING. *WHAT* VERSUS *HOW.*

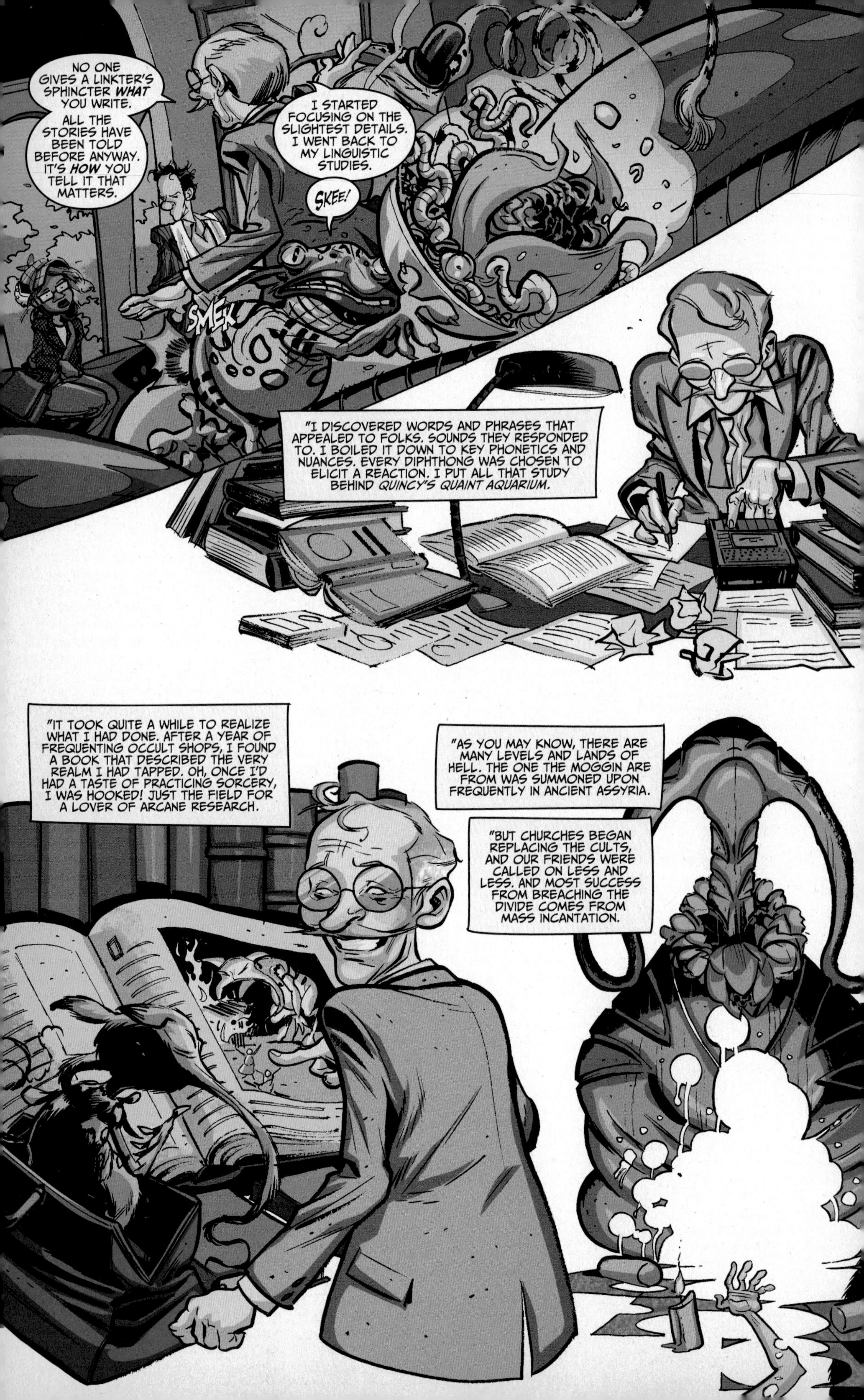
NO ONE GIVES A LINKTER'S SPHINCTER *WHAT* YOU WRITE.
ALL THE STORIES HAVE BEEN TOLD BEFORE ANYWAY. IT'S *HOW* YOU TELL IT THAT MATTERS.
I STARTED FOCUSING ON THE SLIGHTEST DETAILS. I WENT BACK TO MY LINGUISTIC STUDIES.
SKEE!
SMEK
"I DISCOVERED WORDS AND PHRASES THAT APPEALED TO FOLKS. SOUNDS THEY RESPONDED TO. I BOILED IT DOWN TO KEY PHONETICS AND NUANCES. EVERY DIPHTHONG WAS CHOSEN TO ELICIT A REACTION. I PUT ALL THAT STUDY BEHIND *QUINCY'S QUAINT AQUARIUM.*
"IT TOOK QUITE A WHILE TO REALIZE WHAT I HAD DONE. AFTER A YEAR OF FREQUENTING OCCULT SHOPS, I FOUND A BOOK THAT DESCRIBED THE VERY REALM I HAD TAPPED. OH, ONCE I'D HAD A TASTE OF PRACTICING SORCERY, I WAS HOOKED! JUST THE FIELD FOR A LOVER OF ARCANE RESEARCH.
"AS YOU MAY KNOW, THERE ARE MANY LEVELS AND LANDS OF HELL. THE ONE THE MOGGIN ARE FROM WAS SUMMONED UPON FREQUENTLY IN ANCIENT ASSYRIA.
"BUT CHURCHES BEGAN REPLACING THE CULTS, AND OUR FRIENDS WERE CALLED ON LESS AND LESS. AND MOST SUCCESS FROM BREACHING THE DIVIDE COMES FROM MASS INCANTATION.

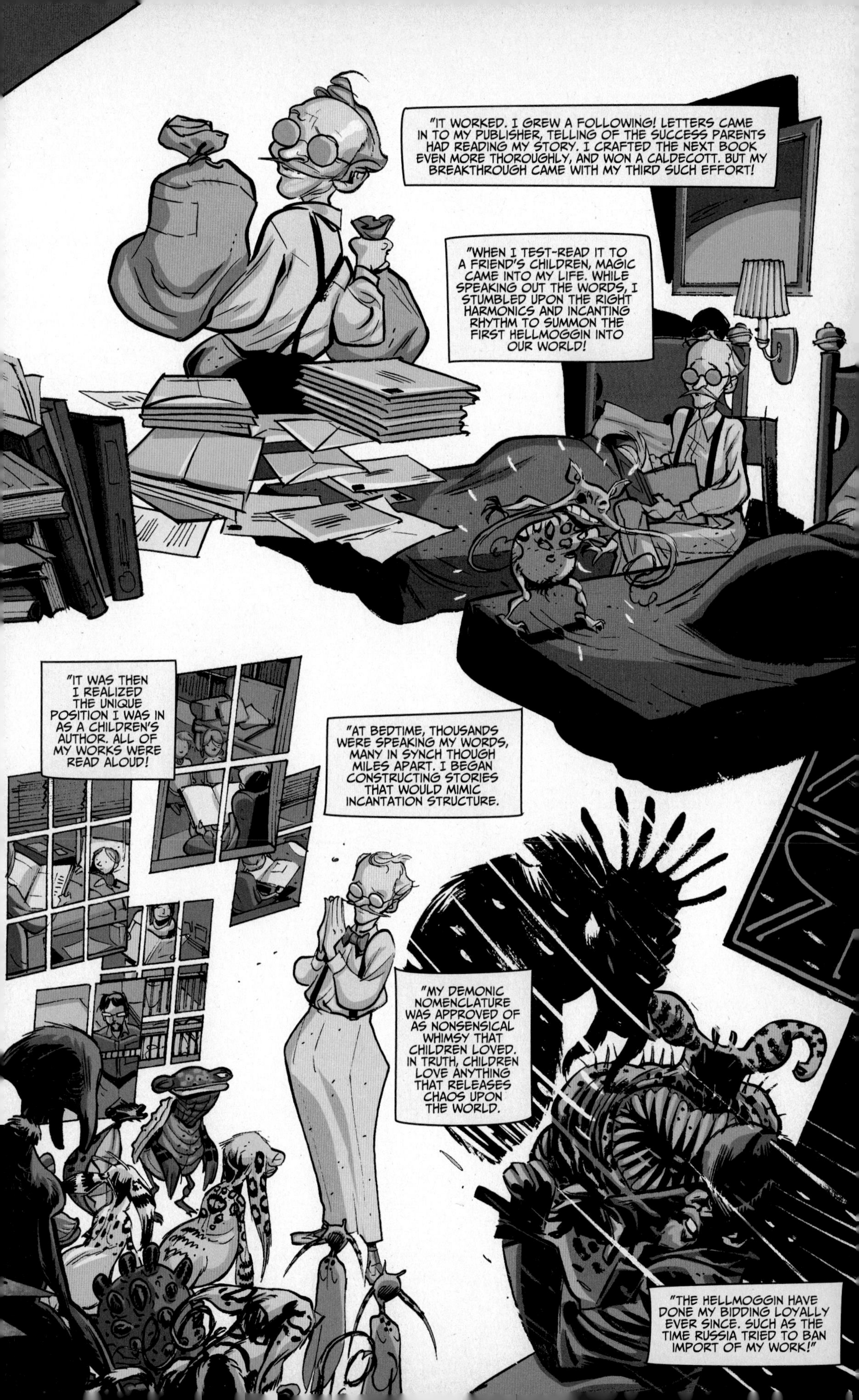
"IT WORKED. I GREW A FOLLOWING! LETTERS CAME IN TO MY PUBLISHER, TELLING OF THE SUCCESS PARENTS HAD READING MY STORY. I CRAFTED THE NEXT BOOK EVEN MORE THOROUGHLY, AND WON A CALDECOTT. BUT MY BREAKTHROUGH CAME WITH MY THIRD SUCH EFFORT!
"WHEN I TEST-READ IT TO A FRIEND'S CHILDREN, MAGIC CAME INTO MY LIFE. WHILE SPEAKING OUT THE WORDS, I STUMBLED UPON THE RIGHT HARMONICS AND INCANTING RHYTHM TO SUMMON THE FIRST HELLMOGGIN INTO OUR WORLD!
"IT WAS THEN I REALIZED THE UNIQUE POSITION I WAS IN AS A CHILDREN'S AUTHOR. ALL OF MY WORKS WERE READ ALOUD!
"AT BEDTIME, THOUSANDS WERE SPEAKING MY WORDS, MANY IN SYNCH THOUGH MILES APART. I BEGAN CONSTRUCTING STORIES THAT WOULD MIMIC INCANTATION STRUCTURE.
"MY DEMONIC NOMENCLATURE WAS APPROVED OF AS NONSENSICAL WHIMSY THAT CHILDREN LOVED. IN TRUTH, CHILDREN LOVE ANYTHING THAT RELEASES CHAOS UPON THE WORLD.
"THE HELLMOGGIN HAVE DONE MY BIDDING LOYALLY EVER SINCE. SUCH AS THE TIME RUSSIA TRIED TO BAN IMPORT OF MY WORK!"

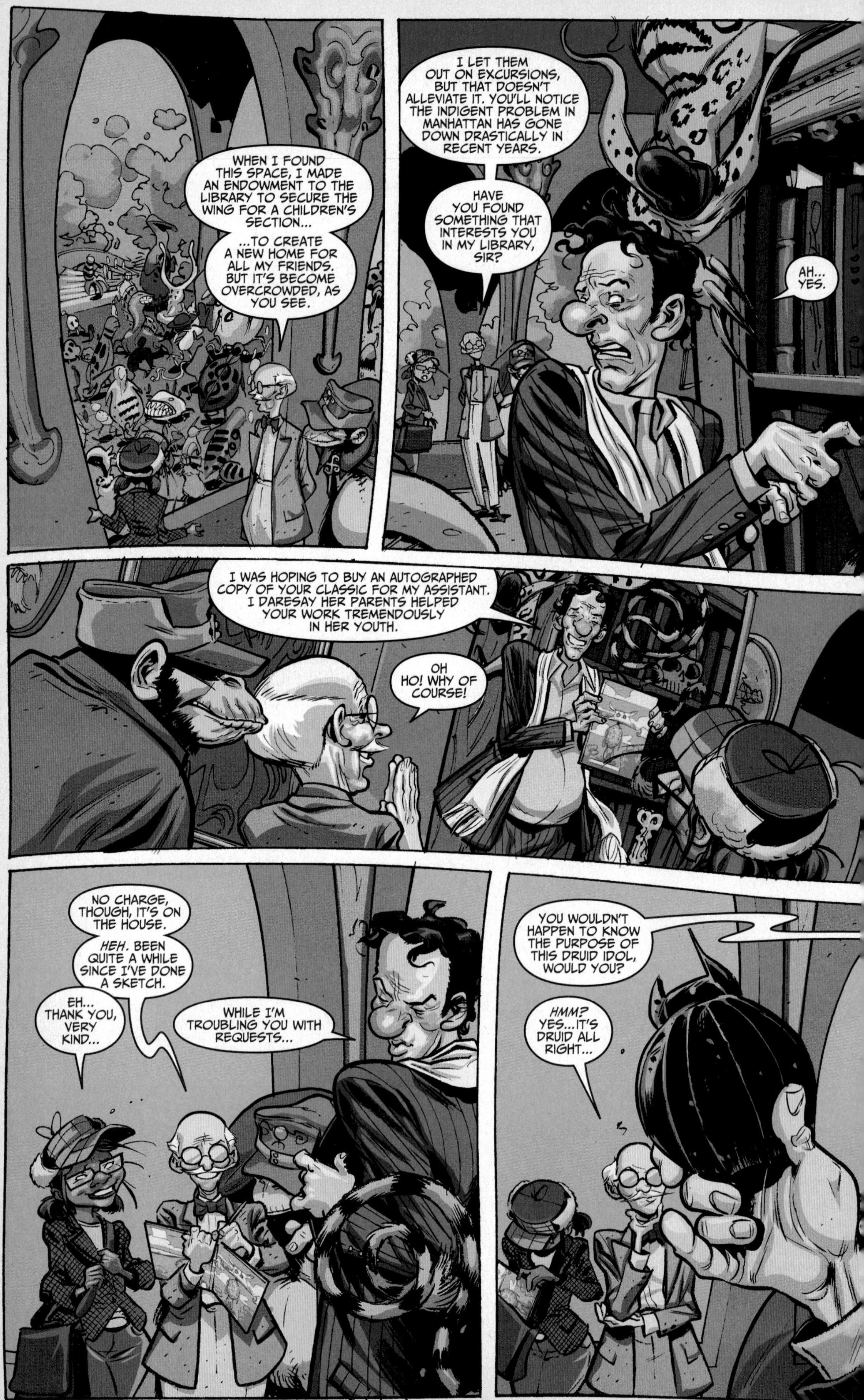
WHEN I FOUND THIS SPACE, I MADE AN ENDOWMENT TO THE LIBRARY TO SECURE THE WING FOR A CHILDREN'S SECTION...
...TO CREATE A NEW HOME FOR ALL MY FRIENDS. BUT IT'S BECOME OVERCROWDED, AS YOU SEE.
I LET THEM OUT ON EXCURSIONS, BUT THAT DOESN'T ALLEVIATE IT. YOU'LL NOTICE THE INDIGENT PROBLEM IN MANHATTAN HAS GONE DOWN DRASTICALLY IN RECENT YEARS.
HAVE YOU FOUND SOMETHING THAT INTERESTS YOU IN MY LIBRARY, SIR?
AH... YES.
I WAS HOPING TO BUY AN AUTOGRAPHED COPY OF YOUR CLASSIC FOR MY ASSISTANT. I DARESAY HER PARENTS HELPED YOUR WORK TREMENDOUSLY IN HER YOUTH.
OH HO! WHY OF COURSE!
NO CHARGE, THOUGH, IT'S ON THE HOUSE.
HEH. BEEN QUITE A WHILE SINCE I'VE DONE A SKETCH.
EH... THANK YOU, VERY KIND...
WHILE I'M TROUBLING YOU WITH REQUESTS...
YOU WOULDN'T HAPPEN TO KNOW THE PURPOSE OF THIS DRUID IDOL, WOULD YOU?
HMM? YES...IT'S DRUID ALL RIGHT...

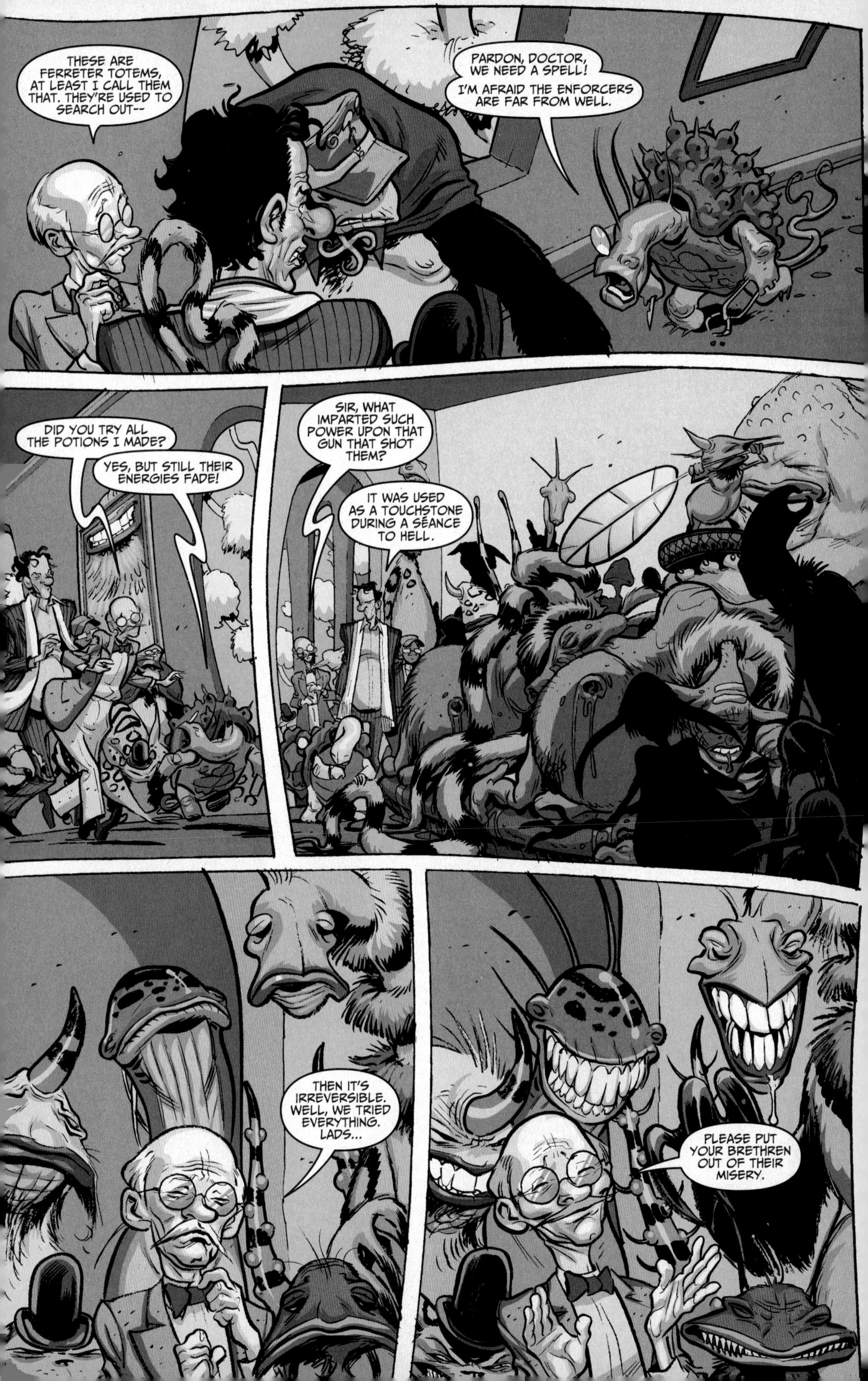
THESE ARE FERRETER TOTEMS, AT LEAST I CALL THEM THAT. THEY'RE USED TO SEARCH OUT--
PARDON, DOCTOR, WE NEED A SPELL!
I'M AFRAID THE ENFORCERS ARE FAR FROM WELL.
DID YOU TRY ALL THE POTIONS I MADE?
YES, BUT STILL THEIR ENERGIES FADE!
SIR, WHAT IMPARTED SUCH POWER UPON THAT GUN THAT SHOT THEM?
IT WAS USED AS A TOUCHSTONE DURING A SÉANCE TO HELL.
THEN IT'S IRREVERSIBLE. WELL, WE TRIED EVERYTHING. LADS...
PLEASE PUT YOUR BRETHREN OUT OF THEIR MISERY.

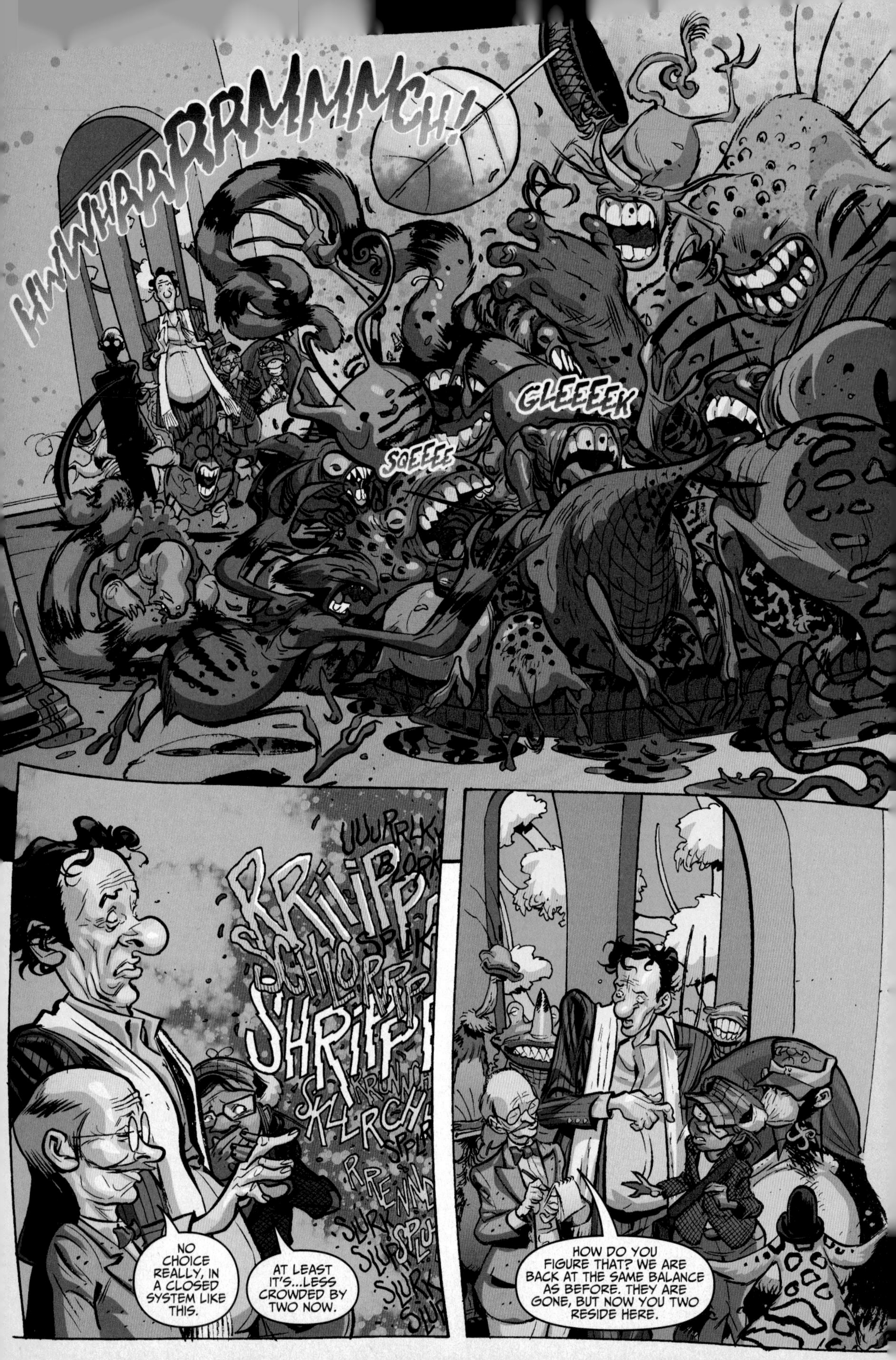
HWWHAARRMMMMCH!
GLEEEEK
SQEEEE
NO CHOICE REALLY, IN A CLOSED SYSTEM LIKE THIS.
AT LEAST IT'S...LESS CROWDED BY TWO NOW.
HOW DO YOU FIGURE THAT? WE ARE BACK AT THE SAME BALANCE AS BEFORE. THEY ARE GONE, BUT NOW YOU TWO RESIDE HERE.

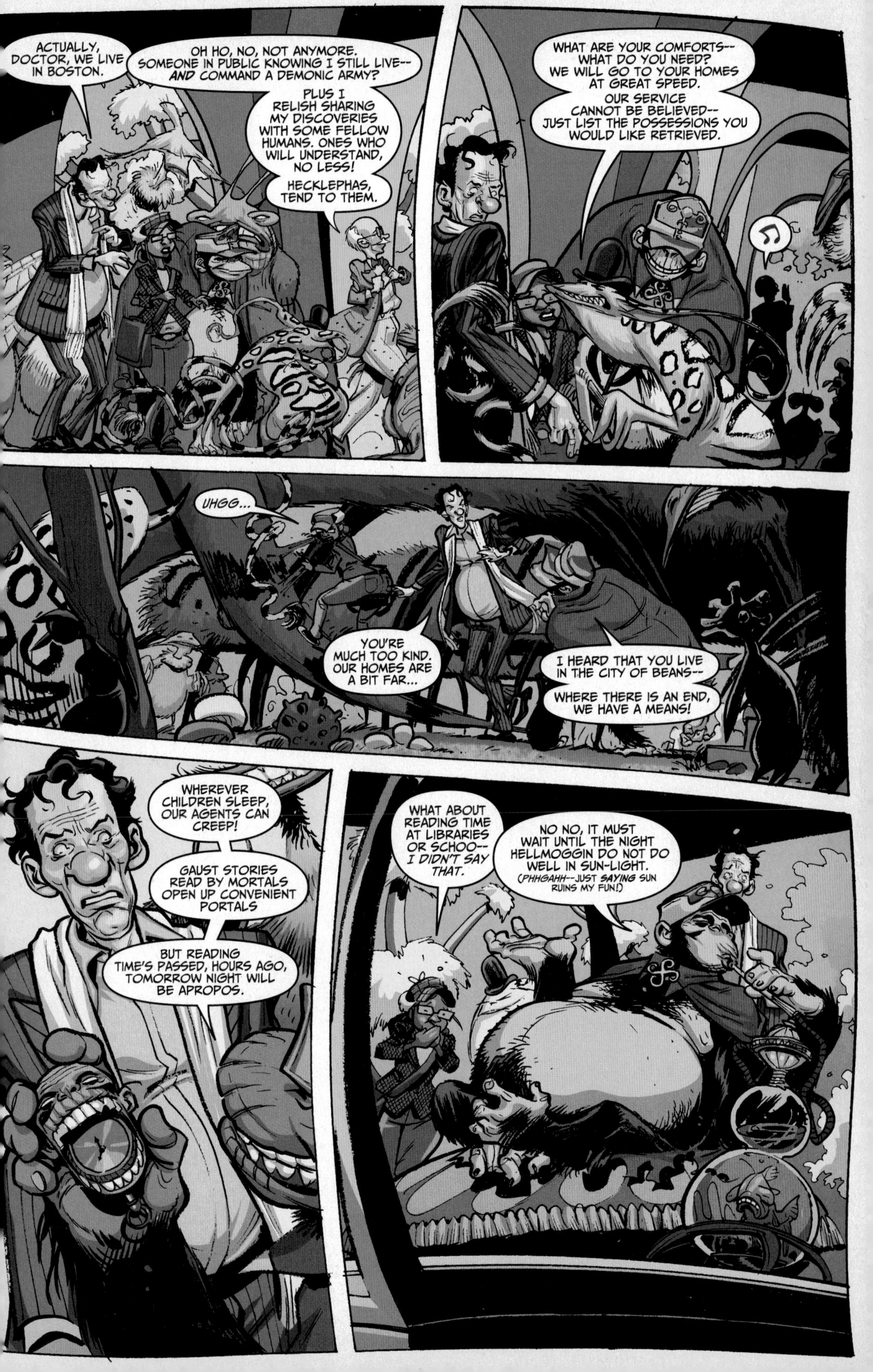
ACTUALLY, DOCTOR, WE LIVE IN BOSTON.
OH HO, NO, NOT ANYMORE. SOMEONE IN PUBLIC KNOWING I STILL LIVE-- *AND* COMMAND A DEMONIC ARMY?
PLUS I RELISH SHARING MY DISCOVERIES WITH SOME FELLOW HUMANS. ONES WHO WILL UNDERSTAND, NO LESS!
HECKLEPHAS, TEND TO THEM.
WHAT ARE YOUR COMFORTS-- WHAT DO YOU NEED? WE WILL GO TO YOUR HOMES AT GREAT SPEED.
OUR SERVICE CANNOT BE BELIEVED-- JUST LIST THE POSSESSIONS YOU WOULD LIKE RETRIEVED.
♫
UHGG...
YOU'RE MUCH TOO KIND. OUR HOMES ARE A BIT FAR...
I HEARD THAT YOU LIVE IN THE CITY OF BEANS--
WHERE THERE IS AN END, WE HAVE A MEANS!
WHEREVER CHILDREN SLEEP, OUR AGENTS CAN CREEP!
GAUST STORIES READ BY MORTALS OPEN UP CONVENIENT PORTALS
BUT READING TIME'S PASSED, HOURS AGO, TOMORROW NIGHT WILL BE APROPOS.
WHAT ABOUT READING TIME AT LIBRARIES OR SCHOO-- *I DIDN'T SAY THAT.*
NO NO, IT MUST WAIT UNTIL THE NIGHT HELLMOGGIN DO NOT DO WELL IN SUN-LIGHT.
(*PHHGAHH--JUST SAYING* SUN RUINS MY FUN!)

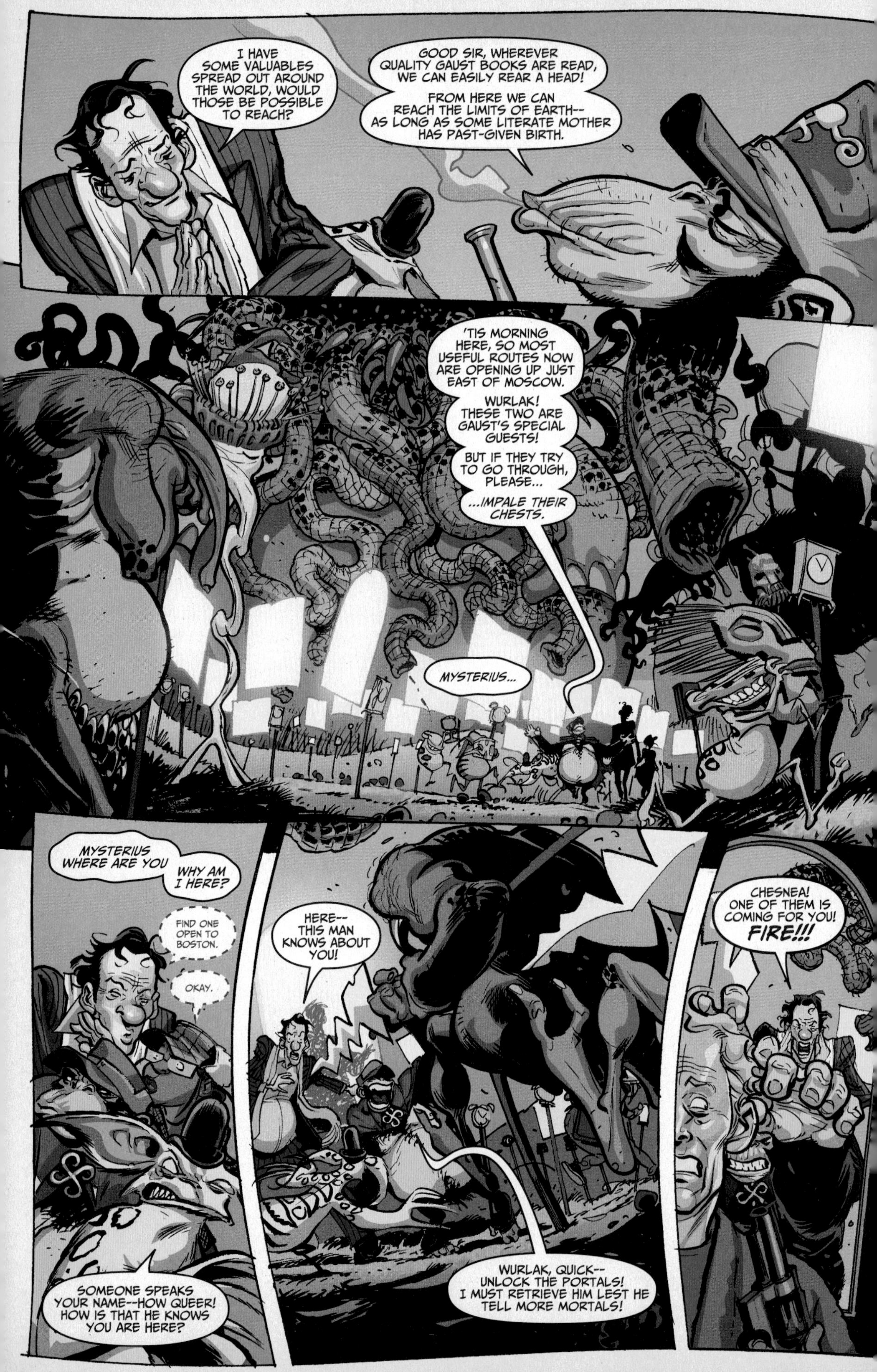
I HAVE SOME VALUABLES SPREAD OUT AROUND THE WORLD, WOULD THOSE BE POSSIBLE TO REACH?
GOOD SIR, WHEREVER QUALITY GAUST BOOKS ARE READ, WE CAN EASILY REAR A HEAD!
FROM HERE WE CAN REACH THE LIMITS OF EARTH-- AS LONG AS SOME LITERATE MOTHER HAS PAST-GIVEN BIRTH.
'TIS MORNING HERE, SO MOST USEFUL ROUTES NOW ARE OPENING UP JUST EAST OF MOSCOW.
WURLAK! THESE TWO ARE GAUST'S SPECIAL GUESTS!
BUT IF THEY TRY TO GO THROUGH, PLEASE...
...IMPALE THEIR CHESTS.
MYSTERIUS...
MYSTERIUS WHERE ARE YOU
WHY AM I HERE?
FIND ONE OPEN TO BOSTON.
OKAY.
SOMEONE SPEAKS YOUR NAME--HOW QUEER! HOW IS THAT HE KNOWS YOU ARE HERE?
HERE-- THIS MAN KNOWS ABOUT YOU!
WURLAK, QUICK-- UNLOCK THE PORTALS! I MUST RETRIEVE HIM LEST HE TELL MORE MORTALS!
CHESNEA! ONE OF THEM IS COMING FOR YOU! FIRE!!!

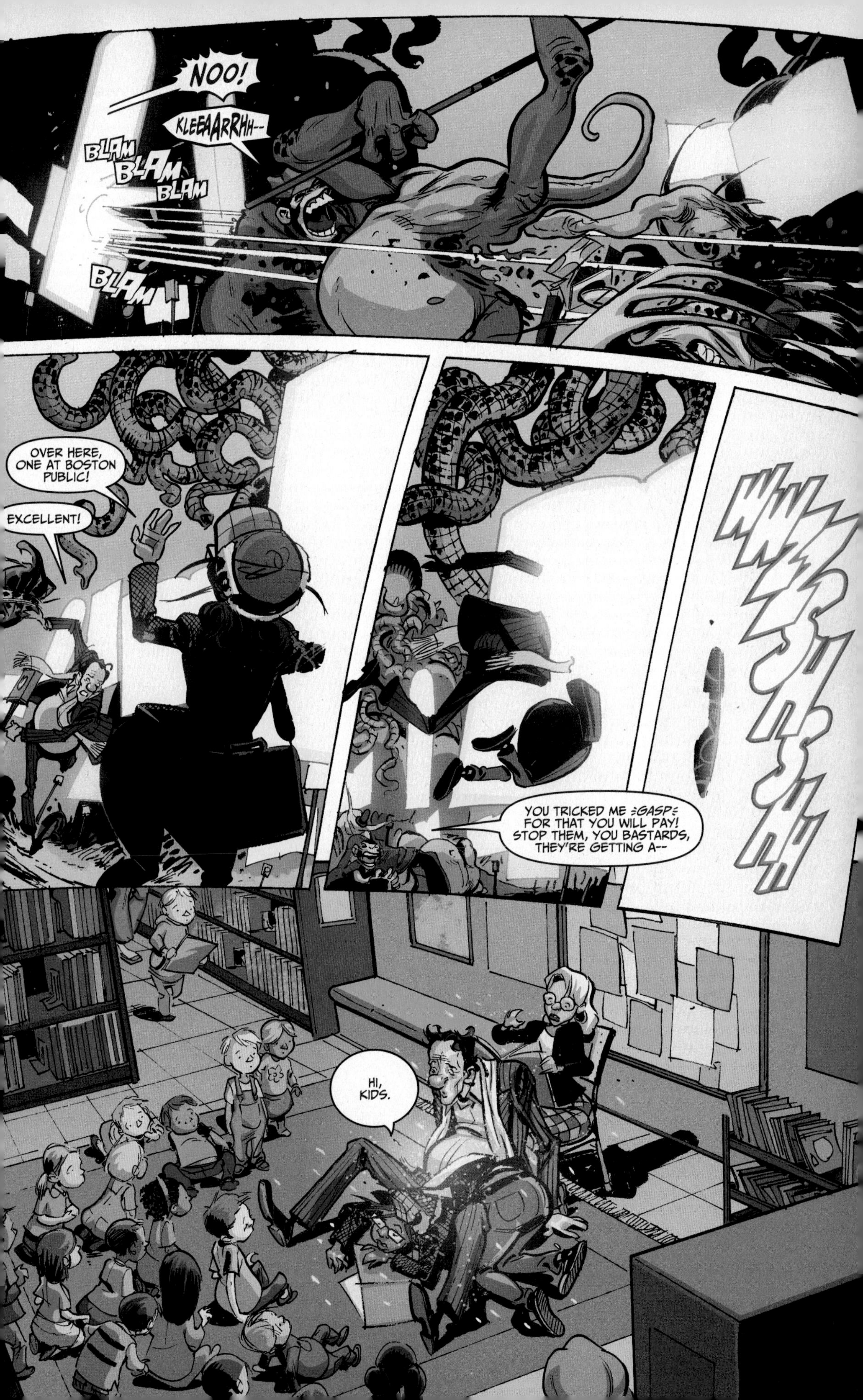
NOO!
KLEEAARRHH--
BLAM BLAM BLAM
BLAM
OVER HERE, ONE AT BOSTON PUBLIC!
EXCELLENT!
YOU TRICKED ME GASP FOR THAT YOU WILL PAY! STOP THEM, YOU BASTARDS, THEY'RE GETTING A--
HI, KIDS.

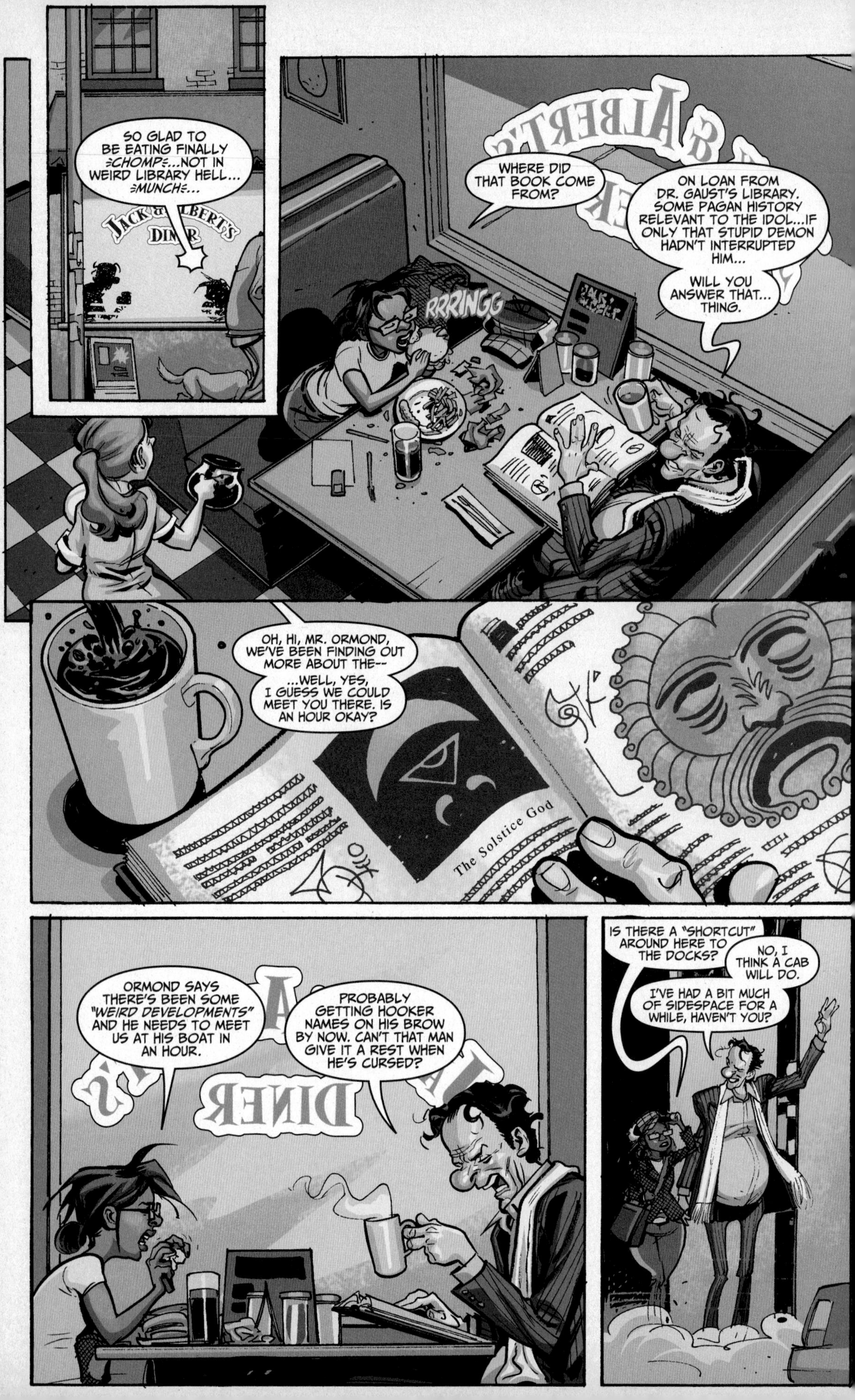
SO GLAD TO BE EATING FINALLY *CHOMP*...NOT IN WEIRD LIBRARY HELL... *MUNCH*...
JACK & ALBERT'S DINER
WHERE DID THAT BOOK COME FROM?
ON LOAN FROM DR. GAUST'S LIBRARY. SOME PAGAN HISTORY RELEVANT TO THE IDOL...IF ONLY THAT STUPID DEMON HADN'T INTERRUPTED HIM...
WILL YOU ANSWER THAT... THING.
RRRINGG
OH, HI, MR. ORMOND, WE'VE BEEN FINDING OUT MORE ABOUT THE--
...WELL, YES, I GUESS WE COULD MEET YOU THERE. IS AN HOUR OKAY?
The Solstice God
ORMOND SAYS THERE'S BEEN SOME "*WEIRD DEVELOPMENTS*" AND HE NEEDS TO MEET US AT HIS BOAT IN AN HOUR.
PROBABLY GETTING HOOKER NAMES ON HIS BROW BY NOW. CAN'T THAT MAN GIVE IT A REST WHEN HE'S CURSED?
IS THERE A "SHORTCUT" AROUND HERE TO THE DOCKS?
NO, I THINK A CAB WILL DO.
I'VE HAD A BIT MUCH OF SIDESPACE FOR A WHILE, HAVEN'T YOU?

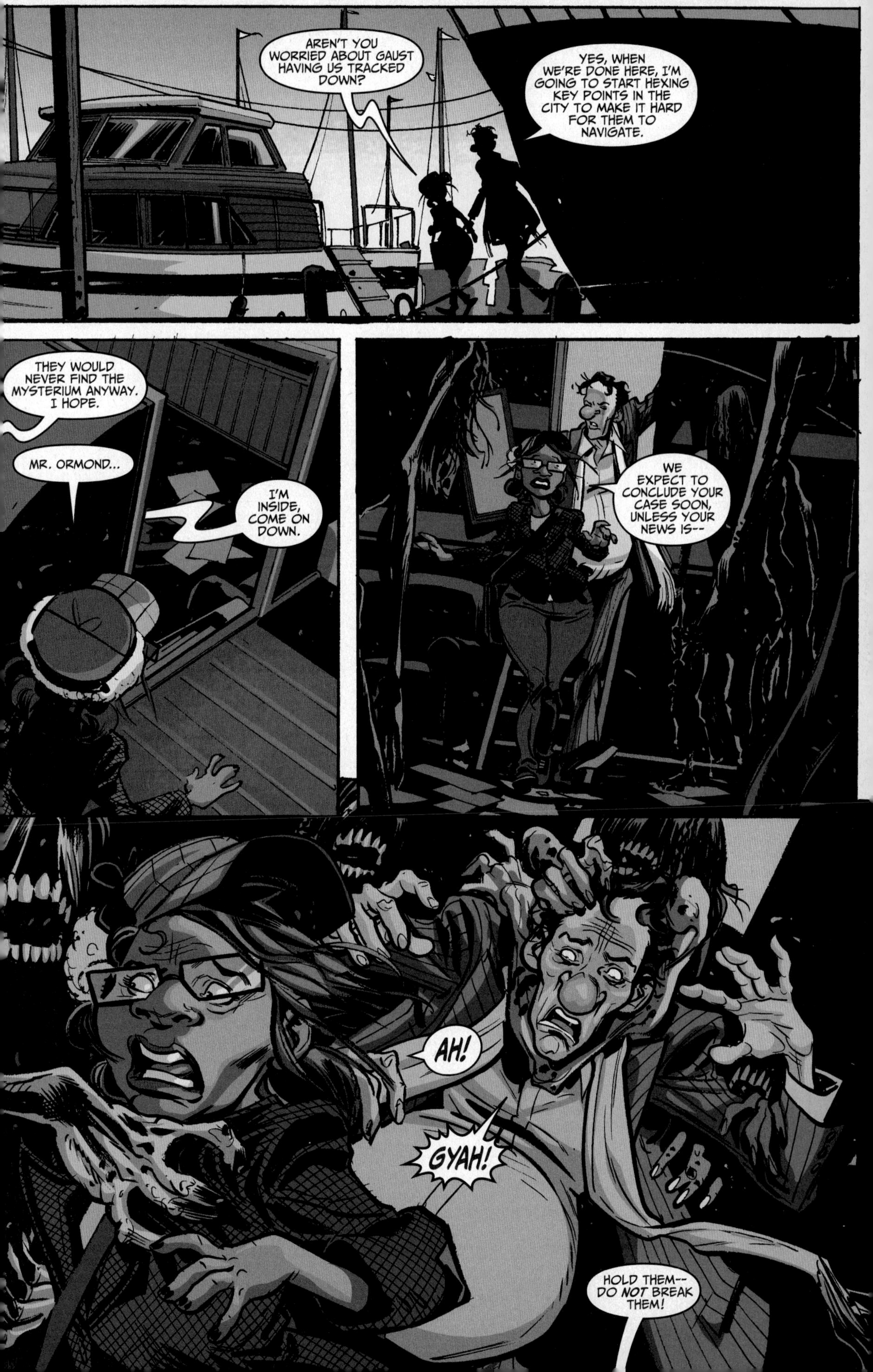

AREN'T YOU WORRIED ABOUT GAUST HAVING US TRACKED DOWN?
YES, WHEN WE'RE DONE HERE, I'M GOING TO START HEXING KEY POINTS IN THE CITY TO MAKE IT HARD FOR THEM TO NAVIGATE.
THEY WOULD NEVER FIND THE MYSTERIUM ANYWAY. I HOPE.
MR. ORMOND...
I'M INSIDE, COME ON DOWN.
WE EXPECT TO CONCLUDE YOUR CASE SOON, UNLESS YOUR NEWS IS--
AH!
GYAH!
HOLD THEM-- DO *NOT* BREAK THEM!

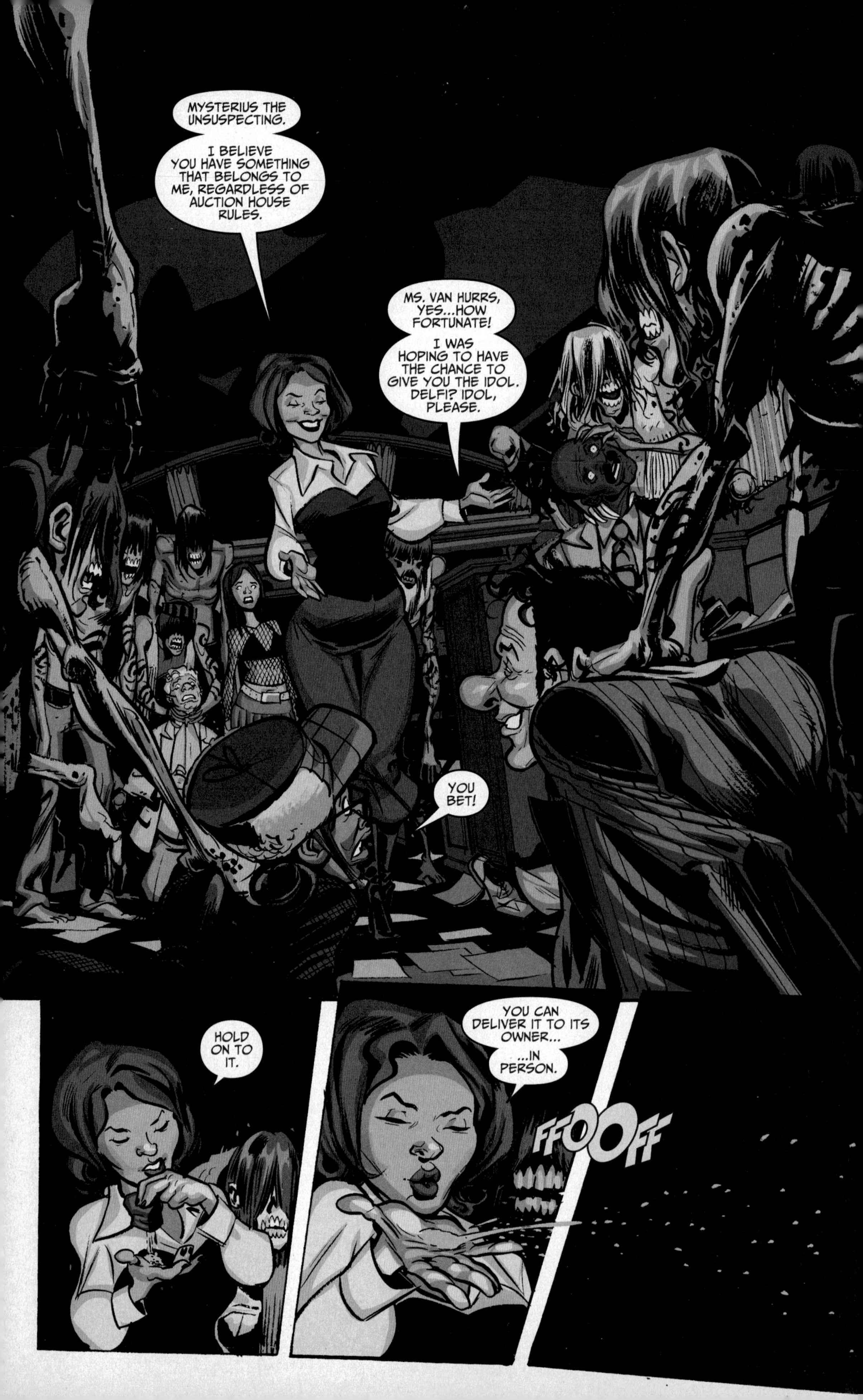
MYSTERIUS THE UNSUSPECTING.
I BELIEVE YOU HAVE SOMETHING THAT BELONGS TO ME, REGARDLESS OF AUCTION HOUSE RULES.
MS. VAN HURRS, YES...HOW FORTUNATE!
I WAS HOPING TO HAVE THE CHANCE TO GIVE YOU THE IDOL. DELFI? IDOL, PLEASE.
YOU BET!
HOLD ON TO IT.
YOU CAN DELIVER IT TO ITS OWNER...
...IN PERSON.
FFOOOFF

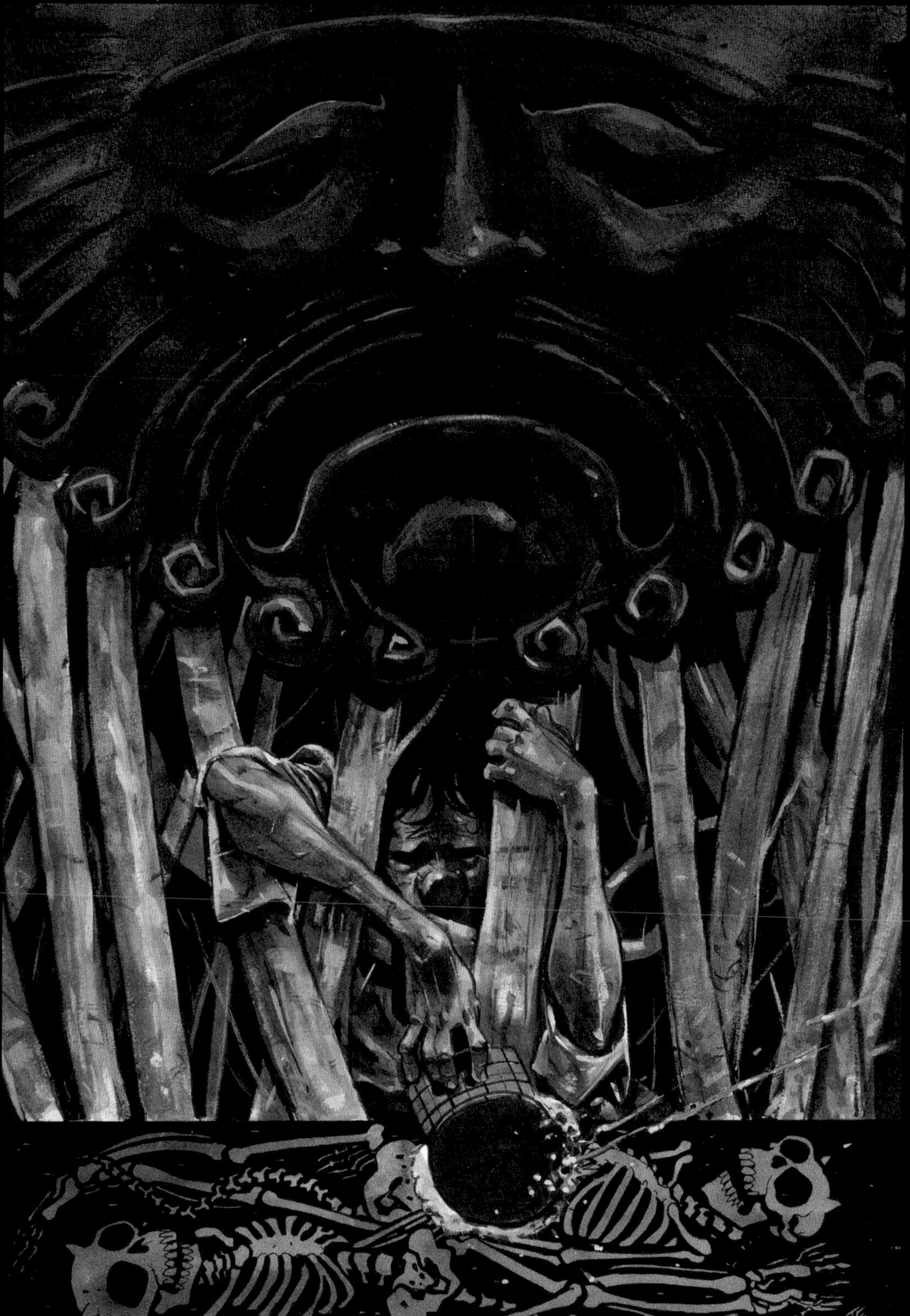

CHAPTER FIVE: FEEL THE BURN

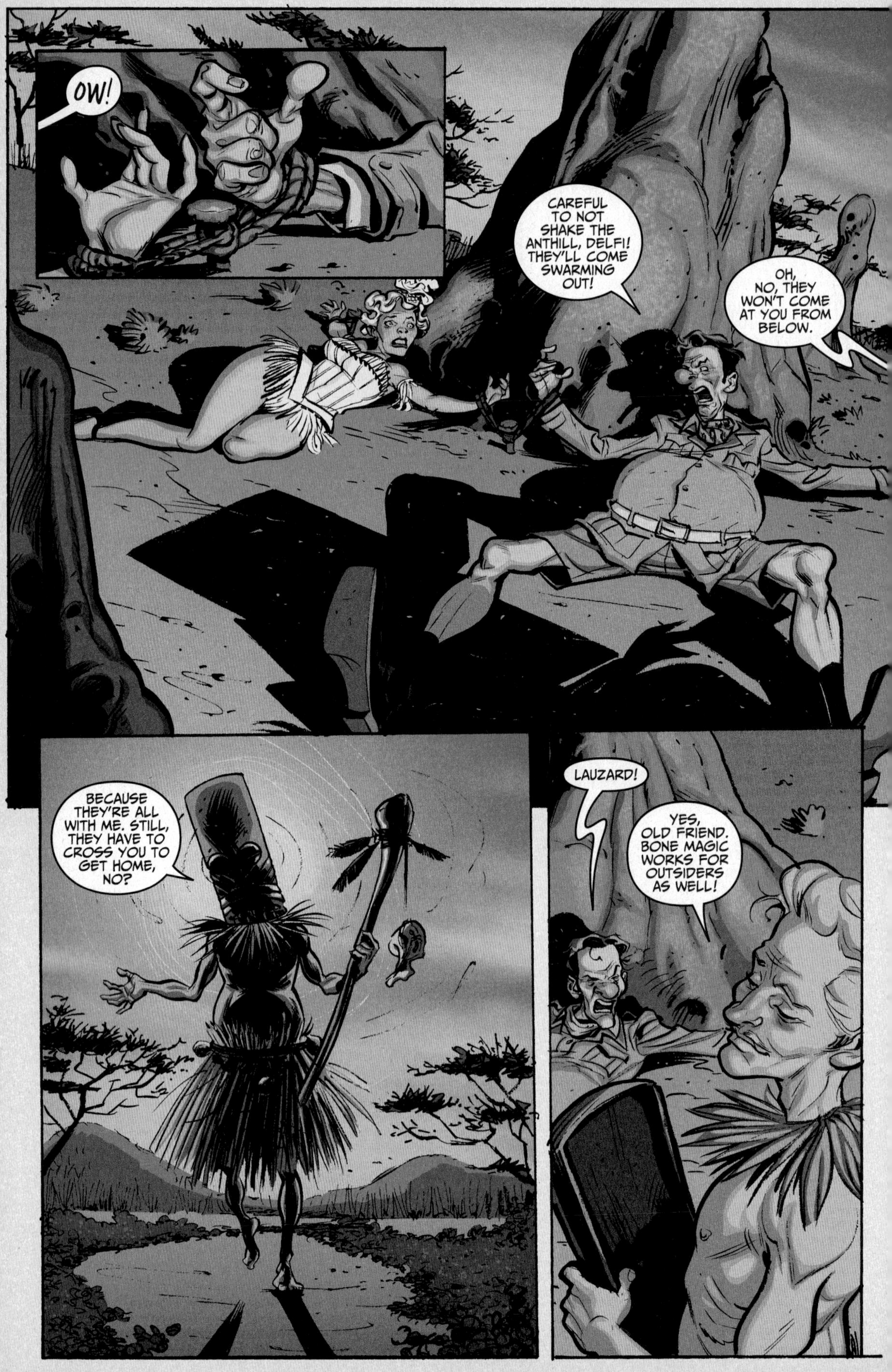
OW!
CAREFUL TO NOT SHAKE THE ANTHILL, DELFI! THEY'LL COME SWARMING OUT!
OH, NO, THEY WON'T COME AT YOU FROM BELOW.
BECAUSE THEY'RE ALL WITH ME. STILL, THEY HAVE TO CROSS YOU TO GET HOME, NO?
LAUZARD!
YES, OLD FRIEND. BONE MAGIC WORKS FOR OUTSIDERS AS WELL!

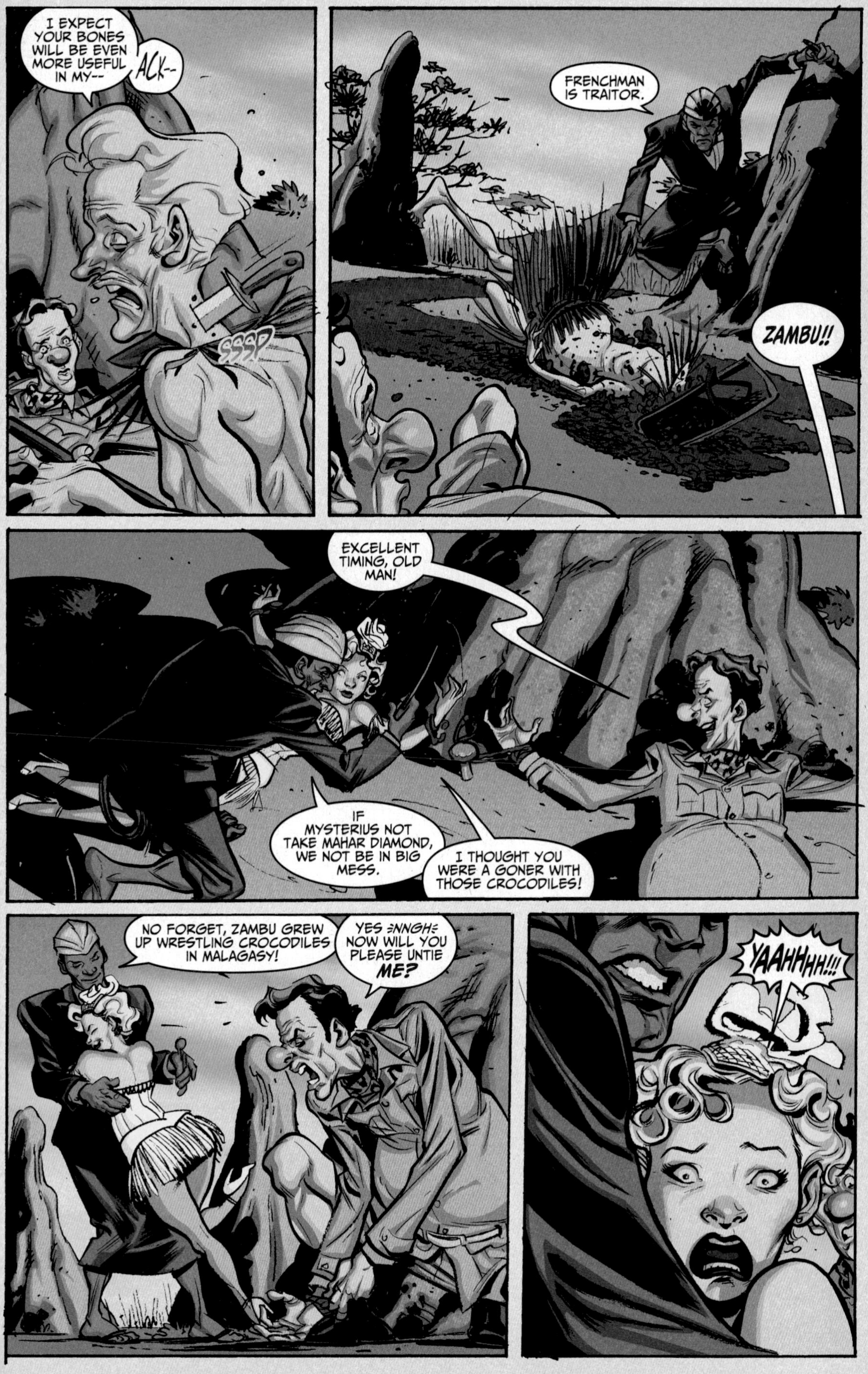

I EXPECT YOUR BONES WILL BE EVEN MORE USEFUL IN MY--
ACK--
SSSP
FRENCHMAN IS TRAITOR.
ZAMBU!!
EXCELLENT TIMING, OLD MAN!
IF MYSTERIUS NOT TAKE MAHAR DIAMOND, WE NOT BE IN BIG MESS.
I THOUGHT YOU WERE A GONER WITH THOSE CROCODILES!
NO FORGET, ZAMBU GREW UP WRESTLING CROCODILES IN MALAGASY!
YES =NNGH= NOW WILL YOU PLEASE UNTIE ME?
YAAHHHH!!!

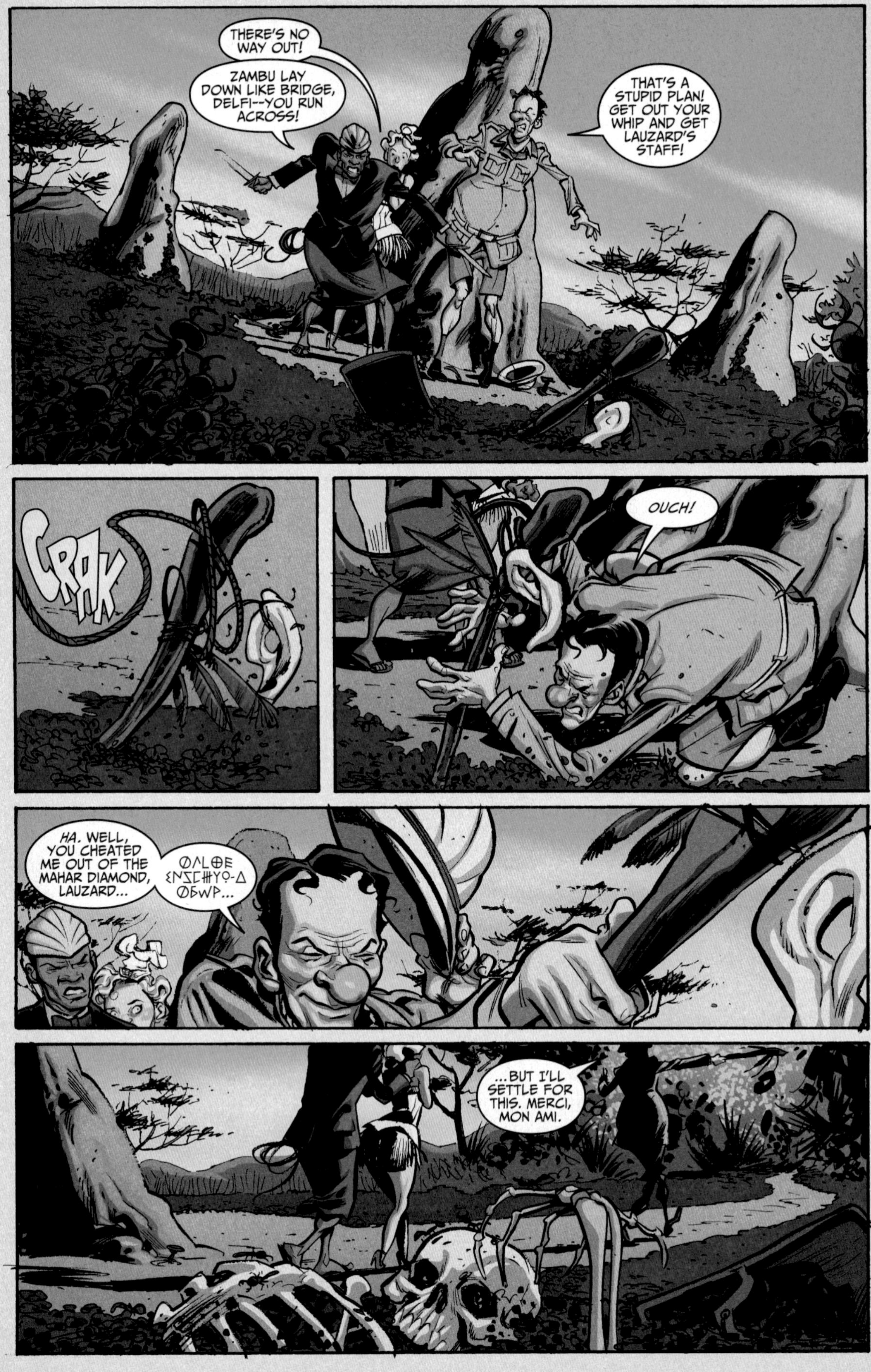
THERE'S NO WAY OUT!
ZAMBU LAY DOWN LIKE BRIDGE, DELFI--YOU RUN ACROSS!
THAT'S A STUPID PLAN! GET OUT YOUR WHIP AND GET LAUZARD'S STAFF!
CRAK
OUCH!
HA. WELL, YOU CHEATED ME OUT OF THE MAHAR DIAMOND, LAUZARD...
...BUT I'LL SETTLE FOR THIS. MERCI, MON AMI.

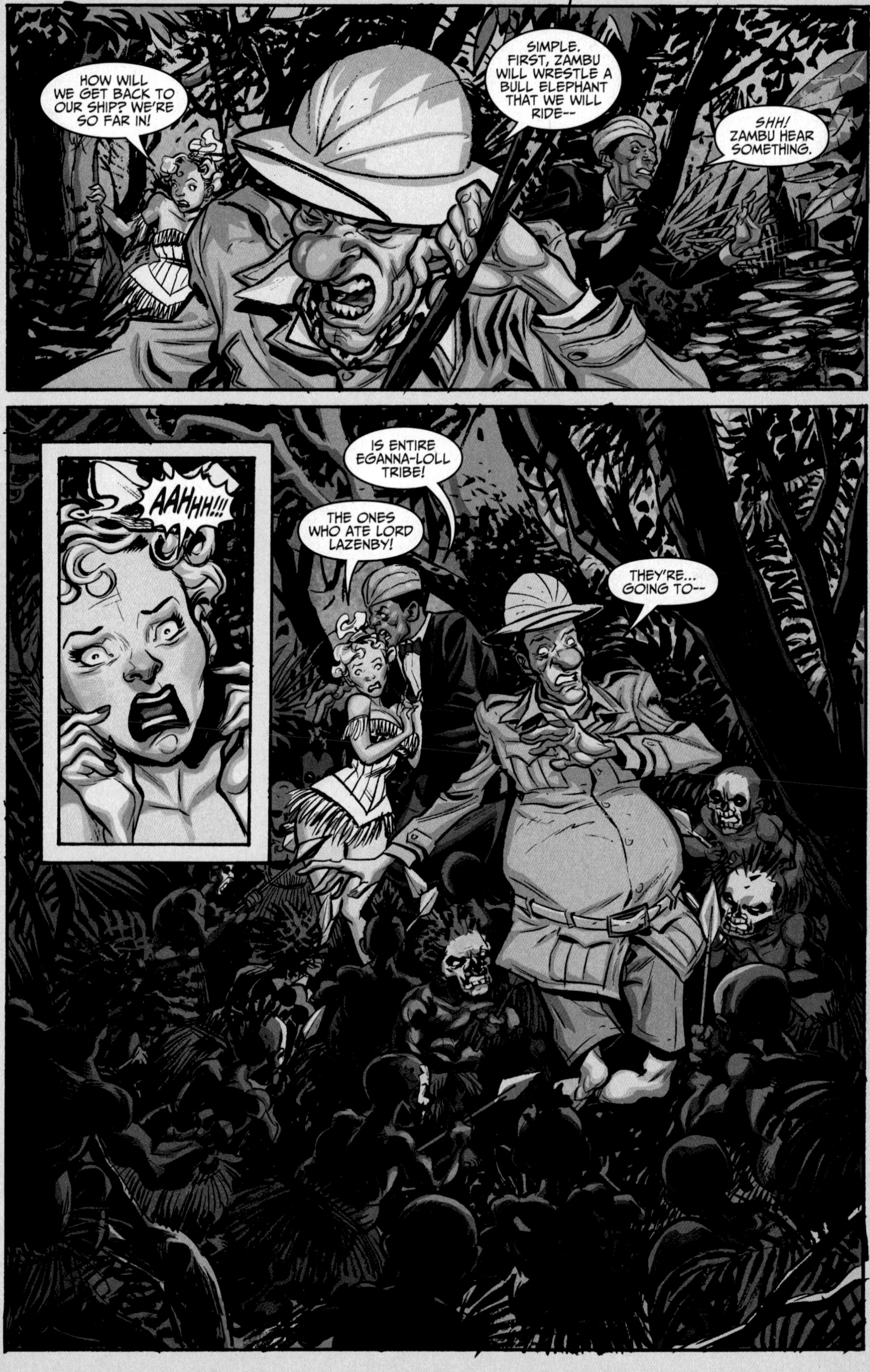
HOW WILL WE GET BACK TO OUR SHIP? WE'RE SO FAR IN!
SIMPLE. FIRST, ZAMBU WILL WRESTLE A BULL ELEPHANT THAT WE WILL RIDE--
SHH! ZAMBU HEAR SOMETHING.
AAHHH!!!
IS ENTIRE EGANNA-LOLL TRIBE!
THE ONES WHO ATE LORD LAZENBY!
THEY'RE... GOING TO--

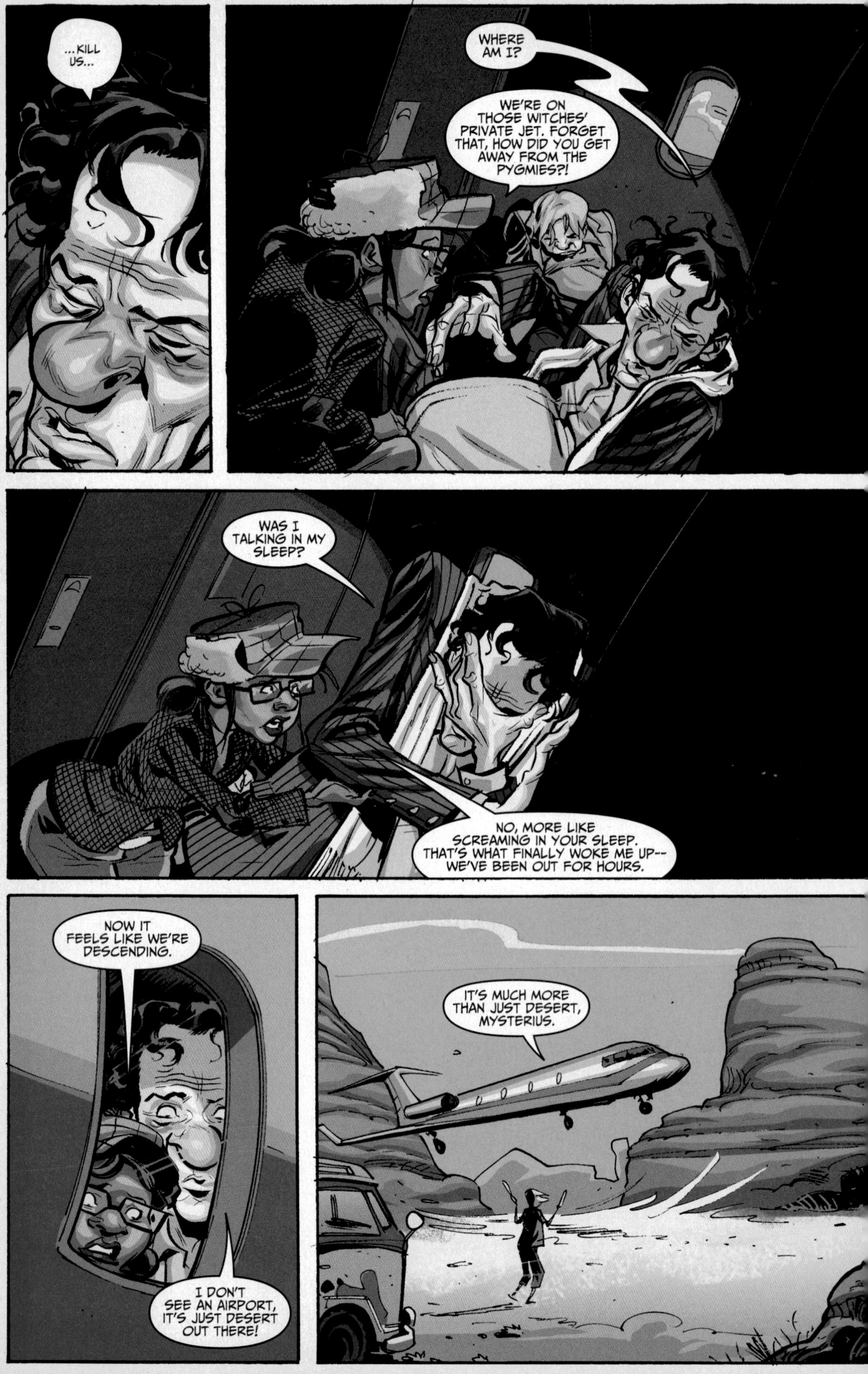
...KILL US...
WHERE AM I?
WE'RE ON THOSE WITCHES' PRIVATE JET. FORGET THAT, HOW DID YOU GET AWAY FROM THE PYGMIES?!
WAS I TALKING IN MY SLEEP?
NO, MORE LIKE SCREAMING IN YOUR SLEEP. THAT'S WHAT FINALLY WOKE ME UP-- WE'VE BEEN OUT FOR HOURS.
NOW IT FEELS LIKE WE'RE DESCENDING.
I DON'T SEE AN AIRPORT, IT'S JUST DESERT OUT THERE!
IT'S MUCH MORE THAN JUST DESERT, MYSTERIUS.

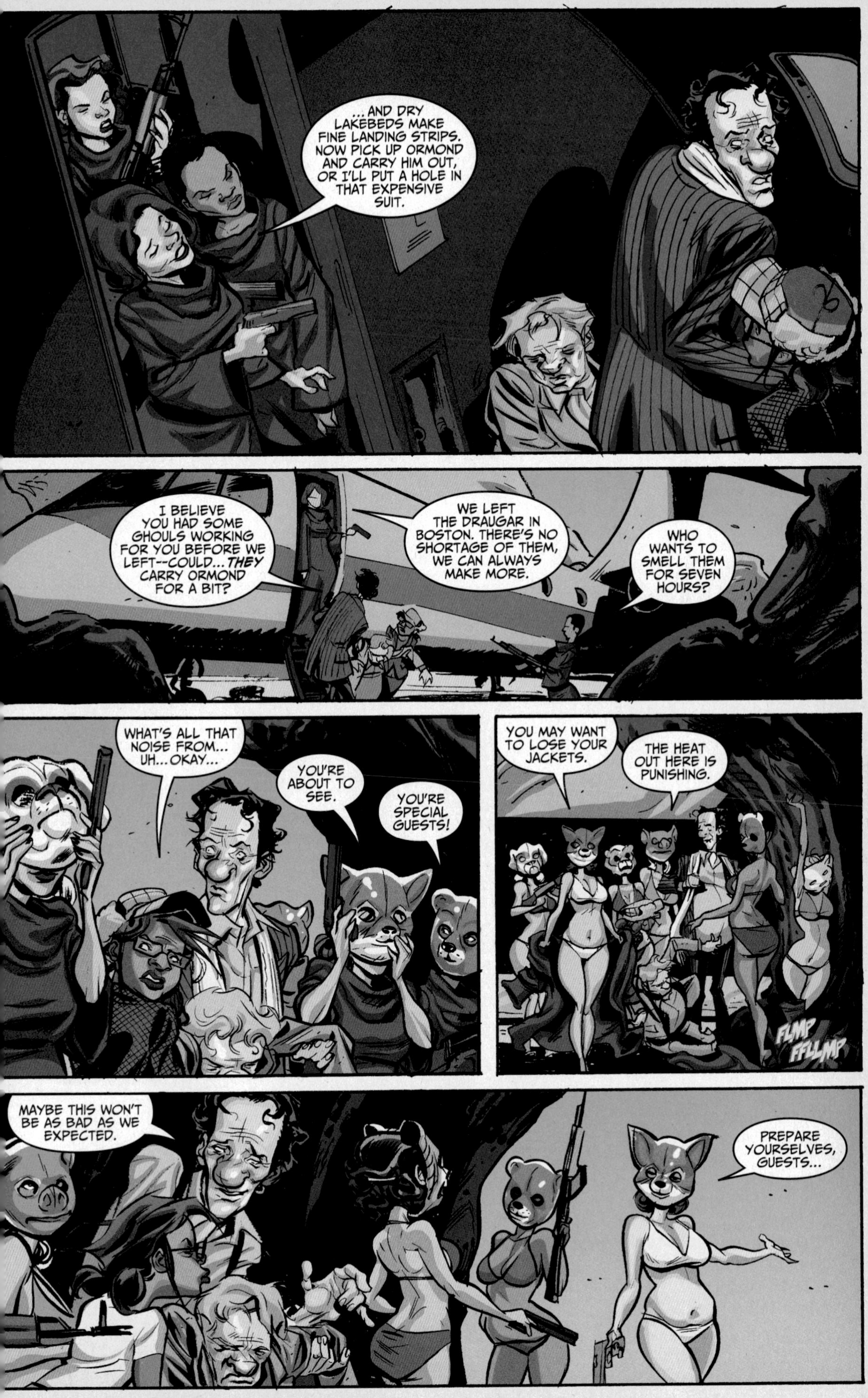
...AND DRY LAKEBEDS MAKE FINE LANDING STRIPS. NOW PICK UP ORMOND AND CARRY HIM OUT, OR I'LL PUT A HOLE IN THAT EXPENSIVE SUIT.
I BELIEVE YOU HAD SOME GHOULS WORKING FOR YOU BEFORE WE LEFT--COULD...THEY CARRY ORMOND FOR A BIT?
WE LEFT THE DRAUGAR IN BOSTON. THERE'S NO SHORTAGE OF THEM, WE CAN ALWAYS MAKE MORE.
WHO WANTS TO SMELL THEM FOR SEVEN HOURS?
WHAT'S ALL THAT NOISE FROM... UH...OKAY...
YOU'RE ABOUT TO SEE.
YOU'RE SPECIAL GUESTS!
YOU MAY WANT TO LOSE YOUR JACKETS.
THE HEAT OUT HERE IS PUNISHING.
FLMP
FFLLMP
MAYBE THIS WON'T BE AS BAD AS WE EXPECTED.
PREPARE YOURSELVES, GUESTS...

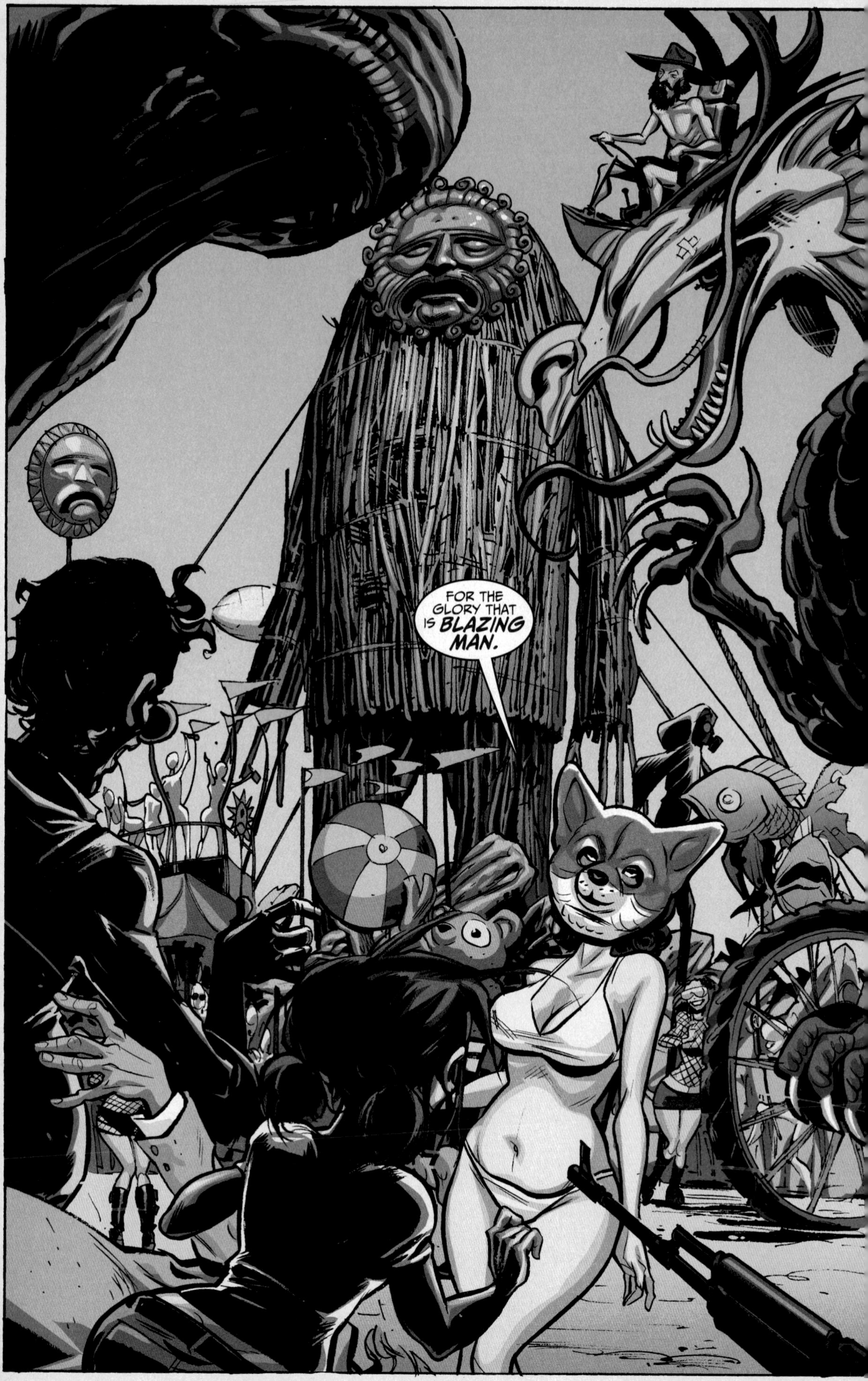
FOR THE GLORY THAT IS BLAZING MAN.

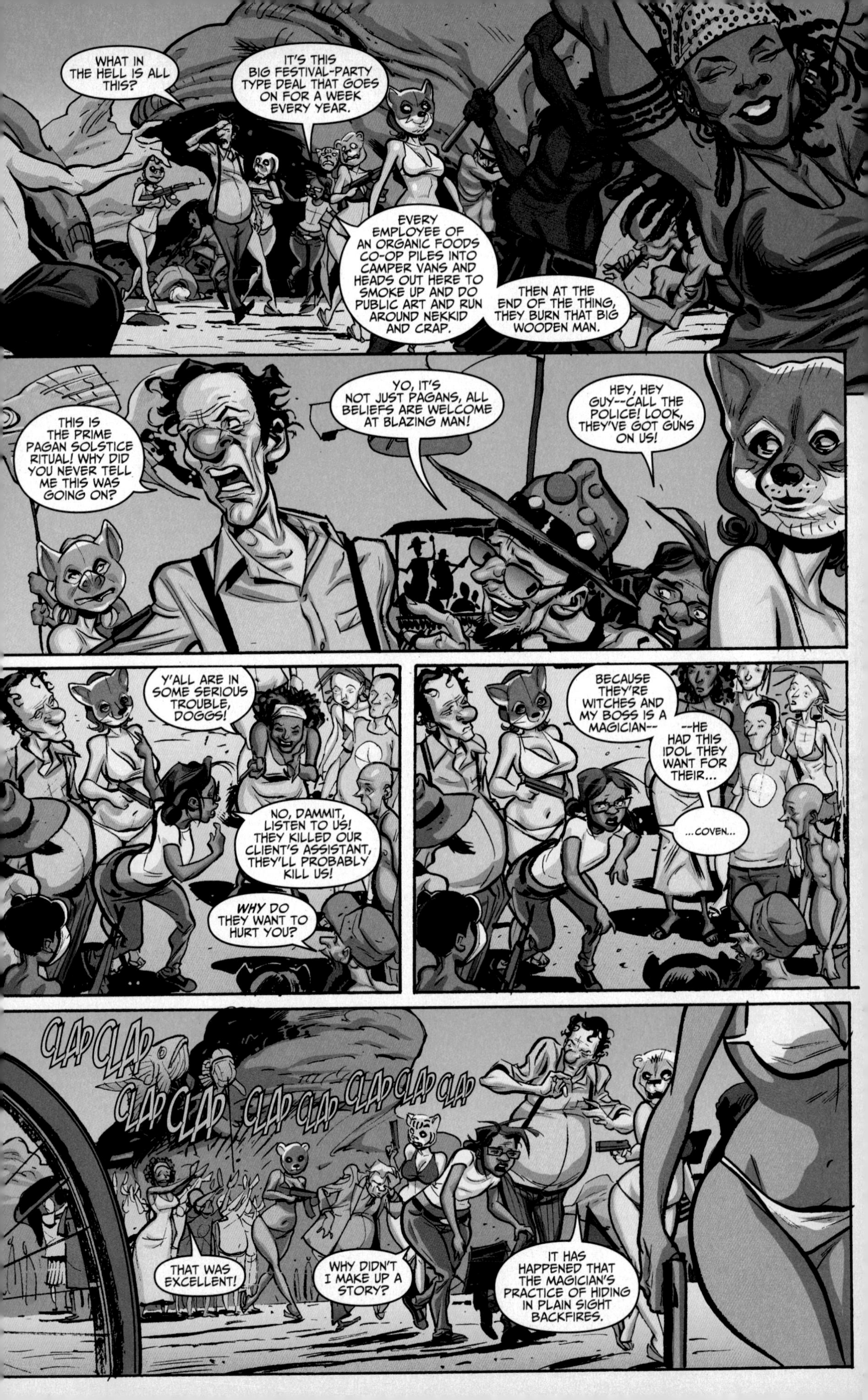
WHAT IN THE HELL IS ALL THIS?
IT'S THIS BIG FESTIVAL-PARTY TYPE DEAL THAT GOES ON FOR A WEEK EVERY YEAR.
EVERY EMPLOYEE OF AN ORGANIC FOODS CO-OP PILES INTO CAMPER VANS AND HEADS OUT HERE TO SMOKE UP AND DO PUBLIC ART AND RUN AROUND NEKKID AND CRAP.
THEN AT THE END OF THE THING, THEY BURN THAT BIG WOODEN MAN.
THIS IS THE PRIME PAGAN SOLSTICE RITUAL! WHY DID YOU NEVER TELL ME THIS WAS GOING ON?
YO, IT'S NOT JUST PAGANS, ALL BELIEFS ARE WELCOME AT BLAZING MAN!
HEY, HEY GUY--CALL THE POLICE! LOOK, THEY'VE GOT GUNS ON US!
Y'ALL ARE IN SOME SERIOUS TROUBLE, DOGGS!
NO, DAMMIT, LISTEN TO US! THEY KILLED OUR CLIENT'S ASSISTANT, THEY'LL PROBABLY KILL US!
WHY DO THEY WANT TO HURT YOU?
BECAUSE THEY'RE WITCHES AND MY BOSS IS A MAGICIAN--
--HE HAD THIS IDOL THEY WANT FOR THEIR...
...COVEN...
CLAP CLAP CLAP CLAP CLAP CLAP CLAP CLAP CLAP
THAT WAS EXCELLENT!
WHY DIDN'T I MAKE UP A STORY?
IT HAS HAPPENED THAT THE MAGICIAN'S PRACTICE OF HIDING IN PLAIN SIGHT BACKFIRES.

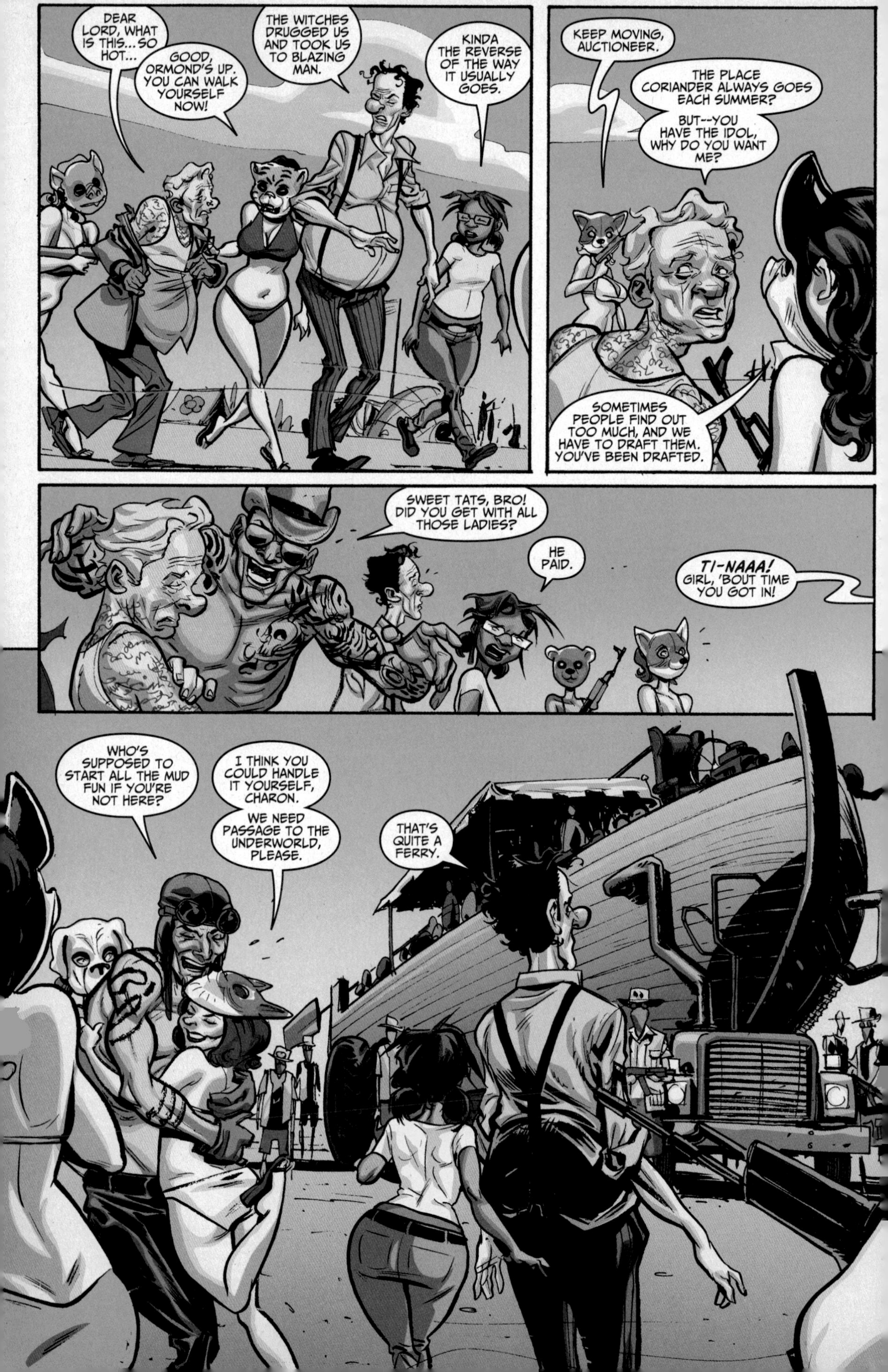
DEAR LORD, WHAT IS THIS... SO HOT...
GOOD, ORMOND'S UP. YOU CAN WALK YOURSELF NOW!
THE WITCHES DRUGGED US AND TOOK US TO BLAZING MAN.
KINDA THE REVERSE OF THE WAY IT USUALLY GOES.
KEEP MOVING, AUCTIONEER.
THE PLACE CORIANDER ALWAYS GOES EACH SUMMER?
BUT--YOU HAVE THE IDOL, WHY DO YOU WANT ME?
SOMETIMES PEOPLE FIND OUT TOO MUCH, AND WE HAVE TO DRAFT THEM. YOU'VE BEEN DRAFTED.
SWEET TATS, BRO! DID YOU GET WITH ALL THOSE LADIES?
HE PAID.
TI-NAAA! GIRL, 'BOUT TIME YOU GOT IN!
WHO'S SUPPOSED TO START ALL THE MUD FUN IF YOU'RE NOT HERE?
I THINK YOU COULD HANDLE IT YOURSELF, CHARON.
WE NEED PASSAGE TO THE UNDERWORLD, PLEASE.
THAT'S QUITE A FERRY.

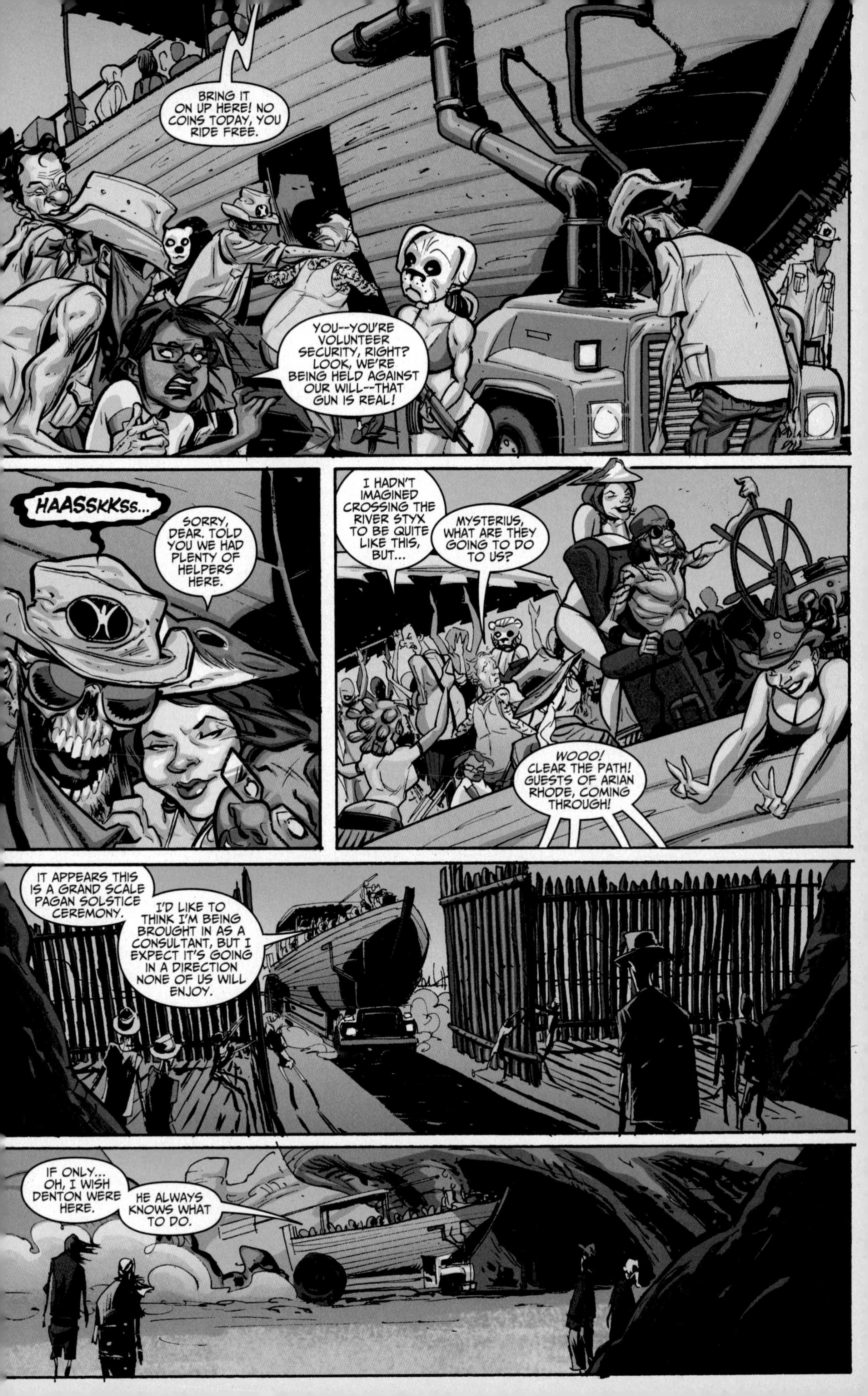
BRING IT ON UP HERE! NO COINS TODAY, YOU RIDE FREE.
YOU--YOU'RE VOLUNTEER SECURITY, RIGHT? LOOK, WE'RE BEING HELD AGAINST OUR WILL--THAT GUN IS REAL!
HAASSKKSS...
SORRY, DEAR. TOLD YOU WE HAD PLENTY OF HELPERS HERE.
I HADN'T IMAGINED CROSSING THE RIVER STYX TO BE QUITE LIKE THIS, BUT...
MYSTERIUS, WHAT ARE THEY GOING TO DO TO US?
WOOO! CLEAR THE PATH! GUESTS OF ARIAN RHODE, COMING THROUGH!
IT APPEARS THIS IS A GRAND SCALE PAGAN SOLSTICE CEREMONY.
I'D LIKE TO THINK I'M BEING BROUGHT IN AS A CONSULTANT, BUT I EXPECT IT'S GOING IN A DIRECTION NONE OF US WILL ENJOY.
IF ONLY... OH, I WISH DENTON WERE HERE.
HE ALWAYS KNOWS WHAT TO DO.

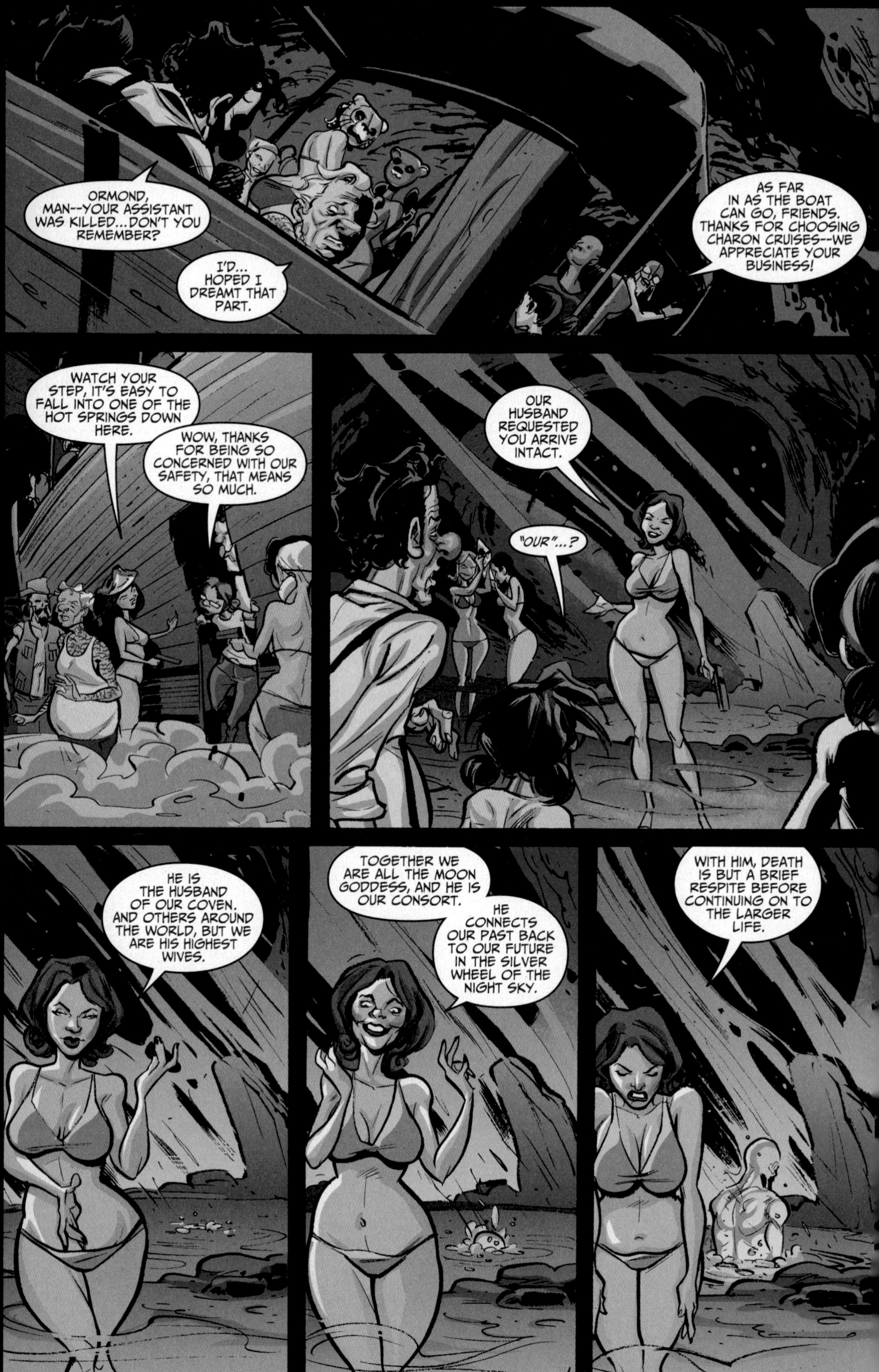
ORMOND, MAN--YOUR ASSISTANT WAS KILLED...DON'T YOU REMEMBER?
I'D... HOPED I DREAMT THAT PART.
AS FAR IN AS THE BOAT CAN GO, FRIENDS. THANKS FOR CHOOSING CHARON CRUISES--WE APPRECIATE YOUR BUSINESS!
WATCH YOUR STEP, IT'S EASY TO FALL INTO ONE OF THE HOT SPRINGS DOWN HERE.
WOW, THANKS FOR BEING SO CONCERNED WITH OUR SAFETY, THAT MEANS SO MUCH.
OUR HUSBAND REQUESTED YOU ARRIVE INTACT.
"OUR"...?
HE IS THE HUSBAND OF OUR COVEN. AND OTHERS AROUND THE WORLD, BUT WE ARE HIS HIGHEST WIVES.
TOGETHER WE ARE ALL THE MOON GODDESS, AND HE IS OUR CONSORT.
HE CONNECTS OUR PAST BACK TO OUR FUTURE IN THE SILVER WHEEL OF THE NIGHT SKY.
WITH HIM, DEATH IS BUT A BRIEF RESPITE BEFORE CONTINUING ON TO THE LARGER LIFE.

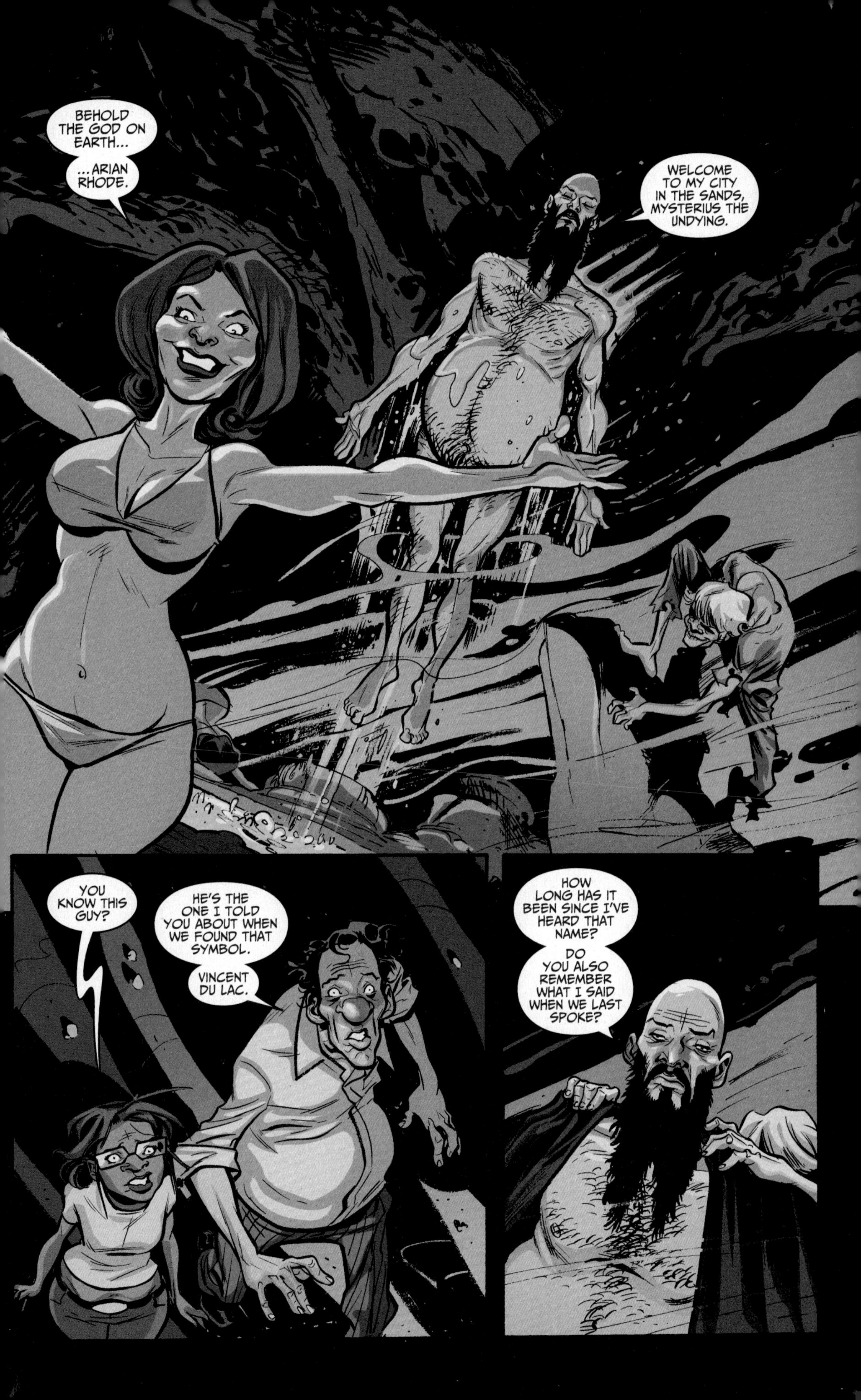
BEHOLD THE GOD ON EARTH...
...ARIAN RHODE.
WELCOME TO MY CITY IN THE SANDS, MYSTERIUS THE UNDYING.
YOU KNOW THIS GUY?
HE'S THE ONE I TOLD YOU ABOUT WHEN WE FOUND THAT SYMBOL.
VINCENT DU LAC.
HOW LONG HAS IT BEEN SINCE I'VE HEARD THAT NAME?
DO YOU ALSO REMEMBER WHAT I SAID WHEN WE LAST SPOKE?

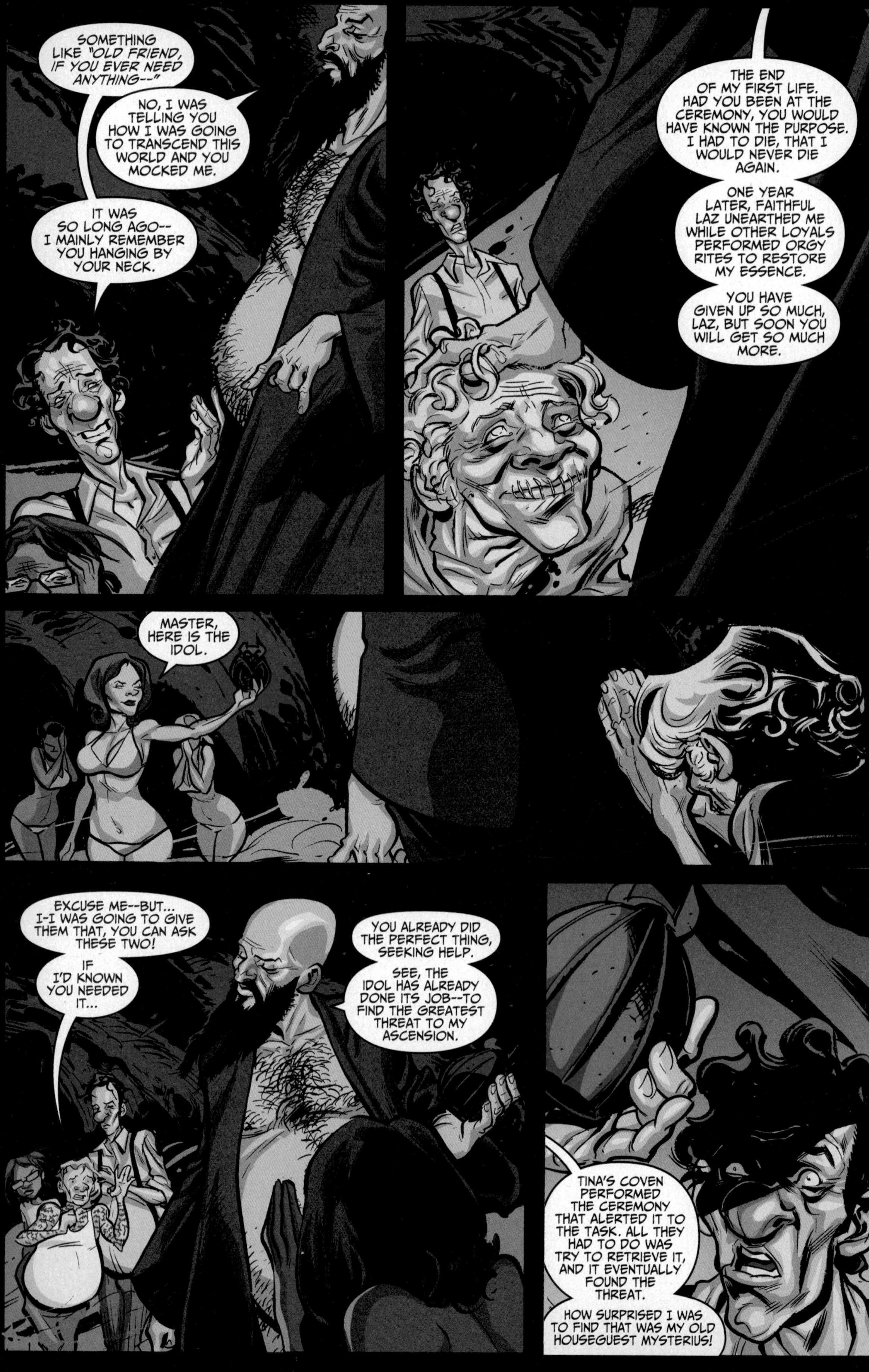
SOMETHING LIKE "OLD FRIEND, IF YOU EVER NEED ANYTHING--"
NO, I WAS TELLING YOU HOW I WAS GOING TO TRANSCEND THIS WORLD AND YOU MOCKED ME.
IT WAS SO LONG AGO-- I MAINLY REMEMBER YOU HANGING BY YOUR NECK.
THE END OF MY FIRST LIFE. HAD YOU BEEN AT THE CEREMONY, YOU WOULD HAVE KNOWN THE PURPOSE. I HAD TO DIE, THAT I WOULD NEVER DIE AGAIN.
ONE YEAR LATER, FAITHFUL LAZ UNEARTHED ME WHILE OTHER LOYALS PERFORMED ORGY RITES TO RESTORE MY ESSENCE.
YOU HAVE GIVEN UP SO MUCH, LAZ, BUT SOON YOU WILL GET SO MUCH MORE.
MASTER, HERE IS THE IDOL.
EXCUSE ME--BUT... I-I WAS GOING TO GIVE THEM THAT, YOU CAN ASK THESE TWO!
IF I'D KNOWN YOU NEEDED IT...
YOU ALREADY DID THE PERFECT THING, SEEKING HELP.
SEE, THE IDOL HAS ALREADY DONE ITS JOB--TO FIND THE GREATEST THREAT TO MY ASCENSION.
TINA'S COVEN PERFORMED THE CEREMONY THAT ALERTED IT TO THE TASK. ALL THEY HAD TO DO WAS TRY TO RETRIEVE IT, AND IT EVENTUALLY FOUND THE THREAT.
HOW SURPRISED I WAS TO FIND THAT WAS MY OLD HOUSEGUEST MYSTERIUS!

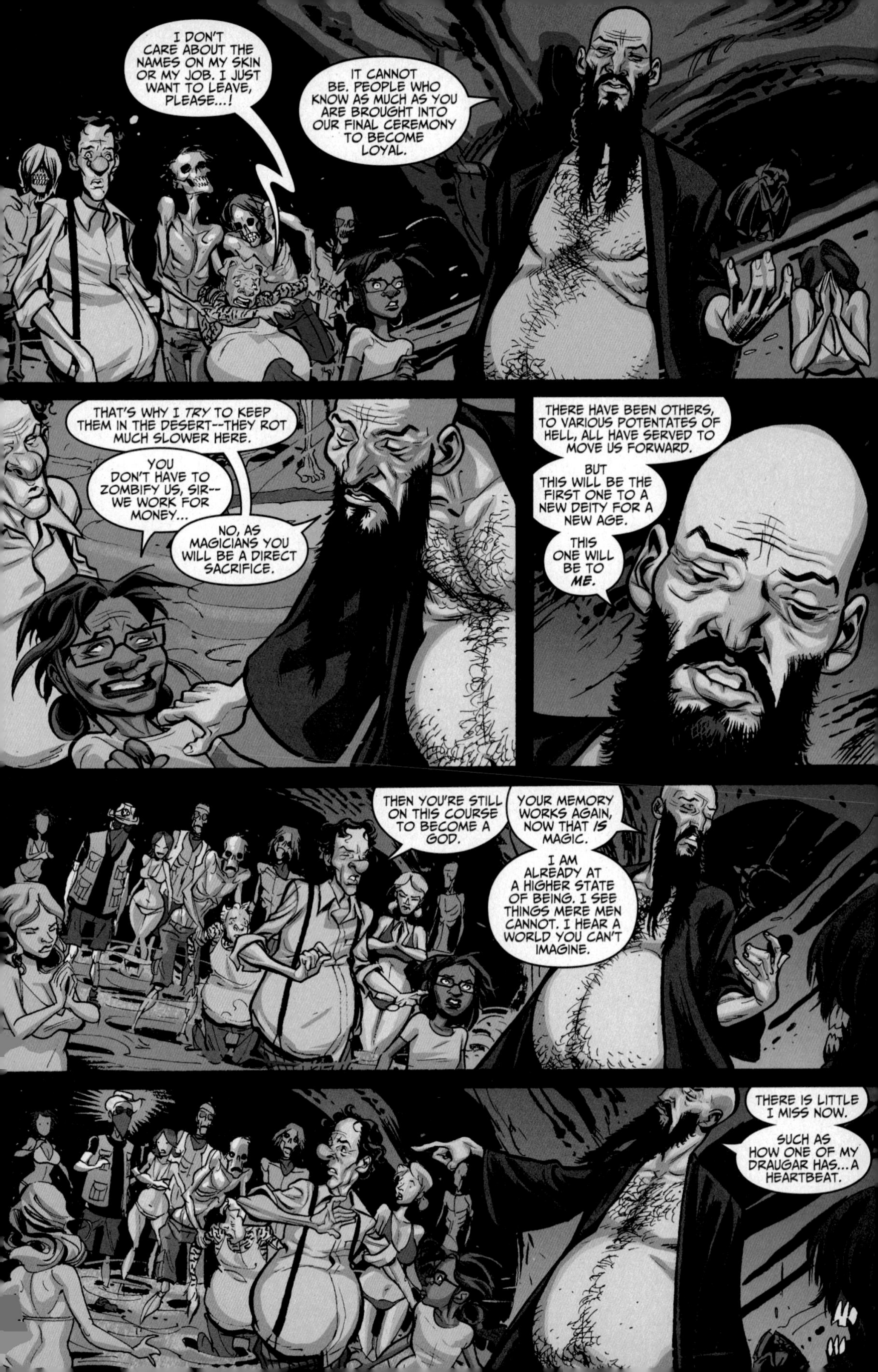
I DON'T CARE ABOUT THE NAMES ON MY SKIN OR MY JOB. I JUST WANT TO LEAVE, PLEASE...!
IT CANNOT BE. PEOPLE WHO KNOW AS MUCH AS YOU ARE BROUGHT INTO OUR FINAL CEREMONY TO BECOME LOYAL.
THAT'S WHY I *TRY* TO KEEP THEM IN THE DESERT--THEY ROT MUCH SLOWER HERE.
YOU DON'T HAVE TO ZOMBIFY US, SIR-- WE WORK FOR MONEY...
NO, AS MAGICIANS YOU WILL BE A DIRECT SACRIFICE.
THERE HAVE BEEN OTHERS, TO VARIOUS POTENTATES OF HELL, ALL HAVE SERVED TO MOVE US FORWARD.
BUT THIS WILL BE THE FIRST ONE TO A NEW DEITY FOR A NEW AGE.
THIS ONE WILL BE TO ***ME.***
THEN YOU'RE STILL ON THIS COURSE TO BECOME A GOD.
YOUR MEMORY WORKS AGAIN, NOW THAT *IS* MAGIC.
I AM ALREADY AT A HIGHER STATE OF BEING. I SEE THINGS MERE MEN CANNOT. I HEAR A WORLD YOU CAN'T IMAGINE.
THERE IS LITTLE I MISS NOW.
SUCH AS HOW ONE OF MY DRAUGAR HAS...A HEARTBEAT.

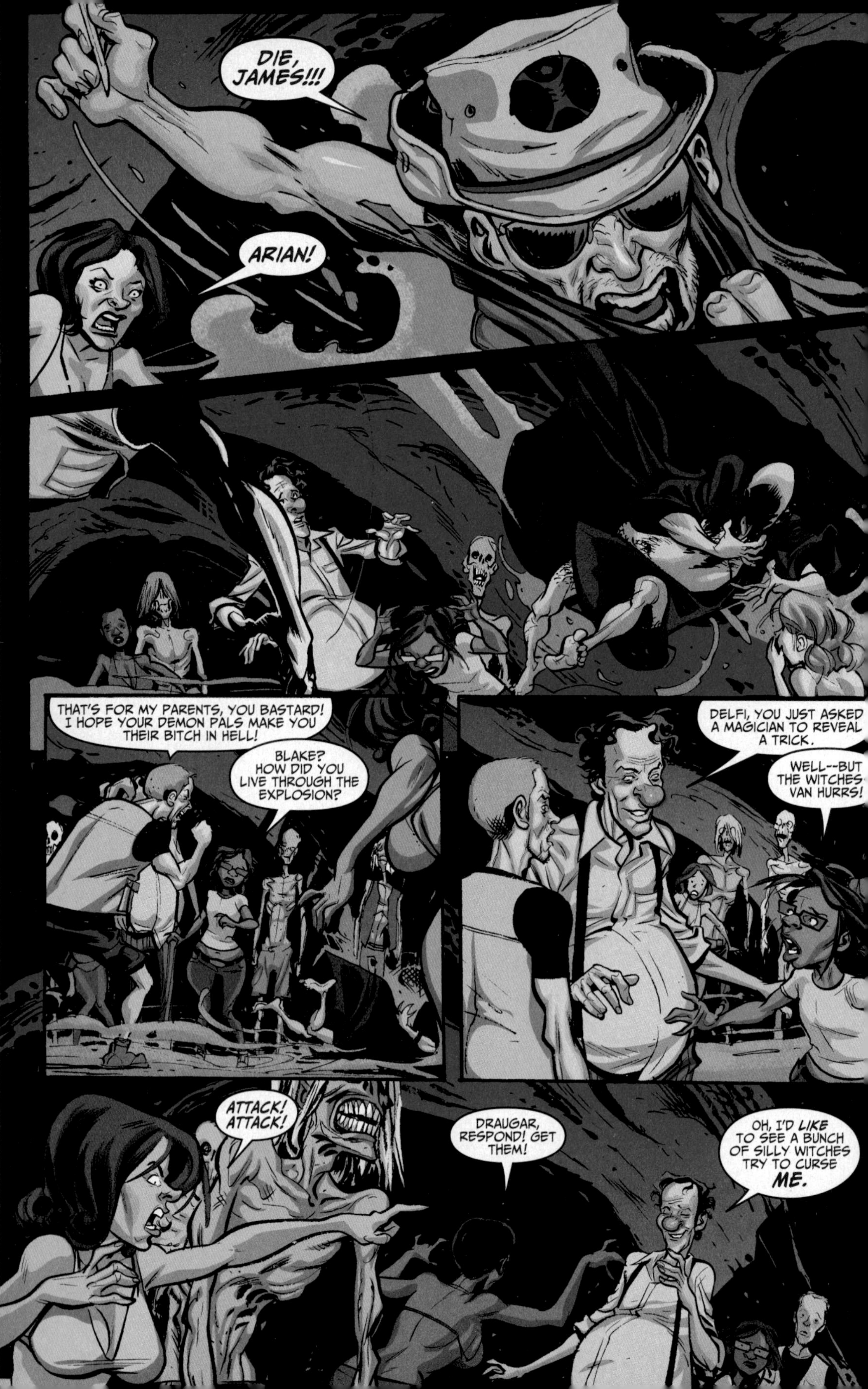
DIE, JAMES!!!
ARIAN!
THAT'S FOR MY PARENTS, YOU BASTARD! I HOPE YOUR DEMON PALS MAKE YOU THEIR BITCH IN HELL!
BLAKE? HOW DID YOU LIVE THROUGH THE EXPLOSION?
DELFI, YOU JUST ASKED A MAGICIAN TO REVEAL A TRICK.
WELL--BUT THE WITCHES VAN HURRS!
ATTACK! ATTACK!
DRAUGAR, RESPOND! GET THEM!
OH, I'D LIKE TO SEE A BUNCH OF SILLY WITCHES TRY TO CURSE ME.

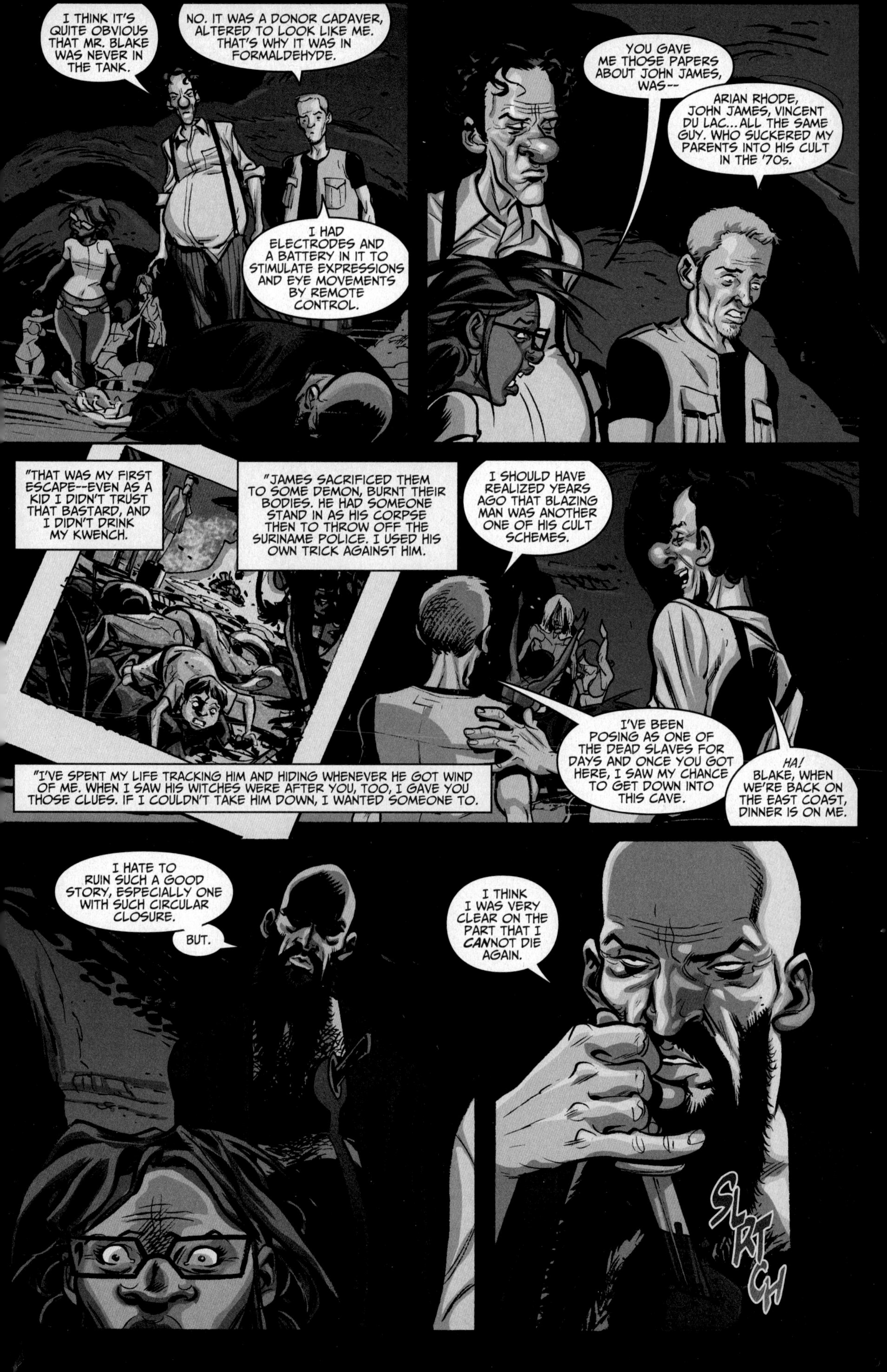
I THINK IT'S QUITE OBVIOUS THAT MR. BLAKE WAS NEVER IN THE TANK.
NO. IT WAS A DONOR CADAVER, ALTERED TO LOOK LIKE ME. THAT'S WHY IT WAS IN FORMALDEHYDE.
I HAD ELECTRODES AND A BATTERY IN IT TO STIMULATE EXPRESSIONS AND EYE MOVEMENTS BY REMOTE CONTROL.
YOU GAVE ME THOSE PAPERS ABOUT JOHN JAMES, WAS--
ARIAN RHODE, JOHN JAMES, VINCENT DU LAC...ALL THE SAME GUY. WHO SUCKERED MY PARENTS INTO HIS CULT IN THE '70s.
"THAT WAS MY FIRST ESCAPE--EVEN AS A KID I DIDN'T TRUST THAT BASTARD, AND I DIDN'T DRINK MY KWENCH.
"JAMES SACRIFICED THEM TO SOME DEMON, BURNT THEIR BODIES. HE HAD SOMEONE STAND IN AS HIS CORPSE THEN TO THROW OFF THE SURINAME POLICE. I USED HIS OWN TRICK AGAINST HIM.
"I'VE SPENT MY LIFE TRACKING HIM AND HIDING WHENEVER HE GOT WIND OF ME. WHEN I SAW HIS WITCHES WERE AFTER YOU, TOO, I GAVE YOU THOSE CLUES. IF I COULDN'T TAKE HIM DOWN, I WANTED SOMEONE TO.
I SHOULD HAVE REALIZED YEARS AGO THAT BLAZING MAN WAS ANOTHER ONE OF HIS CULT SCHEMES.
I'VE BEEN POSING AS ONE OF THE DEAD SLAVES FOR DAYS AND ONCE YOU GOT HERE, I SAW MY CHANCE TO GET DOWN INTO THIS CAVE.
HA! BLAKE, WHEN WE'RE BACK ON THE EAST COAST, DINNER IS ON ME.
I HATE TO RUIN SUCH A GOOD STORY, ESPECIALLY ONE WITH SUCH CIRCULAR CLOSURE.
BUT.
I THINK I WAS VERY CLEAR ON THE PART THAT I CANNOT DIE AGAIN.
SLRTCH

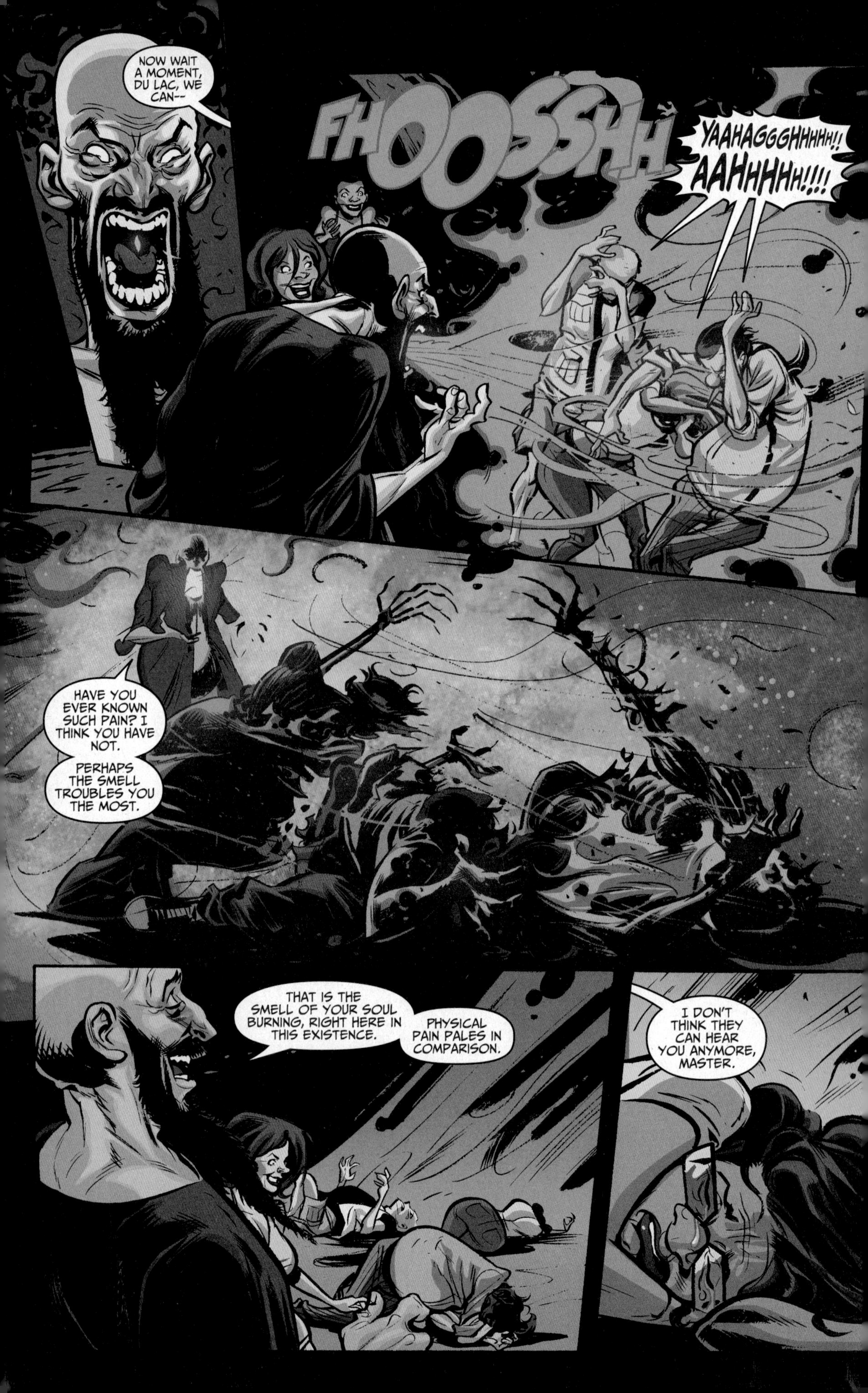
NOW WAIT A MOMENT, DU LAC, WE CAN--
FHOOSSHH
YAAHAGGGHHHHH!! AAHHHHH!!!!
HAVE YOU EVER KNOWN SUCH PAIN? I THINK YOU HAVE NOT.
PERHAPS THE SMELL TROUBLES YOU THE MOST.
THAT IS THE SMELL OF YOUR SOUL BURNING, RIGHT HERE IN THIS EXISTENCE.
PHYSICAL PAIN PALES IN COMPARISON.
I DON'T THINK THEY CAN HEAR YOU ANYMORE, MASTER.

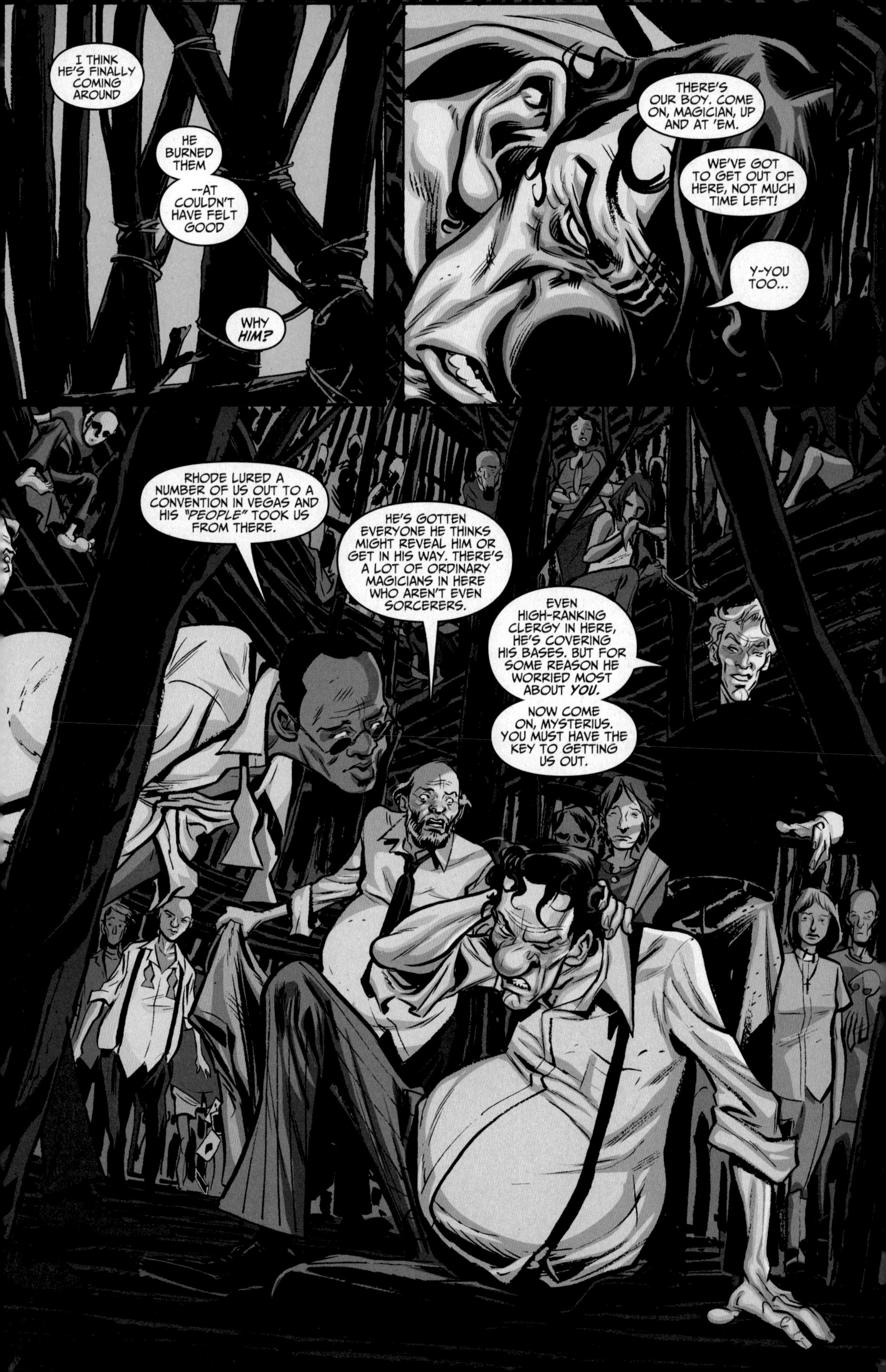
I THINK HE'S FINALLY COMING AROUND
HE BURNED THEM
--AT COULDN'T HAVE FELT GOOD
WHY *HIM?*
THERE'S OUR BOY. COME ON, MAGICIAN, UP AND AT 'EM.
WE'VE GOT TO GET OUT OF HERE, NOT MUCH TIME LEFT!
Y-YOU TOO...
RHODE LURED A NUMBER OF US OUT TO A CONVENTION IN VEGAS AND HIS *"PEOPLE"* TOOK US FROM THERE.
HE'S GOTTEN EVERYONE HE THINKS MIGHT REVEAL HIM OR GET IN HIS WAY. THERE'S A LOT OF ORDINARY MAGICIANS IN HERE WHO AREN'T EVEN SORCERERS.
EVEN HIGH-RANKING CLERGY IN HERE, HE'S COVERING HIS BASES. BUT FOR SOME REASON HE WORRIED MOST ABOUT *YOU.*
NOW COME ON, MYSTERIUS. YOU MUST HAVE THE KEY TO GETTING US OUT.

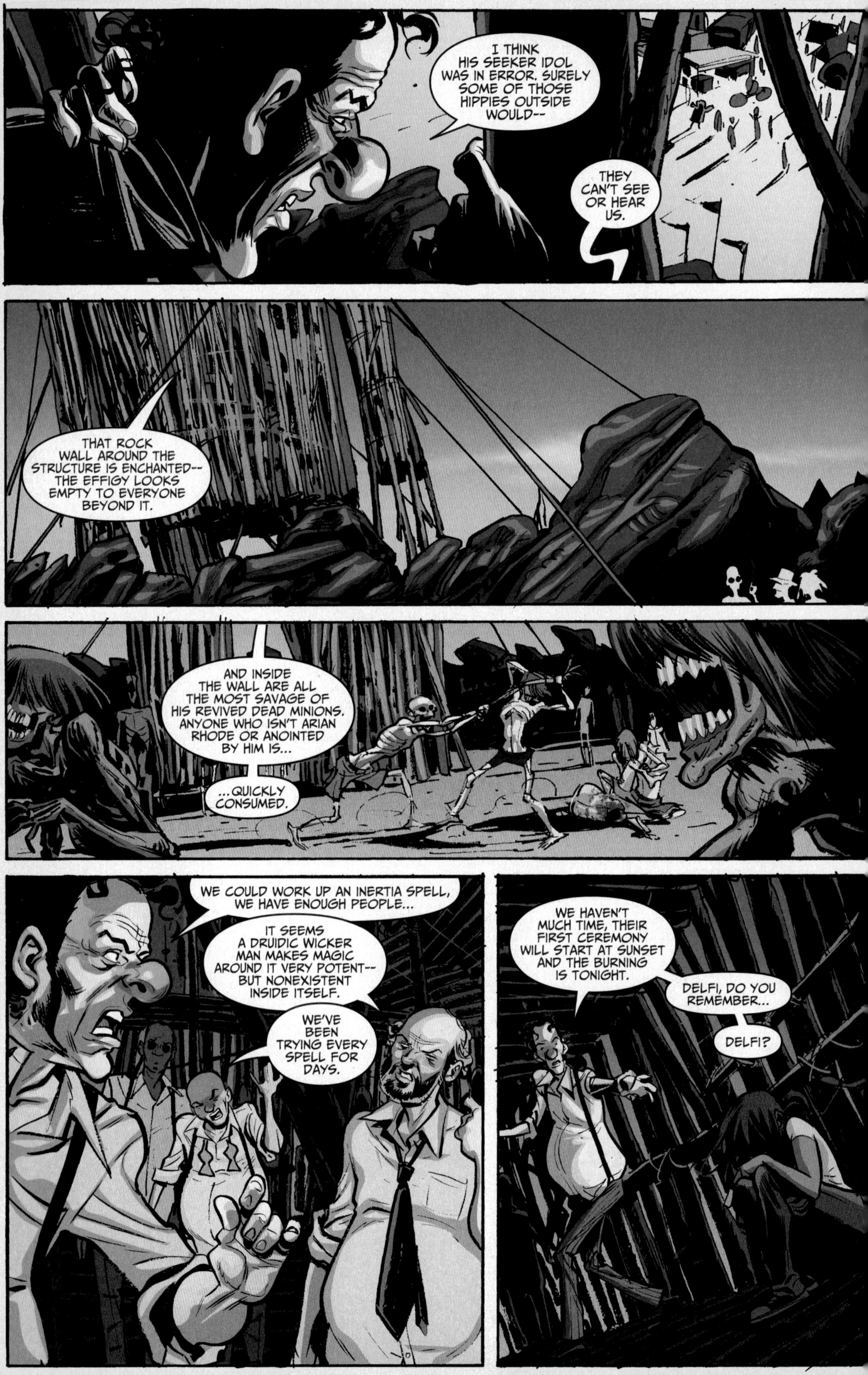
I THINK HIS SEEKER IDOL WAS IN ERROR. SURELY SOME OF THOSE HIPPIES OUTSIDE WOULD--
THEY CAN'T SEE OR HEAR US.
THAT ROCK WALL AROUND THE STRUCTURE IS ENCHANTED-- THE EFFIGY LOOKS EMPTY TO EVERYONE BEYOND IT.
AND INSIDE THE WALL ARE ALL THE MOST SAVAGE OF HIS REVIVED DEAD MINIONS. ANYONE WHO ISN'T ARIAN RHODE OR ANOINTED BY HIM IS...
...QUICKLY CONSUMED.
WE COULD WORK UP AN INERTIA SPELL, WE HAVE ENOUGH PEOPLE...
IT SEEMS A DRUIDIC WICKER MAN MAKES MAGIC AROUND IT VERY POTENT-- BUT NONEXISTENT INSIDE ITSELF.
WE'VE BEEN TRYING EVERY SPELL FOR DAYS.
WE HAVEN'T MUCH TIME, THEIR FIRST CEREMONY WILL START AT SUNSET AND THE BURNING IS TONIGHT.
DELFI, DO YOU REMEMBER...
DELFI?

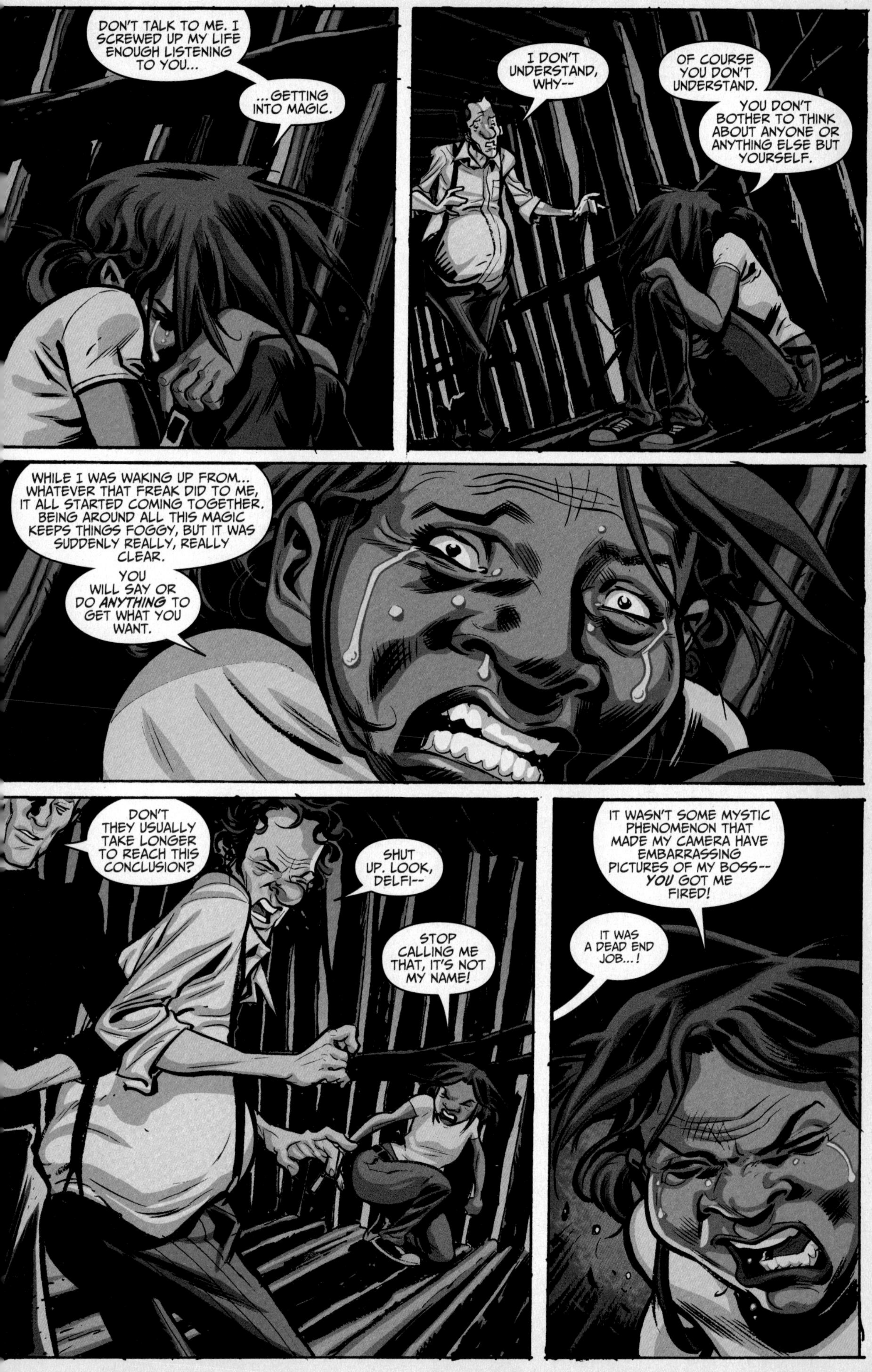
DON'T TALK TO ME. I SCREWED UP MY LIFE ENOUGH LISTENING TO YOU...
...GETTING INTO MAGIC.
I DON'T UNDERSTAND, WHY--
OF COURSE YOU DON'T UNDERSTAND.
YOU DON'T BOTHER TO THINK ABOUT ANYONE OR ANYTHING ELSE BUT YOURSELF.
WHILE I WAS WAKING UP FROM... WHATEVER THAT FREAK DID TO ME, IT ALL STARTED COMING TOGETHER. BEING AROUND ALL THIS MAGIC KEEPS THINGS FOGGY, BUT IT WAS SUDDENLY REALLY, REALLY CLEAR.
YOU WILL SAY OR DO *ANYTHING* TO GET WHAT YOU WANT.
DON'T THEY USUALLY TAKE LONGER TO REACH THIS CONCLUSION?
SHUT UP. LOOK, DELFI--
STOP CALLING ME THAT, IT'S NOT MY NAME!
IT WASN'T SOME MYSTIC PHENOMENON THAT MADE MY CAMERA HAVE EMBARRASSING PICTURES OF MY BOSS-- *YOU* GOT ME FIRED!
IT WAS A DEAD END JOB...!

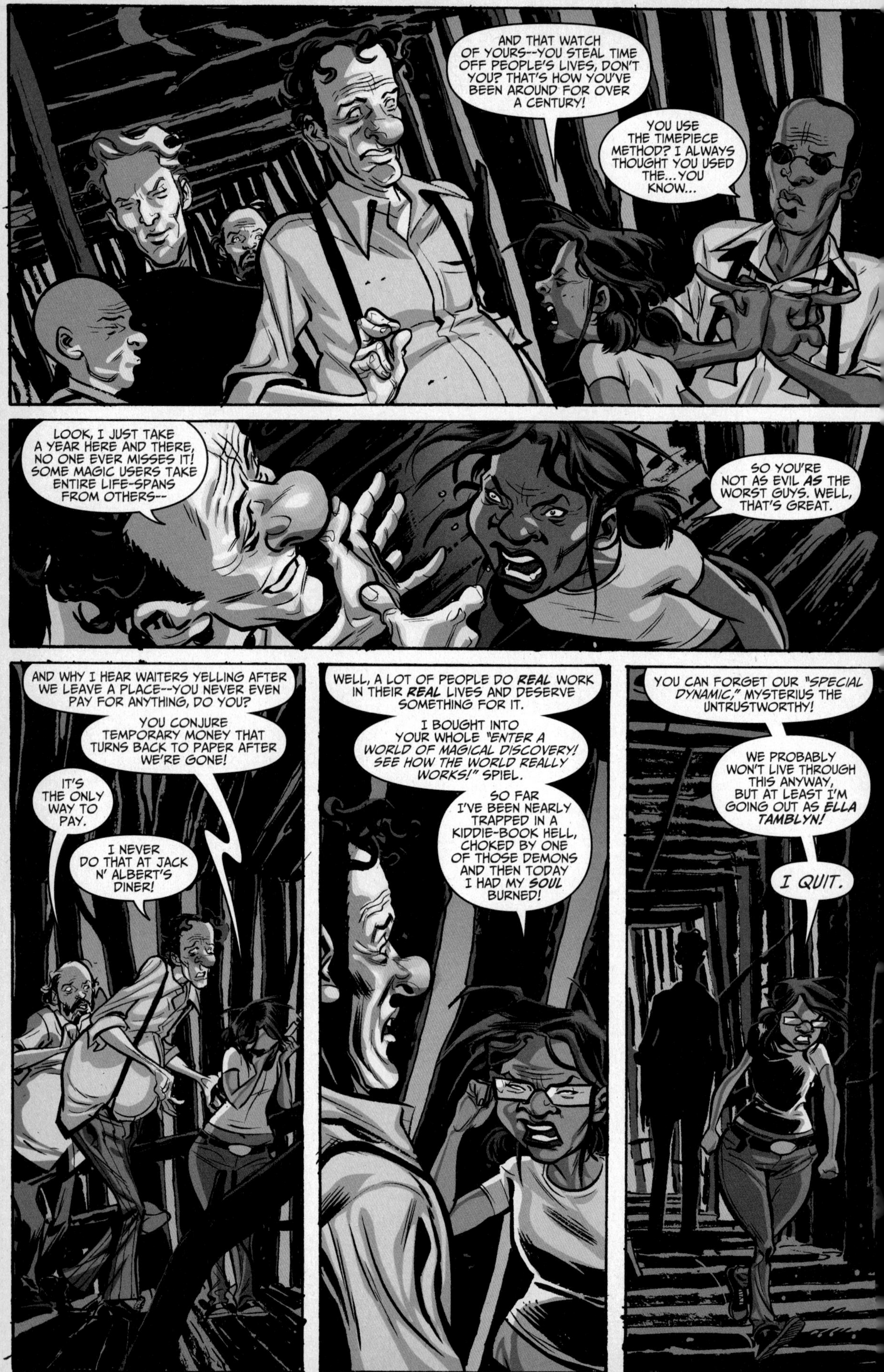
AND THAT WATCH OF YOURS--YOU STEAL TIME OFF PEOPLE'S LIVES, DON'T YOU? THAT'S HOW YOU'VE BEEN AROUND FOR OVER A CENTURY!
YOU USE THE TIMEPIECE METHOD? I ALWAYS THOUGHT YOU USED THE...YOU KNOW...
LOOK, I JUST TAKE A YEAR HERE AND THERE, NO ONE EVER MISSES IT! SOME MAGIC USERS TAKE ENTIRE LIFE-SPANS FROM OTHERS--
SO YOU'RE NOT AS EVIL *AS* THE WORST GUYS. WELL, THAT'S GREAT.
AND WHY I HEAR WAITERS YELLING AFTER WE LEAVE A PLACE--YOU NEVER EVEN PAY FOR ANYTHING, DO YOU?
YOU CONJURE TEMPORARY MONEY THAT TURNS BACK TO PAPER AFTER WE'RE GONE!
IT'S THE ONLY WAY TO PAY.
I NEVER DO THAT AT JACK N' ALBERT'S DINER!
WELL, A LOT OF PEOPLE DO *REAL* WORK IN THEIR *REAL* LIVES AND DESERVE SOMETHING FOR IT.
I BOUGHT INTO YOUR WHOLE *"ENTER A WORLD OF MAGICAL DISCOVERY! SEE HOW THE WORLD REALLY WORKS!"* SPIEL.
SO FAR I'VE BEEN NEARLY TRAPPED IN A KIDDIE-BOOK HELL, CHOKED BY ONE OF THOSE DEMONS AND THEN TODAY I HAD MY *SOUL* BURNED!
YOU CAN FORGET OUR *"SPECIAL DYNAMIC,"* MYSTERIUS THE UNTRUSTWORTHY!
WE PROBABLY WON'T LIVE THROUGH THIS ANYWAY, BUT AT LEAST I'M GOING OUT AS *ELLA TAMBLYN!*
I QUIT.

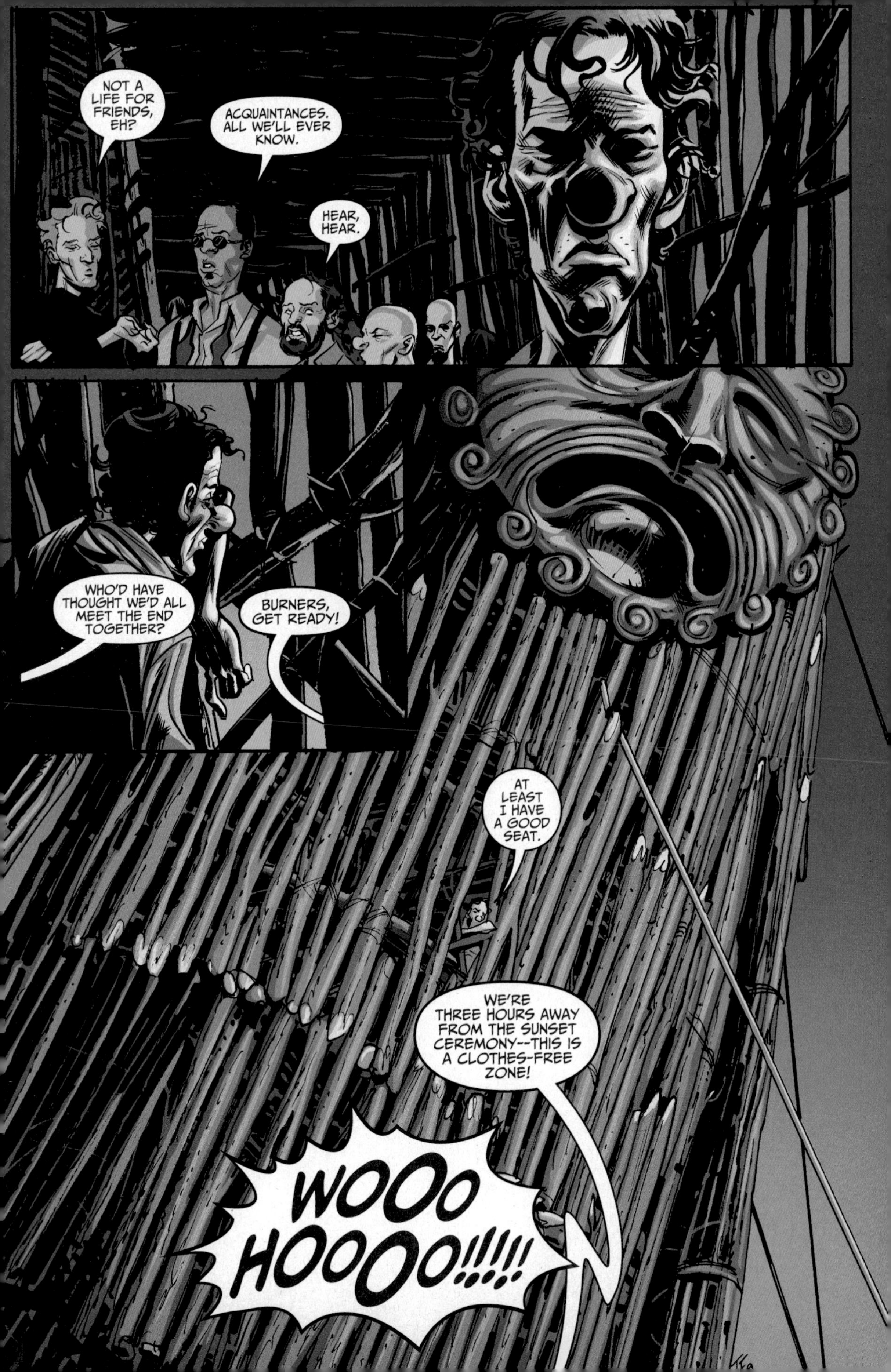
NOT A LIFE FOR FRIENDS, EH?
ACQUAINTANCES. ALL WE'LL EVER KNOW.
HEAR, HEAR.
WHO'D HAVE THOUGHT WE'D ALL MEET THE END TOGETHER?
BURNERS, GET READY!
AT LEAST I HAVE A GOOD SEAT.
WE'RE THREE HOURS AWAY FROM THE SUNSET CEREMONY--THIS IS A CLOTHES-FREE ZONE!
WOOO HOOOO!!!!!

The room erupted in chaos. Actors with prop spears poked at the Neanderthal, causing him to leap the orchestra pit, and the audience rolled over itself to avoid him. An usher tried to grab the primitive's arm only to be served a backhand that sent him over three rows of seats. "See, I was right about the propmaster," said Delfi, standing in her own seat to watch the turmoil. Now she saw the white of Mr. Garland's head emerge from the sea of people, pushing Belgand and pointing, his lips clearly mouthing an order. Brave little Belgand grabbed at a mass of rust-colored hair only to be sent into the curtains with one smooth kick. The Neanderthal bared his fangs and bellowed, spittle flying. Delfi felt sure that someone was going to be mortally wounded—the diva already looked dead, but was only frozen in shock. The worried assistant looked over to her boss standing still, a lone calm rock in a swirling ocean of madness. She felt reassured—someone was keeping his head and assessing the true nature of this event.

"He made me pick the surrounding cards...I even went with the ends, that usually thwarts any trick."

"Boss! Do you not see what is happening here?! Someone is going to get hurt!"

"We will be those someones if we try to stop the Neanderthal. Look, he's heading back down into...

Seven pages from the copy of **Diabolic Tales** *were largely obliterated here. From what survives, the gist of the missing section is Mysterius and Delfi finding another trap door under the stage that opens to a deep hole. Mysterius explains a legend about distant times connecting and how Freemasons sought to build over such natural wonders to keep them secret. Frantic that no women will ever want to perform at The Mammoth, Garland throws money at the magician until he and Delfi descend a ladder. The two feel gravity invert halfway down. They emerge in the distant past and find the frightened understudy with a Neanderthal tribe trying to indoctrinate her into their lifestyle. Mysterius frightens them with flash powder and other sleight-of-hand tricks that make most kneel in reverence. At this point the original missing diva emerges from the cave with what appears to be a loving Neanderthal mate, surprised to find the two investigators.*

"Of course!" blurted Delfi. "He wasn't kidnapping you—you've been having an affair for some time! You brushed his fur in your dressing room!" At that, the buxom singer scratched her mate's head.

"Gorru has been visiting me for weeks. My song carried through the ages and enchanted him, and he finally found the tunnel that led to me. His tribe began to think his stories insane—which apparently they discourage by killing the afflicted—so when he heard last night's performance he came for me. This era is the true time of romance, whenever it is."

Mysterius fought to hold in a smile. "Ah. Then your companion's friends realized they could also find...healthy partners in the 20th Century." Greta picked at Gorru's nits without looking up.

"No...I asked Kra-Ga there if he wouldn't fetch my understudy. No one plays Brunnhilde at The Mammoth but Greta Saxton. No one."

The understudy's eyes widened. She shook. Her mouth closed tight and then she snatched a large femur from a bone pile and lunged at Greta. Gorru shielded his mate and took the full blow in his wide face, blood gushing from his broad nose. Mysterius and Delfi wrestled with the understudy, pulling on her armored breastplate to drag her back.

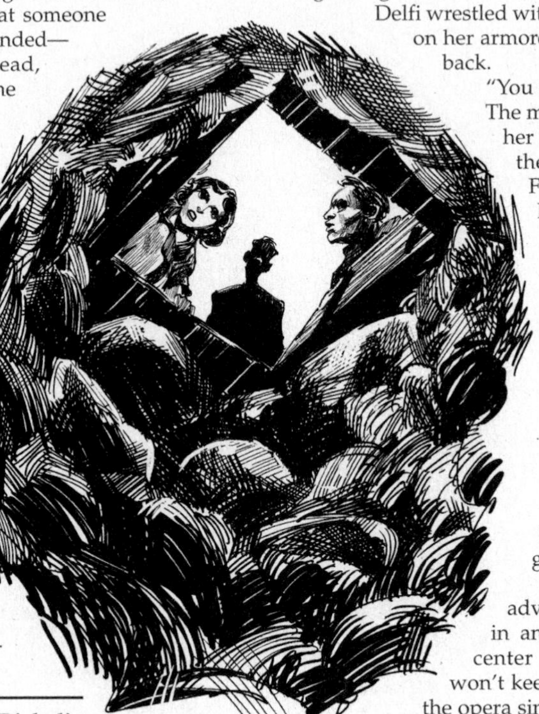

"You fool, they'll rip us apart!" The mystic investigators pulled her Rubenesque frame down the hill towards the pit. From the tall grass, several Neanderthals began to emerge, now less impressed at the otherworldliness of the visitors. Many began to growl. Mysterius reached down to grab the long ladder and his hand found nothing. Looking across he saw a group of apish children swinging the ladder around and breaking it apart. "We're going to die here."

Delfi looked back at the advancing cavemen. "Jump in anyway! Remember at the center gravity switches, we won't keep falling!" Mysterius and the opera singer stood at the precipice and wavered as more Neanderthals arrived. Delfi took in a breath and lunged at her fellow time-travelers, plunging them all into the hole.

"Only had a short climb," explained Mysterius as Garland poured the brandy. "We had such speed approaching the inversion point that we continued most of the remaining feet to where your brother had lowered the rope." Belgand paused a moment to appreciate his crucial place in the story, then placed another nail down on the trap door and resumed hammering the hatch closed.

"What if Greta wants to return?" asked Delfi. "Do Neanderthals have...ladder technology?" Garland swung his brandy snifter around and swallowed. "She should have thought of such things before having assignations with primitives in this hall. She sounds happy with her new...old boyfriend, and I'll say nothing of this to the papers. I'll not have busybodies tearing apart The Mammoth to explore some dead-end natural occurrence, anyway." He sipped his brandy. "Now a hole that led to the Baroque Period, that would be something."

Delfi took a drink and turned to say something to her boss, and then kept it to herself. Mysterius was laying out playing cards on the stage, contorting his face as he kept drawing and shuffling in frustration. The understudy knelt down to the stage and smiled as she handed Belgand more nails.

THE END

CHAPTER SIX· THE END

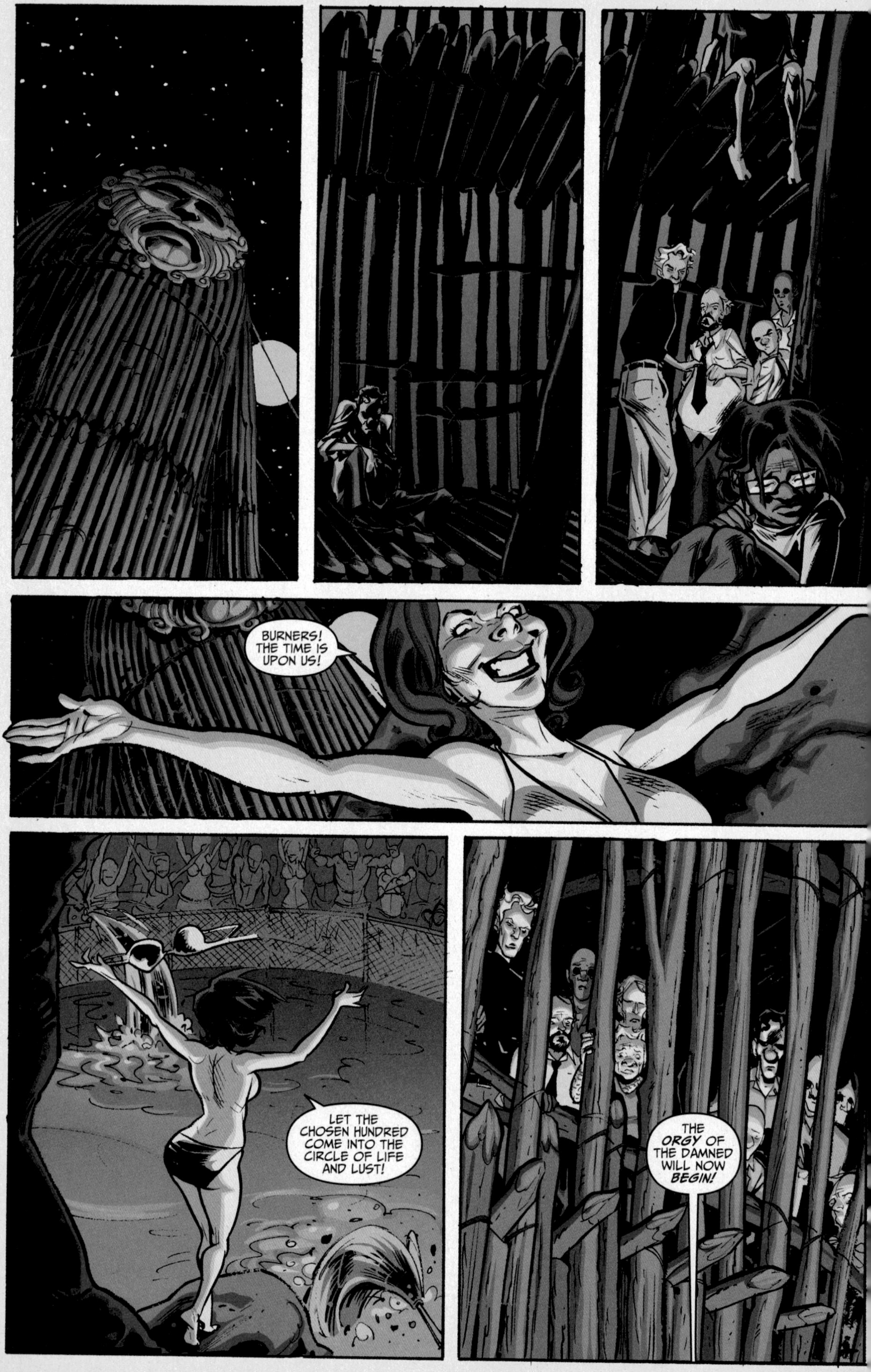
BURNERS! THE TIME IS UPON US!
LET THE CHOSEN HUNDRED COME INTO THE CIRCLE OF LIFE AND LUST!
THE *ORGY* OF THE DAMNED WILL NOW *BEGIN!*

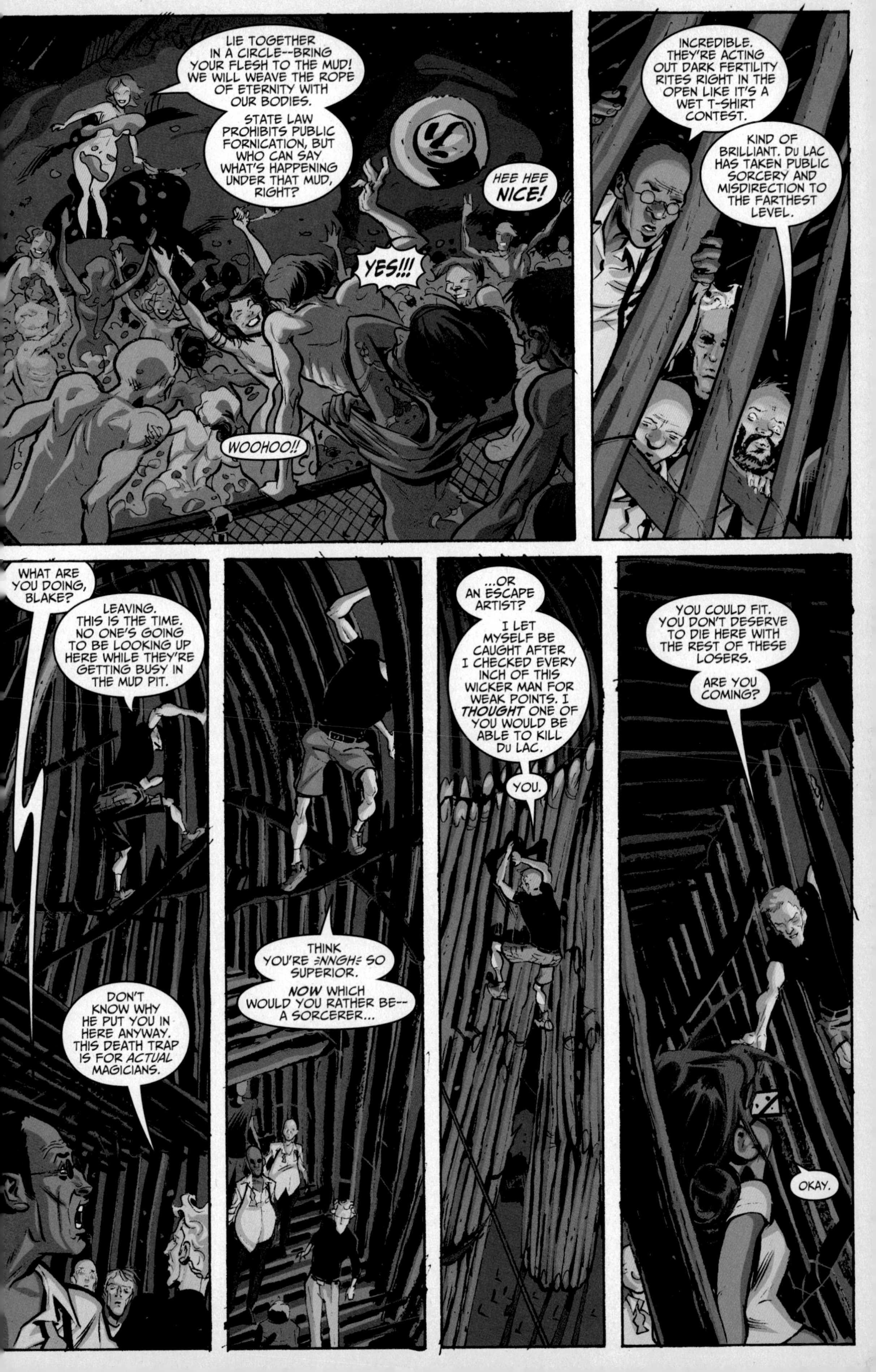
LIE TOGETHER IN A CIRCLE--BRING YOUR FLESH TO THE MUD! WE WILL WEAVE THE ROPE OF ETERNITY WITH OUR BODIES.
STATE LAW PROHIBITS PUBLIC FORNICATION, BUT WHO CAN SAY WHAT'S HAPPENING UNDER THAT MUD, RIGHT?
HEE HEE NICE!
YES!!!
WOOHOO!!
INCREDIBLE. THEY'RE ACTING OUT DARK FERTILITY RITES RIGHT IN THE OPEN LIKE IT'S A WET T-SHIRT CONTEST.
KIND OF BRILLIANT. DU LAC HAS TAKEN PUBLIC SORCERY AND MISDIRECTION TO THE FARTHEST LEVEL.
WHAT ARE YOU DOING, BLAKE?
LEAVING. THIS IS THE TIME. NO ONE'S GOING TO BE LOOKING UP HERE WHILE THEY'RE GETTING BUSY IN THE MUD PIT.
DON'T KNOW WHY HE PUT YOU IN HERE ANYWAY. THIS DEATH TRAP IS FOR ACTUAL MAGICIANS.
THINK YOU'RE =NNGH= SO SUPERIOR.
NOW WHICH WOULD YOU RATHER BE--A SORCERER...
...OR AN ESCAPE ARTIST?
I LET MYSELF BE CAUGHT AFTER I CHECKED EVERY INCH OF THIS WICKER MAN FOR WEAK POINTS. I THOUGHT ONE OF YOU WOULD BE ABLE TO KILL DU LAC.
YOU.
YOU COULD FIT. YOU DON'T DESERVE TO DIE HERE WITH THE REST OF THESE LOSERS.
ARE YOU COMING?
OKAY.

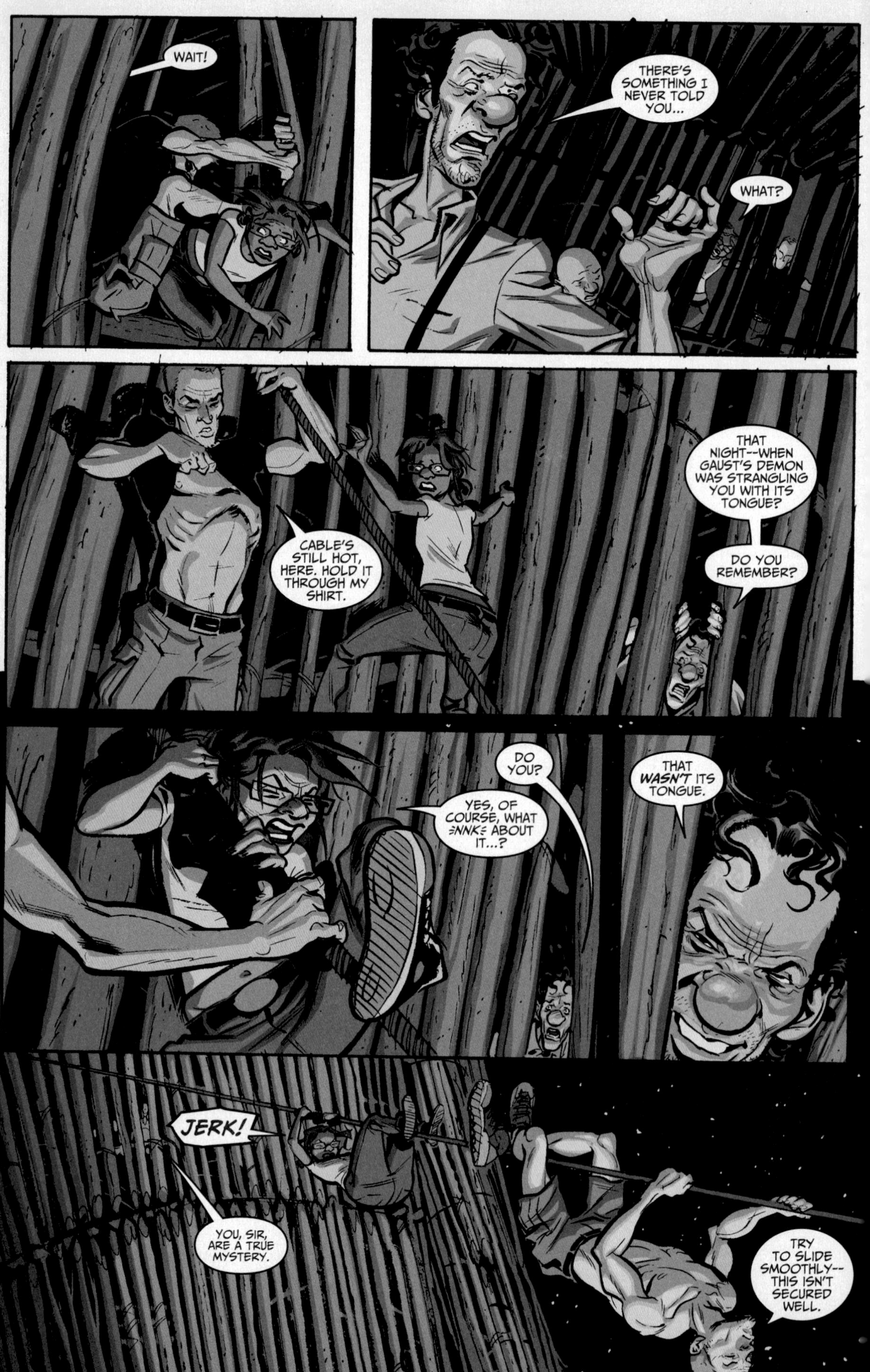
WAIT!
THERE'S SOMETHING I NEVER TOLD YOU...
WHAT?
THAT NIGHT--WHEN GAUST'S DEMON WAS STRANGLING YOU WITH ITS TONGUE?
DO YOU REMEMBER?
CABLE'S STILL HOT, HERE. HOLD IT THROUGH MY SHIRT.
DO YOU?
YES, OF COURSE, WHAT NNK ABOUT IT...?
THAT WASN'T ITS TONGUE.
JERK!
YOU, SIR, ARE A TRUE MYSTERY.
TRY TO SLIDE SMOOTHLY-- THIS ISN'T SECURED WELL.

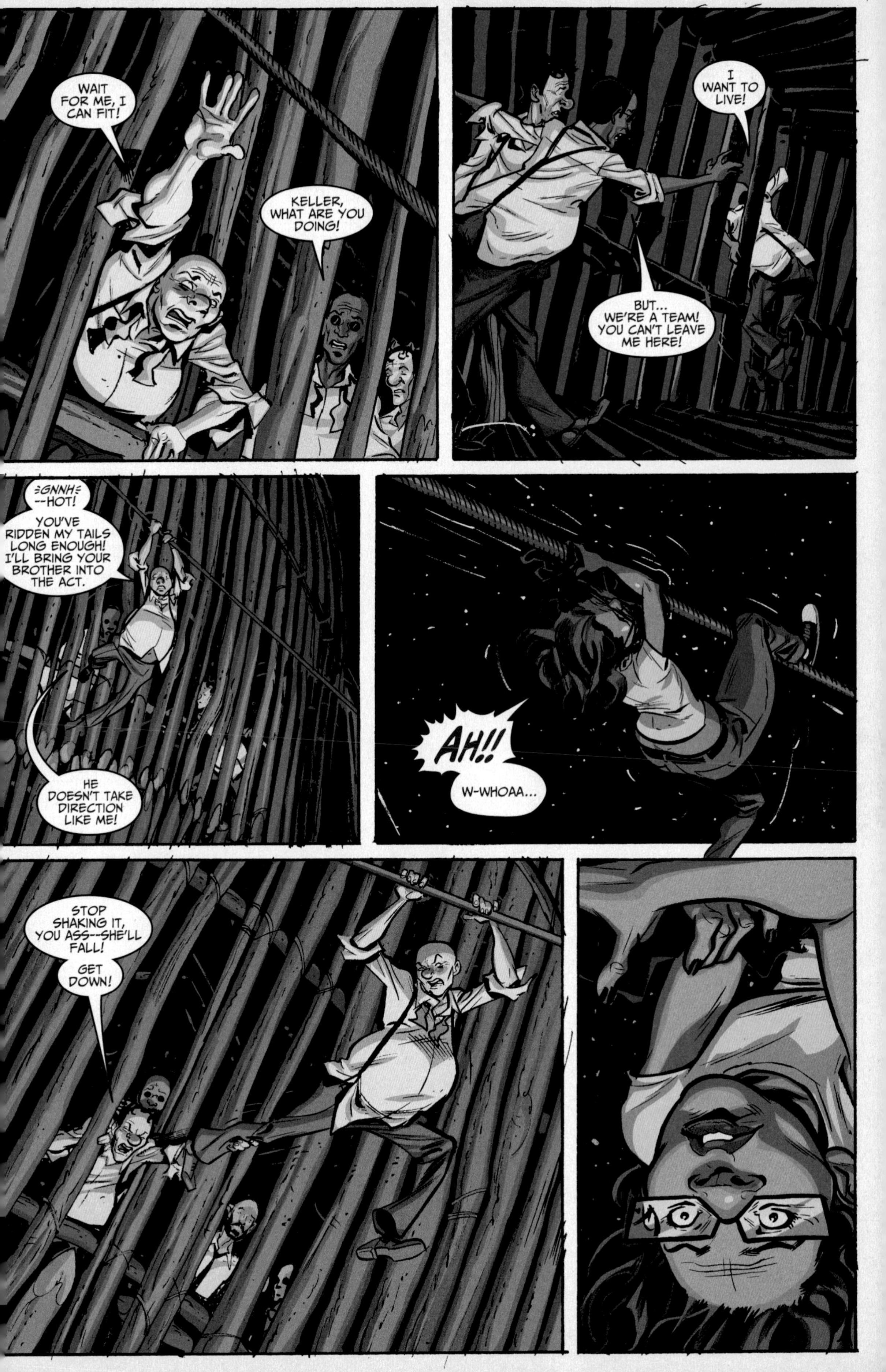
WAIT FOR ME, I CAN FIT!
KELLER, WHAT ARE YOU DOING!
I WANT TO LIVE!
BUT... WE'RE A TEAM! YOU CAN'T LEAVE ME HERE!
GNNH --HOT!
YOU'VE RIDDEN MY TAILS LONG ENOUGH! I'LL BRING YOUR BROTHER INTO THE ACT.
HE DOESN'T TAKE DIRECTION LIKE ME!
AH!!
W-WHOAA...
STOP SHAKING IT, YOU ASS--SHE'LL FALL!
GET DOWN!

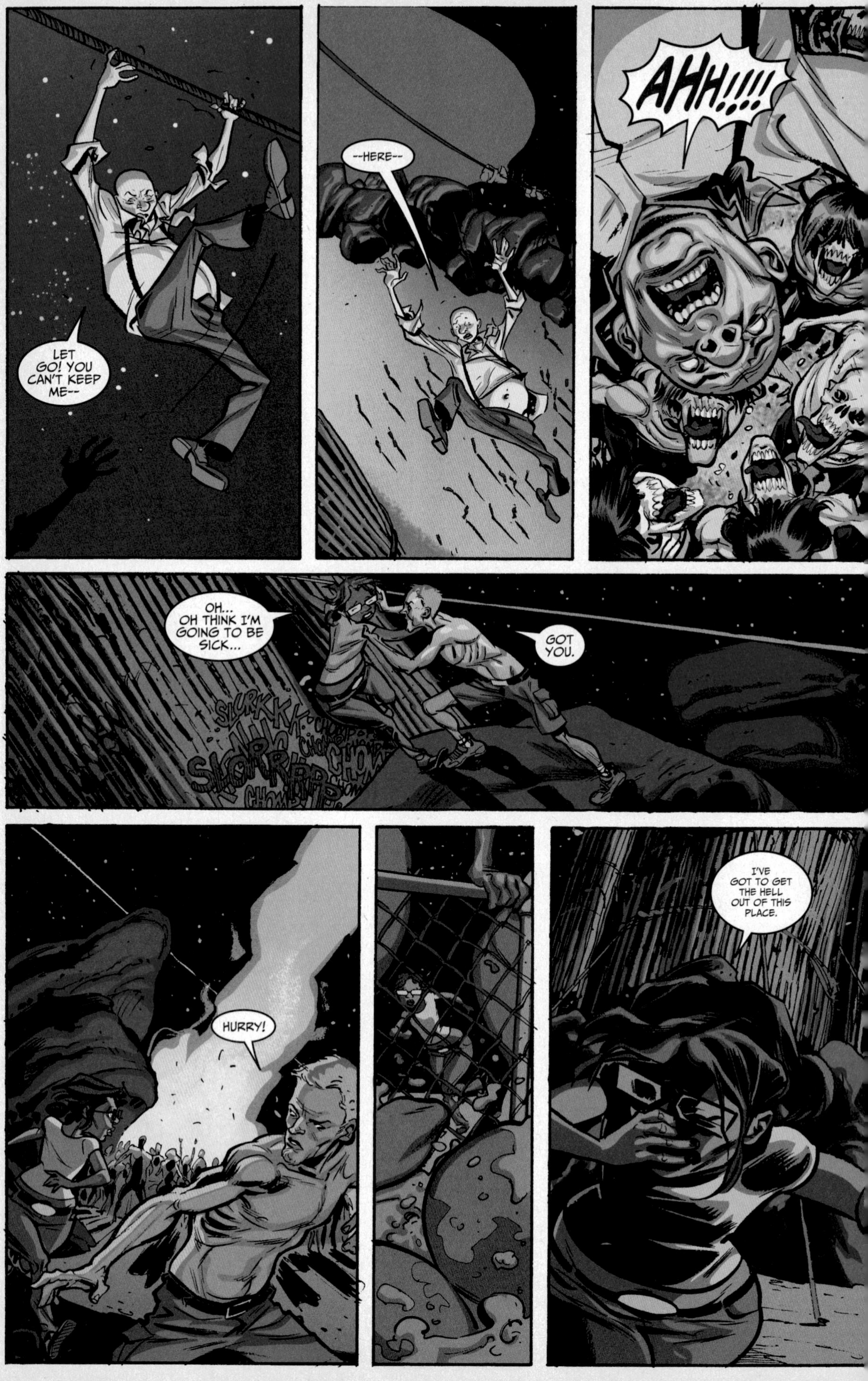
LET GO! YOU CAN'T KEEP ME--
--HERE--
AHH!!!!
OH... OH THINK I'M GOING TO BE SICK...
GOT YOU.
SLURKKK
HURRY!
I'VE GOT TO GET THE HELL OUT OF THIS PLACE.

MORE! LET MORE SOULS JOIN THE WORLD'S LOVE!

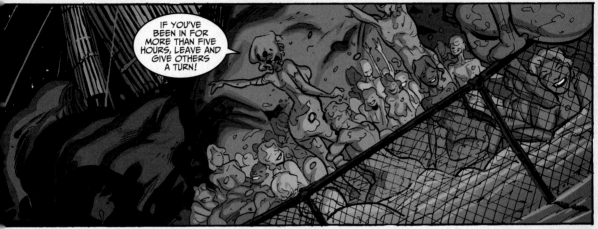

IF YOU'VE BEEN IN FOR MORE THAN FIVE HOURS, LEAVE AND GIVE OTHERS A TURN!

THEY'VE GONE ALL NIGHT! I BET THERE HAVEN'T BEEN ORGY RITES OF THIS SCALE SINCE THE FOURTH CENTURY.

IDIOTS. THEY'RE CHURNING UP UNIMAGINABLE POWER FOR DU LAC.

THAT BASTARD OVER THERE HAS *THREE* WOMEN!

THEY ALL LOOK BETTER UNDER MUD.

KEEP TELLING YOURSELF THAT.

WHAT CAN DU LAC DO WITH SO MUCH RAW POWER? HE'S ALREADY IMMORTAL!

YOU'RE THINKING LIKE SOMEONE WHO WANTS TO BE HUMAN, NOT A GOD. HE'LL BE ABLE TO DRAW ON LONG-LOST POWER.

START REMAKING CIVILIZATION TO HIS OWN TASTES.

I LIKE THE WAY YOU THINK.

FOR IT IS EXACTLY HOW I DO.

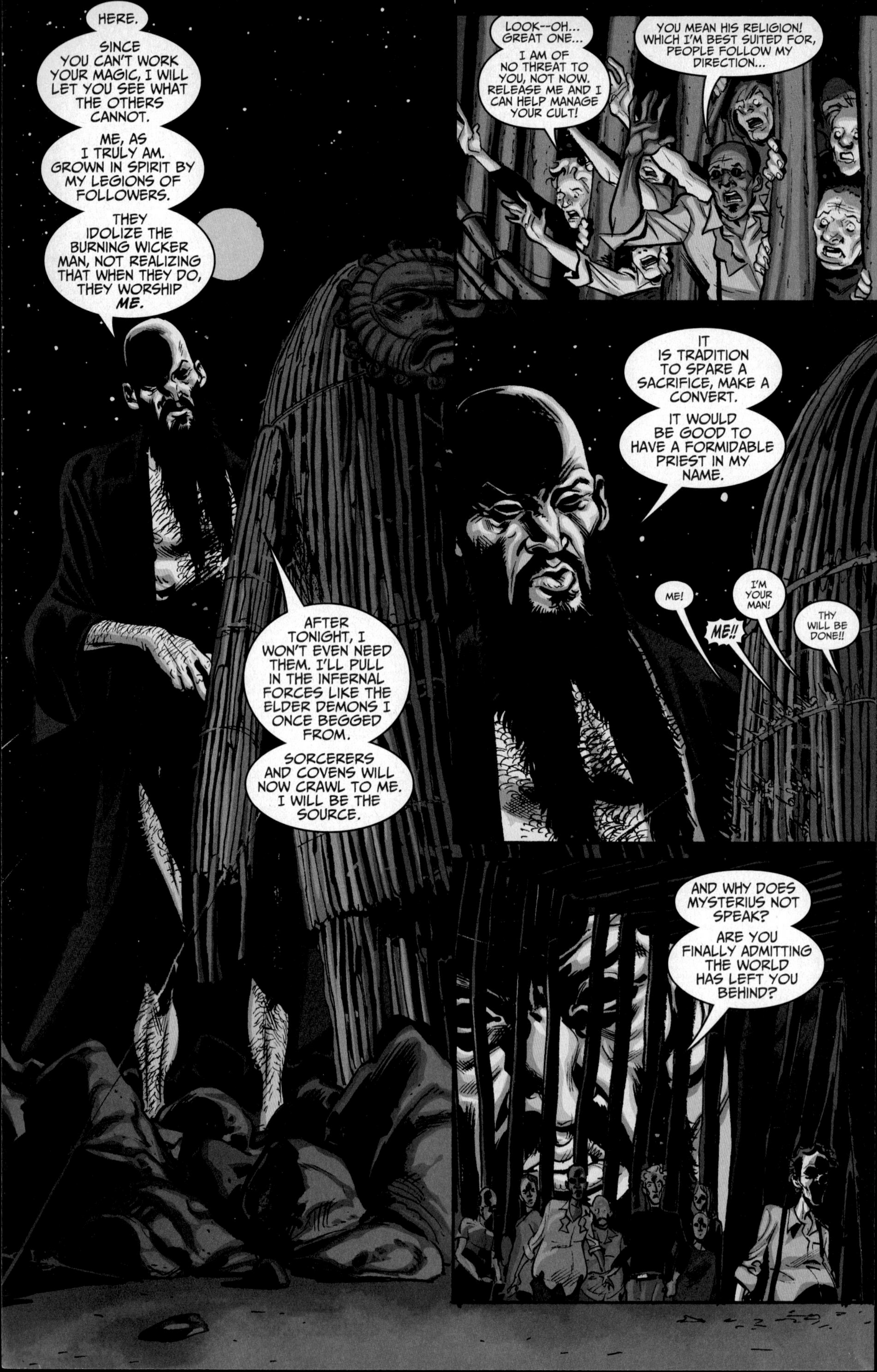
HERE.
SINCE YOU CAN'T WORK YOUR MAGIC, I WILL LET YOU SEE WHAT THE OTHERS CANNOT.
ME, AS I TRULY AM. GROWN IN SPIRIT BY MY LEGIONS OF FOLLOWERS.
THEY IDOLIZE THE BURNING WICKER MAN, NOT REALIZING THAT WHEN THEY DO, THEY WORSHIP *ME.*
AFTER TONIGHT, I WON'T EVEN NEED THEM. I'LL PULL IN THE INFERNAL FORCES LIKE THE ELDER DEMONS I ONCE BEGGED FROM.
SORCERERS AND COVENS WILL NOW CRAWL TO ME. I WILL BE THE SOURCE.
LOOK--OH... GREAT ONE...
I AM OF NO THREAT TO YOU, NOT NOW. RELEASE ME AND I CAN HELP MANAGE YOUR CULT!
YOU MEAN HIS RELIGION! WHICH I'M BEST SUITED FOR, PEOPLE FOLLOW MY DIRECTION...
IT IS TRADITION TO SPARE A SACRIFICE, MAKE A CONVERT.
IT WOULD BE GOOD TO HAVE A FORMIDABLE PRIEST IN MY NAME.
ME!
ME!!
I'M YOUR MAN!
THY WILL BE DONE!!
AND WHY DOES MYSTERIUS NOT SPEAK?
ARE YOU FINALLY ADMITTING THE WORLD HAS LEFT YOU BEHIND?

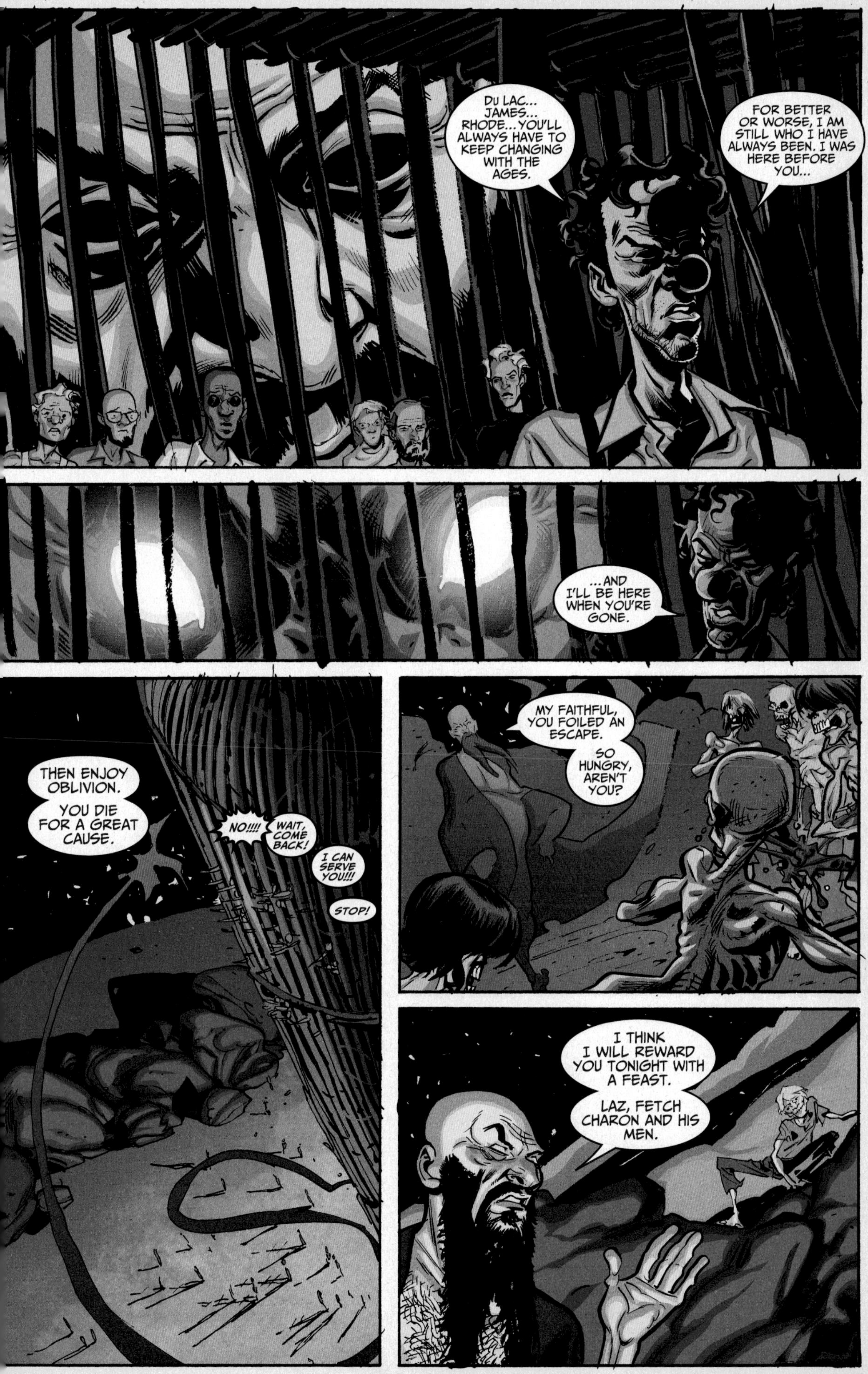
DU LAC...
JAMES...
RHODE...YOU'LL ALWAYS HAVE TO KEEP CHANGING WITH THE AGES.
FOR BETTER OR WORSE, I AM STILL WHO I HAVE ALWAYS BEEN. I WAS HERE BEFORE YOU...
...AND I'LL BE HERE WHEN YOU'RE GONE.
THEN ENJOY OBLIVION.
YOU DIE FOR A GREAT CAUSE.
NO!!!!
WAIT, COME BACK!
I CAN SERVE YOU!!!
STOP!
MY FAITHFUL, YOU FOILED AN ESCAPE.
SO HUNGRY, AREN'T YOU?
I THINK I WILL REWARD YOU TONIGHT WITH A FEAST.
LAZ, FETCH CHARON AND HIS MEN.

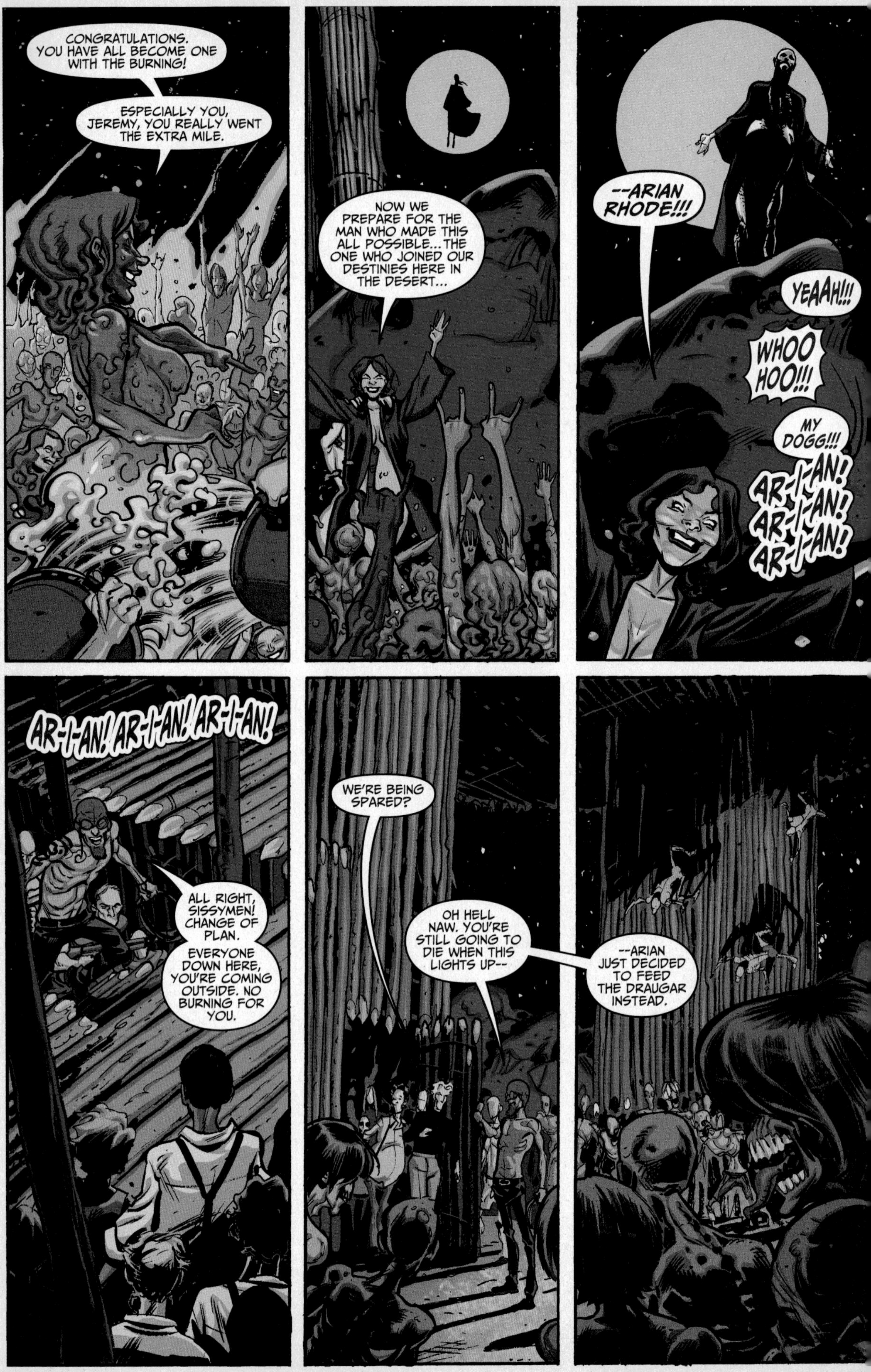
CONGRATULATIONS. YOU HAVE ALL BECOME ONE WITH THE BURNING!
ESPECIALLY YOU, JEREMY, YOU REALLY WENT THE EXTRA MILE.
NOW WE PREPARE FOR THE MAN WHO MADE THIS ALL POSSIBLE... THE ONE WHO JOINED OUR DESTINIES HERE IN THE DESERT...
--ARIAN RHODE!!!
YEAAH!!!
WHOO HOO!!!
MY DOGG!!!
AR-I-AN! AR-I-AN! AR-I-AN!
AR-I-AN! AR-I-AN! AR-I-AN!
ALL RIGHT, SISSYMEN! CHANGE OF PLAN.
EVERYONE DOWN HERE, YOU'RE COMING OUTSIDE. NO BURNING FOR YOU.
WE'RE BEING SPARED?
OH HELL NAW. YOU'RE STILL GOING TO DIE WHEN THIS LIGHTS UP--
--ARIAN JUST DECIDED TO FEED THE DRAUGAR INSTEAD.

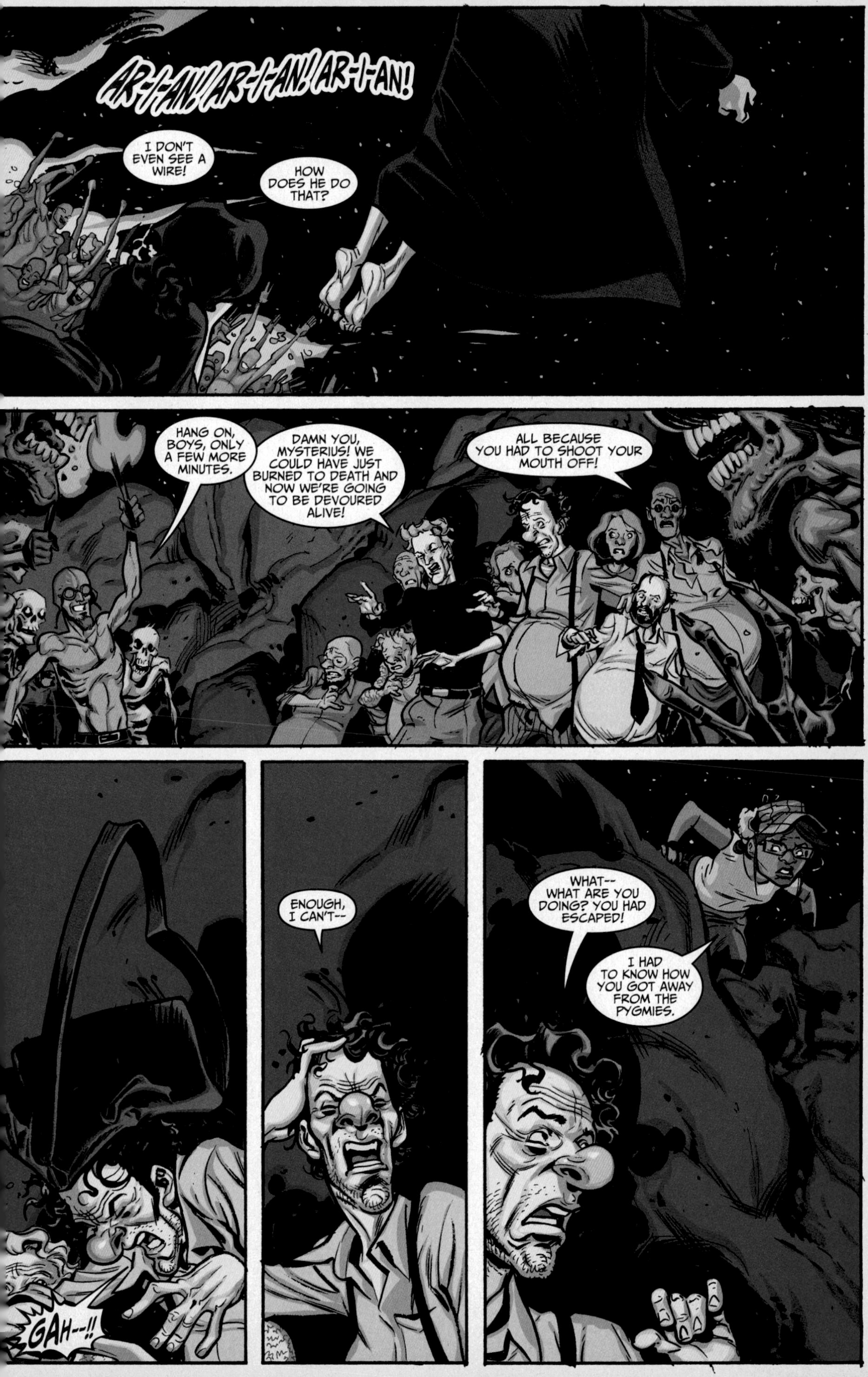
AR-I-AN! AR-I-AN! AR-I-AN!
I DON'T EVEN SEE A WIRE!
HOW DOES HE DO THAT?
HANG ON, BOYS, ONLY A FEW MORE MINUTES.
DAMN YOU, MYSTERIUS! WE COULD HAVE JUST BURNED TO DEATH AND NOW WE'RE GOING TO BE DEVOURED ALIVE!
ALL BECAUSE YOU HAD TO SHOOT YOUR MOUTH OFF!
GAH--!!
ENOUGH, I CAN'T--
WHAT-- WHAT ARE YOU DOING? YOU HAD ESCAPED!
I HAD TO KNOW HOW YOU GOT AWAY FROM THE PYGMIES.

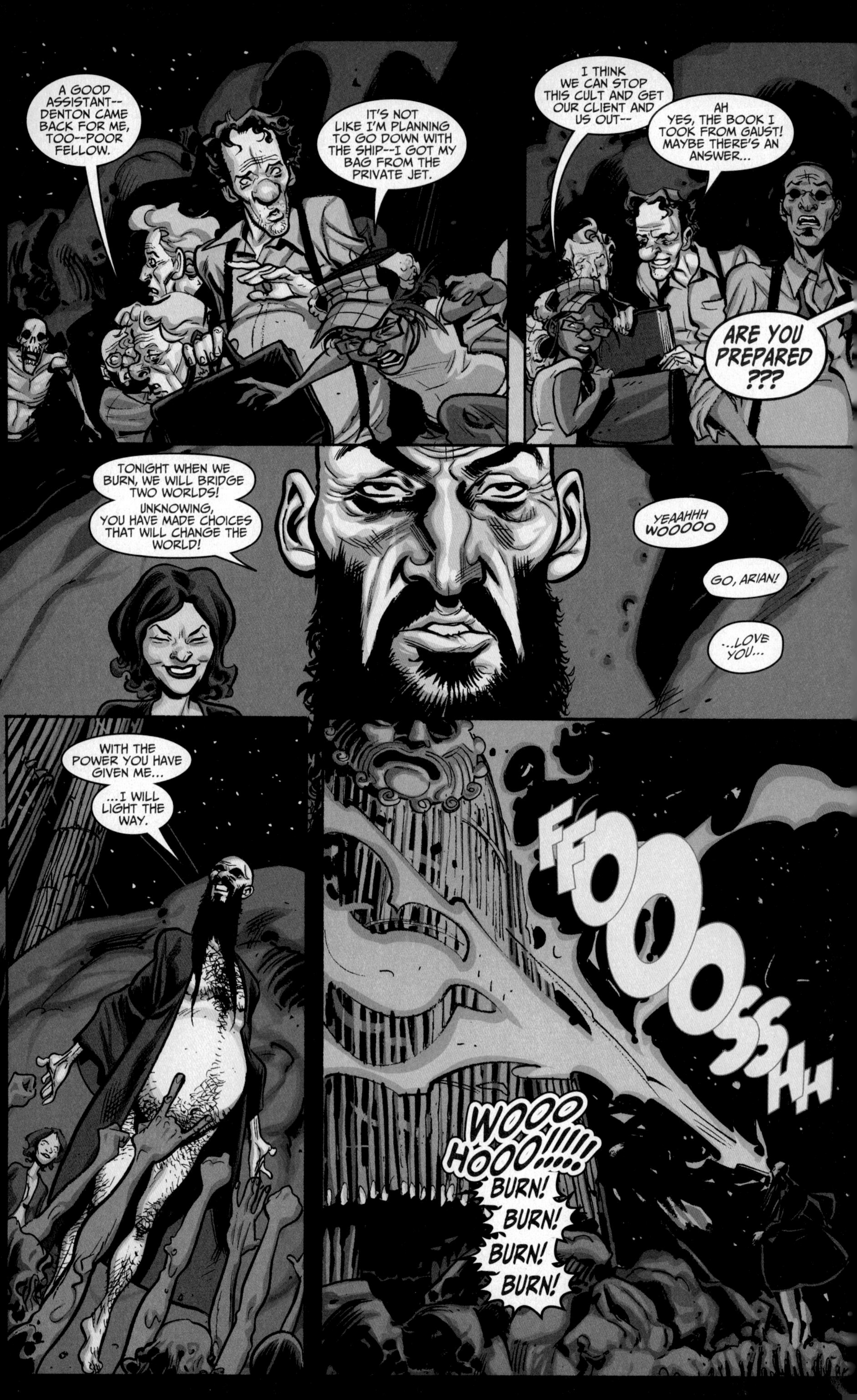

A GOOD ASSISTANT--DENTON CAME BACK FOR ME, TOO--POOR FELLOW.
IT'S NOT LIKE I'M PLANNING TO GO DOWN WITH THE SHIP--I GOT MY BAG FROM THE PRIVATE JET.
I THINK WE CAN STOP THIS CULT AND GET OUR CLIENT AND US OUT--
AH YES, THE BOOK I TOOK FROM GAUST! MAYBE THERE'S AN ANSWER...
ARE YOU PREPARED ???
TONIGHT WHEN WE BURN, WE WILL BRIDGE TWO WORLDS!
UNKNOWING, YOU HAVE MADE CHOICES THAT WILL CHANGE THE WORLD!
YEAAHHH WOOOOO
GO, ARIAN!
...LOVE YOU...
WITH THE POWER YOU HAVE GIVEN ME...
...I WILL LIGHT THE WAY.
FFOOOOSSHH
WOOO HOOO!!!!!!....
BURN!
BURN!
BURN!
BURN!

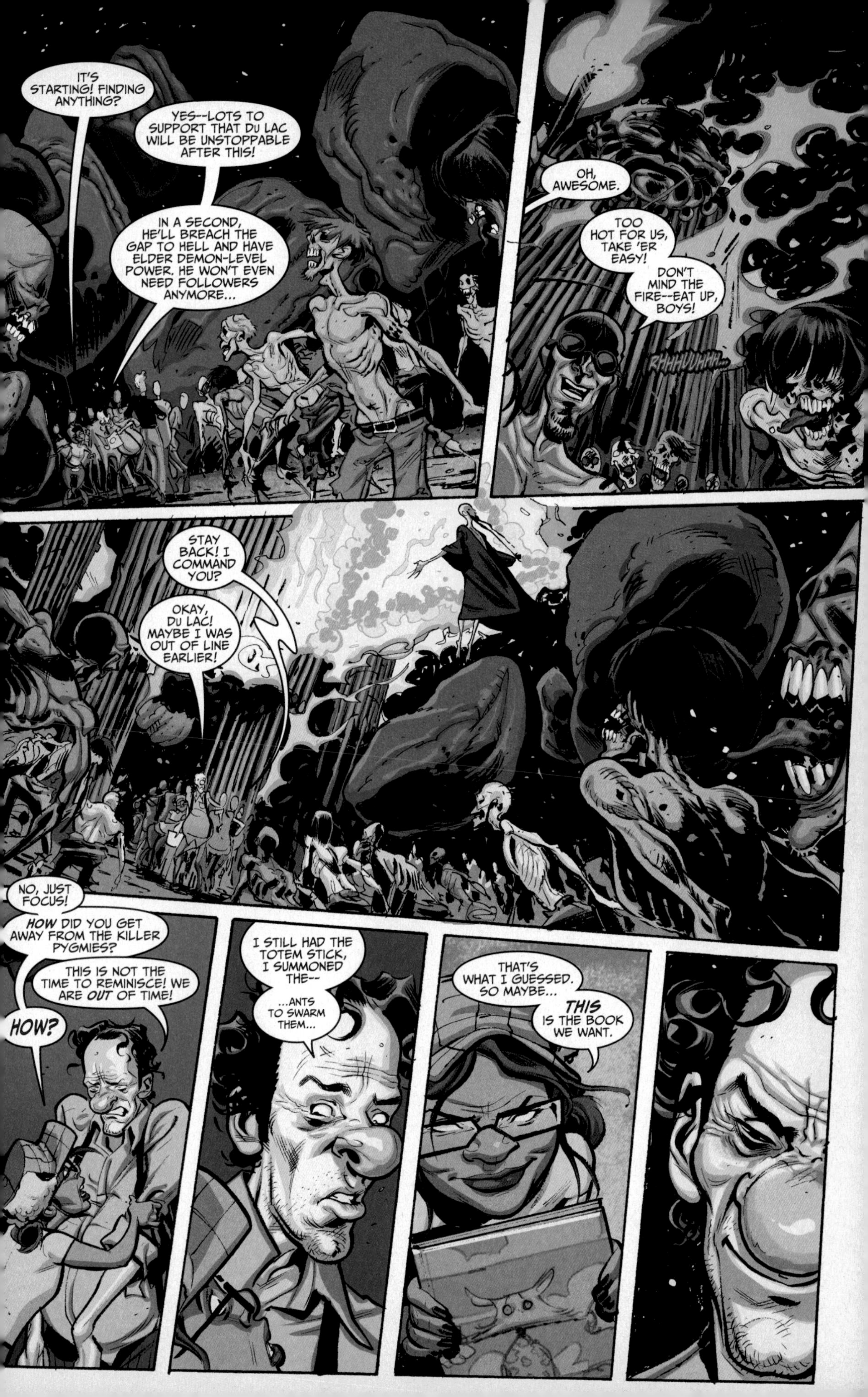
IT'S STARTING! FINDING ANYTHING?
YES--LOTS TO SUPPORT THAT DU LAC WILL BE UNSTOPPABLE AFTER THIS!
IN A SECOND, HE'LL BREACH THE GAP TO HELL AND HAVE ELDER DEMON-LEVEL POWER. HE WON'T EVEN NEED FOLLOWERS ANYMORE...
OH, AWESOME.
TOO HOT FOR US, TAKE 'ER EASY!
DON'T MIND THE FIRE--EAT UP, BOYS!
RHHHUUHHH...
STAY BACK! I COMMAND YOU?
OKAY, DU LAC! MAYBE I WAS OUT OF LINE EARLIER!
NO, JUST FOCUS!
HOW DID YOU GET AWAY FROM THE KILLER PYGMIES?
THIS IS NOT THE TIME TO REMINISCE! WE ARE OUT OF TIME!
HOW?
I STILL HAD THE TOTEM STICK, I SUMMONED THE--
...ANTS TO SWARM THEM...
THAT'S WHAT I GUESSED. SO MAYBE...
THIS IS THE BOOK WE WANT.

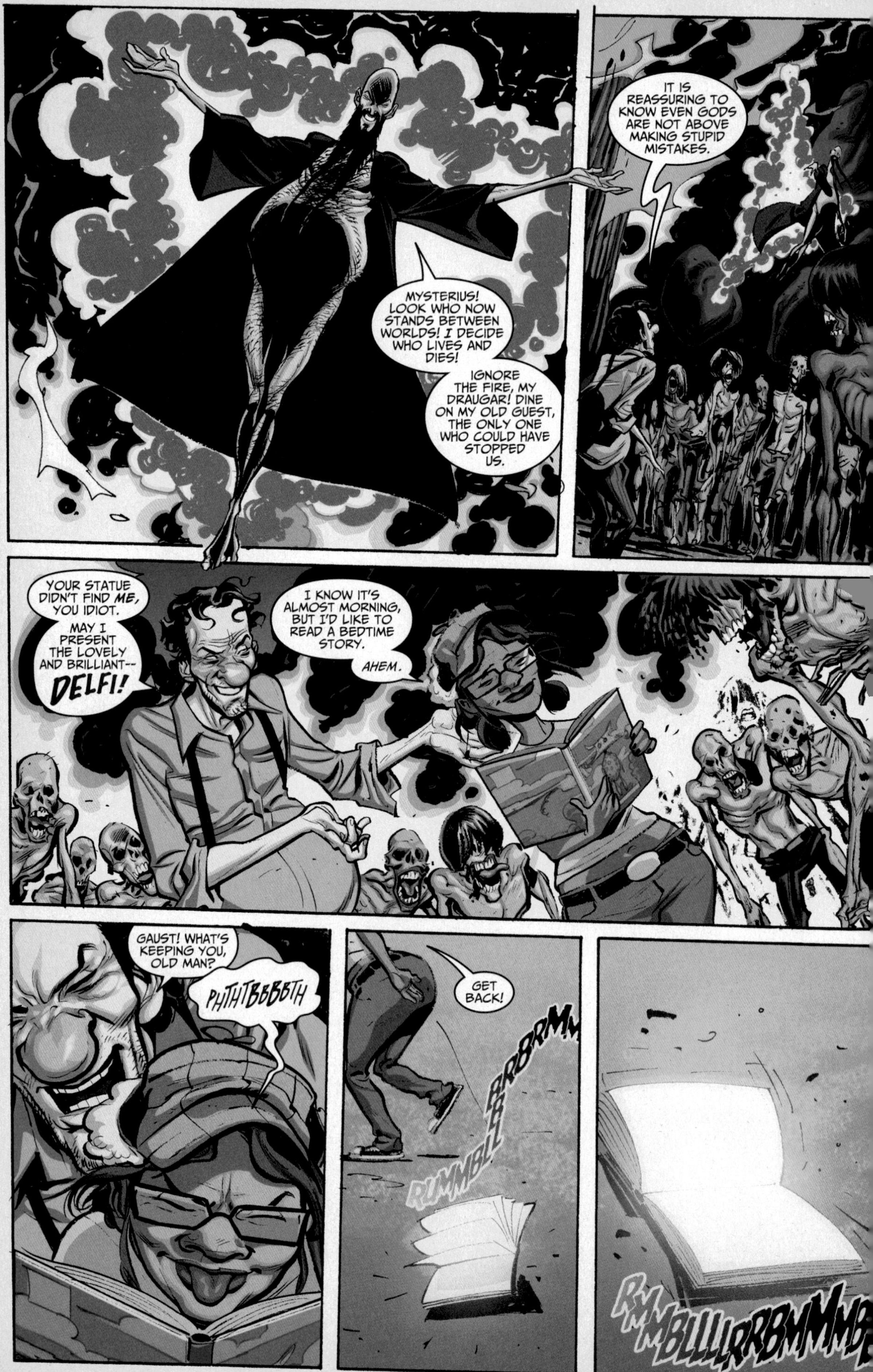
MYSTERIUS! LOOK WHO NOW STANDS BETWEEN WORLDS! I DECIDE WHO LIVES AND DIES!
IGNORE THE FIRE, MY DRAUGAR! DINE ON MY OLD GUEST, THE ONLY ONE WHO COULD HAVE STOPPED US.
IT IS REASSURING TO KNOW EVEN GODS ARE NOT ABOVE MAKING STUPID MISTAKES.
YOUR STATUE DIDN'T FIND *ME,* YOU IDIOT.
MAY I PRESENT THE LOVELY AND BRILLIANT--
DELFI!
I KNOW IT'S ALMOST MORNING, BUT I'D LIKE TO READ A BEDTIME STORY.
AHEM.
GAUST! WHAT'S KEEPING YOU, OLD MAN?
PHTHTBBBBTH
GET BACK!
RRBRRMM
RUMMBLL
RMMBLLLLRRBMMMB

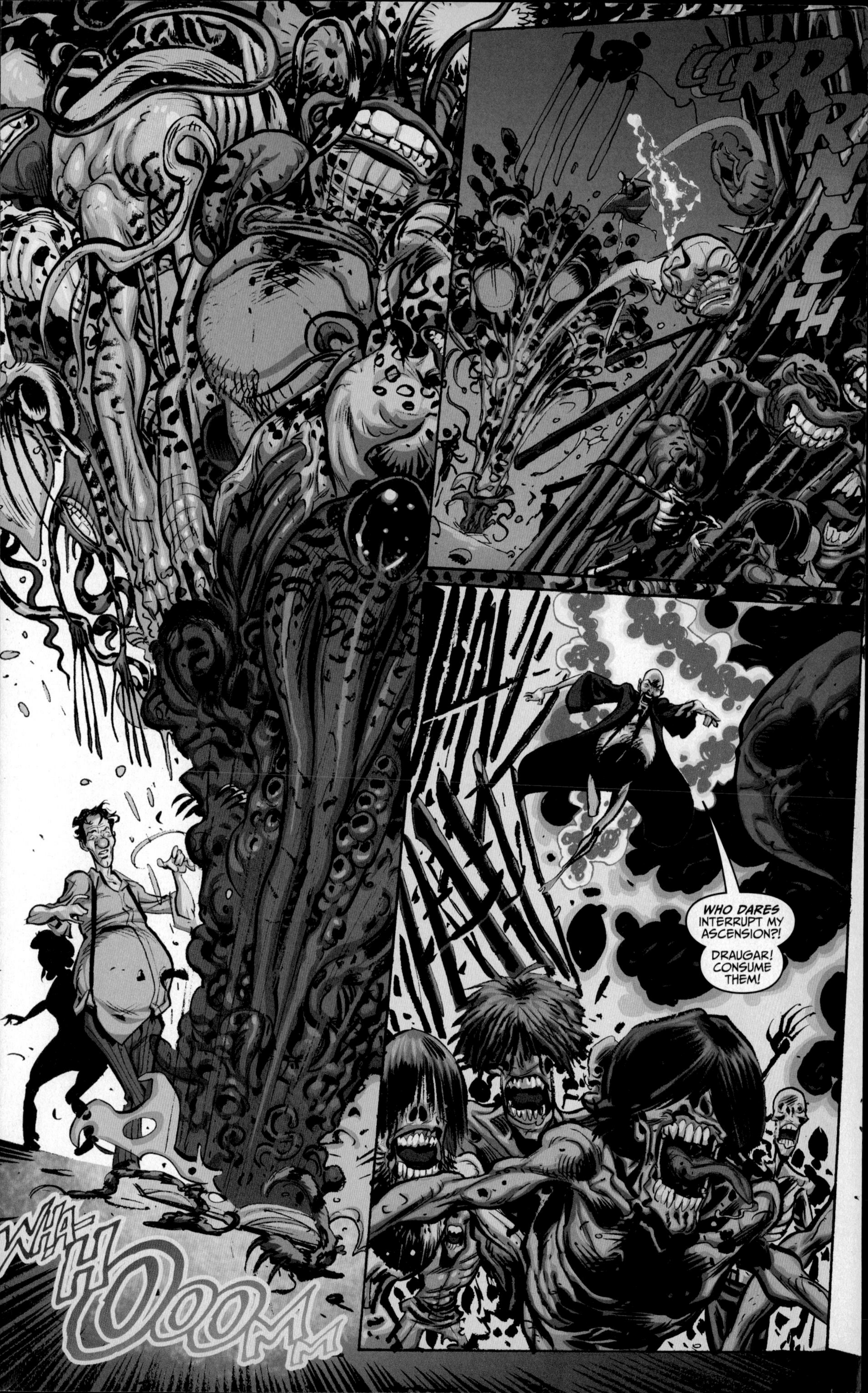
WHO DARES INTERRUPT MY ASCENSION?!
DRAUGAR! CONSUME THEM!

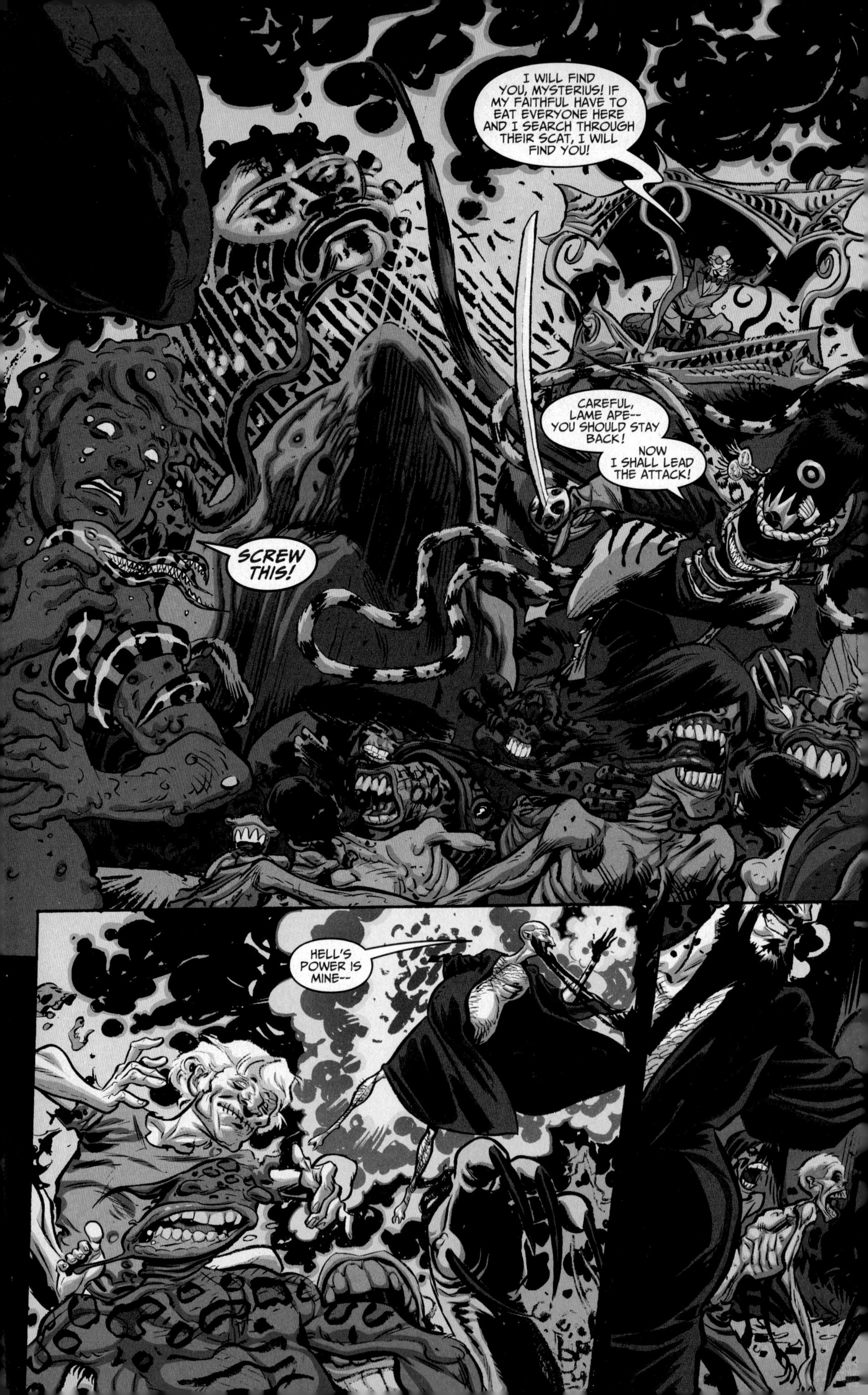
I WILL FIND YOU, MYSTERIUS! IF MY FAITHFUL HAVE TO EAT EVERYONE HERE AND I SEARCH THROUGH THEIR SCAT, I WILL FIND YOU!
CAREFUL, LAME APE-- YOU SHOULD STAY BACK!
NOW I SHALL LEAD THE ATTACK!
SCREW THIS!
HELL'S POWER IS MINE--

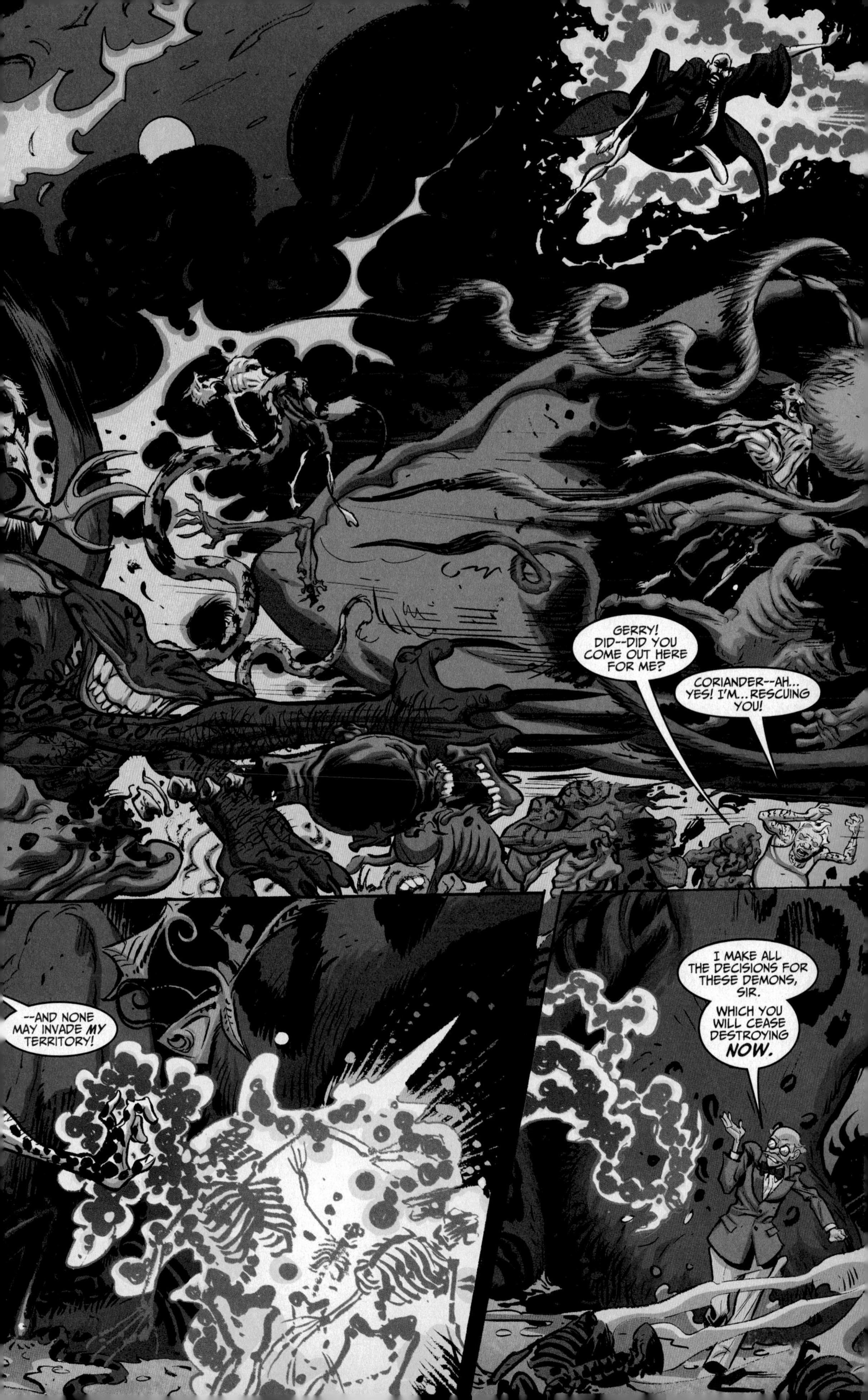
GERRY! DID--DID YOU COME OUT HERE FOR ME?
CORIANDER--AH... YES! I'M...RESCUING YOU!
--AND NONE MAY INVADE *MY* TERRITORY!
I MAKE ALL THE DECISIONS FOR THESE DEMONS, SIR.
WHICH YOU WILL CEASE DESTROYING **NOW.**

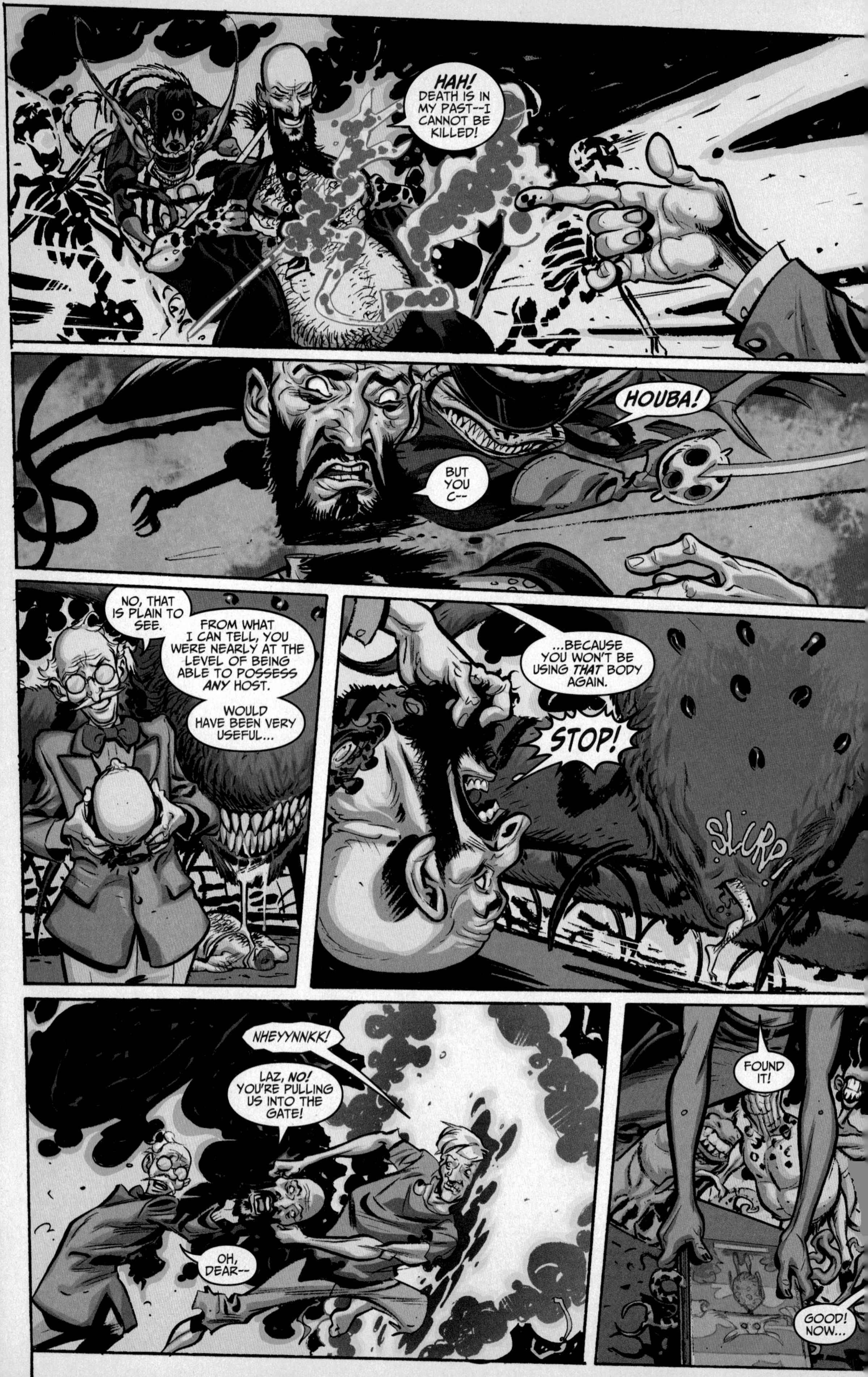
HAH! DEATH IS IN MY PAST--I CANNOT BE KILLED!
HOUBA!
BUT YOU C--
NO, THAT IS PLAIN TO SEE.
FROM WHAT I CAN TELL, YOU WERE NEARLY AT THE LEVEL OF BEING ABLE TO POSSESS ANY HOST.
WOULD HAVE BEEN VERY USEFUL...
...BECAUSE YOU WON'T BE USING THAT BODY AGAIN.
STOP!
SLURP!
NHEYYNNKK!
LAZ, NO! YOU'RE PULLING US INTO THE GATE!
OH, DEAR--
FOUND IT!
GOOD! NOW...

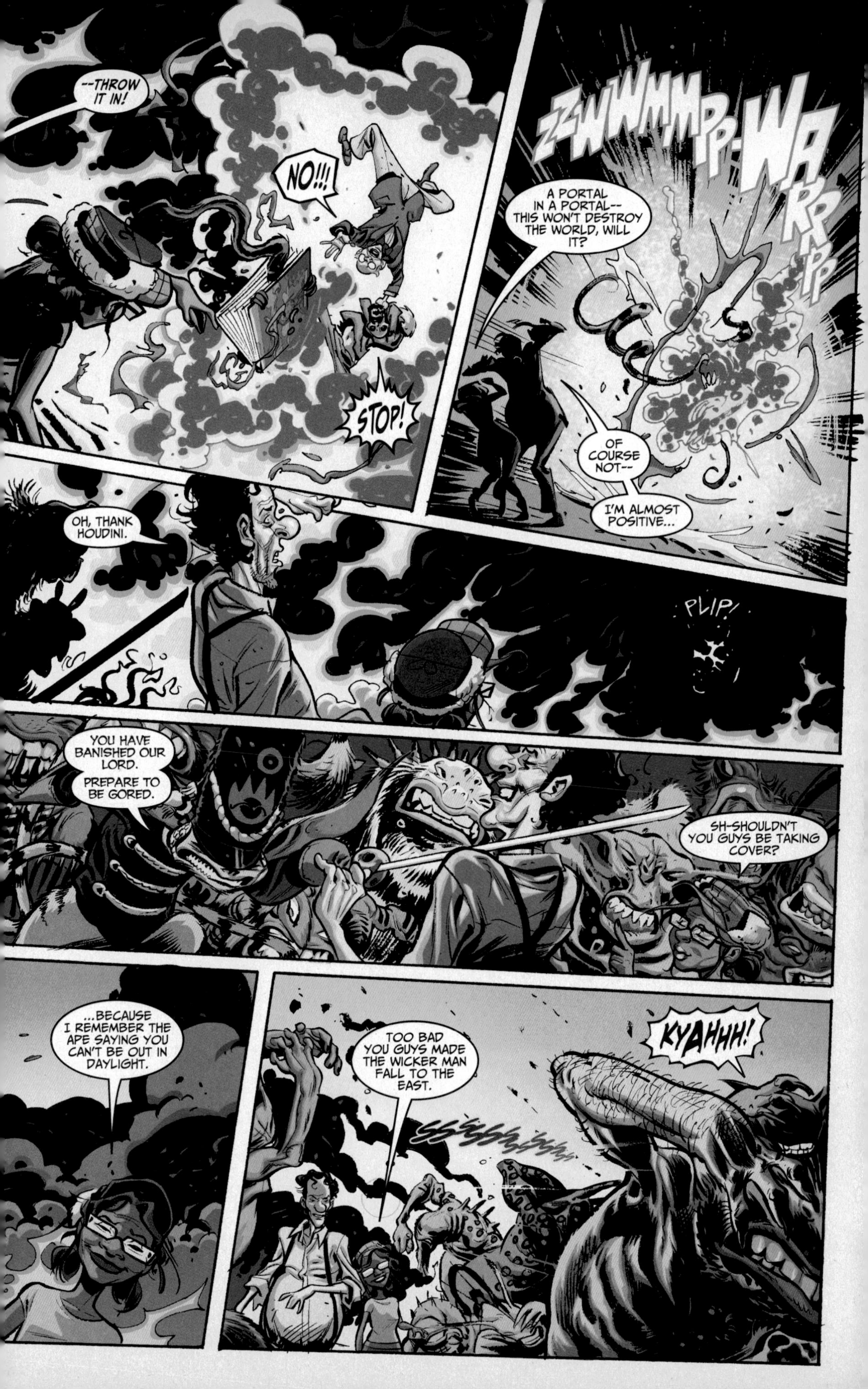
--THROW IT IN!
NO!!!
STOP!
ZZWWMMPP-WARRPP
A PORTAL IN A PORTAL-- THIS WON'T DESTROY THE WORLD, WILL IT?
OF COURSE NOT--
I'M ALMOST POSITIVE...
OH, THANK HOUDINI.
PLIP!
YOU HAVE BANISHED OUR LORD.
PREPARE TO BE GORED.
SH-SHOULDN'T YOU GUYS BE TAKING COVER?
...BECAUSE I REMEMBER THE APE SAYING YOU CAN'T BE OUT IN DAYLIGHT.
TOO BAD YOU GUYS MADE THE WICKER MAN FALL TO THE EAST.
KYAHHH!

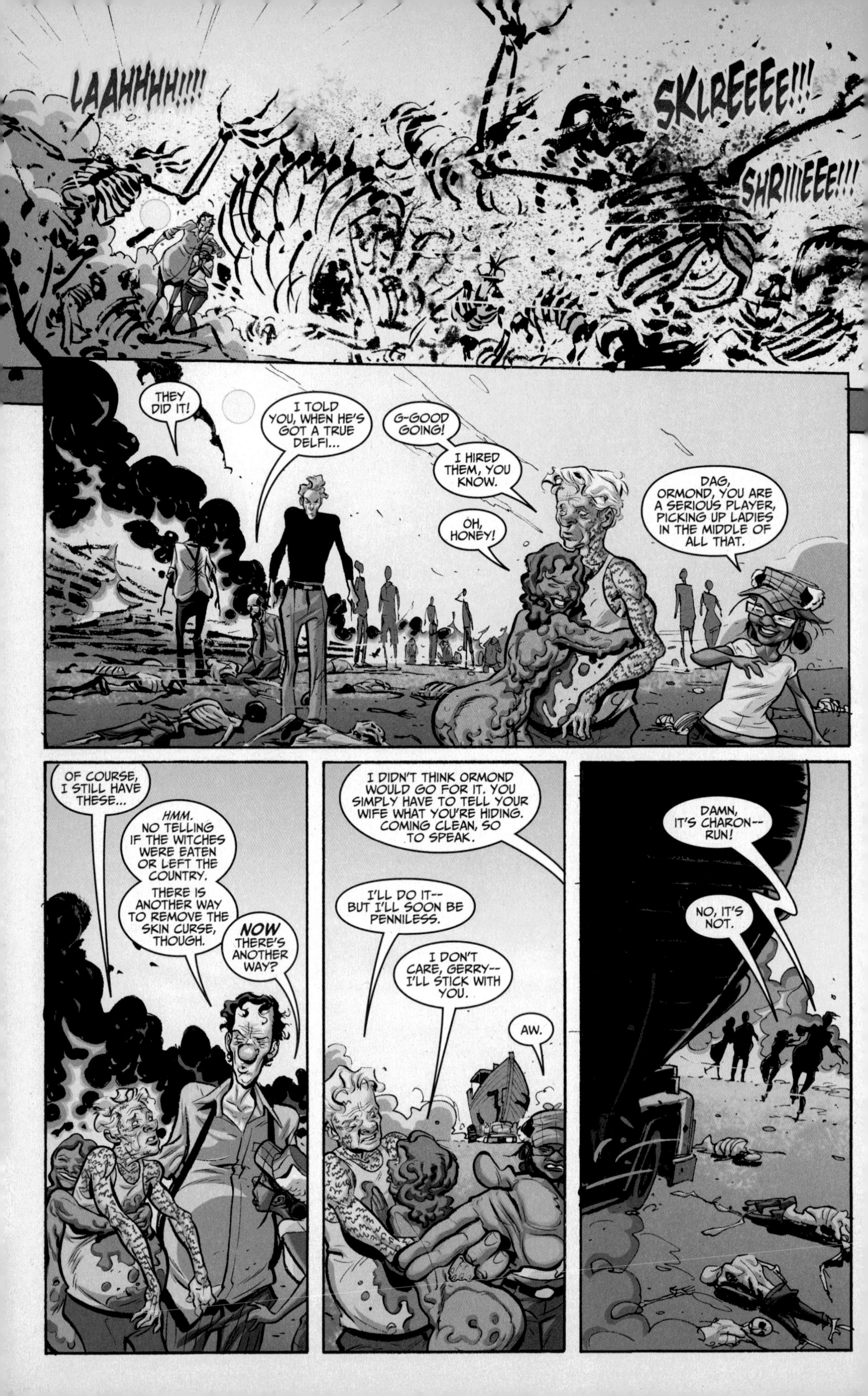
LAAHHHH!!!!
SKLREEEEE!!!
SHRIIIEEE!!!
THEY DID IT!
I TOLD YOU, WHEN HE'S GOT A TRUE DELFI...
G-GOOD GOING!
I HIRED THEM, YOU KNOW.
OH, HONEY!
DAG, ORMOND, YOU ARE A SERIOUS PLAYER, PICKING UP LADIES IN THE MIDDLE OF ALL THAT.
OF COURSE, I STILL HAVE THESE...
HMM. NO TELLING IF THE WITCHES WERE EATEN OR LEFT THE COUNTRY.
THERE IS ANOTHER WAY TO REMOVE THE SKIN CURSE, THOUGH.
NOW THERE'S ANOTHER WAY?
I DIDN'T THINK ORMOND WOULD GO FOR IT. YOU SIMPLY HAVE TO TELL YOUR WIFE WHAT YOU'RE HIDING. COMING CLEAN, SO TO SPEAK.
I'LL DO IT-- BUT I'LL SOON BE PENNILESS.
I DON'T CARE, GERRY-- I'LL STICK WITH YOU.
AW.
DAMN, IT'S CHARON-- RUN!
NO, IT'S NOT.

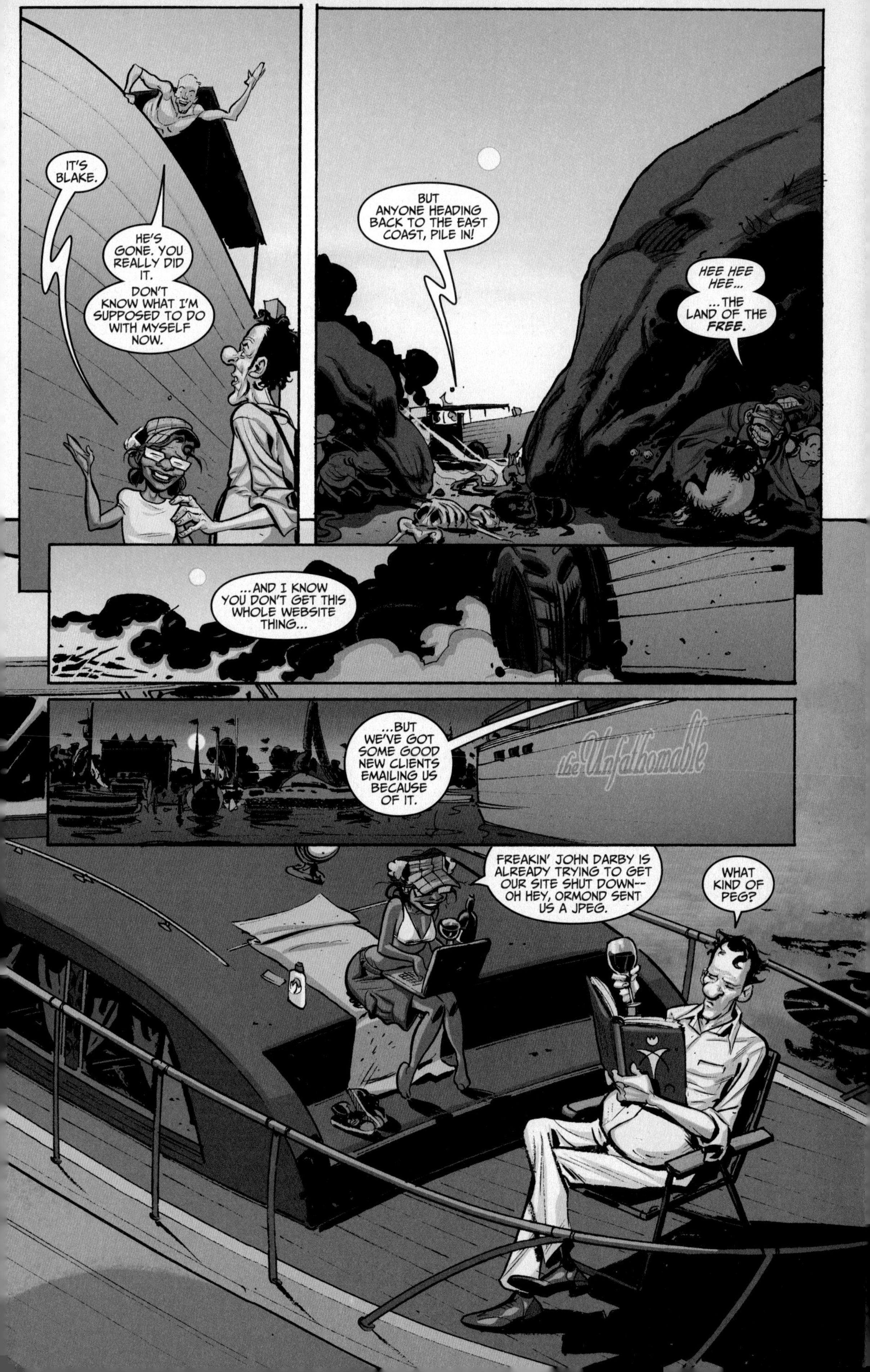
IT'S BLAKE.
HE'S GONE. YOU REALLY DID IT.
DON'T KNOW WHAT I'M SUPPOSED TO DO WITH MYSELF NOW.
BUT ANYONE HEADING BACK TO THE EAST COAST, PILE IN!
HEE HEE HEE...
...THE LAND OF THE FREE.
...AND I KNOW YOU DON'T GET THIS WHOLE WEBSITE THING...
...BUT WE'VE GOT SOME GOOD NEW CLIENTS EMAILING US BECAUSE OF IT.
the Unfathomable
FREAKIN' JOHN DARBY IS ALREADY TRYING TO GET OUR SITE SHUT DOWN-- OH HEY, ORMOND SENT US A JPEG.
WHAT KIND OF PEG?

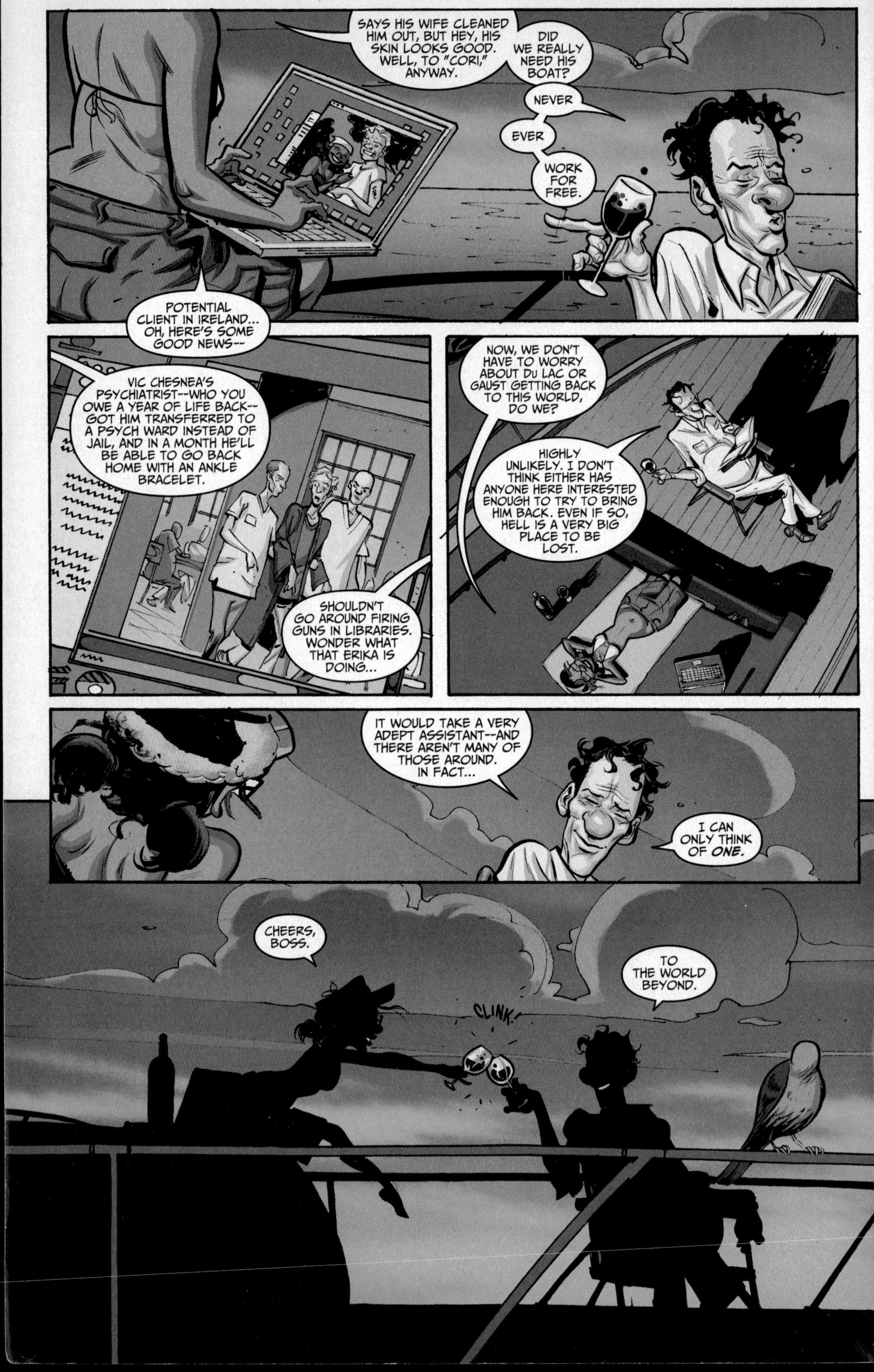
SAYS HIS WIFE CLEANED HIM OUT, BUT HEY, HIS SKIN LOOKS GOOD. WELL, TO "CORI," ANYWAY.
DID WE REALLY NEED HIS BOAT?
NEVER
EVER
WORK FOR FREE.
POTENTIAL CLIENT IN IRELAND... OH, HERE'S SOME GOOD NEWS--
VIC CHESNEA'S PSYCHIATRIST--WHO YOU OWE A YEAR OF LIFE BACK--GOT HIM TRANSFERRED TO A PSYCH WARD INSTEAD OF JAIL, AND IN A MONTH HE'LL BE ABLE TO GO BACK HOME WITH AN ANKLE BRACELET.
SHOULDN'T GO AROUND FIRING GUNS IN LIBRARIES. WONDER WHAT THAT ERIKA IS DOING...
NOW, WE DON'T HAVE TO WORRY ABOUT DU LAC OR GAUST GETTING BACK TO THIS WORLD, DO WE?
HIGHLY UNLIKELY. I DON'T THINK EITHER HAS ANYONE HERE INTERESTED ENOUGH TO TRY TO BRING HIM BACK. EVEN IF SO, HELL IS A VERY BIG PLACE TO BE LOST.
IT WOULD TAKE A VERY ADEPT ASSISTANT--AND THERE AREN'T MANY OF THOSE AROUND. IN FACT...
I CAN ONLY THINK OF *ONE.*
CHEERS, BOSS.
TO THE WORLD BEYOND.
CLINK!

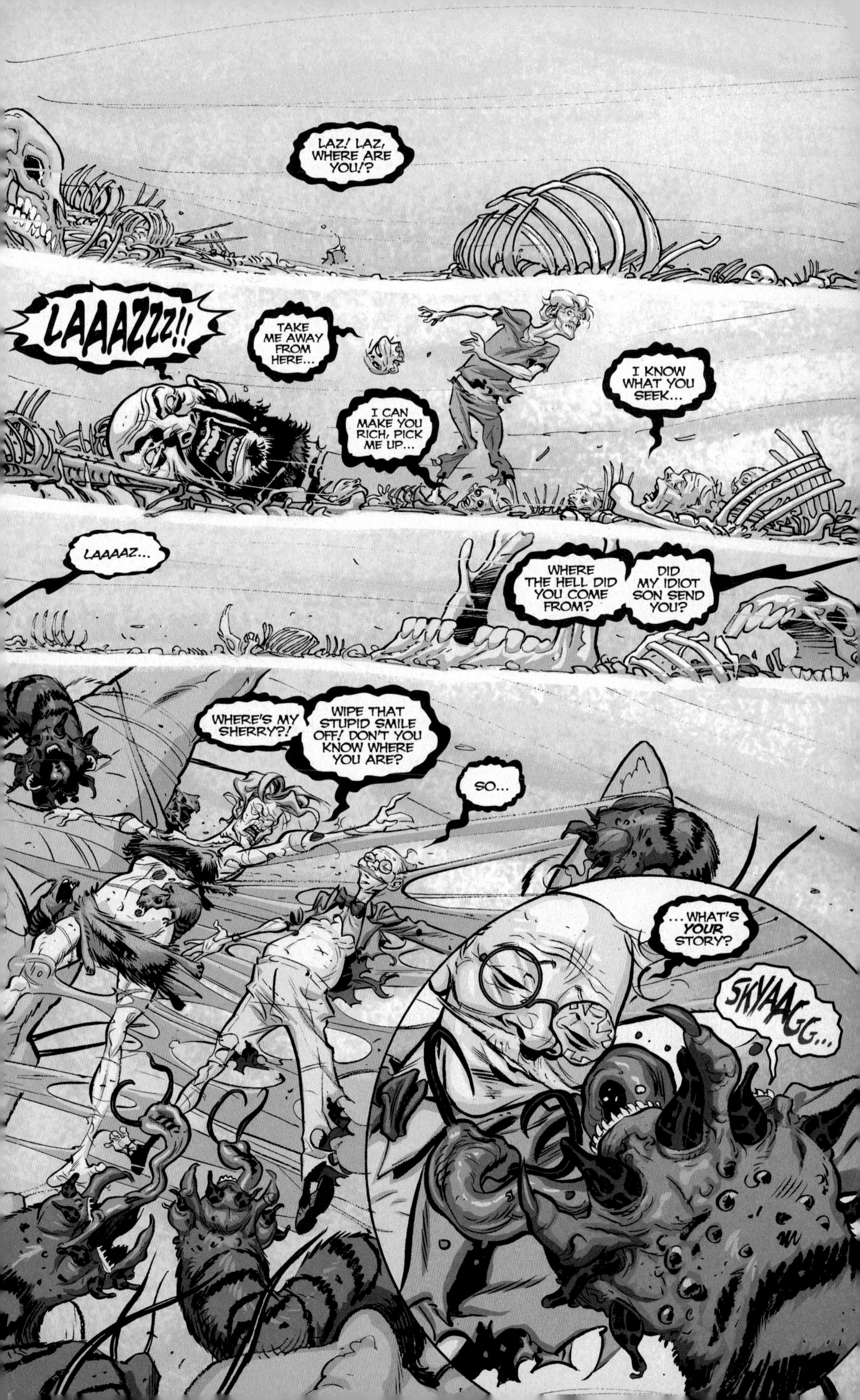
LAZ! LAZ, WHERE ARE YOU!?
LAAAZZZ!!
TAKE ME AWAY FROM HERE...
I CAN MAKE YOU RICH, PICK ME UP...
I KNOW WHAT YOU SEEK...
LAAAAZ...
WHERE THE HELL DID YOU COME FROM?
DID MY IDIOT SON SEND YOU?
WHERE'S MY SHERRY?!
WIPE THAT STUPID SMILE OFF! DON'T YOU KNOW WHERE YOU ARE?
SO...
...WHAT'S YOUR STORY?
SKYAAGG...

For Hilary and John Fowler for their endless support and patience.
And for Monique and Graham. I love you.

-Tom

For Kenny Parker, who appreciated pure bastards like Mysterius.
-Jeff

The creators would like to thank Bill Angus, Kin Jee, Chris Butcher, James Sime, John Siuntres, Evie and Aaron, and the 11 O'Clock Comics podcast. Thanks to Kristy, Ed and Chris for this edition, and to Ben Abernathy and Hank Kanalz for giving Mysterius a shot. And, most importantly, thank you to all of the fans who expressed support for this book.